MEANS TO A KILL

An Encyclopedia of Murder Methods

Also by Jon E Lewis

Red Handed
True War Stories
The Mammoth Book of the Western
The Mammoth Book of Modern War Stories
Cult TV
Eye-witness D-Day
True Stories of the Elite Forces
Raising the Flag

MEANS TO A KILL

An Encyclopedia of Murder Methods

Jon E Lewis

HEADLINE

First published in 1994
by HEADLINE BOOK PUBLISHING

10 9 8 7 6 5 4 3 2 1

British Library Cataloguing in Publication Data

Lewis, Jon E.
  Means to a Kill
  I. Title
  364.1523

ISBN 0-7472-0942-1

Typeset by
Letterpart Limited, Reigate, Surrey

Printed and bound in Great Britain by
Mackays of Chatham PLC, Chatham, Kent

HEADLINE BOOK PUBLISHING
A division of Hodder Headline PLC
338 Euston Road
London NW1 3BH

Contents

Introduction	1
Acid	5
Aconitine	9
Aircraft	12
Air Embolism	13
Alcohol	15
Animals	16
Antimony	18
Antipyrine	24
Arsenic	24
Asphyxia	33
Atropine	35
Axes	35
Bacterial Poisoning	40
Barbiturates	44
Biting	46
Blunt Instruments	47
Burning	51
Cannibalism	58
Cantharidin	60
Carbon Monoxide	61
Caustic Potash	65
Chloral Hydrate	67
Chloroform	67
Choking	71
Concrete	71
Crossbows	72
Curare	74
Cut-throat	77
Cyanide	78
Defenestration	84
Digitalis	85
Dismemberment	87
Drowning	93
Electrocution	98
Explosives	101

Firearms	105
Fungi	120
Glass	122
Hanging	123
Hemlock	127
Hit-and-run	129
Hyoscine	132
Insulin	137
Interring	142
Karate	146
Kicking	148
Kidnapping	149
Knives	155
Mercury	164
Morphine	165
Mummification	170
Nicotine	175
Paraquat	178
Phosphorus	180
Poisoning	185
Quicklime	193
Refrigeration	198
Ricin	200
Sharp Instruments	203
Snakes	207
Spiders	212
Starvation	214
Strangulation	216
Strychnine	224
Succinylcholine Chloride	232
Suffocation	235

Thallium   243   Water   264
Trains   248
Trunks   251   Select Bibliography   271
                               Index   273

Introduction

In *Homicide* (1991), his account of a year spent shadowing the Baltimore murder squad, the journalist David Simon noted that real detectives, unlike their fictional counterparts, were peculiarly uninterested in the whys and whos of sudden death. The real detective's concern was physical evidence, his creed: 'find out the how, and nine times out of ten it'll give you the who'. Nor are the cops from Baltimore alone in their obsessions. For homicide departments everywhere the working rule is that to catch the killer you must first establish the method of murder. It is the essential, inviolable link between victim and perpetrator.

This book is a how- and whatdunnit of murder. In truth there are only nine or so basic ways of criminally arresting life – shooting, stabbing, bludgeoning, burning, electrocution, poisoning, explosion, asphyxiation, starvation – and all murders are variations on these basic means. But the variations are myriad. As the following pages show, there is a positive pharmacopoeia of poisons and drugs that can be used to lethal effect (not a few of them can be found in any garden shed or household medicine chest), while bludgeoning can be accomplished by any number of blunt instruments from a brick to a golf club. Defenestration, where a body is pushed to earth from a high place, and hit-and-run with a car are also, in their way, types of bludgeoning. It can be said with some safety that every murder method conceivable has at some time, somewhere, been attempted by someone. A report in the *South Wales Echo* of 5 June 1990 detailed the case of a Texas pizza delivery man, Troy Brewer, who had been robbed and threatened with his life by an assailant wielding a large turtle. A year later, in 1991, England's Norwich Crown Court sentenced Susan Whybrow and her lover Dennis Saunders to a lengthy term in prison for trying to murder Whybrow's husband by sabotaging the brakes on his ride-on lawnmower.

Most murderers, though, when they come to kill are subject to definite constraints which dictate their choice of killing method. The overwhelming majority of murders – possibly as high as 90 per cent – are impulsive, committed in the heat of the moment, with the perpetrator using the nearest available deadly weapon – the kitchen knife, the poker, even his or her own hands. In 1991 40 per cent of Britain's 708 homicides were committed with a knife or sharp instrument, 10 per cent were strangled and 1 per cent axed to death. In the USA, where guns are readily available, 70 per cent of its average 23,000 homicides per annum are shootings. It is only the premeditated murder which allows for sophistication or esotericism. Not that all premeditated murders are sophisticated; male sado-sex killers who go hunting humans often do so with a common-or-garden knife which allows stabbing (symbolic penetration), butchery, the desecration of the victim. A number of serial sex killers have evidenced a liking for strangling, including the Boston Strangler, since this method allows complete control over the victim's life. If the strangler loosens his grip, the subject lives a little longer; if he tightens it, the subject dies a little sooner.

The type of killer and the type of crime to be committed all have a bearing on homicidal method. A killer who wants to go on a mass-murdering 'spree' does not usually choose a lead cosh; he or she seizes a firearm, preferably an automatic with a rapid rate of fire – as did Michael Ryan in Hungerford in 1987, Howard Unruh in New Jersey in 1949. It goes without saying, of course, that the technological base of a society is a limiting factor (an AK47 assault rifle is the prerogative of the 20th century killer only), but that technological base has advanced unerringly. Since Cain's killing of Abel with a Neanderthal club, the history of society can be measured by humankind's search for more and more devastating ways of dealing death.

Conversely, one of the most overlooked factors in the murderer's choice of method is gender. Although there are cases of hefty woman servants battering their employers in the 19th century, in general the 'weaker sex' – at least when killing men – has had to find ways and means which do not depend on brute strength. If homicidal technology has benefited anybody, it has benefited the lady killer. The prime example is the firearm, where the puller of the trigger does not even need to get close to the victim. Historically, however, the main means of murder for woman has been poison; as maker of meals and dispenser of drinks she was in the ideal position to give a large dose of something deadly to her unwanted spouse. Poison has also proved fatally attractive to the medical fraternity who, when they decide on the crime most foul, almost invariably open their dispensary door. Presumably their easy access to poison drugs is simply too tempting. A sobering number of murdering medics, armed with poisons simple (arsenical weedkiller) and poisons cunning (insulin, succinylcholine chloride), appear in this encyclopedia.

It is perhaps poisoning which is most often held to offer the killer's equivalent of the philosopher's stone: the perfect murder, the unlawful death which is undetectable. And for thousands of years, a sort of perfect death with poison was possible because law enforcement agencies, such as they were, had no means of detecting whether the cadaver before them had been poisoned or had died from natural causes. The free, dark reign of the poisoner did not begin to end until the 19th century with the gradual invention of reliable chemical tests to determine the presence – or not – of poison. (A major theme throughout this book is the history, development and diligence of forensic science in its catching of criminals.) At the end of the 20th century it would only be a fool, a highly accomplished medic or a toxicologist who would try and get away with a poison death.

Which begs the question, is the perfect murder possible? Inevitably, all the cases put under the microscope here are failures. Their perpetrators were caught. Not that this should allow any satisfaction. Some of the killers stalking these pages only met with justice when stricken by conscience, or loss of nerve, and volunteered a confession. Their means was sound. It is a paradox that the most 'successful' murders have often tended to be the most basic: South Africa's Carolyn Laurens wrenching the wheel and jumping out of a moving car – leaving it, and her husband, to plunge into a ravine, for instance. It was not until Laurens murdered her sister some years later (with poison spiders) and confessed to the earlier crime that the police realized it had been something other than an accident. And this is exactly what the perfect murder has to achieve: the semblance of an accident. The bullet left tragically in the chamber of the gun being cleaned, the foot which slips on the cliff path, the overdose of prescribed drugs.

Of course, the perfect murder takes more than a good method. It requires certain characteristics in the killer, notably an iron nerve and a lack of conscience. A none-too-obvious motive is a help, and if the victim lacks nosy and suspicious relatives and friends, so much the better. And then there is the small matter of the disposal of the corpse. A quite reassuring line-up of killers is brought to book, even if it is later rather than sooner, by their lack of foresight and care in dispensing of the tell-tale cadaver. Disposing of the body is as murderously important as dispatching the victim. Consequently, methods of corpse disposal are treated in requisite fullness in this dossier of murder, from the depraved (cannibalism) to the desperate (trunks). Some, like the freezing of the body of Helle Crafts and its subsequent feeding into a woodchipper, are morbidly inventive. It was Nietzsche who pointed out that the urge to destroy was a creative one. Some of the foul deeds which follow can be seen as a backhanded compliment to the creativity of humanity.

It is intended that this book should appeal to the armchair criminologist, though the professional associated with the business of murder should find it of more than memory-jogging interest. It gives much of the flavour of forensic investigation, including post-mortem appearances, and explains the effects and mechanics of each murder mode. The contents are arranged alphabetically by method of murder or disposal, and are accompanied by case files which are illustrative, famous or fascinating. Cross-referencing allows the reader to follow a particular interest or divert to an associated method or case. The book is rounded off with a bibliography and full index to maximize its usefulness as a reference source for the dedicated reader.

It only remains for me to thank my editor at Headline, Lorraine Jerram, for her patience and guidance, Clifford Elmer Books (8 Balmoral Avenue, Cheadle, Cheshire SK8 5EQ), an indispensable port of call for the true-crime devotee in search of a particular title, and the usual suspects: Julian Alexander of Jacintha Alexander Associates, my parents, Michele Lowe, and Penny Stempel.

A

ACID

An acid is a substance which in solution with water produces protons (hydrogen ions). The practical importance of this chemical definition for the homicidally minded is that acids – and particularly mineral acids, such as sulphuric acid – are corrosive poisons which extract water from human tissue. Or, put less delicately, they 'burn' flesh.

With the exception of prussic acid (a form of CYANIDE), the actual procuring of murder by means of acid is rare – but not unknown. In 1887, a Jewish immigrant to London's East End, Israel Lipski, forced his neighbour Miriam Angel to swallow nitric acid with fatal result. Australian Martha Rendall 'washed' the throats of three of her stepchildren with hydrochloric acid – in each case the doctor gave diphtheria as the cause of death – between 1908 and 1909. Such ingestions of acid, or corrosive poisonings are lethal because they dissolve the larynx (causing ASPHYXIA) and the digestive system, which retards gastric functions and/or causes internal haemorrhaging, with the speed of death largely determined by the sort and the strength of the acid used. A death from acid poisoning can take short, merciful minutes or long, writhing weeks.

Nor is poisoning the only homicidal possibility of acid. The notorious Dr Geza de Kaplany (see Case File, The Acid Doctor) indulged in the 'wet' BURNING to death of his wife in 1962 by applying nitric acid to her skin. And in one bizarre, but gruesome, British killing from the 1950s the victim was murdered by means of a hydrochloric acid enema. However, these cases aside, acid is a most uncommon choice for a homicide. Where acid is the agent of death it is invariably the result of suicidal or accidental ingestion.

It is as a means of disposal, rather than dispatch, that acid has tended to attract the murderer. Among the first to show an appreciation of the corrosive properties of acid in dealing with the perennial problem of the unwanted corpse was American serial-killer H.H. Holmes (a.k.a. Hermann Mudgett), who installed an acid bath in the cellar of his Chicago death-house, or 'Holmes' Castle as it became known, in the 1890s. Acid, Holmes discovered, was just the right stuff to reduce a human corpse to an easy, pourable-down-the-drain sludge. (The bath can rarely have been empty; Holmes was probably the USA's greatest mass-murderer.)

Like Holmes, the French lawyer Maître Georges Sarret was an insurance fraudster as well as one of the *cognoscenti* of acid. In 1933 – contrary to the old adage, there is no honour amongst thieves – Sarret shot dead two of his confederates and placed their bodies in a bath, which was then filled with 25 gallons of sulphuric acid. Sarret would have got away with his crime, but he and his female collaborators, Catherine and Philomene Schmidt, were later caught perpetrating an insurance scam and the whole dark deed came out. Maître Sarret was executed in Marseilles in April 1934 and the two Schmidts each received a ten-year prison sentence.

Perhaps the most infamous 'acid-bath murderer' of all was John George Haigh, who dissolved Mrs Durand-Deacon in 1949 (see Case File, The Acid Bath Murders). It should not be supposed, though, that acid-baths are a quaint eccentricity of bygone times. As recently as 1987, 33-year-old Swiss chauffeur Erwin Spengler murdered his wealthy 74-year-old employer, Frau Kornagel, at her Lake Constance home. Afterwards he placed her in the upstairs bath and added several gallons of hydrochloric acid. The resultant process – which, incidentally, would have generated intense heat, making Frau Kornagel's bath extremely hot to the touch – reduced her to a state where she flushed down the plughole.

Hydrochloric, nitric and sulphuric acid – these are the acids most frequently encountered in the crime annals. All are used widely in legitimate industry and, consequently, relatively easily available:

Hydrochloric acid (HCl) or Spirit of Salts. This aqueous solution of the gas hydrogen chloride is used in the production of chlorines and the recovery of zinc from scrap metal.
Sulphuric acid (H_2SO_4) A colourless, viscous liquid also known as Oil of Vitriol, which is extensively used by petroleum, chemical and manufacturing industries. In the 19th century, vitriol was frequently thrown at employers and strike-breakers by protesting workers, until, in 1861, its use became a felony punishable by life imprisonment.
Nitric acid (HNO_3) Sometimes called Aqua Fortis, this brown liquid is employed in the manufactures of explosives, fertilizers and plastics. It is so corrosive that it eats metal (and is thus of little use in an acid bath).

CASE FILE: The Acid Bath Murders

John George Haigh was regarded as being quite a charmer by the well-heeled lady residents of Onslow Court Hotel, Kensington, where he lived in 1949. A particular admirer of the 39-year-old engineer was elderly Mrs Henrietta Olivia Durand-Deacon, who had inherited £40,000 on the death of her husband – money which Haigh intended to make his own.

Under the pretext of helping Mrs Durand-Deacon in her scheme for making false fingernails, Haigh lured her down to his 'workshop' outside Crawley, Sussex, on Friday, 18 February 1949. There he shot the unsuspecting 69-year-old widow through the neck with a .38 Enfield revolver. After stripping her body of valuables he placed it in a 45-gallon oil drum and, donning a rubber apron and gas mask, proceeded to pump sulphuric acid into the drum until the corpse was covered. Haigh knew this would dissolve and destroy the human body. After all, he had done it before.

At the Onslow Court Hotel, Henrietta Durand-Deacon's absence increasingly worried her friend Constance Lane. Asked if he had seen Henrietta, Haigh said she had failed to keep their appointment to visit his Crawley workshop. When Durand-Deacon had not turned up by Sunday morning breakfast, Mrs Lane decided to go to the police. She also made Haigh go with her. Lane did not like Haigh, whom she found 'oily', and she had started to become suspicious of his story.

The police also formed a poor impression of Haigh and his unctuous concern for Henrietta Durand-Deacon's wellbeing. After interviewing him on several occasions, and checking with the Criminal Records Office, their impression was even poorer. John George Haigh had a record for swindling.

A visit to Haigh's two-storey brick workshop revealed the .38 revolver, and a receipt from a firm of cleaners for Durand-Deacon's Persian lamb coat. Further inquiries revealed that her jewellery had been sold by Haigh to a shop in Horsham. Haigh was arrested and taken to Chelsea police station. Under questioning, he suddenly announced: 'Well, if I told you the truth you wouldn't believe me . . . Mrs Durand-Deacon no longer exists . . . I have destroyed her with acid!' He looked at the incredulous policemen with a sly smile. 'How can you prove murder if there is no body?' Like many murderers before him, Haigh made the mistake of believing the old fallacy of 'no corpse, no case'. This was not Haigh's only mistake, however, for Mrs Durand-Deacon had not entirely dissolved.

It was true, she had been reduced to a greasy residue, which Haigh had poured over ground near his workshop, but the expert eye of pathologist Keith Simpson noticed lying in it an object about the size of a marble: it was a human gallstone. After this, the sludge was shovelled into boxes to be examined at Scotland Yard's laboratory. There it was found to contain part of a left foot, more gallstones, eighteen fragments of human bone, a lipstick container, a set of acrylic dentures and the red handle of a handbag. Haigh had failed to take into account the longer time needed to destroy plastic and fat-protected gallstones. (The fragments of bone probably survived because the foot was above the level of the acid in the drum.) The dentures were identified by Durand-Deacon's dentist, and the red handbag handle by her friends. A plaster cast of the foot fitted Mrs Durand-Deacon's shoe perfectly. There was more than enough of Mrs Durand-Deacon left to hang Haigh.

In his statement to the police, Haigh also admitted five other murders: three members of a family called McSwann, and a Dr and Mrs Henderson, each involving disposal of the body with acid. His claim, however, that he drank glasses of his victims' blood – hence his tabloid newspaper nickname, 'The Vampire Murderer' – was simply an obvious and crude ruse to establish a defence of insanity. The jury at his trial at Lewes Assizes were not so easily duped, and took only seventeen minutes to bring in a guilty verdict. On 10 August 1949, John George Haigh was hanged by Albert Pierrepoint. The latter made a red ink entry in his diary that day, to indicate, as he said, 'more than a formal interest in this particular execution'.

From five years of committing murder, Haigh had made a mere £12,000. The last killing, of Henrietta Durand-Deacon, had brought him in about £150 for the coat and jewellery. Almost any honest occupation would have made him more.

CASE FILE: The Acid Doctor

Dr Geza de Kaplany, a 36-year-old Hungarian anaesthetist working for a hospital in San Jose, California, became besotted with a local beauty queen, whom he finally persuaded to accompany him to the altar in August 1962. But, according to a statement de Kaplany later made, after only a few days of marriage he found himself impotent and became paranoid that every male in their apartment block was making love to his wife when he was out. Consequently, he decided to 'fix her' so that no man would ever look at her again.

On the morning of 28 August 1962, neighbours heard loud music in the de Kaplanys' apartment – but not loud enough to drown out the sound of human screaming. When the police arrived, they pounded on the door until it was opened by de Kaplany, who, sweating and grinning, was nude except for underpants and hands covered in thick rubber gloves. Pushing their way inside, the police found that the de Kaplanys' bedroom had been turned into a virtual torture chamber. Tied to the bed was Geza de Kaplany's wife, Hajna, horribly mutilated but alive. On the floor stood three pint bottles of sulphuric, hydrochloric and nitric acid – the latter almost empty from being poured into dozens of small incisions de Kaplany had made all over his wife's body. A note by the pillow instructed her: 'If you want to live – do not shout; do what I tell you or else you will die.' Around the bed the carpet was in a chaos of acidic disintegration.

On admission to hospital, Hajna de Kaplany was found to have third-degree corrosive burns covering 60 per cent of her body, her breasts and genitals being particularly badly affected. When the hospital attendants tried to apply ointment to the injuries they burnt their hands on her acid-coated body. She lived for twenty-one days, her mother by her bedside praying for her to die.

Following his wife's death, de Kaplany was charged with murder and tried in January 1963. He pleaded not guilty by reason of insanity. The court, however, after hearing the calculated preparations de Kaplany had made for the torture – including the fact that he manicured his fingernails so that they would not puncture the rubber gloves he used when handling the acid – found him guilty. De Kaplany was sentenced to life imprisonment. However, in a controversial decision, he served only thirteen years of this sentence before being released to work in Taiwan as a medical missionary.

ACONITINE

In a celebrated 19th-century poison trial, the eminent toxicologist Professor Sir Robert Christison remarked to the judge: 'My Lord there is but one deadly agent of this kind which we can not trace in the body after death, and that is –' At which point Christison was hastily stopped by the judge who, not unnaturally, feared a spate of murders if the poison was named. The agent the learned professor had in mind was aconitine.

Aconitine – or aconite, as it is sometimes known – is a white crystalline vegetable POISON derived from the roots and leaves of the monkshood (*Aconitum napellus*) or wolfsbane plant, which grows wild in Europe and North America. The foliage of the plant looks a little like parsley, its root like radish. Ancient Greeks are thought to have given the plant its name because it was found growing on rocks which they called *aconas*. Certainly, the old Hellenics were quite aware of the deadly properties of aconitine, nicknaming it 'the Queen of poisons'. It was used extensively in Classical Greece, and later in Rome, for the elimination of political rivals. Indeed, by the time of the Emperor Trajan it was so prevalent as an assassin's tool that he was obliged to forbid the cultivation of wolfsbane in Roman gardens.

The homicidal popularity of aconitine derives not only from its difficulty of detection in the human body after death, but from its extreme potency: a dose of 1–5 mg, if taken orally, will cause death in approximately eight minutes. Large doses kill almost instantaneously. The chief symptoms of aconitine poisoning are a weakened pulse, clammy skin, tingling and numbness of the mouth and face. There may also be vomiting, and visual disturbance. Death is caused by the paralysis of the heart or lungs.

As aconitine can be absorbed through the skin, it has a medicinal use in the form of liniments and ointments to treat rheumatism and sciatica, or for pain relief. A small amount rubbed on the skin stimulates the nerve endings and produces a warm, anaesthetic effect. Patent liniments such as ABC, which are composed of about 2 per cent aconitine, are still available but not much favoured since if over-applied they can produce mild aconitine poisoning.

In the modern almanac of murder history, aconitine does not figure prominently, save for the exploits of a trio of Victorian gaslight medics, Doctors Lamson, Pritchard, and Warder. (It is often said that poison is a woman's weapon for murder; an equally strong claim can be made for it being the doctor's weapon.) The most notable of these was Lamson (see Case File). Dr Edward William Pritchard used both aconitine and ANTIMONY to poison his wife and mother-in-law, a crime for which he was hanged in Glasgow in 1865. In the following year, Dr Alfred Warder, an authority on toxicology and forensic medicine, poisoned his wife over several months by administering Fleming's Tincture of Aconite internally. Before the police could arrest Warder at his Brighton home he committed suicide by taking prussic acid. His timely exit also left unanswered certain pertinent questions about the untimely demises of the first two Mrs Warders.

Aconitine was probably chosen by the three doctors because of lack of tests at the time that could detect the poison. Although the Belgian chemist Jean Servais Stas had, in 1851, devised a method of detecting aconitine and other vegetable poisons, the knowledge of this breakthrough remained limited for a number of years. Almost certainly Dr Pritchard would have got away with his murder if he had not used antimony as well, and Warder with his if another doctor had not seen him misapplying the aconite tincture. By the time Dr Lamson came to try his hand at murder in 1881, Victorian toxicology was able to show, albeit in an extremely basic fashion, aconitine poisoning. Not until the 1920s was a proper test for detecting aconitine available in Britain.

CASE FILE: The Blenheim School Poisoning

George Henry Lamson was born in 1850, and from an early age seems to have been possessed of a restless – if affable – nature. He left Britain in his teens to study medicine in Paris. In 1876 and 1877 he served as a volunteer army-surgeon in Serbia and Romania, where his work won him awards for humanitarianism. It also introduced him to the recreational use of MORPHINE, to which he became addicted. Lamson would later attribute his downfall to the drug.

After his Balkan sojourn, Lamson set up in England as a general practitioner and married Kate John, a wealthy ward in Chancery. Lamson gained not only £1500 by his marriage, but also a sister-in-law, Margaret, and two brothers-in-law, Herbert and Percy John.

Lamson proved to have no head for business and his medical practice failed to flourish. Financial disaster was only averted by the fortuitous death of Herbert John, who left £700 to his sister

Kate. Since the Married Woman's Property Act had not yet been passed, the money came into the control of her husband. Lamson used it to buy a new practice in Bournemouth, but this went the way of its predecessor. All the while his morphine habit ate at his capital. In 1881, Lamson had to sell his practice and home, and was reduced to borrowing from friends and passing false cheques. He briefly tried his luck in the USA, but arrived back in Britain with nothing but £5, borrowed from the ship's surgeon. His many creditors were pressing for payment. Lamson badly needed a new – and large – source of cash . . .

If his remaining brother-in-law Percy, a seventeen-year-old crippled with curvature of the spine, were to die unmarried – as Herbert had done – then Lamson would inherit £1500 through his wife. To Lamson it must have seemed a desperate but effective remedy. At a stroke all his money troubles could be cured.

Lamson first tried to kill Percy in the summer of 1881 during a holiday on the Isle of Wight. The means was a dose of quinine sulphate and aconitine disguised as a quinine pill. The boy recovered after severe vomiting. Perhaps this was a trial run or even a botched job.

Lamson then made another trip to the USA, this time returning home even poorer than before, and having to pawn his set of surgical instruments and watch. He now needed money more urgently than ever. If after his initial failure he had abandoned the plan to murder Percy, he now definitely resolved to do it.

On 1 December, Lamson wired Percy John at Blenheim Special School, Wimbledon, where the boy boarded. Lamson's message indicated that he was planning a trip to Paris and would like to visit Percy before he went. The message signed off, 'Your loving brother, George Lamson'. Two days later, Lamson arrived at the school, and took evening refreshment with Percy and the headmaster. Lamson produced some ready sliced pieces of Dundee cake which he passed around. After they had eaten, Lamson mentioned some gelatine capsules he had brought back from the USA, and ostentatiously filled a capsule with sugar. He gave it to Percy with the words, 'Percy, you are a champion pill-taker, take this.' The boy swallowed the pill and Lamson left for the boat train to France.

Twenty minutes after Lamson's departure, Percy John complained of heartburn. At 11.20 p.m., after some three hours of agony, he died. The police were called and Lamson sought for questioning. On 8 December, Lamson, believing the crime was unprovable, returned from Paris and boldly marched into Scotland Yard to announce his innocence. He was immediately placed under arrest.

Lamson was tried for murder at the Old Bailey in March 1882, with much of the court's time taken up by the argument as to whether it was possible to detect alkaloid poisons. Appearing for the prosecution was Home Office pathologist Dr Thomas Stevenson, whose method of identifying them was primitive but effective: he did so by taste. To some astonishment he testified that he had extracted and isolated the poison from the dead boy's body organs. 'Some of this extract I placed on my tongue,' he said, 'and it produced the effect of aconitia.' (This included four hours of acute illness.) As an additional test he had injected mice with the extract, and in each case the injections produced symptoms identical to those of an injection from aconitine. The pathologist also correctly divined, as later proved by Lamson's gallows confession, that the poison had been injected into a raisin and pushed into a slice of the Dundee cake that was specially earmarked for Percy John. In addition to Stevenson's testimony, the prosecution was also able to prove that Lamson had brought two grains of aconitine from Allen & Hanbury's pharmacy in the City of London on 2 November.

Although the evidence against Lamson was only circumstantial it was strong, and the jury returned after forty-five minutes with a verdict of guilty. It is probable that Lamson's pantomime with the gelatine capsule on the evening of Percy John's death was intended, should his design be discovered, to lead the prosecution to maintain that the poison was in the pill, and then compel them to prove it. In the event the jury was satisfied that the boy had been poisoned, but not greatly troubled by the way in which it was done.

While in prison awaiting his execution Lamson suffered badly from morphine withdrawal and lost all composure. Even as the hangman Marwood pulled the lever beneath his feet on 18 April 1882, Lamson tried to snatch another moment of life by begging the chaplain to recite one more prayer.

AIRCRAFT

Though only a mediocre gangster, Brian Donald Hume merits a footnote in the crime annals for his unusual method of corpse disposal. On 5 October 1949, Hume had a falling-out with Stanley Setty – his partner in a London stolen car racket – which resulted in Hume stabbing Setty to death. Hume then undertook the DISMEMBERMENT of the corpse, severing the head and legs from the torso. Believing that the only way to avoid the long arm of the law was to dispose of the body properly, Hume, an ex-RAF airman, hired a private plane from the United Services Club in Elstree. Over the next two days he flew the aircraft out over the English Channel, dropping three parcels into the WATER of the deep blue sea. Landing for the last time at Elstree, Hume thought he had committed the perfect disposal.

Unfortunately for Hume, however, one of his parcels was washed on to the Essex coast some days later, to be discovered by a labourer on his way to work. Fingerprints showed the dead man to be

Stanley Setty, also known as Sulman Seti, whose known associates included one Brian Donald Hume. The police traced Hume's movements and learned about him hiring the light aircraft. Arrested on 27 October, Hume emphatically denied murder, saying that he had been forced by three men to dump parcels, containing – he thought – parts of a press which had been used to print petrol coupons. The evidence at Hume's trial in January 1950 was insufficient to convict him of murder. A new jury was sworn in, and Hume was found guilty on the lesser charge of accessory and sentenced to twelve years. On his release in 1958, and knowing that he could not be tried for the same crime again, he confessed to the *Sunday Pictorial* newspaper that he had indeed killed Setty. After a series of bank robberies and the shooting of a taxi driver in Zurich, Hume was sentenced by a Swiss court to life imprisonment in 1959.

With the exception of Hume, the potential of aircraft has been largely neglected by the murderer. Usually where an aircraft enters homicidal affairs it is as a means of escape. There have, however, been a number of killers, beginning with Albert Guay in 1949, who have placed EXPLOSIVES aboard aircraft with devastating results. Guay's bomb aboard a Quebec Airways DC3 on a flight from Montreal to Seven Island killed twenty-three passengers – including Mrs Guay – and crew. A similar, if larger-scale, crime was committed by John Gilbert Graham when he secreted a bomb aboard an American airliner in 1955.

In an unusual case of DEFENESTRATION, 51-year-old Belgian millionaire Alfred Loewenstein was pushed from a Fokker FU11 in 1928. Loewenstein fell 4000 feet into the English Channel. The case is a classic, for nobody knows which of his six co-passengers gave the fatal push. Moreover, legal opinion of the time was that anything that happened on board an aircraft over international waters was nobody's affair.

AIR EMBOLISM

There is a common belief that just a tiny bubble of air injected into a vein will cause death. In fact, a whole syringe-full – about 10 cc – will only discomfort a healthy person. Opinions on what *does* constitute the minimum fatal volume range between 40 cc and 300 cc, but, as Dr John Thomson observed in his book *Crime Scientist*, the person intent on homicide by air embolism might do better to be equipped with a bicycle pump rather than a syringe.

If air is introduced into the circulatory system it travels through the bloodstream until it reaches the right side of the heart, where the injected air forms bubbles and froth, resulting in an air-lock, or blockage. The air may also be pumped through the lungs to form bubbles in other vital organs, including the brain, and so block their blood supply.

Accidental air embolism from wounds in the neck or from

surgery, where air is sucked into opened veins, is not unknown. In the days of the backstreet abortionist, death from air embolism was a common consequence of Higginson syringing if air, instead of fluid, was accidentally pumped into the womb, gaining access to the circulatory system via the placental bed. The few homicidal instances of air embolism are usually so-called 'mercy-killings' by doctors, as in the cases of Doctors Montemerano and Sander (see Case File) in the USA.

Embolism can also be caused by fat particles released into the circulation following injury or BURNING to subcutaneous fat or bones. The fat particles can then impede the blood supply to vital organs in the same way as air embolism.

CASE FILE: The Sander Mercy Killing

In late 1949, Dr Hermann Sander attended the bed of a cancer patient, Mrs Abbie Borroto, at the New Hampshire Hospital where he worked. Mrs Borroto was terminally ill, with only days – perhaps even hours – to live. In the presence of a nurse, Sander tied a tourniquet around Mrs Borroto's arm and injected 10 cc of air into her arm – four times. Each time, Mrs Borroto gave a groan, then she made no more sound or movement.

A death certificate was made out, giving carcinoma of the large bowel as the cause of death, and Mrs Borroto was embalmed and buried. Some days later, Dr Sander filled out her medical record, giving a full account of the injections performed to induce air embolism. The confession to the killing of Mrs Borroto – since this is, in effect, what the completed medical record amounted to – was noticed by a vigilant hospital clerk. Then the newspapers got hold of it and very soon Dr Sander was in court in what became known worldwide as 'The Mercy Killing Trial'.

The trial opened in February 1950 and was dominated by expert testimonies on the subject of air embolism. Dr Milton Helpern, representing the Attorney-General, pointed out that since the post-mortem examination of Mrs Borroto's corpse had shown no other cause of death, the most probable cause was the air embolism which Dr Sander admitted to inducing. Thus he was guilty of murder. Events then took a dramatic turn with Sander changing his story: Mrs Borroto, he now said, was already dead when he injected air into her arm. Why, then, had he done it? To make sure she was dead. If this was so, then Sander could not have possibly murdered her. Controversy continued over the amount of air necessary to cause an embolism. Some doctors suggested 200–300 cc. Milton Helpern believed it was much less and anyway depended on the condition. In the case of Dr Sander's patient, 40 cc was obviously enough – that is, if he really did kill her. Much to the approval of the public the jury brought in a verdict of not guilty.

AIR GUNS *See* **FIREARMS**

ALCOHOL

As the 19th-century writer Thomas De Quincey observed, 'Sobriety disguiseth man.' Alcohol, at least in small to moderate amounts, depresses controls in the highest centres of the brain, leading to the paralysis of rationality and inhibition. The behavioural effects of alcohol are complex, but some people when inebriated are more prone to violence than at other times. Certainly, a drunken person is more likely to have and to cause accidents than a sober one.

The alcohol (ethyl alcohol, or ethanol) which is drunk as a recreational drug is formed from the fermentation of sugar. Alcohol is rapidly absorbed after drinking, both from the stomach lining and (especially) the first part of the intestine. The drug is toxic, but, outside sustained chronic abuse by the alcoholic, is only fatal in relatively enormous quantities. How each individual will be affected by alcohol depends to a large extent on gender, physical size, whether food is taken as well as drink, the dilution of the alcohol and whether the person is used to drinking. But in general an individual with over 250 mg of alcohol per 100 ml of blood is likely to be severely drunk, grossly uncoordinated, incoherent and vomiting (the latter condition carrying with it the danger that the subject may choke to death on his or her vomit, particularly if lying on the back). A further rise of alcohol levels to 350–400 mg/100 ml causes a progressive passage through stupor to coma. The complexion becomes pallid and the body temperature very low. Death from paralysis of the lower brain function of breathing control can occur from any point onwards. To achieve a level of 400 mg/100 ml an average subject would have had to have drunk approximately eleven pints of beer.

It should come as no surprise, then, that ethyl alcohol is not the substance the prospective poisoner is likely to reach for. However, a number of murderers have encouraged victims into heavy drinking which has made them more amenable – i.e., more defenceless, more passive – to their own death. The 19th-century grave-robbers Burke and Hare made their human prey senseless with drink convivially offered before crushing them (a form of ASPHYXIA), while the South African killer Carolyn Laurens jumped out of a speeding car . . . leaving her inebriated – and unwanted – husband too stupefied to move before it crashed – a variation of HIT-AND-RUN.

Methyl alcohol (methanol) and isopropyl alcohol (isopropenol), however, are very different jars of poison to ethyl alcohol. Methyl alcohol – also known as wood alcohol or Columbian Spirits – is a common industrial chemical which is broken down in the body much more slowly than ethyl alcohol and can thus accumulate from even a moderate intake. Lower blood levels than ethyl alcohol are dangerous or fatal, 80 mg/100 ml being a dangerous level. A fatal dose is 60–200 ml. A small amount of methyl alcohol is present in methylated spirits. Pure methyl alcohol is sometimes used as a motor anti-freeze and deaths – accidental, suicidal and homicidal – have occurred from drinking it.

Like methyl alcohol, isopropyl alcohol is used in anti-freeze preparations, although it is most commonly found in industrial solvents. It is less poisonous than methyl alcohol, a fatal dose being 250 ml or more.

ALKALOIDS   *See* POISONING

ANIMALS

When Michael Onufrejczyk, a Polish ex-soldier living as a farmer in Wales, murdered his business partner Stanislaw Sykut in 1953, he adopted an unusual means of disposing of the corpse: he fed it to the pigs. No body was ever found at Cefn Hedre Farm and the case was of notable legal significance. The defence counsel said that he could find no case in the last 300 years where there had been a conviction of murder without identification of the body or part of the body, or an admission by the accused indicating that the victim was dead. Nonetheless, Onufrejczyk was found guilty.

Not that this has deterred others from using the farmyard pig as a corpse-disposal machine. The voracious – and indiscriminate – appetite of the pig, for instance, might also be testified to by the Hosein brothers. After murdering their kidnap victim Muriel McKay in 1970 they are believed to have cut up her corpse and fed it to their herd of Wessex Saddlebacks at Rooks Farm. More recently, in 1987, John Lawrence David added his erstwhile girlfriend to the food at a Berkshire piggery (see Case File).

The pig is not alone in the animal kingdom in being used to eat human corpses. In more temperate climes, there are documented cases of bodies being deliberately left out for the enjoyment of sharks and lions. And crocodiles. When American sociopath and mass murderer Carl Panzram (personal motto: 'Rob 'em all, rape 'em all and kill 'em all') took six African blacks as porters on a crocodile hunt in 1920, he shot the porters and fed their bodies to the crocodiles. Sixteen years later, Texan alligator breeder and tavern owner Joe Ball shot himself rather than answer Sheriff John Klevenhagen's pressing questions concerning the whereabouts of a string of Ball's ex-wives and waitresses; it turned out that no less than five of them had been fed to the alligators the forty-year-old

Ball kept in a pool to entertain guests at his misnamed Sociable Inn, near Elmendorf. A one-time neighbour later revealed how he had stumbled across Ball one night as he was hacking up the body of a woman and feeding chunks to the alligators: '. . . He shoved a gun in my face . . . said he would let me go because I had a big family.' The neighbour wisely fled to another state. After Ball's suicide, his reptile pets were donated to the San Diego Zoo, where they became a main attraction.

It is not just as methods of disposal that animals feature in the crime annals. A number of imaginative killers, and would-be killers, have used animals as homicidal weapons. A British man was reported by the *Daily Mail* in 1993 as having trained his Alsatian dog to attack his wife; she survived the canine fury. (An Alsatian, incidentally, appears as the most improbable excuse ever offered by a murderer for his deed; in 1979 Suresh Nair, a Singaporean living in Earls Court, London, claimed that an Alsatian jumped up behind him, knocked him forwards – thus causing the knife Nair happened to be holding to be driven into the throat of his landlord.) More successful than dog-users have been murderers who have employed poisonous animals, or the POISON extracted from animals. Poisonous BACTERIA, SPIDERS and SNAKES have a notable pedigree in crime, as do the beetles *Cantharis vesicatoria* and *Mylabris sidea*, both of which are used to make CANTHARIDIN, or 'Spanish Fly'.

More esoteric – at least for modern Westerners – than these terrestrial sources of animal poison are marine sources, such as the stone fish, the weever fish and the puffer fish. The puffer fish and other members of the family Tetraodontoidea, such as globe fish, contain one of the deadliest poisons known, tetrodotoxin. The poison halts nerve transmission and death is usually due to respiratory failure. The Ancient Egyptians certainly knew about the puffer fish (or *fugu*), since it is depicted on the tomb of the Pharaoh Ti, built around 2500 BC. Eating the toxic parts of the puffer fish – the liver, ovaries and roe – was a common method of suicide in medieval China and Japan. In 1774, natives tried to poison the explorer Captain James Cook by giving him puffer fish. Such poisoning is not only of historical interest, since the puffer fish is virtually Japan's national poison. The Japanese consider stewed puffer a great delicacy, but if the fish is incorrectly prepared it is extremely dangerous (as little as 8 mg of poison is lethal). There are as many as 100 fatalities each year in Japan from eating puffer fish. The police, by their own admission, have little chance of determining whether each fatality was suicidal, accidental or homicidal.

Another marine animal, the plankton *Gonyaulaux catenella*, has the distinction of producing a toxin, saxitoxin, used by the CIA. When U-2 spy pilot Gary Powers was captured by the Russians in

1960 he had a tiny suicide pin containing traces of saxitoxin in its grooves. The pin was discovered before Powers could use it. To test its efficacy the Russians pricked a large guard dog with it; the dog died in under ten seconds. It is probably only the relative inaccessibility of the marine animals which produce such toxins that has precluded their greater homicidal importance.

CASE FILE: The Disappearance at McCarthy's Farm

It was on the morning of 8 April 1987 that Mrs Miriam Jones was first reported missing. A 24-year-old barmaid at a Hell's Angels pub in Reading, she had failed to turn up for work, having spent the previous night with an ex-lover, John Lawrence David. David was not a Hell's Angel himself – in fact, he had been prevented from joining the Windsor Chapter because he was not 'tough' enough – but hung around the organization for his social life.

Several days after Mrs Jones' disappearance the police, acting on a tip-off, began an intensive search of McCarthy's pig farm outside Reading. During a week of inch-by-inch examination of the farm property, much of it inches deep in liquid pig manure, a number of chewed pieces of human bone were found. Also found were a blue suspender belt and some tatters of clothing. These were later identified by the victim's mother. Meanwhile, the forensic laboratory confirmed that the bone pieces were human. And so John Lawrence David, who had been seen driving out to the farm, was charged with Mrs Jones' murder. He confessed to the crime during the subsequent police interrogation.

At John David's trial at Reading Crown Court in December 1988, Nicholas Purnell QC, prosecuting, said that David had gone to Mrs Jones' bedsit and demanded sex. When she refused, David strangled her and drove her body, wrapped in a blanket, to the pig farm. There he doused it in petrol, BURNING it, before leaving it to the pigs. Mr Purnell added: 'Among the trees were over 100 pigs and piglets. Pigs will eat anything – flesh, clothing, bones, absolutely anything.' Including Mrs Miriam Jones.

John David was sentenced to life imprisonment on 6 December 1988.

ANTI-FREEZE   *See* **ALCOHOL**

ANTIMONY
Antimony is a metallic poison closely related to ARSENIC. Like arsenic, it is an odourless, colourless irritant poison which tends to preserve the body after death and cause symptoms which may be

mistaken for gastro-enteritis. As with arsenic, antimony can be detected by the Marsh Test (see page 26).

While the history of murder is full of cases of arsenical poison, death by antimony is scarce. Unlike arsenic, antimony, which is extracted from the ore stibnite and used to harden alloys in the metallurgical industry, was not available at every 19th century corner chemist as a pesticide. In the Victorian era, when most of the classic modern antimony poisonings occurred, it was invariably acquired as tartar emetic (potassium antimonyl tartrate). As its name suggests, this crystalline, metallic-tasting, soluble salt was used to induce vomiting and to purge the system. Not that the use of antimony as an emetic was peculiar to the Victorians; it dated back to Imperial Rome, when bloated revellers drank wine which had stood in antimony cups, vomited – and then carried on feasting.

The emetic character of antimony gives it a signal disadvantage for the poisoner; the victim is equally likely to vomit up the poison as ingest it. For that reason, the criminal user of antimony has tended to administer it in small frequent doses, bit by bit. A fatal amount might be as little as two grains (although there are recorded cases of 400 grains being taken without fatal results).

The symptoms of antimony poisoning are a burning pain in the throat, great thirst, abdominal pains and cramps, violent vomiting, diarrhoea, giddiness, and spasms in the arms and legs, all of which lead to an emaciated, exhausted state. The poison depresses the heart and breathing action, the fatal collapse being likely to be precipitated by circulatory failure.

Celebrated poisoners who employed antimony are Dr William Palmer ('The Rugeley Poisoner', hanged in 1856); Thomas Smethurst, who gave it to his bigamous wife in 1859; Dr Edward William Pritchard (see Case File); George Chapman (see Case File, George the Poisoner); and Florence Bravo. The latter, it is true, was never tried for the death of her London barrister husband, Charles, in 1876, but she remains the prime suspect of the prescriber of the lethal single dose of around thirty grains. The case became a Victorian scandal, not least because Mrs Bravo was discovered to have had an affair with her husband's elderly physician, Dr Gully.

CASE FILE: Doctor Edward William Pritchard

It was long Dr Edward Pritchard's ambition to be the most talked about man in Glasgow and on 28 July 1865 he realized his ambition: he was hanged before a crowd of 100,000 people for the murder of his wife and mother-in-law.

Born in 1815, Pritchard graduated from the Royal College of Surgeons in 1846, and served for several years as a naval assistant surgeon before marrying Mary Taylor, the daughter of a prosperous Scottish merchant. After resigning his commission he set up in private practice in Yorkshire.

In 1860, Pritchard bought a practice in Glasgow, and actively began his seeking of eminence. He lectured on medicine and his own travels abroad (the flavour and verisimilitude of which may be gauged from his claim that 'I have plucked the eaglets from their eyries in the deserts of Arabia and hunted the Nubian lion in the prairies of North America'), joined the Freemasons, and wrote for the local press. To all who met him he handed out photographs of himself. Such conceit did little to endear him to the city's medical fraternity.

In May 1863, Pritchard's house was badly damaged by fire, and the body of a servant girl found: 'The face, arms and trunk were badly charred, and only the legs encased in stockings had resisted the action of the flames.' The police believed that the girl had fallen asleep while reading a book by candlelight. Others scented wrongdoing: Who was responsible for her pregnant condition? Why was she only wearing stockings in chilly May? Why was there no trace of the supposed book? Couldn't Pritchard – who was alone with her in the house when she died – have done more to save her? The insurance company was suspicious enough to refuse to pay up for the fire damage.

Pritchard then moved his family to a house on Sauchiehall Street. This was to be the scene of the crime which would take him to the gallows. It was also where he made fifteen-year-old servant girl Mary McLeod pregnant, then performed an abortion on her with the promise that she would become the next Mrs Pritchard.

In October 1864, the actual Mrs Pritchard, thirty-eight and hitherto healthy, became violently ill with nausea and cramps. Over the following months her condition gradually declined. On 1 February 1865, she had a particularly severe attack of cramp. Her husband suggested irritation of the stomach, and another doctor called diagnosed gastric fever. As Mrs Pritchard failed to improve, her mother, Mrs Taylor, decided to come to Glasgow to nurse her.

Within two weeks of arriving *chez* Pritchard the redoubtable Mrs Taylor was dead. The old woman had been in the habit of imbibing the morphine-based Battley's Sedative Solution, and to a Dr Paterson who was called in Pritchard suggested she had 'had a good swig' of it and accidentally overdosed. As would be discovered later, Mrs Taylor's particular bottle of sedative had some extra ingredients in it, in the form of antimony and ACONITINE, courtesy of her son-in-law.

Mrs Taylor thus disposed of, Pritchard resumed the slow poisoning of his wife. On 17 March, after progressively aggravated symptoms, Mary Pritchard died. The signatory to her death certificate – which stated that she had died of gastric fever – was none other than Dr Pritchard himself. As the mourning husband he gave a convincing performance, even having Mary's coffin opened so that he could give her one last kiss before she was lowered into the ground.

But if Pritchard thought he had got away with murder he was wrong. An anonymous letter had already arrived with the Procurator Fiscal pointing out that two sudden deaths at Pritchard's house were 'at least very suspicious'. (The sender was quite possibly Dr Paterson, who had had doubts about the 'accidental' nature of Mrs Taylor's demise, but failed to air them publicly.) Whoever was its author, the letter was enough to persuade the police to order a post-mortem on the body of Mrs Pritchard. A Reinsch Test (similar to the test for arsenic pioneered by James Marsh; see page 26) revealed the presence of antimony in the form of tartar emetic in her urine, blood, kidney, liver and other organs. The distribution of the poison suggested that she had been poisoned over many months. On 22 March, Dr Pritchard found himself a prisoner.

Mrs Taylor was also exhumed, and organ analysis again revealed the presence of antimony. Although Pritchard protested his innocence at his trial, the scientific evidence of antimony poisoning weighed against him. The prosecution was also able to show that the doctor had purchased tartar emetic on 16 November 1864 and 7 February 1865 from Glasgow apothecaries. Dr Pritchard was duly convicted.

There are few more puzzling poisoners. Nobody was ever able to establish a satisfactory motive for Pritchard's evil and he seemed as bewildered by it as anybody else. He gained nothing financially from the murders (his wife was uninsured), and he never seriously intended to make Mary McLeod an 'honest woman'.

Equally perplexing is his use of both aconitine *and* antimony. Aconitine, as subsequently found in Mrs Taylor's bottle of Battley's Sedative Solution, would have been undetectable given the state of toxicology in 1865.

It is almost as if Pritchard wanted to be caught. After all, he wouldn't have been famous if the crimes had gone undiscovered. Maybe Dr Edward Pritchard just killed for the sheer fame of it.

CASE FILE: George the Poisoner

Although possessed of looks which led the famous lawyer Sir Edward Carson to compare him to 'an evil wild beast', George Chapman could apparently persuade women to perform sex with him at will. His list of lovers was long; so was his list of dead brides.

Chapman's real name was Severin Antoniovich Klosowski, and he was born in Poland in 1865, the son of a carpenter. In 1888, after six years' apprenticeship to a surgeon (and, it was later discovered, beheading a paramour), Klosowski arrived in Britain where he took up a job as barber in London's East End. It was the same year that Jack the Ripper started his career.

The following year, 1889, Klosowski went through a form of marriage with a Polish immigrant woman, Lucy Baderski. Not long after they tied the knot, Klosowski's real wife – whom he had married back in Poland – arrived on the scene. For a time, it seems, the trio lived in Cable Street in some sort of harmony, until his legal wife moved out. Klosowski and Lucy went to the USA, where they parted, with Klosowski returning to the East End alone. In 1892 he was living with a woman called Annie Chapman, whose name he adopted for himself.

When working in Leytonstone in 1895, 'Chapman' met Mary Spink, his first known English victim. Doubtless part of her attraction was the £600 she had in trust, which Chapman used to buy his own barber's salon in Hastings. While George cut hair, 'Mrs Chapman' played to the customers on the piano. For a while these novelty 'musical shaves' proved popular, but not popular enough to keep the business afloat. Within six months the couple were back in the East End where Chapman took over as landlord of the Prince of Wales Tavern off City Road. Before leaving Hastings Chapman had bought antimony in the form of an ounce of tartar emetic, costing twopence.

Towards the end of 1897, Mrs Spink fell ill with vomiting and stomach pains. On Christmas Day of that year she succumbed to what the doctor certified as consumption.

Not long after Mrs Spink was buried in a common grave, Chapman advertised for a barmaid, selecting farmer's daughter Bessie Taylor from the applicants. As well as installing Bessie behind the bar, Chapman quickly installed her in his bed. As 'Mr and Mrs Chapman' the couple ran, briefly, the Grapes public house at Bishop's Stortford, before moving back to London and management of the Monument Tavern. In the process Bessie had been struck by attacks of vomiting, and become emaciated. On 13 February 1901, Bessie died, aged thirty-six. Her death certificate, signed by one Dr Stoker, attributed death to 'exhaustion from vomiting and diarrhoea'.

The next to take over the role of George's barmaid-cum-wife was nineteen-year-old Maud Marsh, the couple 'marrying' in a Roman Catholic room in Bishopsgate. In 1902, George and Maud took over the Crown, where Maud started to go the way of previous 'Mrs Chapmans', vomiting and wasting away. The symptoms mysteriously abated when she was admitted to hospital, although doctors could not discover their cause. On her return home to George Maud relapsed. By this time Maud's mother had become thoroughly alarmed by her daughter's illness and descended from Croydon to look after her. After drinking a glass of brandy and soda prepared for Maud by Chapman, Mrs Marsh became very ill. Thus was the first seed of doubt sown. Mrs Marsh called in her own physician who quickly concluded that Maud was indeed being poisoned, probably, he thought, by arsenic. He telegrammed his concern to Maud's doctor, Stoker, but it was too late to save her. Maud died on 22 October 1902.

Alerted by the telegram, however, Dr Stoker refused to write a death certificate. He also carried out an unofficial post-mortem and discovered what he thought to be arsenic. As well as informing the coroner, Stoker informed the Metropolitan Police.

George Chapman was arrested at the Monument on 25 October. A police search of his room revealed many powders and medicines. Meanwhile, a second post-mortem on the remains of Maud, this time undertaken by Home Office analyst Dr Thomas Stevenson, revealed the fatal poison to be antimony, not arsenic. Post-mortems were also carried out by Stevenson on the corpses of Mary Spink and Bessie Taylor, whose exhumed bodies were found to contain respectively 3.83 and 29.12 grains of antimony. In his report on Spink, Stevenson made note of the high state of preservation of her body caused by the antimony. Her body was 'altogether remarkable, her face and hands were those of a woman who might have been coffined that day'.

Chapman's trial opened at the Old Bailey on 16 March 1903. He was charged, convicted and sentenced to death only for the murder of Maud Marsh, although evidence was admitted of the deaths of Bessie Taylor and Mary Spink. Dr Stevenson testified that he believed that much of the poison which killed Maud Marsh had been injected via the anus. The jury deliberated for only eleven minutes before returning with the inevitable verdict. Chapman was hanged at Wandsworth Prison on 7 April 1903.

Chapman's name is sometimes mentioned as a candidate for the role of Jack the Ripper. No less than Chief Inspector Abberline, leader of the Ripper inquiry, said, on Chapman's arrest, 'You've got Jack the Ripper at last.' It is true, there were several similarities between the two. The Ripper started his murder spree in the year that Klosowski/Chapman washed up in London. Chapman had surgical knowledge, so did the Ripper. The Ripper used American slang expressions, so did Chapman. The motive for both killers could be construed as sadistic woman-hating.

The problem with the Ripper/Chapman theory is the difference in killing methods. The Ripper was a frenzied murderer who liked SHARP INSTRUMENTS and hot blood. Chapman preferred poison and slow, cold, calculated deaths. It is unlikely that the needs of the one would have been satisfied by the means of the other.

ANTIPYRINE

First synthesized in 1884, antipyrine is an analgesic and anti-inflammatory compound used until relatively recently in medicine for the treatment of rheumatic fever, lumbago, and dysmenorrhoea (painful or difficult menstruation).

The most infamous misuse of antipyrine was in 1911 by Lieutenant Henry Lovell William Clark, a Eurasian doctor with the Indian Subordinate Medical Service. Lieutenant Clark had formed a *liaison* with one Augusta Fullam, the impediment to their eternal future happiness being their respective spouses. In time-honoured fashion, and wishing to avoid the scandal of divorce, the lovers conspired to murder.

It was decided to remove Mr Fullam first. With Clark living in Agra and the Fullams in Meereut, the task devolved to Mrs Fullam with Clark – who, because of his job, had full access to drugs and poisons – sending her various harmful substances, plus letters of instruction. And she replied regularly, reporting progress and declarations of lust and love.

Mr Fullam was injected with a veritable cocktail of poisons including the depressant gelsemium, ATROPINE, cocaine, and ARSENIC, and spent several weeks in extreme agony, which his physician diagnosed as heatstroke. Eventually, Lieutenant Clark decided to remove Mr Fullam in person, travelling to Agra and administering four drams of antipyrine, which had the desired effect.

Then the lovers turned their homicidal attentions to Clark's wife, but she proved stubborn to poisoning so they hired four assassins to murder her. Following her demise, however, tongues began to wag, and the police searched Mrs Fullam's bungalow. Under her bed was a tin box containing some 400 of her letters to Clark, which he had given her for safekeeping. These proved damning in their subsequent trial, containing as they did such lines as: 'You assure me you are determined to win me at any cost. Come what may I will help you achieve that end. I don't approve of your powders at all. How many hundred years will it take?' And: 'Oh! what a different wife your second one will be. The stakes are high, but the prize is well worth striving after.'

Mrs Fullam turned King's Evidence and Clark, belatedly doing the decent thing, made a full confession, stressing that the burden of responsibility for the murders lay with him. Both were convicted, and Clark was executed at Allahabad on 26 March 1913. Medical evidence showed that Mrs Fullam was pregnant, and her sentence was commuted to life imprisonment. She died ten months after the birth of her baby. It is something of an irony that she died of heatstroke.

ARSENIC

In his famous essay 'The Decline of the English Murder', published in 1946, George Orwell listed the ingredients that made up the classic English homicide. The murderer, he thought, should be a man of the professional classes – a dentist or a solicitor – living in the suburbs, who goes astray because of some 'secret passion for his secretary or the wife of a rival'. Having decided on murder, he should plan it all with the utmost cunning, and only slip up over some tiny unforeseen detail. The means, of course, should be poison.

In fact, Orwell might have been more specific, for many of the truly vintage English murders – those by Frederick Seddon (see Case File), Major Herbert Armstrong (see Case File) and Co – have been committed not with any old poison, but with arsenic. Arsenic is, at it were, the classic murderer's weapon of choice.

Yet it is not just the quality of arsenical murders which is remarkable, but their quantity. No poison has been so much used by those of murderous intent.

If the 'golden age' of the arsenic murder might roughly be said to be 1850–1950, there are many instances before and after these dates. Arsenic compounds were favoured by murderers in Imperial Rome, the Borgias raised their employment to an art form, and in the 16th century the woman Neapolitan robber Toffana admitted to killing 600-plus people (including two popes) by sprinkling arsenic on their food. In *ancien* France the poison became known as *poudre de succession* ('inheritance powder').

Arsenic is a metallic poison, occurring naturally in an ore called realgar. In ancient times, arsenic was administered in the form of yellow sulphide but in the 8th century an Arab alchemist, Gber, devised a method of producing arsenious oxide, a white, odourless powder. Arsenious oxide is the most common form of arsenic in the poisoner's cupboard.

The early signs of arsenical poisoning may include burning lips, difficulty in swallowing, and skin discoloration. Gastric pains, violent vomiting and watery diarrhoea follow. A raging thirst, cramps and cyanosis develop. In the last stages the victim goes into coma. Where poisoning is severe, death can sometimes ensue in an hour. More usually, however, severe poisoning leads to death in around twenty-four hours. The fatal dose is around two to three grains.

Arsenic possesses several qualities which endear it to the poisoner. The symptoms it produces, described above, can easily be confused with those of ordinary illnesses such as gastro-enteritis, dysentery or cholera. The white powder looks innocuous, is virtually tasteless and may be mistaken for flour or sugar. Arsenic can be administered (though with difficulty) as a vapour, or it can be passed via the skin. The poison also has a cumulative effect, so it can be built up in the victim's body by small doses administered over a long period of time. For centuries there was no means of detecting arsenic in the body. It was also easily obtainable.

Until the 1851 Arsenic Act the poison was freely available in Britain from any pharmacy. By the terms of the Act, the sale of arsenic was forbidden unless the purchaser was known to the pharmacist. Additionally, all arsenic compounds were required to be mixed with a colourant – which went some way to preventing people 'sugaring' their unwanted one's tea with the poison. The Act, however, left loopholes: anybody could set themselves up as a pharmacist, and arsenic was present in all manner of non-controlled household and industrial goods, including ant poison, rat poison, flypapers, sheep dip, medicines (it was, for example, present in the first cure for syphilis, Salvarsan), weedkiller, dyes . . . Napoleon even died from exposure to an arsenic-based paint in his room on Elba.

Unsurprisingly, perhaps, arsenic retained its popularity as a means of homicide even after the 1851 Act; instead of scuttling off to the pharmacist's the murderer only had to go next door to the ironmonger's for a packet of rat poison or flypapers . . .

In 1857, Madeleine Smith poisoned her lover in Glasgow with a cup of cocoa laced with arsenic; in 1873, Mary Cotton poisoned fifteen members of her family; in 1899, Florence Maybrick was convicted of giving her husband arsenic in Valentine's Meat Juice; Frederick Seddon also found Valentine's Meat Juice – suitably fortified with arsenic – just the ticket for murder in 1912.

Over in the United States in 1917, Amy Archer-Gilligan murdered five patients at a home for the elderly. Going several hundred corpses better, fifty Hungarian peasant women – 'The Angel Makers of Nagyrev' – employed arsenic potions to acquire land and lose husbands until caught in 1929. Back in Britain, in 1922, Major Herbert Armstrong used weedkiller not on his lawn but on his wife, while the same year saw Edward Black executed for the arsenical homicide of Mrs Black, sweetshop owner. In 1936 Ada Applegate found that the arsenic-based 'Rough on Rats' poison was especially rough on her, administered as it was by her husband and his lover.

Progressive restrictions on the sale of arsenic and arsenic-based goods, and its removal from many everyday articles, has severely curtailed the arsenically inclined murderer. Moreover, ever since James Marsh developed an accurate test for arsenic in 1836 – whereby arsenic traces are converted into arsine gas, with the arsenic presence revealed as a 'metallic' mirror on a piece of glass – it has been possible to prove evidence of arsenical poisoning in a court of law. The Marsh Test is sensitive enough to detect a presence of arsenic as small as one-fiftieth of a milligram, and was first used in 1840 to convict Marie Lafarge of the death of her French industrialist husband, Charles.

The Marsh Test brought the free reign of the arsenic poisoner to a timely end. Unless, that is, the murderer had a very clever lawyer. In 1961 the French advocate Gautrat got 'The Black Widow of

Loudon' (see Case File) acquitted by proving that the graveyard soil around her victims' coffins contained arsenic, and this was responsible for arsenic traces in their bodies.

The Marsh Test is still used today, although most contemporary forensic scientists prefer the improved versions – which still involve the principle of reducing arsenic to arsine gas – by Reinsch or Gutzeit, which are easier to conduct and more accurate.

It should not be supposed, though, that arsenic poisoning belongs exclusively to the past. When Sandy Coulthard died in suspicious circumstances in North Carolina, USA, in 1988, the autopsy discovered that she had been poisoned with arsenic over a considerable period. Her husband had killed her for the insurance money.

CASE FILE: Frederick Seddon

In 1910, the household at 63 Tollington Park, London N4, appeared to be the epitome of Edwardian lower-middle class respectability. The paterfamilias, Frederick Henry Seddon, was the district superintendent for the London & Manchester insurance company. A wife, Margaret Ann, four children, a servant, and Seddon's 73-year-old grandfather made up the rest of the ménage.

The Seddons would have been unremarkable except for a personality trait of Frederick himself. He was obsessed with acquiring money – so much so that he supplemented his already sizeable income by running a second-hand clothes business and speculating in property.

But it was still not enough. To make more money Seddon decided to rent out the second floor of No. 63.

His choice of tenant was Miss Eliza Barrow, a 49-year-old spinster of unhygienic ways and a fondness for the gin bottle. Accompanying her was a young nephew, Ernie Grant, and two friends, Mr and Mrs Hook. Within a fortnight, after a blazing row, the Hooks left. No sooner had they gone than Seddon was advising Miss Barrow on financial matters, she apparently grateful for the opinions of someone who was an expert and her social better. On 14 October 1910, after just three months in the house, Barrow transferred £1600 of India Stock into Seddon's name in return for a small annuity and a remission of rent. Three months later, she turned over the leases of a pub and barber's shop in Camden for an annuity of a further £50 per annum. In June 1911, Seddon took possession of her tenement building in exchange for another annuity. On Seddon's advice Miss Barrow also withdrew all her savings from her bank, £216, and placed them alongside the jewellery and gold coin in her strong box at No. 63. The spinster's entire £4000 fortune was now within Seddon's grasp.

In August, in an uncharacteristic fit of generosity, Seddon took his family, Miss Barrow and little Ernie to Southend-on-Sea for a holiday weekend. A few days after their return Seddon sent his daughter Maggie to buy a threepenny packet of Mather's Fly Paper, a preparation containing a large quantity of arsenic. (Florence Maybrick was accused of using the same flypaper in the 1889 murder of her husband.)

On 1 September 1911, Miss Barrow was taken ill with stomach pains and diarrhoea. Mrs Seddon summoned her own family doctor, Dr Henry Sworn, to examine her. He said it was nothing serious and prescribed a variety of stomach mixtures, including a nightly dose of Valentine's Meat Juice. Days passed, but Miss Barrow showed no sign of improvement. The state of her rooms, meanwhile, deteriorated in the summer heat from unpleasant to squalid, with an infestation of flies attracted by the constant vomiting and diarrhoea. Seddon would later claim that the Mather's flypapers were to combat the infestation.

At around midnight on 13 September Mrs Seddon heard a cry of 'I'm dying!' from upstairs, and found Mrs Barrow writhing around on the floor. Mrs Seddon managed to get the tenant back to bed. On his return from the theatre, where he had spent the evening, Seddon was unperturbed by Miss Barrow's condition. Instead, he complained over and over about being swindled out of sixpence. Throughout the night the Seddons attended to Miss Barrow. At 6.15 a.m. on the 14th, rasping thickly, she died.

The same morning Seddon got a death certificate from Dr Sworn, who did not bother to examine his erstwhile patient. The certificate gave the cause of death as epidemic diarrhoea.

It was then that Seddon made the slips that would lead him to the gallows. With typical meanness he buried Miss Barrow in a common grave, even taking a 2s 6d commission from the undertaker for introducing new business. He also informed Miss Barrow's nearest relatives, the Vonderahes, that all her stocks and property had been transferred to him, and that there was only £10 in liquid cash and valuables left. From this Seddon had deducted funeral expenses and the cost of Ernie's upkeep – leaving him, he claimed, out of pocket. In fact, they owed *him* £1 1s 10½d. He refused to show them the will.

The Vonderahes, who were Miss Barrow's cousins, were outraged – they had hoped to gain much from the will – and wasted no time in communicating their suspicions to the police. An autopsy on Eliza Barrow's corpse was carried out by Dr Bernard Spilsbury, who had just made his reputation on the Crippen case, and a Dr Willcox. The body was remarkably well preserved, a fact attributed to some preserving agent – such as arsenic – and sufficient traces of arsenic were found in the body to suggest that the cause of death was not epidemic diarrhoea but 'acute arsenical poisoning'. Seddon was arrested on 4 December, and his wife some weeks later.

The Seddons were tried at the Old Bailey over ten days in March 1912. Leading the defence was the flamboyant and brilliant Edward Marshall Hall, who claimed that the arsenic found in Miss Barrow's body was a result of her taking very small doses over a long period, probably from some medicinal preparation. Arsenic had been found in the roots of her hair, and it took as long as twelve months to appear there.

This was an ingenious theory and might have got Seddon's head out of the noose if Dr Willcox had not come up with the solution: while in her coffin Eliza Barrow's hair had become soaked with her own arsenic-containing blood. As it was, Willcox and Spilsbury were firm in their opinion that the poisoning of Barrow had been acute, and the 131.57 mg of arsenic in her remains was sufficient evidence of deliberate poisoning. In return, Marshall asked: 'Why did not Seddon, were he guilty of poisoning Miss Barrow, have the body cremated?' Seddon must have wished that he had.

In all probability the outcome of the trial was uncertain until the moment Seddon stepped into the witness box. The jury had already heard from no less than forty-five prosecution witnesses about Seddon's meanness of spirit and parsimony. In person he was proof and more of everything said against him: arrogant, conceited, cold, vain, hypocritical, calculating – all too obviously a man who would murder for money.

Frederick Seddon was found guilty as charged. His wife, against whom no real case had been put, was acquitted. After hearing the verdict Seddon addressed the judge, a fellow Mason, with a Masonic salute, saying, '. . . I declare before the Great Architect of the Universe I am not guilty, my lord.' The judge replied, 'You and I know we both belong to one brotherhood. But our brotherhood does not encourage crime.'

On the evening before his execution Seddon was informed that his house had been sold for less than its market value. 'That's finished it!' he exclaimed.

He was hanged on 28 April 1912 at Pentonville Prison.

CASE FILE: Herbert Armstrong

Major Herbert Rowse Armstrong was a practising solicitor in the Welsh border town of Hay-on-Wye. Dapper, with eyes of 'forget-me-not blue' and a waxed moustache, he cut quite a figure on the local scene, where he was much regarded for his conviviality. But as close acquaintances knew, Armstrong was completely under the thumb of his wife, Katherine, a domineering hypochondriac who ordered him around. On one notorious occasion she had interrupted a tennis party at their house, Mayfield, to tell him: 'Time to stop. Six o'clock, Herbert. How can you expect punctuality in the servants if the master is late for his meals?'

In July 1920 Katherine Armstrong became ill, and was certified insane. With his wife in a Gloucester asylum, Armstrong found he had more time to indulge the vices she forbade him (smoking, drinking) and one she knew nothing about (adultery). He also paid much attention to the lawns at Mayfield, tackling the dandelions with a variety of concoctions.

After several months Katherine was returned home – at Armstrong's insistence – to Hay, only to die of an agonizing illness. The Major noted briefly in his diary for 22 February 1921 – 'K. died'. Though Mrs Armstrong's illness bore all the signs of chronic arsenic poisoning – nausea, loss of weight, peripheral neuritis, skin discoloration – the cause of death was given as gastritis, and Mrs Armstrong was duly buried.

Free of his wife, Armstrong took a holiday in Italy and Malta, where he philandered with a vengeance. After returning to England, the Major asked a certain Mrs Gale of Bournemouth – with whom he had had a long illicit liaison – to marry him. She, perhaps wisely in the light of events, demurred.

In the autumn of 1921, Armstrong found himself in a professional dispute over the sale of a house with rival Hay solicitor, Oswald Martin, whose office was directly opposite his on Broad Street. Armstrong invited Martin to discuss the matter over tea at Mayfield, during which he handed Martin a buttered scone with the apology, 'Excuse fingers'. When Martin returned home he was violently ill, and failed to respond to treatment in the following days. His father-in-law, the town chemist, was suspicious of Armstrong on account of his purchases of arsenic, and conveyed this to the local physician, Dr Hincks. A sample of Martin's urine tested positive for arsenic.

The result got the doctor thinking about Katherine Armstrong's sudden death earlier in the year. Armed with as many facts as he could find, Hincks went to the police. They were sceptical – after all, the Major was a pillar of the local community, and Clerk to the Justice – but eventually put into motion a secret investigation. Unaware that he was suspected, Armstrong bombarded Martin with more invitations to tea. When it was discovered that Martin had been anonymously sent a box of chocolates with arsenic centres, Armstrong was arrested in his office at Hay, and charged with murder. A packet of arsenic was found in his jacket, while a search of Mayfield found more arsenic and a syringe-nozzle which fitted exactly the holes made in the chocolates sent to Martin.

Two days later, on 2 January 1922, Mrs Armstrong's body was dug up in the presence of Dr Hincks and the pathologist Bernard

Spilsbury. A post-mortem and tests showed it to contain three-and-a-half grains of arsenic. The body was phenomenally well preserved for one which had lain in the earth for ten months.

Armstrong was tried at the Hereford Assizes for his wife's murder. In a dexterous display of the medical evidence, Spilsbury showed clearly that Katherine Armstrong had been killed by a large final dose of arsenic, taken less than twenty-four hours before her death. Armstrong had the means and he also had the motive. Not only did he dislike his wife, he had forged a will by which she left him her £2000 estate. He, himself, was insolvent.

Major Armstrong was found guilty. An appeal was held, but Mr Justice Avory had the same difficulty with Armstrong's 'innocence' as his trial judge. To account for his purchases of arsenic the Major gave the poor excuse of his using it to kill the dandelions on his lawn. Above all, he was unable to explain the packet of arsenic on his person when arrested. As Mr Justice Avory drily noted, 'To find a packet of three and half grains of white arsenic in a solicitor's pocket is surely rare.'

On 31 May 1922, Major Armstrong gained the distinction of being the only solicitor in Britain to be executed for murder.

As a postscript, it is worth noting that another Welsh solicitor, Harold Greenwood, was acquitted of poisoning his wife with arsenic in 1920. It is quite probable that the Greenwood case gave Armstrong the idea to murder his spouse, and that he brought her home from the asylum for that express purpose.

CASE FILE: The Black Widow of Loudon

Among the most extraordinary of the arsenic cases is that of Marie Besnard of Loudon, France. In 1947 Madame Besnard's second husband, Leon, died of a heart attack. Not long after M. Besnard was committed to the earth an anonymous letter reached the public prosecutor alleging that Besnard had been poisoned. His body was exhumed, and traces of arsenic found – 39 mg per kg. The exhumation of Marie Besnard's mother was ordered; her body contained even more arsenic than Leon's. A spate of exhumations of Marie's relatives and friends followed – in each case arsenic was found in the remains. From the deaths of all these people Marie Besnard had gained financially.

Marie Besnard faced twelve murder charges at her trial in Poitiers in 1952. She denied every single one. As nobody was able to come forward to say that they had seen her administer arsenic, the case came to rest on the scientific evidence the prosecution presented. This was briskly demolished by Besnard's wily defence lawyer, Maître Albert Gautrat, who asserted that the specimen jars used by the police analyst were dirty. He also tricked the police analyst into saying that he could distinguish by sight between arsenic and ANTIMONY – and then theatrically demonstrating in a courtroom test that he could not.

The trial was adjourned, while four new scientific experts could be appointed. The bodies were exhumed again. To try and strengthen its case the prosecution dropped seven charges because the evidence of a fatal dose of arsenic in the corpses concerned was dubious. Two years later, Madame Besnard was put on trial again. Maître Gautrat followed on where he had left off in Poitiers, casting doubt on the scientific procedures used, particularly a new radio-chemical one to establish the presence of fatal quantities of arsenic in the hair of exhumed bodies. The lawyer then called his own experts, but the evidence had become so complex that the judges again adjourned the hearing, this time until the prosecution toxicologists could present clearer proof of arsenic poisoning. The Nobel Prize winner, Frederic Joliot-Curie, was asked to check the earlier radio-chemical analysis for arsenic. The arguments and tests dragged on for months, then years, and the soil of Loudon cemetery was analysed over and over. Each test showed a high natural presence of arsenic in the earth.

Then, in November 1961, Marie Besnard was tried for the third time, with all the original twelve murder charges back in the indictment. By now the Besnard trial had become a battle between scientific experts about research findings, with the defence side bringing in a troop of independent experts who testified – out of honesty, not bias – that too little was known about arsenic and its behaviour in soil to reach definite conclusions in a criminal case. Since the arsenic in the twelve bodies *could* have come from the soil in Loudon cemetery Marie Besnard was acquitted of the charges of murder.

The same grounds for acquittal had obtained in an earlier case in Britain. In 1931, at the trial of Annie Hearn for poisoning her friend and neighbour, Alice Thomas, with an arsenic seasoned tinned-salmon sandwich, the advocate Norman Birkett got the defendant acquitted by proving that the soil in which the deceased was interred yielded a high concentration of natural arsenic. As Gautrat did at the trial of Marie Besnard, Birkett also suggested that the analysis jars had become contaminated. 'Am I right in saying', asked Birkett of the prosecution pathologist, Dr Eric Wordley, 'that a piece of soil, so small you could hold it between your fingers, dropped onto the body would make every single calculation wrong?' A question to which Wordley could only reply, 'Yes'.

SOME NOTABLE CASES OF MURDER BY ARSENIC

Name	Date	Victim(s)
Toffana (Ita)	1500s	600+
Marquise de Brinvilliers (Fra)	1676	100+ (relatives and strangers)
Mary Blandy (UK)	1752	1 (father)
Anne Marie Zwaniger (Ger)	1811	11
Marie Lafarge (Fra)	1840	1 (husband)
Helene Jagado (Fra)	1851	23
Madeleine Smith (UK)	1857	1 (not proven)
Dr William King (Can)	1859	1 (wife)
Dr Thomas Smethurst (UK)	1859	1
Mary Ann Cotton (UK)	1873	20 (lovers and relatives)
Dr Philip Cross (Ire)	1887	1 (wife)
Florence Maybrick (UK)	1889	1 (husband)
Edith Carew (Jap)	1896	1 (husband)
Cordelia Botkin (USA)	1898	2
Johann Hoch (USA)	1905	15 (wives)
Bingham Poisoning Case (UK)	1911	3 (same family; unsolved)
Frederick Seddon (UK)	1912	1 (lodger)
Angel-Makers of Nagyrev (Hun)	1914/29	200+
Dr Arthur Warren Waite (USA)	1916	2 (in-laws)
Amy Archer-Gilligan (USA)	1917	5
Harold Greenwood (UK)	1920	1 (wife; acquitted)
Herbert Armstrong (UK)	1922	1 (wife)
Ernest Edward Black (UK)	1922	1 (wife)
Ronald Greeves Griggs (Aus)	1928	1 (wife; acquitted)
Croydon Poisonings (UK)	1928/29	3 (same family; unsolved)
Annie Hearn (UK)	1931	1 (neighbour; acquitted)
Daisy de Melker (SA)	1932	3 (relatives)
Charlotte Bryant (UK)	1936	1 (husband)
Mary Creighton and Everett Applegate (USA)	1936	1 (wife)
Frederick Radford (UK)	1949	1 (wife)
Marie Besnard (Fra)	1950s	12 (relatives; acquitted)
Marcus Marymont (UK)	1959	1 (wife)
Maria Groesbek (SA)	1969	1 (husband)
Marie Hilley (USA)	1975	1 (husband)
Rob Coulthard (USA)	1986/89	1 (wife)

ASPHYXIA
A term which has come to mean 'deprivation of air', although its

original Greek meaning is 'absence of pulsation'. In forensic science, asphyxia is generally regarded as manual asphyxia (or anoxic anoxia), where the air supply is interrupted as a result of CHOKING, STRANGULATION, SUFFOCATION or DROWNING. These are the basics of murder and are dealt with in separate entries. A rare homicidal form of manual asphyxia is HANGING, and rarer still is crush or traumatic asphyxia, where the chest is fixed or weighed down to prevent breathing. As a method of killing, its most notorious users were Burke and Hare, the two Irish labourers who provided cadavers for Edinburgh's anatomical school at 10 Surgeon's Square (Principal: Dr Knox) in the 1820s. Their *modus operandi* was to lure a vagrant back to their lodgings, encourage him or her to imbibe large quantities of ALCOHOL and, when the victim was senseless, sit on his chest. This deflated the lungs, and, by covering the mouth and nostrils with a blanket, the respiratory system was violently arrested (a homicide technique which became known as 'Burking'). Traumatic asphyxia is also seen in homicidal circumstances where a bomb has caused great destruction and collapsing masonry has pinned and crushed victims in the rubble.

Medical authorities sometimes class as asphyxia a number of disorders not caused by manual means, but which affect the blood's capacity to carry oxygen or to take it up. These are:

Stagnant Anoxia The circulation of blood is stopped as a result of shock, for example ELECTROCUTION, AIR EMBOLISM, heart failure.
Histotoxic Anoxia Where body tissues are unable to utilize oxygen in the blood due to paralysis from poisons such as CYANIDE.
Anaemic Anoxia Either an insufficient supply of oxygen to the body as a result of severe blood loss (for instance, from a stab wound), or the prevention of oxygen into the blood. The latter can be caused by CARBON MONOXIDE poisoning.

Additionally, medicine may classify the action of poisons such as MORPHINE and BARBITURATES in paralysing the respiratory system as a form of manual asphyxia.

Whatever the cause, the signs of asphyxia are uniform. Classically, these are congestions (reddening of skin and tissues), cyanosis (bluish coloration), and petechial haemorrhages (burst blood vessels) in the eyes, heart, lungs and on the face. A post-mortem may also show distension of the right-hand side of the heart.

The time taken for asphyxia to occur is extremely variable. Pressure on the carotid artery, for instance, in some forms of strangulation can bring almost instantaneous death, while suffocation may require upwards of five minutes. In the process, the victim will experience death in three stages: firstly, an increase in pulse rate and blood pressure as he or she struggles for breath; secondly, congestion and cyanosis of the face, bulging eyes, semi-consciousness, and convulsions; thirdly, shallow respiration, unconsciousness, and involuntary twitching of the muscles as death occurs.

ATROPINE

Atropine is an alkaloid POISON extracted from belladonna (*Atropa belladonna*), the plant whose name, translated from Italian, means 'beautiful woman'.

For centuries, women used eye drops of belladonna – also known as deadly nightshade – to widen their pupils and so enhance their attractiveness. The poison also figures prominently in the history of the occult. Medieval witches rubbed atropine ointment – the poison is easily absorbed through the skin – into their vaginas, the resulting hallucinations giving the sensation of flight.

In its pure form, atropine can cause death with as little as 100 mg in an adult, 10 mg in a child. The symptoms of atropine poisoning are dryness of the mouth and throat, an increase in the heart rate, delerium and, later, coma. A distinctive symptom is the same dilation of the pupils which made it valued as a cosmetic, making the eyes appear almost totally black. Death occurs from respiratory or heart failure.

Atropine was much valued as a poison in the classical world, and the long list of victims who suffered at the hands of Agrippina, wife of Claudius, is a testament to its power. In modern times, atropine poisoning is something of a forgotten homicidal art. Among the very few documented instances are those of Nurse Steele, who added belladonna to the milk drink of a surgeon she worked for at a London hospital in 1872, and Frenchman Dr Eustachy, who injected atropine into some thrushes which he sent as a present to a rival, Dr Tournatoire, in 1884. Madame Tournatoire and her cook devoured one thrush each and suffered chronic hallucinations and head pains. Despite his protestations ('It's all a joke'), Dr Eustachy was convicted of attempted murder and served eight years in prison.

AXES

> *Lizzie Borden took an axe*
> *And gave her mother forty whacks*
> *And when she saw what she had done*
> *She gave her father forty one.*

Thus runs the popular rhyme about the most famous axe murders in crime history, those attributed to Lizzie Borden in 1893. The axe

– with its combination of heavy weight, sharp edge and association with the executioner – is a particularly horrific weapon (hence its prominence in nightmare movies). And once upon a time, in the days when domestic heating consisted of a wood fire and an axe was to be found by almost every back door, it was commonly pressed into homicidal service.

In an axe murder the head and upper torso are usually the prime targets, with the skull being penetrated, even the carotid artery severed, if the weapon is sharp. The axe will always split or lacerate the skin and underlying tissues unless, as in the abdomen, they are capable of 'give'. Sometimes the split from the axe is so deep that it amounts to a cleft, leaving a clue to its dimensions (useful if the murder weapon is to be found).

Axe murder is invariably a bloody business. The crime scene will be marked by blood-splashes, as will the attacker. And, since the axe is most often wielded with two hands, the attacker may have defence wounds on his or her forearms.

The axe is not only an instrument of death. It can, as Kate Webster discovered in 1879 (see Case File), double up as an aid to mutilation and DISMEMBERMENT.

Although Lizzie Borden was acquitted of murdering her family at Fall River, Massachusetts, other axe-men and women have not been so judicially fortunate. Louis Wagner killed two women friends in New Hampshire, USA, in 1873 with his axe – wielding it so brutally that the handle broke – in a robbery which netted him $20. After various stays of execution he was hanged in 1875. Herbert Glasson, the ex-butcher who slaughtered two people while trying to rob a bank ('Money I want. And money I must have') in New South Wales in 1893, also had an assignment with the hangman, despite a defence claim of insanity. In the infamous Ruahine Axe Murders in New Zealand, 1914, farm labourer Arthur Rottman killed three members of his employer's family – including a two-year-old baby – with a selection of cleavers and axes. Rottman claimed that he was drunk at the time and could not remember what happened. His trial was dominated by medical debates over mania and the effects of ALCOHOL. He was hanged in 1915 nonetheless.

More recently, David Masters, a clinically depressed veterinary surgeon, struck his wife at least twelve times with an axe as she lay asleep at their Wiltshire home on 26 July 1993, before committing suicide by DEFENESTRATION.

CASE FILE: Kate Webster

At the time of her 1879 infamy, Kate Webster was a thirty-year-old habitual thief and prostitute who had gone into service with Mrs

Thomas, a gentlewoman of 2 Vine Cottages, Park Road, Richmond, London. It was a decision that Mrs Thomas would live – but only for a very short time – to regret. With malice aforethought and robbery in mind, Kate Webster battered her employer to death with a coal axe, and dragged the body into the scullery. There, with the aid of the axe, a carving knife and a meat saw, she hacked the corpse apart. The resulting portions were then boiled down in the kitchen copper, and parcelled up. Some of the parcels were packed into a wooden box which was thrown in the river, the rest were put on the fire for BURNING. The fat from these was then, apparently, skimmed off and sold in a local public house as two jars of 'dripping'.

The wooden box consigned to the Thames, however, surfaced to give Kate's game away. Mrs Thomas's head, thrown off Hammersmith Bridge, was never found, but Kate Webster's head was placed in the hangman's noose on 29 July 1879 at Wandsworth Prison. Webster had made a small fortune from the sale of her late mistress's goods and chattels – including her false teeth (sold for 6s) – but, unfortunately for her, she did not live to enjoy the proceeds of her crime.

The Webster case has a certain culinary similarity with that of American Roxanna Druse, who, in 1889, took a hatchet to her farmer husband, John. Neighbours made suspicious by his absence and the black clouds billowing from the Druse chimney, questioned her young boy, who blurted out the whole tale. Not only had John Druse been killed, but Mrs Druse and her mentally retarded daughter had – with the offending axe – dismembered his corpse, then boiled the pieces and placed them on the farmhouse fire.

CASE FILE: The Axeman of New Orleans

Between the years 1911 and 1919 the American city of New Orleans was subjected to a reign of Ripper-like terror by 'The Axeman'. His targets were unusual, and his *modus operandi* distinctive. Almost all his victims were Italian grocers, and he invariably broke into their premises by smashing a door panel with an axe – which he then used to strike his victims.

In 1911, the Axeman murdered three Italian grocers and their wives, the Cutis, the Rosettis, and Schiambras. Then, for seven years, it seemed that the Axeman's depredations had stopped.

However, on 28 May 1918, an Italian grocery couple called Maggio were attacked in the night while they slept, the perpetrator chiselling out a door panel to gain entry. Mrs Maggio's head was virtually severed from her shoulders. To ensure that they were dead – the axe is not the most reliable means of homicide – the killer had cut their throats. The bloody axe was left on the backyard steps.

The next morning the police discovered a chalked message on a nearby pavement: 'Mrs Maggio is going to sit up tonight just like Mrs Toney'. 'Mrs Toney', it occurred to the police, might be Mrs *Toni* Schiambra, one of the Axeman's 1911 victims. The Axeman had commeth back.

On 28 June 1918, the grocer Louis Besumer was discovered in his apartment with a headwound from an axe, while his common-law-wife, Harriet Lowe, was lying on the bed, badly injured and unconscious. A week later, Harriet Lowe died, but before she did so she mumbled that Louis Besumer had killed her. As it would later turn out, this was just the first of several bizarre allegations made by victims in the case. Besumer was arrested – but on the very same day, the Axeman battered a Mrs Schneider. Besumer was acquitted.

The next to be visited by the Axeman, in a break from his usual routine, was Joseph Romano. In the early morning of 10 August, Pauline and Mary Bruno were awakened by noises of struggling from their Uncle Joseph's room. When, with trepidation, they peeked out into the corridor a man they described as 'dark, tall, heavy-set, wearing a dark suit and a black slouch hat' ran past them. The sisters immediately called for help, and Joseph Romano was sped to hospital but he died of brain injuries. As in the previous cases, a panel had been cut from the door and the weapon discarded at the scene of the crime.

For seven months there were no attacks; but it was a false peace, for on 10 March 1919 the Axeman started again. The victims this time were the Cortimiglia family. Charles Cortimiglia – a grocer – and his wife Rosie both sustained severe head injuries, while their baby daughter was killed outright by a single blow. All the usual hallmarks – the forced door panel, the discarded bloody axe – were present. Possibly as a result of her split skull, Mrs Cortimiglia began to accuse her neighbours, Iorlando Jordano and his son, Frank, of the crime. Charles Cortimiglia denied that they were responsible – he had after all grappled close up with the Axeman – but the Jordanos were arrested and tried for the murder of the Cortimiglia baby. The jury found them guilty and Frank was sentenced to death, Iorlando to imprisonment for life.

Yet it soon became clear to the inhabitants of New Orleans that the Axeman was still among them, not safely behind bars: on 10 August 1919, grocer Steve Bocca had his head split open while he slept; on 3 September, Sarah Laumann was found unconscious with head injuries; on 29 October Mike Pepitone was murdered, his wife disturbing the killer just after he had landed the fatal blow. This was the last time the Axeman would attack.

But it is not the end of the story. On 7 December, Rosie Cortimiglia confessed in a wail of tears to New Orleans' *Times-Picayune* newspaper that she had falsely accused the Jordanos, who were accordingly released. Meanwhile, in Los Angeles the police had arrested a woman for shooting dead a man in the street. The woman was Mrs Mike Pepitone, widow of the Axeman's last victim, and the dead man was Joseph Mumfre. 'He was the Axeman,' said Mrs Pepitone. 'I saw him running from my husband's room.'

The police checked on Mumfre, who had a long criminal record. Although he had many periods of imprisonment, he was always free when the axe murders were committed . . . It will probably now never be known for sure whether Mumfre was the Mad Axeman of New Orleans, and intriguing questions remain about the most prolific exponent of the art of the axe murder. What was his motive, for he never took money? Above all: Why single out Italian grocers?

B

BACTERIAL POISONING

Bacteria are primitive forms of micro-organisms, first observed by the Dutch scientist Anthony van Leeuwenhoek in about 1687. In 1842, Scottish anatomist John Goodsir linked bacteria with disease, describing sarcinae in the stomach. Their work came to fruition in the hands of Louis Pasteur (1822–1895), the brilliant French bacteriologist who was the first to understand how micro-organisms cause disease by producing toxins which are harmful to tissues.

One group of toxins, endotoxins, are retained in the bacterial cells and can do damage wherever the bacteria are sited in the body. Another group, exotoxins, of which diphtheria is an example, pass from the bacteria and circulate throughout the body. The poison from the bacterium *Clostridium botulinum* – botulism – is generally believed to be the most powerful in the world, seven million times more potent than cobra venom. The bacterium causing the poison lurks in soil, but is only active under certain defined conditions and is killed by exposure to oxygen. If the poison is absorbed by humans it interferes with the production of the nerve transmission fluid called acetylcholine. As a result, fewer and fewer impulses reach the muscles, and the muscles which control breathing are paralysed.

Pasteur used his understanding of bacteria to pioneer methods of immunizing against killer diseases such as rabies and anthrax. In a sense, Henri Girard (see Case File) built on Pasteur's work, using micro-organisms not to save life but to commit murder. An incorrigible swindler who had been dishonourably discharged from the French 10th Hussars, Girard poisoned an insurance broker in 1912 with typhoid. For this exploit Girard has been accorded the title of 'the first scientific murderer'.

But there are earlier cases of bacterial poisoners than Girard. The German germ slayer, Karl Ropf, had pressed bacteria into homicidal service at the turn of the twentieth century, while, in 1909, Dr Bennett Clarke Hyde employed typhoid in his personal quest to be a millionaire. His wife's family, the Swopes, were the richest in Kansas and if they died all the Swope wealth would come to her – and thus to him. He began his project with STRYCHNINE and CYANIDE, but then administered bacterial poison to five members of the family, one of whom died, the rest recovered. Suspicion began to fall on Hyde and he was observed trying to throw away a cyanide capsule. The case made headlines across the world. Found guilty of first-degree murder, Hyde won an appeal and was granted two retrials. At both the jury failed to agree a verdict and the charge against him was dropped.

Dr Hyde was probably the role model for two other killers who were likewise motivated by a desire to remove family members standing between them and a father-in-law's fortune. Patrick O'Brien de Lacey hired a needy Petrograd physician, Dr Pachenko, in 1910 to poison family members through inoculation. Selecting de Lacey's brother-in-law as the first victim, Pachenko substituted diphtheria poison for anti-cholera medicine. On 16 May 1910, the brother-in-law died, but Pachenko and de Lacey were exposed by the former's mistress. Six years later diphtheria – along with influenza and tuberculosis bacteria – was used by New York's Dr Arthur Waite to murder his mother and father-in-law.

A more recent case of bacterial poisoning comes from Texas in the 1960s. At the beginning of that decade, Joan Robinson, adopted daughter of oil millionaire Ash Robinson, married surgeon John Hill. But their relationship quickly crumbled. In 1969 Joan Hill died as a result of a 'fulminating infection of unknown origin' and her grieving father accused Hill of 'murder by omission', alleging that he had caused his wife's death by deliberately withholding medical treatment. Although a rushed first post-mortem disclosed nothing suspicious, a second post-mortem found signs of meningitis in the brain.

Dr Hill was tried in 1971 after his second wife alleged that he had attempted to murder her by HIT-AND-RUN. She testified that he had confided to her that he had killed Joan Hill by injecting her with a bacterial culture made from 'every form of human excretion . . . urine, faeces . . . and even pus taken from a boil on a patient's back'. All this resulted in a mistrial, and before Hill could be retried he was shot in his home by a hired gunman who, in turn, was shot by the police.

It is, of course, significant that John Hill, like Hyde, Arthur Waite (see Case File) and Pachenko, was a physician. Who better to know which germs to use, in which quantities, and how to inject them than a doctor? Not that bacterial poisoning hasn't been tried by the keen amateur. And there was no amateur more keen than Henri Girard.

CASE FILE: The First Scientific Murderer

Forty-six-year-old Henri Girard entertained his friends lavishly. He also kept three Parisian mistresses. He pretended to be a bookmaker, but actually made his money from more-or-less legal insurance schemes. His family, who were comfortably bourgeois, also sent occasional money treats his way.

But, alas, it was not enough to keep Girard in the excessive

manner to which he had become accustomed, so, like others before
him, he added murder to his means of making more lucre. Equipping
himself with test tubes and other laboratory apparatus, Girard began
.looking for a victim, who came in the unsuspecting shape of Louis
Pernotte, an insurance broker and admirer of Girard's. In 1910,
Pernotte handed over all his financial affairs to Girard, giving him
power of attorney. Soon after Girard insured Pernotte's life for a total
of 300,000 francs. At the same time, Girard obtained cultures of
typhoid bacteria from a laboratory supplier.

In 1912, Pernotte, his wife and two children became ill with
typhoid after drinking water from a carafe into which Girard had
infiltrated typhoid bacteria. Girard attended them, bringing with
him a syringe of 'camphorated camomile'. Although the wife and
children recovered, Louis Pernotte died in December 1912, despite
the injections from his good friend Girard. As well as collecting on
the life policy, Girard brazenly told Madame Pernotte that her
husband had died owing him 200,000 francs. There was no
suspicion at all that Pernotte had been deliberately killed, and this
is the great advantage of bacterial poisoning for the murderer – by
its very nature, it is a death open to confusion with 'natural causes'.

Girard's next pre-insured victims were given *Amanita phalloides*,
a type of poisonous fungus (see FUNGI), but, despite severe
illness, managed to survive. Then, in 1918, Girard's murderous eye
fell on war widow, Madame Monin. This time, he enlisted the help
of one of his mistresses, Jeanne Droubin, who took out a policy on
Monin's life. Safely insured, Madame Monin was invited to
Girard's apartment, where she was given an aperitif with a dash of
bacteria. She collapsed in the Metro on the way home and died. Her
demise, coming so soon after the purchase of insurance, prompted
the company to investigate. Girard was arrested in August 1918,
and while in custody made a number of confessions. He insisted,
though, that he was a misunderstood man 'with a very warm heart'.
He killed himself before he could go to trial. Naturally, he used
germ cultures.

CASE FILE: Arthur Warren Waite

On trial for his life, accused of double murder, Dr Arthur Warren
Waite took the witness stand in the New York courtroom. He
smiled broadly and looked relaxed, just as he had done over the
previous three days of trial in that hot summer of 1916, even when
the prosecution was detailing his crimes.

Yes, it was, he agreed, all true. He had murdered his mother-in-
law, using germs of diphtheria and influenza. Some week later he
had tried 'similar methods' on his father-in-law, but when the old
man proved rather tougher than expected, plied him with doses of

the somewhat less novel ARSENIC and CHLOROFORM. Asked why he had killed, Waite replied simply, 'For the money'.

Waite was a native of Grand Rapids, Michigan, the son of middle class parents. At the age of nineteen he enrolled at the dental school of the University of Michigan. He then went to Glasgow, and worked in South Africa before returning home to Grand Rapids. There he met Clara Peck, daughter of millionaire drug manufacturer, John Peck. In September 1915, the couple married, and set up home in a luxurious apartment on fashionable Riverside Drive in New York.

On 17 September 1915 – just eight days after his wedding – Waite began studying bacteriology. Through contacts at the Cornell Medical School he acquired quantities of diphtheria and typhoid bacilli and put these under his microscope at his apartment, where he had set up a small private laboratory. 'Doctor' Waite, as he styled himself, also got an introduction to Dr Percival de Nyce, a skilled bacteriologist at New York's Flower Hospital. Dr Nyce was impressed by the 28-year-old's keenness. He did think it was odd, however, that Waite only wanted to study dangerous bacteria.

Early in January 1916, Waite invited Clara's parents, John and Hannah Peck, to New York. No sooner had they arrived than Mrs Peck began feeling ill. Waite explained why at his trial: 'I started poisoning her from the very first meal after she arrived. I gave her six assorted tubes of pneumonia, diphtheria and influenza germs in her food.' He added that he also gave her Veronal, a BARBITU-RATE, for good measure. Her death on 30 January was certified as being from kidney disease.

After the funeral in Grand Rapids, Arthur and Clara Waite returned to New York, accompanied by the distressed and inconsolable Mr Peck. With Mrs Peck in the ground, Waite now turned his attention on 'Father', subjecting him to doses of germs. Waite recalled later, with some pride, a refinement in the form of 'a nasal spray filled with tuberculosis bacteria'. Still Mr Peck would not die, so Waite let off tubes of chlorine gas in his room, and tried to give him pneumonia by damping his sheets with water. Exasperated and impatient, Waite gave John Peck a whacking 18 g of arsenic. The old man was dead within thirty-six hours. Once again, death was ascribed to kidney failure.

John Peck left his children over $1,000,000. Waite tried to have his father-in-law cremated, but the family were firmly opposed. An anonymous telegram had been sent to John Peck's son which read: 'Suspicions aroused. Demand autopsy. Keep telegram secret. – K. Adams'. K. Adams was in fact Elizabeth Hardwicke, a relative of the Pecks, who had seen Waite dining at the Plaza Hotel in New York with his beautiful mistress, Margaret Horton. It was this entanglement which led to his downfall. Waite tried to pass Horton off as his nurse, but Elizabeth Hardwicke was too clever to be taken in by such a flustered lie. She also added 'Mistress' and the 'Sudden Deaths' of the Pecks together to equal 'Murder'.

John Peck's son did as the telegram demanded, and had an autopsy performed on his father. The arsenic was easily detected, and it was this which betrayed Waite. If he had persisted with bacteria it would have been well nigh impossible to prove that John Peck's death was not from 'natural causes'.

Waite tried to escape capital punishment by pleading insanity, claiming that he had been compelled to murder the Pecks by 'The Man from Egypt'. But it was to no avail and he went to the electric chair at Sing Sing Prison on 24 May 1917. As the warders strapped on the electrodes, Waite asked: 'Is this all there is to it?'

BARBITURATES

With the gradual control of 'old-fashioned' poisons such as ARSENIC, ANTIMONY and STRYCHNINE, criminal toxicologists had seemed to have earned themselves a respite; it was not so. The widespread use of barbiturates from the 1950s and their easy availability on prescription caused them to eclipse CARBON MONOXIDE poisoning from coal gas fires as the most frequent means of committing suicide. Barbiturates also began to be more widely identified as the agents of homicide, as a procession of killers descended on the unwary, prescription bottle in hand.

Barbiturates are a category of drugs which depress the central nervous system, inducing in the taker a mild sense of wellbeing and calm. They trace their origin back to 1863 when the German chemist Adolf von Bayer synthesized Barbituric acid (named after a girlfriend, Barbara). Some forty years later, von Mering and Fischer isolated two derivatives of the acid, barbital (Veronal) and phenobarbital (Luminal). These were found to be excellent sedatives. Many other barbiturate preparations have since been developed. These are divided into four main types, according to their speed of action:

Long-acting, such as barbital and phenobarbital. A therapeutic dose of phenobarbital is about 50–100 mg, a fatal dose upwards of 1–4 g. *Intermediate-acting*, such as butobarbitone (Soneryl) and amylobarbitone (Amytal). A dangerous dose is around 1–2 g. *Short-acting*, such as pentobarbitone (Nembutal), which have a dangerous dose of about 1 g. *Ultra-short-acting*, given as intravenous injection for the induction of anaesthesia in operations.

All tend to be addictive over prolonged use, and are easy to overdose on, especially if taken in conjunction with alcohol. The short-acting barbiturates may cause death from heart failure (ventricular fibrillation) within twenty minutes in large doses. Other barbiturate drugs cause extended coma which may result in respiratory depression. In a long coma, bronco-pneumonia may be the mode of death.

Evidence of barbiturate poisoning is likely to be shown in the subject's corpse by oedema, froth and pus in the lungs and congestion of the brain. The subject's urine will show strongly red when it is in an acid solution.

Although mainly a post-war murder weapon, the barbiturate was introduced into the world of crime as early as 1916, when Dr Arthur Warren Waite used Veronal on his in-laws (although his preferred method was BACTERIAL POISONING). In a celebrated French case from 1934, Violette Nozière, a part-time Parisian prostitute, drugged her parents' coffee with massive doses of Veronal with the intention of using her inheritance to buy a car for a boy she fancied. Although she did kill her father, her mother survived. Nozière would have been the first woman to have been executed in France for fifty years, but at the last minute President Lebrun, at the pleading of her mother, commuted her sentence to life imprisonment.

CASE FILE: The Unwanted Child

The victim was Terence Armstrong, a five-month-old baby who died at his home in Gosport, Hampshire, 22 July 1955. The doctor could not identify the cause of death, and accordingly notified the Gosport coroner. Examining the tiny corpse the local pathologist, Dr Harold Miller, discovered a shrivelled red shell in the child's throat. It reminded Dr Miller of the skin of the highly toxic daphne berry. There were more shells in the stomach and berry poisoning seemed the most likely cause of death. An officer from the coroner's office duly called at the child's home to see if he had had access to daphne berries. The officer was amazed to find Terence's parents, 26-year-old John and nineteen-year-old Janet Armstrong, watching television without an apparent sorrow in the world. However, there was a daphne tree in the garden. The officer reported his finding to Dr Miller.

The case would have been closed there except for the fact that the 'berries' and child's stomach contents had behaved unusually when stored in formaldehyde, causing Dr Miller to send samples to a laboratory. Analysis showed the berry 'skins' to be made from cornstarch and a red dye, eosin – ingredients found in red medical capsules. At this point Superintendent L.C. Nicholls, Director of Scotland Yard's Forensic Laboratory, was called in. After five days of tests he found a trace – $1/50$ of a grain – of the barbiturate Seconal in a vomit stain on the dead child's pillow.

Alerted by Superintendent Nicholls, the Gosport police went to John Armstrong's place of work, which happened to be the local naval hospital where he was a sick-bay attendant. Armstrong was known to have access to Seconal and, it transpired, fifty Seconal capsules had mysteriously disappeared from the medicine cupboard. However, since Armstrong denied having Seconal in his house there was no substantial proof against him and the inquest on Terence Armstrong's death returned an open verdict.

It was only open for a year. In July 1956, Janet Armstrong applied for a separation order against her husband, on the grounds that he repeatedly assaulted her. The order was refused, so Janet went to the Gosport police in a fit of revenge and informed them that her husband *had* brought Seconal capsules home. Furthermore, after Terence's death, he had made her dispose of the remaining capsules.

At the trial of the Armstrongs at Winchester Assizes, the jury heard that Terence had been the innocent victim of inadequate parents, who were completely unable to cope with family life. One child had been stricken by a mysterious illness, and another had died after developing the same symptoms. The Armstrongs were also in debt, and John Armstrong at least regarded the latest child as a costly inconvenience. John Armstrong was pronounced guilty, Janet was acquitted. A month later, however, Janet Armstrong revealed that she had given Terence Armstrong a Seconal capsule 'to help him sleep'.

BELLADONNA   *See* **ATROPINE**

BITING
Human-on-human biting is a common feature of sexual killings. Such bites tend to be inflicted for deliberate, sadistic pleasure, with a characteristic 'sucking' action. Invariably, the bites will be congregated around the subject's genitalia or erogenous zones. Nipples may be injured, even bitten off.

Biting is also a characteristic of child abuse, though the targeted areas here tend to be the extremities, chest and thorax. Bite-mark analysis forms a whole branch of forensic odontology since, if the impression left in the victim's flesh is clearly enough defined, it can be compared with an impression of a suspect's teeth. Additionally, saliva may be present around the bite; if this contains antigens it will identify the attacker's blood group. (In the future, profiling from saliva may be able to give a DNA 'fingerprint' of the assailant.)

In one case, at least, a killer has progressed from simply biting his victims as a sado-sexual turn-on to biting them to death. This is the notorious Fritz Haarmann, a meat smuggler and mass killer who stalked Hanover in the dark years after World War I. Posing as a policeman, Haarmann preyed on the young male refugees who flocked to the city's railway station, enticing them to his seedy lodgings on the Kellerstrasse with promises of food. Once they were inside, Haarmann sexually assaulted them before biting through their throats until they were dead (the wounds inflicted would have been similar to those of a CUT-THROAT). Afterwards, Haarmann sold their clothing – and the meat from their bodies, which, carried in buckets to Hanover's open market, was purveyed by Haarmann as 'horseflesh' to starving citizens. Unusable portions of the bodies, such as bones and skulls, were dumped in the River Leine.

In the autumn of 1919, Haarmann was joined in his CANNIBALISM, and his bed, by a homosexual petty crook called Hans Grans, the duo taking up a joint lodging on Neuestrasse. It has been estimated that over the following sixteen months Haarmann and Grans disposed of two bodies every week. In the chaos of post-war German society the gruesome twosome's business might have gone on for years, but in June 1924 Haarmann was arrested for indecently assaulting a boy in the street. As a matter of course, the Neuestrasse apartment was searched and articles belonging to the missing bodies found. As if to prove that Haarmann's luck had run out, bones from his victims were coincidentally discovered by boys fishing in the Leine.

Haarmann now decided it was time to confess and implicated Hans Grans, who was promptly arrested. At their trial in December 1924, Haarmann seemed bemused by the fact that he was only being charged with twenty-seven murders; his recollection was that he had committed more than forty. Whatever the total, it was enough to earn him a decapitation. Grans, who had been careful always to let Haarmann do all the really dirty work, was given a twelve-year sentence.

BLUNT INSTRUMENTS

The infamous 'blunt instrument' is one of the commonest homicidal weapons; one of the earliest too, dating back to the Neanderthal's club. It is usually, though not exclusively, associated with unpremeditated attacks carried out by a person in whom the killer instinct is suddenly roused and who grabs the nearest heavy implement to hand: the hammer, the fireside poker, the iron bar, the wooden bough on the ground.

Unlike poison or firearms, the blunt instrument is a weapon of intimacy, of naked fury: it allows the satisfaction of violence. By their brief, impulsive nature, homicidal wieldings of the blunt instrument – whether bludgeonings or batterings – tend to be remarkable only in their quantity. There is, in general, no refinement to them. Exceptions include transvestite Margaret 'Bill'

Allen's battering of a Rawtenstall widow in 1949 because she was
'in a funny mood'; the *folie à deux* of New Zealand lesbian teenagers
Pauline Parker and Juliet Hulme (see Case File); sex-killer DeWitt
Clinton Cook's use of a piece of 2 ft × 4 ft wood for his murder of
Los Angeles college girl Anna Sosoyeva, the length of wood clearly
being a symbolic sexual organ (Cook's penis was exceptionally
small).

Occasionally, too, bludgeonings are distinguished by the novel
choice of blunt instrument. As a prelude to robbing them, Edgar
Edwards battered London grocer John Darby and his wife to death
in 1902 with a lead window-sash weight. Peter Griffiths, aged
twenty-two, killed three-year-old Anne Devaney of Blackburn in
1948 by beating her against the wall of the hospital in which she was
a patient. Teenager Michael Queripel used an iron tee-marker to
murder a woman walking her dog on a Birmingham golf course in
1955. In 1994, Clwyd police sergeant Stephen Jones, aged thirty-
four, found his wife Madallin an inconvenience to his relationship
with a teenage barmaid, so he killed her – with his truncheon.

Exotic, but as yet unidentified, blunt implements are featured in
two of the great unsolved crimes of the century: the murders of Sir
Harry Oakes and Marilyn Sheppard. Oakes, an American-born
millionaire, was found burned and battered to death in his home in
the Bahamas in 1943. Four triangular-shaped wounds were made in
the head by an unknown weapon. Eleven years later, in Cleveland,
Ohio, Mrs Sheppard was similarly done in by an unidentified blunt
implement, although a surgical instrument of some sort was
suggested. Her husband – a surgeon – was tried for the murder and
found guilty. At a second trial, in 1966, Sheppard's claim that the
murder was committed by an intruder was believed and the
conviction overturned. The case formed the basis for the TV serial
– and subsequent movie – *The Fugitive*.

In the homicidal wielding of the blunt instrument the head is the
natural target; in fact, bludgeoning is rarely fatal unless it is, the
brain being the vital organ that is least protected by flesh and bone.
However, the physical strength needed to wield a single 'killer
blow' is prodigious and usually a flurry of blows is needed to
dispatch the victim. As a result, the crime scene and the victim are
likely to be a gory mess, and the assailant blood-splattered.

In blows to the head from a blunt instrument, the epidermis and
subcutaneous tissue are crushed against the underlying skull,
causing lacerated wounds. Characteristically, these are ragged and
surrounded by bruising, with strands of skin, hair, and blood
vessels lying at their base. Where blows have been delivered with
great force – or the instrument is extremely heavy – such strands
may be impacted into fractured or broken bone.

Often a great deal about the type of blunt instrument can be
gathered from the shape of the wound. An X-ray examination may

also reveal the number and direction of injuries not obvious to the naked eye. Meanwhile, the blunt weapon used in the assault will invariably have crushed skin, broken or detached hairs and blood adhered to its surface. In the famous 'Wigwam Girl' case of 1942, a birch bough found 300 yards from the body – in a wood with boughs lying around in profusion – had bark crushed at one end, and caught in the splintered bark were a number of human head hairs identical to those of the dead girl. The bough 'fitted' the solitary crushing head wound which caused her death. This forensic work by Keith Simpson resulted in a Canadian soldier of Red Indian stock stationed in Britain, August Sangret, being convicted of the girl's murder.

Death from bludgeoning of the head is almost always from brain injury. This can occur without the skull being fractured, where haemorrhaging of blood vessels results in internal bleeding between the skull and the membrane covering the brain, the dura. Brain injury is inevitable if fracturing occurs, either from haemorrhaging, or from the brain being 'pulped' through an opening in the skull, or from fragments of skull being driven into the brain. In cases where the head injury is not fatal but the subject becomes unconscious amnesia sometimes follows. Impact injuries to the head, it might be noted, are also a feature of attacks by other weapons, in addition to the blunt instrument, including the motor-car in HIT-AND-RUN, and personal weapons, such as fists and feet (see KICKING).

CASE FILE: Folie à Deux

It was common knowledge at the Girls' High School in Christchurch, New Zealand, in 1954 that Pauline Parker had a crush on Juliet Hulme and the feeling was reciprocated. But what seemed to teachers and schoolmates a typical schoolgirl friendship was something much deeper, much darker. It was an obsession that would breed murder.

Pauline Yvonne Parker was, at sixteen, the elder of the two by a year. She was also the shorter, if the more dominant. She lived with her mother Honora Parker and the man she called Father, wholesale fishmonger Herbert Rieper. Although Honora and Herbert weren't married, they had lived together for twenty years. Pauline was a reserved and uncommunicative girl at home, where the only outlet for her thoughts was her diary.

Juliet Hulme was the younger and taller of the two girls who would make courtroom history. Her father was an eminent British scientist who had moved to New Zealand for Juliet's health; she had a tendency to tuberculosis. At first her home life was happy. Then, one afternoon, she opened a door and found her mother in the arms of the lodger. Although Juliet said nothing to her father

about the incident, he quickly became aware that his wife was
having an affair. In early 1954 he decided to move back to England,
taking with him Juliet's brother. Juliet – because of her health –
would remain behind in New Zealand, although she would accompany her brother and father on their voyage as far as South Africa.
The long holiday, Mr Hulme thought, would be good for her.

More importantly, it would get her away from Pauline Parker.
Both girls' parents had become uneasy about their friendship,
about the hours they spent together locked away in the bedroom. It
was, the parents all agreed, 'unnatural'.

If the parents thought it was a good idea that Juliet went on the
voyage to South Africa, Juliet and Pauline were horrified. No one
was going to split them up, ever. They went into one of their secret
sessions and Juliet gave her father an ultimatum: 'I'm not going
with you to South Africa unless Pauline comes with us.'

His answer was an emphatic No.

The girls then made an entreaty to Pauline's mother, hoping to
get her to intercede on their behalf. She, however, was even more
opposed to the idea. No, Pauline could not go. Absolutely not.

Little did she know it, but Honora Parker had just ensured that
she would be murdered.

Almost immediately, Pauline and Juliet began plotting the deed,
examining the various possible methods of murder. After much
discussion they settled on a makeshift blunt instrument: a brick in a
stocking.

On 22 June 1954, the two girls and Honora Parker went to
Victoria Park on the outskirts of Christchurch for the afternoon. At
about 3 p.m. the two girls and Mrs Parker left the refreshment hut,
with Juliet going on in front. When she came to a bend in the path
she scattered some pink pebbles.

Pauline Parker stayed by her mother's side. In her pocket was
the half-brick shoved into the toe of a stocking. At the bend in
the path, Mrs Parker saw the pretty pink pebbles and stooped to
pick them up. As she did so, Pauline swung the brickbat on to
her mother's lowered head, using all the strength she could. Mrs
Parker pitched forward, helpless. Pauline struck her again and
again, raining down a frenzy of blows. Juliet rushed up and
seized the stocking and she too beat the unconscious woman on
the head.

Panting, the two blood-spattered girls ran back to the refreshment kiosk, telling the woman there that Mrs Parker had tripped
over. 'She kept falling and banging her head as she went down,'
shouted Pauline. 'I'll never forget her head banging,' exclaimed
Juliet. The kiosk owner sent her husband to investigate. Even at a
glance he could tell that Mrs Parker had suffered no accident, not
with head wounds like that.

So could the police when they arrived: the girls were taken

into custody immediately. At the hospital where Mrs Parker's body was taken a surgeon counted forty-five separate wounds to the head. Most of them were smeared with brickdust. Pauline admitted to the police that she had planned the murder days ahead. Asked how many times she had hit her mother, she replied: 'A great many, I imagine.'

At the trial, Pauline's diary was the main exhibit for the prosecution. The entries were chillingly explicit. On 21 June, she wrote: 'We decided to use a brick in a stocking rather than a handbag . . . Feel quite keyed up.' On 22 June, the entry read: 'The Day of the Happy Event'. The diary also illustrated their sex life, and there were passages which suggested that they were living in a kind of never-neverland. The defence pleaded that such entries showed paranoia, insanity and 'moral disease'. In short, Parker and Hulme were unable to form true moral judgements.

Throughout the trial the girls were calm. When they were found guilty and sentenced to be detained during Her Majesty's pleasure they seemed unconcerned. In fact, they sniggered.

BOILING   *See* **WATER**

BURIAL   *See* **INTERRING**

BURNING
Homicide by burning is rare, with the exception of India, where hundreds of women are murdered in 'kitchen accidents' every year so that their husbands can gain another dowry through remarriage. The most common use of fire by the murderer is in fact to destroy the victim's corpse.

As a means of homicide, burning is slow and painful, although the actual cessation of life may be quickened by the inhalation of CARBON MONOXIDE or by shock to the heart. It is almost exclusively a man's weapon. Bobbie Ryan, a female Chicago secretary who picked up Peter Hoban in a singles' bar in 1978, stupefied him with ALCOHOL, robbed him and then set him alight, is one of the very few women to have indulged in murder by burning.

There are several classification systems for burn injuries from dry or flame heat but the best known of them is that devised by the French surgeon Baron Guillaume Dupuytren (1777–1835). Dupuytren catalogued six degrees of burns, ranging from inflammation of the skin and transitory swelling (first degree) to deep burns with muscular, nerve and bone damage (sixth degree). In general any burning which destroys over 30 per cent of the total skin surface is likely to be fatal in an average adult.

A characteristic of badly burned corpses is that they assume a boxing-type pose – the so-called 'pugilistic attitude', which is caused by heat contraction of the muscles. In cases of extreme charring, identification may only be made from the teeth which, as the 20th-century forensic pathologist Francis Camps pointed out, are 'the most difficult things to destroy'. Teeth are almost as good as fingerprints for identification purposes; the chances of two people producing identical bite-marks are 2.5 billion to 1. Naturally, however, this system of corpse identification is useless unless a set of the victim's *ante*-mortem dental records exists.

Moreover, teeth and the whole human body *can* be completely burned to ashes if the murderer is able to burn the body at a high enough temperature. It helps, of course, if the murderer is a janitor like Joe Nischt (see Case File, The Disappearance of Rose Michaelis), and has access to an apartment block's heating furnace, but at a pinch a smaller fire will do if it can be used for long enough. Easier, cheaper and usually more convenient than ACID – who, with the exception of a volume killer like John Haigh, happens to have a dozen carboys of sulphuric acid lurking in the cellar? – burning is the murderer's most effective means of disposing of, or severely disfiguring, the corpse.

For the police and the pathologist one of the problems in cases of burning is to establish whether the corpse was alive or dead at the time of the fire. This can be established by the presence – or lack – of carbon monoxide in the victim's windpipe and lungs. Simply put, only a body which was actually breathing at the time of the fire will contain carbon monoxide in the air passages. The killer may claim, as in the 'Burning Car Murder' (see Case File) from 1930 that the victim died in the fire, but forensic science can show that he was dead before the match was struck.

Homicidal burning by the application of 'wet' or chemical agents to the skin is a very rare entry in the crime almanac. Where it does occur, acid is invariably the guilty substance, as it is in those cases where murderers have tried to dissolve the evidential corpse by chemical burning. But on occasion other chemical burning-agents are used for the murderer's tasks. A 49-year-old French vagrant, Jules Quinart, was burned to death in Lille in 1981 by a mixture of caustic soda and sodium hypochlorite. The pathologist's report noted: 'The skin has been completely eaten away in many places, all hair on the scalp is lacking and irreversible damage was done to the eyes.' Quinart had been killed by drunken associates after he refused to leave their squat.

In one of the most sensational murders of the first part of the 20th century, sausage-maker Adolph Luetgart used CAUSTIC POTASH to dissolve his victim, a method of some uniqueness. QUICKLIME has also been tried by several killers as a disposal aid, though probably not with the success they wished for.

CASE FILE: The Burning Car Murder

The year 1930 saw one of the most dramatic fire deaths in criminal history. At 2 a.m. on the morning of 6 November two young men walking home to the village of Hardingstone in Northamptonshire saw a bright blaze ahead of them. At first they thought nothing of it, since the previous evening had been Guy Fawkes Night. Then they were surprised to see a smartly dressed man carrying a small case climb out of a ditch and come hurrying towards them. As he passed, he called out: 'Looks like someone's having a bonfire up there.'

Rounding the bend the men saw that the glow was caused by a burning car which was so completely enveloped in flames that it was impossible to tell if anyone was inside.

When the police arrived and doused the fire it could be seen that the car was a Morris Minor. On the front seat were the charred remains of a person. Although the car was all but destroyed the licence plate was still legible. When the police traced the number, MU 1468, they discovered that it was owned by Alfred Arthur Rouse, a 36-year-old travelling salesman who lived in Finchley, North London. Rouse's wife said she had no idea where he was.

In fact, Alfred Rouse was at the home of one of his mistresses, Ivy Jenkins, at Gelligaer in Wales. When he saw that the morning newspapers of 7 November mentioned him by name and that the police were anxious to get in touch with the man seen near the burning car in Northampton, he realized that his 'vanishing trick' was in jeopardy. On the 7th he returned to London, where he was met off the bus by police. He said, 'I'm glad it is all over. I was going to Scotland Yard about it.' He claimed that on the night of the car fire he had given a lift to a man travelling to Leicester. At Hardingstone, Rouse had got out of the car to relieve himself down the lane and the man had accidentally set fire to a can of petrol in the car, probably with a cigarette. 'I saw the man was inside, and I tried to open the door', said Rouse, 'but I could not, as the car was a mass of flames.' He had then panicked and run away.

It sounded plausible enough and he might have got away with it, except for the fact that the police had meanwhile uncovered the remarkable secret life of Alfred Arthur Rouse. Not only was he a bigamist, with numerous illegitimate children, but he had had, according to the police's estimation, affairs with more than eighty women over the years he worked as a travelling salesman for a brace and garter company. More suspicious than ever, the police brought in the leading forensic scientist of the day, Sir Bernard Spilsbury, to examine the remains of the unidentified corpse. Spilsbury found that fine particles of soot were present in the lungs, proving beyond doubt that the man had been alive when the car burst into flames. (Rouse had been more cunning than Sidney Fox, who had murdered his mother the year before and then simply lit a fire which he thought would explain the death; the post-mortem, of course, showed that she had breathed no trace of smoke or carbon monoxide and had therefore already been dead when the fire broke out.) Spilsbury also found a scrap of cloth between the corpse's legs which smelled of petrol. An expert fire-assessor discovered that the petrol union joint of the carburettor had been deliberately loosened, and petrol splashed from the can to the roadside, which had then been ignited. Rouse's flawless murder had not been so flawless after all.

Rouse was brought to trial at Northampton Assizes in January 1932, where the evidence of Spilsbury and the fire-assessor destroyed Rouse's claim that the fire was an accident. He was found guilty and sentenced to death. He was hanged at Bedford on 10 March. Financial pressures, he confessed before dying, from his various wives had made him stage a suicide; he had hoped that the burnt corpse in the car would be mistaken for him. The identity of the fire victim was never established.

There are strong similarities between the Burning Car Murder and the case of Erich Tetzner in Germany, who staged a 'pseudocide' by burning an unknown tramp to death in his car in 1929. The autopsy revealed that the badly charred body was that of a youth (Tetzner was twenty-six) of small build (Tetzner was big). The air passages did not contain soot, and blood samples tested negative for carbon monoxide. Tetzner was also found to have taken out life insurance for the vast sum of 145,000 marks. Their suspicions aroused, the police set a trap by tapping his wife's phone, and traced Tetzner to Strasbourg, where he was arrested. Like Rouse he was executed.

CASE FILE: The Disappearance of Rose Michaelis

The only good thing to come out of the murder of Rose Michaelis in Chicago in 1945 was a development in forensic science. On 28 February of that year, Milton Michaelis rang the local police station to report that his wife had been missing for several hours. It was the first time in thirty-six years of married life that Rose had gone off without telling him. The police called by, and the husband showed them a shoe and some keys he had found in a nearby alleyway. The door to the basement of the apartment building on the alleyway was open, and the janitor there, Joe Nischt, told them he had seen nothing. The police asked to look in his furnace room. It was empty.

Working on the assumption that Rose Michaelis had been a victim of a HIT-AND-RUN, the police searched the alleyway again, and this time they found a hairpin and shards of glass from a bottle Rose Michaelis was thought to be carrying. They also found some bloodstains.

Joe Nischt was interviewed again, and his alibi checked. He was about to be ruled out of the inquiry when a check of criminal records revealed a history of assaults on women by him when drunk. His behaviour was uncooperative and the police decided to book him on suspicion of murder. His union promptly filed a writ of *habeas corpus*, and Nischt was out of the hoosegow that same day.

The following day, the 30th, a woman came into the police station with a copy of the evening paper reporting the case. It carried a picture of Nischt. Nischt, she said, had called at her house on the evening of the 28th and babbled: 'I just killed a woman.' At the time the woman had thought nothing of it, it was just the meanderings of a drunk. But now . . .

Nischt was again brought in for questioning, and when told about the woman witness he broke down. He then described how he had tried to pick up the attractive Rose Michaelis and when she rebuffed him he had struck her, knocking her out against a telegraph pole. He had then dragged her into his apartment and put her in the furnace. He thought she was alive at the time.

After Nischt's statement the furnace was doused – but not the smallest trace of a human body could be found in it. Without such evidence, the chance of Nischt being convicted seemed slim. Seizing his chance, Nischt repudiated his confession, claiming that it had been obtained under duress. His lawyer declared that it was impossible to totally destroy a body.

But was it? So wondered the State Prosecutor, who approached an anthropologist at the University of Chicago, Wilton Krogman. At the State Prosecutor's behest, Krogman did some research at various crematoria in Chicago and found that a human body could be reduced to ashes at a temperature of 3000° in an hour or so. The temperature at the Clyde Street furnace would have been much less but it would have had more time to do its job.

Krogman then staged a gruesome reconstruction, taking from the city morgue the unclaimed body of a woman, placing it in Nischt's furnace, and turning up the heat. Within four hours the body had disappeared into ashes, with not one identifiable fragment to be found. A human body could, indeed, be totally destroyed. Janitor Joe Nischt was sentenced to life imprisonment for the murder of Rose Michaelis.

In fact, as the British pathologist Professor James Cameron proved in an experiment over forty years later, in 1987, the murderer does not even need a furnace to completely destroy a corpse. A domestic fire is sufficient. Cameron burnt an 11-stone male pig – calculated as the physical equivalent of an average adult man – in a household fireplace in thirteen hours. The temperature in the fire reached a surprising 1000°. 'We ended up with remains of ash, bone and whatnot', said Cameron, 'which filled two large plastic bags. We then went over it twice with the hammer . . . and eventually finished up with a small plastic bag of ash with not a remnant of teeth or bone visible to the naked eye.' The process did not even smell unduly.

CASE FILE: Hi, I'm Chucky. Wanna Play?

They were petty grudges, a dispute over a pink duffle coat, lice and an Arab boyfriend. But they cost Suzanne Capper her life, taken from her in December 1992, after days of brutal torture.

At the age of sixteen, Suzanne Capper, who lived with her stepfather in Manchester's Moston district, had started to drift around the local streets and had become friendly with Clifford Pook, also 16. Through Pook Suzanne Capper met Pook's married sister, Jean Powell, 26, and her husband, Glyn, 28. The Powells lived at 97 Langworthy Road, Moston, where Bernadette McNeilly, aged 24, her boyfriend, Anthony Dudson, 16, and former prison inmate Jeffrey Leigh, 26, were regular visitors. The group, the best that Suzanne Capper could find in the way of friends, were big drug users, especially of amphetamines.

For a while Suzanne's new friendships went smoothly. But then the little, nagging problems started. In late November, Jean Powell gave Suzanne Capper what she later described to the police as 'a bloody good hiding', after Suzanne suggested she had sex with a friend of a friend, Mohammed Yussif, they had met at a party. Not long after, McNeilly and Dudson were angry because they had become infected by pubic lice, which they concluded had been caught from Suzanne, who regularly slept in a bed they used at No. 97. McNeilly also thought Suzanne had stolen a pink duffle coat belonging to her. The household of No. 97 decided to punish her.

Bernadette McNeilly and Jean Powell found Suzanne at her stepfather's home on 7 December 1992. They managed to lure her to 97 Langworthy Road, telling her a boy she fancied was there. He was not.

As soon as the damaged and vengeful McNeilly and Powell got Suzanne through the door, they beat her, stripped her and hit her with a 3-foot fork. Her hair was hacked off, her head shaved and she was forced to shave off her pubic hair. She was then locked overnight in a cupboard. Already Capper had been more than punished for any imagined wrongs she had committed, but the residents of No. 97 had only just started.

The next day, Capper was moved to 91 Langworthy Road, McNeilly's former house and to which she still had the keys. Suzanne Capper would spend the rest of her incarceration here, a further six days and nights of relentless violence. She was gagged with socks in her mouth, bound to a bed base with cord, rope, electric flex, belts and a chain. She was bathed in neat disinfectant and rubbed so hard with a yard brush that the marks were visible days later. As forensic experts later testified, Suzanne had a deep burn inflicted between the eyes, probably by a cigarette. The residents then decided to act out a scene from the horror film, *Child's Play*, in which a felon uses voodoo to transfer his being into a battery-powered doll which can recite three sentences, including: 'Hi, I'm Chucky. Wanna play?' A cassette endlessly played this line to Suzanne through headphones. At one point, Bernadette McNeilly, high on drugs, decided to assume the character of Chucky as she filled a hypodermic needle with amphetamines and jabbed into Suzanne's arm. 'I'm Chucky', said McNeilly, 'and Chucky wants to play.'

On 14 December, Suzanne's last day of captivity, two of her front teeth were pulled out with pliers. This was done not only to hurt her, but to make identification more difficult. The decision had by now been made to kill her. The logic of events demanded it. She could not be held for ever in that rundown terraced house. And she could not be freed, not after the things her five 'friends' had done to her.

In the afternoon of the 14th Suzanne, wearing only leggings, was bundled into the boot of a stolen car and driven to Werneth Low, an area of scrubland outside Stockport. On arriving there, she was pushed through brambles and down a slope. McNeilly doused her with petrol from a canister. One of the three others present from the gang at No. 97 – Glyn Powell, Jean Powell or Anthony Dudson – set Suzanne alight.

As Suzanne's killers drove away, they turned around and saw her in a sheath of flame, screaming. But she did not die as they intended, quickly and anonymously. An hour or so after she was set alight she was found wandering around, and was rushed to hospital, suffering 80 per cent burns. She survived for four days, long enough to tell the police who she was and who had done these things to her. As Suzanne slipped into a coma on 17 December, her penultimate day of life, the police arrived at 97 Langworthy Road, Moston. They found five of the six residents who had tortured and murdered Suzanne. On a shelf near the Christmas tree were the pliers used to pull her teeth. Outside, in the wheelie-bin, was her hair.

A year later to the day, Jean Powell, Glyn Powell, Bernadette McNeilly and Anthony Dudson were found guilty of Suzanne Capper's murder. Jeffrey Leigh was found guilty of false imprisonment, Clifford Pook of false imprisonment and conspiracy to commit grievous bodily harm. Mr Justice Potts, sentencing the six defendants to lengthy terms of imprisonment, described the crime 'as appalling a murder as it is possible to imagine'.

C

CANCER *See* **POISONING**

CANNIBALISM

'. . . t'other piece I fried and it was very nice,' wrote Jack the Ripper in a letter to the Whitechapel Vigilance Committee about one of his victims' kidneys. The eating of human flesh in association with a homicide is usually the result of sado-sexual perversion (*à la* Jack the Ripper), though cannibalism has also been used as both a symbolic and practical means of body disposal. It has even be done for financial advantage, as illustrated by the German 'meat vendor' Fritz Haarmann, who sold his victims' surplus flesh to unwary neighbours as horse meat.

Morally repugnant it might be, but the eating of human flesh has an uncomfortably long history. Cannibalism was rife when early hominoid *Pithecanthropus erectus* trod the dawns of the African plain – the practice being either a form of magical rite or, more prosaically, simply a way of ensuring a good square meal. In more recent times, Victorian and early 20th-century explorers have recorded South American Oceanic and African tribes feasting on their defeated enemies. Sir James Frazer noted in his monumental anthropological study, *The Golden Bough* (1922), that the 'flesh and blood of dead men are eaten and drunk to inspire bravery, wisdom or other qualities'. This cannibalistic eating of the enemy not only asserted the superiority of the victors but ensured that the consumed enemy could not have vengeance.

In modern homicide, an unpleasantly large cast of killers have enjoyed cannibalism as a form of perverted sexual pleasure. The pleasant-looking Peter Kurten began his reign as the 'Monster of Dusseldorf' in 1929 with the stabbing of nine-year-old Rosa Ohliger, and soon graduated to drinking the blood of another twenty-two victims. Dubbed 'a king of sexual perverts' by the psychologist Professor Karl Berg, Kurten was beheaded in 1931.

Almost as inoffensive to the eye as Kurten was meek, middle-aged New York serial-killer Albert Fish, who consumed parts of his child victims for more than one meal, even writing to the mother of one child, ten-year-old Grace Budd, 'I cut her up and ate part of her flesh. I didn't fuck her. She died a virgin.' This was presumably small consolation. A psychopath, Albert Fish was strapped to the 'Chair' at Sing Sing in 1936. As a psychiatrist pointed out, this was no punishment for Fish – whose perversions included masochism – since 'he is looking forward to the electric chair as the final experience of true pain.'

A cannibalistic *cause célèbre* was provided in 1981 by 32-year-old Issei Sagawa, a Japanese student studying in Paris. Sagawa was disturbed trying to dump two overlarge TRUNKS into the Bois de Boulogne's Lac Inferieur. These were subsequently discovered to contain parts of the body of a Dutch student, Renne Hartevelt.

When police arrested Sagawa at his apartment they found his refrigerator full of human flesh. Sagawa told them he had shot fellow-student Hartevelt after she rejected his sexual advances. He had then committed necrophilia and dismembered her corpse. While engaged in this labour he had snacked on strips of her flesh. Before dumping her body in the Bois de Boulogne, Sagawa had refrigerated some tasty morsels for use at a later date. Sagawa spent three years in a French hospital, before being returned to Japan, where he was released.

Although the complete eating of a human body by a murderer as a means of disposing of the evidence is not entirely practical, it has provided a semi-solution in cases where a tendency to anthropophagy has already existed. For instance, Moenchengladbach's Martina Zimmermann.

The morning's work of 27 February 1984 was rather ruined for municipal gardener Karl Mandel by finding a human foot among the rhododendrons. Nearby, wrapped in plastic bags, was the skeleton belonging to the foot. The Moenchengladbach pathologist was surprised to find that the flesh had been deliberately and painstakingly stripped off the bones with a knife. From matching the corpse's fingerprints against police records, it was determined that the dead person was Josef Wirtz, a hairdresser who had once been arrested in connection with a minor fraud. Wirtz had been missing for ten months. Police, meanwhile, interviewed the video-shop owner whose plastic bags had been used to wrap and carry the victim's inedible remains. The shop's shelves were amply stocked with horror flicks and porn movies, so it seemed possible that one of its customers was Wirtz's killer. A check through the list of registered customers turned up Walter Krone, who had already served a prison sentence for eating flesh from a traffic accident victim.

To the police's astonishment and dismay Krone was not their man; his alibi proved that he could not possibly have murdered Wirtz. There was another cannibal loose in Moenchengladbach. Another trawl through the video shop's customers netted 26-year-old Martina Zimmermann – who just happened to be Josef Wirtz's landlady and girlfriend. A search of her home revealed a menagerie of poisonous spiders and snakes, a library of books and videos on the occult – and some of the choicer bits of Herr Wirtz in the deep-freeze (refrigeration must be an absolute boon to the modern cannibal). In fact, a number of Wirtz 'cutlets' had already been consumed. To aid the carving up of the whole Mr Wirtz, Zimmermann had used an electric knife and electric saw. In total, she managed to fill four dozen plastic boxes with 'cuts' and offal for home-freezing. At her trial for murder, Zimmermann threw herself on the mercy of the court, pleading extenuating circumstances. Herr Wirtz had wanted to be helped on to 'a higher plane'. Killing him had not been murder. It had been an act of love. This was not an original defence, but the court was impressed, and the charge against her was reduced from murder to manslaughter. She was found guilty on this charge and sentenced to eight years' imprisonment.

As a means of disposing of the corporeal evidence of murder, the selling of human flesh to customers blissfully unaware of its provenance has largely gone out of fashion. Aside from Victorian London's Kate Webster, who allegedly sold the 'dripping' from her murdered employer (see AXES), the most celebrated practitioners come from the chaotic years of Weimar Germany. As noted, Fritz Haarmann, who distinguished himself by BITING his victims to death in Hanover, made considerable profit out of misery on the meat black-market in the 1920s. Haarmann's compatriot and contemporary, Georg Grossmann, murdered over fifty Berlin prostitutes before being caught, likewise marketing his victims as cheap meat. The inevitable bones he dumped in the River Spree. It is even claimed that the so-called 'Butcher of Berlin' had a frankfurter stand at the railway station so that he could pick up his next victim as he sold off his last.

CANTHARIDIN

Cantharidin is the active component of cantharides, a powder made from the dried wings and body of the beetle, *Cantharis vesicatoria*, found in southern Russia, Italy and Spain. The beetle's Spanish habitat gives the powder its popular name of Spanish Fly. In the East, the dried beetle *Mylabris sidea* is used as a source of cantharidin.

An irritant, cantharidin acts on the parts of the body it contacts and, when passed out of the urinary system, irritates the genitals. For this reason cantharidin has long – but undeservedly – had the reputation for being an aphrodisiac. In truth, a dose of cantharidin is more likely to produce blistering of the mouth, nausea, vomiting, bloody diarrhoea and death, rather than blistering passion and the *petit mort* of orgasm. The lethal dose is considered to be about 60 mg of cantharidin, or 162 mg of Spanish Fly powder. Such an amount will literally burn the victim's insides out.

Most occasions of cantharidin poisoning have taken place where the poison has been supplied with the intention of sexual stimulation, not murder. The Marquis de Sade (1740–1814) decided to liven up the inmates of a brothel by the administration of a cantharidin *philtre amoureux*, a prank which caused many of the

women to throw themselves out of the building (DEFENESTRA-
TION) in agony. The criminal misuse of cantharidin as an aphrodisiac at a dance in Uxbridge in 1830, where it was mixed in the
beer to excite the womenfolk, resulted in the death of a girl.
Neither the prostitutes nor the girl dancer, it appears, noticed any
aphrodisiac effects.

A fatal and famous case from Britain in 1954 was also the
outcome of the administration of cantharidin with intent to sexually
excite. Arthur Kendrick Ford, a 44-year-old married man, had
developed a lustful desire for Betty Grant, a girl who worked at the
wholesale chemist's business where he was a manager. In his army
days Ford had heard much about the legendary Spanish Fly
aphrodisiac, and because of his work had now learned that its active
ingredient was cantharidin. He had also learned that stocks of
cantharidin were kept at his very own workplace. The Spanish Fly
in the ointment, as it were, was that cantharidin was a listed poison.
A request by Ford to the firm's senior chemist for a quantity of
cantharidin to help his neighbour's rabbits through a patch where
they seemed reluctant to breed was turned down. The chemist,
however, had let Ford see where the poison was kept; at lunchtime
Arthur Ford returned and stole some.

With the aid of a pair of scissors, Arthur Ford inserted a small
quantity of cantharidin into a bar of coconut ice confectionery.
Ford now thought that he was about to have the time of his life;
unfortunately, two girls were about to have the time of their death.
On 26 April, Ford gave a piece of the sweet to Betty Grant and her
friend June Malins, and ate some himself. Within hours all three
were taken to hospital, where Betty Grant and June Malins died
within twenty-four hours. Arthur Ford just survived. When the
post-mortems revealed cantharidin, Ford was obliged to confess. At
his trial at the Old Bailey he pleaded guilty to manslaughter and was
sentenced to five years' imprisonment.

CARBON MONOXIDE

In the days when coal gas was used for domestic cooking and
heating, gassing was the most common means of suicide. As a way
of ending your own life, 'putting one's head in the oven' was almost
a cliché. But not for nothing was coal gas the suicide's favourite. Its
active killing component is carbon monoxide, an odourless, non-
irritating gas of quick lethality.

Carbon monoxide kills in two ways: firstly, it has a direct toxic
effect on the internal body tissues it comes into contact with;
secondly, and more importantly, it combines with haemoglobin in
the blood to prevent the red blood cells carrying oxygen. Carbon
monoxide has 300 times more affinity for combining with haemoglobin than oxygen. In other words, carbon monoxide poisoning
causes death by oxygen starvation. If coal gas – which contains

about 7–10 per cent carbon monoxide – is inhaled, death is likely to result in between two and five minutes.

In Britain, suicide in the kitchen through the inhalation of domestic gas was virtually abolished after the national conversion to 'natural gas' in 1967. Accidental poisonings by carbon monoxide also dropped markedly. Today, the main sources of carbon monoxide are faulty gas appliances in unventilated rooms, and motor vehicle exhaust fumes, which contain 4–7 per cent monoxide. The gas is no less dangerous for being less domestically available, however: a 1.5-litre car engine will generate a fatal level of monoxide in a closed single garage in about five minutes.

There is another dangerous aspect to carbon monoxide poisoning: it is cumulative, and the inhalation of minute quantities can build up dangerous levels. One part of carbon monoxide per 1000 of air can cause a lethal concentration of 60 per cent in the blood within three hours. So, for instance, a person unaware of carbon monoxide leaking into the room – say, from a defective butane heater – will become drowsy, fall asleep unsuspectingly, and thus enter into a coma, followed by death. Where carbon monoxide is more than one part of air it can cause coma within a few minutes. In house fires, people are more often killed by the carbon monoxide fumes than by the flames themselves.

The indications of carbon monoxide poisoning in the corpse are distinctive. The skin has a bright pink aspect and the blood is cherry-red and extremely free-flowing. Proof of carbon monoxide poisoning is made by chemical and spectroscopic tests on the blood, which will show the presence of carbon monoxide for up to six months after death.

Murderously intended carbon monoxide poisonings are extremely unusual, and most cases come from the coal gas era; for instance, the insurance-motivated gassing of Mike Malloy in 1932 by the members of the New York 'Murder Trust' (see Case File). In the tragic 'Ritual Murder Case', 1953, thirteen-year-old epileptic John Conroy was found buried in a mattress in his London home. A post-mortem examination revealed a 55 per cent saturation of carbon monoxide in the boy's blood, plus a large quantity of barbiturate. The boy had been gassed by his mother who was found guilty but insane at her trial.

A rare modern case was that of Ian Smith, a Leeds lecturer in physics. In early 1981, Smith's wife was found dead in a caravan from carbon monoxide poisoning, the cause of which was initially attributed to the faulty ignition of a butane heater – as Smith intended. Suspicion descended on Smith, however, because of the extremely high saturation level of carbon monoxide in his wife's blood – 80 per cent – and the relatively low level in his blood of 14 per cent on the morning of the 'accident', although they had been in the caravan together. As Smith later confessed, he had subjected his wife to the inhalation of *pure* carbon monoxide, stolen from his laboratory, while she slept. He was convicted of manslaughter.

More common than murders by gas are murders where the gas is turned on to give the appearance of suicide. Or cases where gas, like ALCOHOL, has been used to knock out the victim so that he or she may then be killed by some other means. The classic example of the murder-dressed-up-as-gas-suicide ruse was provided by Reginald Hincks, a vacuum cleaner salesman, who coveted his father-in-law's property. After trying to kill the 85-year-old James Pullen by long, tiring walks, Hincks decided on murder. On 1 December 1933, Hincks telephoned the Bath fire brigade to say that Pullen was dead, with his head in the kitchen stove, adding that any bruise on Pullen's head 'happened when I pulled him out of the gas oven'. Pullen had indeed died of gas poisoning, but the pathologist was able to show that the bruise was inflicted before death. The old man's head had been put in the oven by his son-in-law. Notable murderers who have used gas to render victims unconscious are American mass-murderer H.H. Holmes, who piped gas into the rooms of the victims at his Chicago hotel (see also ACID), and John Christie, the sex murderer of 10 Rillington Place, London (see Case File).

CASE FILE: 10 Rillington Place

The murders committed by John Christie at 10 Rillington Place, a seedy Graham-Greenish street in North London, were probably England's most widely publicized crimes of the 1950s. John Reginald Halliday Christie was a bald-headed, bespectacled hypochondriac and long-term sexual inadequate. In his teens in Halifax he had been known as 'Reggie-no-dick'. Such was Christie's inadequacy that he preferred his sex with women who were dead or unconscious. In his initial murders he seems to have achieved this by a clever contraption which enabled him to bubble coal gas through a mixture of Friar's Balsam – an anti-catarrh medicament – in a large glass sweet jar. The Balsam masked the smell of the gas. Ruth Fuerst, an Austrian evacuee, was the first to be lured back to the ground floor flat at Rillington Place, in September 1943, when Christie's wife was away. There she was persuaded to sit in a chair with her head covered with a cloth, breathing in the stream of Friar's Balsam mixed with coal gas. When she was unconscious, she was killed – in what would become Christie's *modus operandi* – by STRANGULATION with a ligature and her corpse raped. She was buried in the back garden. So too was Muriel Eady, a co-worker of Christie's at Ultra Radio in Acton, three months later.

For nine years, Christie committed no more murders, probably because his wife was more or less permanently in the house.

However, after strangling *her* in December 1952 – without a preliminary gassing – he seemed to lose all control. Between 2 January 1953 and 6 March 1953 he murdered three prostitutes, Rita Nelson, Kathleen Maloney and Hectorina Maclennan. All were gassed beforehand by being enticed into sitting in an old deck chair, which had a canopy over the head, in Christie's kitchen. He then ran coal gas from the oven stove via a rubber hose to the lethal deck chair. Christie placed the bodies of these women in a large kitchen cupboard, then wallpapered it over and abandoned the flat, becoming a vagrant. The bodies were discovered almost immediately by the landlord. A massive public alarm and police search followed. Christie, all instinct of self-preservation gone, was recognized by a policeman wandering near Putney Bridge, and offered no resistance to his arrest.

Christie was tried at the No. 1 Court at the Old Bailey for his wife's murder in June 1953. He pleaded insanity. Among the revelations to come out in the courtroom was his confession to the murder of Mrs Beryl Evans, a resident of the upper-floor flat at 10 Rillington Place in 1949. Her death, and that of her child Geraldine, had been blamed on her husband Timothy John Evans, for which Evans had been executed. Christie's claim to have gassed Beryl Evans resulted in a legal inquiry, and her being exhumed for a second autopsy. There were no traces of carbon monoxide poisoning; Beryl Evans had not been gassed. (In fact, it was inconceivable that if she *had* been gassed, the distinctive cherry-pink sign of carbon monoxide poisoning would have been missed by the eminent pathologist, Donald Teare, who did the original autopsy just after her death.) The conclusion of the legal inquiry had been that Evans had killed his wife, and that Christie had only claimed to do so to help his defence of insanity. Christie was hanged by Albert Pierrepoint at Pentonville on 15 July 1953. Timothy Evans was granted a posthumous pardon in 1966.

CASE FILE: The Murder Trust

Mike Malloy, an alcoholic Irish vagrant, looked the perfect victim for the insurance murder plotted by four New York get-ahead-types in the Prohibition era. Based at a 'speakeasy' on 171st Street, the four men – bootlegger Tony Marino, bartender Red Murphy, undertaker Frankie Pasqua, and thug Daniel Kriegsburg – otherwise known as 'The Murder Trust', insured Malloy's life for $1200. They then set about killing him – but Malloy proved to be almost indestructible. Instead of dying from the copious quantities of anti-freeze (the main ingredient of which is poisonous methyl ALCOHOL) given to him as free 'whisky' at the speakeasy on New Year's Eve 1932, the alcoholic Malloy actually developed a taste for it and returned the next day wanting more. And the next day and the next. The Trust next tried to kill him by BACTERIAL POISONING, from a tin of sardines which had gone off, and then with metal fragments in his food. Neither had any effect on Malloy. He was then left out in the open, unconscious from drink, naked and soaking wet during a winter's night to die of hypothermia. It was to no avail. 'Durable', as the plotters grudgingly nicknamed him, was back at the speakeasy next day looking for free drinks, without even a chill. In desperation, the Murder Trust tried to kill Malloy by a HIT-AND-RUN. But this only succeeded in breaking his arm, and fracturing ribs and one leg. As a last gamble, the gang inveigled Malloy into visiting a room in a boarding-house on Fulton Avenue on the pretext of sampling a new brand of alcohol. After he had sampled much and fallen into unconsciousness, two of the gang brought out a length of rubber hosing, fastened it to a gas jet, and then put the other end in Malloy's mouth. For an hour gas was pumped into Mike Malloy. At long, long last Malloy died. Even he could not survive carbon monoxide poisoning.

The gang got a dubious doctor to certify the cause of death as pneumonia, and duly collected the insurance. They did not escape the electric chair at Sing Sing, however. One of the gang bragged about the murder and word filtered through to the police. An order was issued to exhume Mike Malloy's body. There was no doubt about the cause of death. The corpse was still bright pink.

CAUSTIC POTASH

In 1897, Chicago businessman Adolph Louis Luetgart decided to dispose of his wife's body by a method that showed some originality.

The owner of a sausage factory on Hermitage and Diversey Street, Luetgart was a man of insatiable sexual appetites, a condition which is known clinically as satyrism. In addition to sleeping with his wife, his maid, a Mrs Christine Feldt, and a saloon-owner's wife called Agatha Tosch, he also paid regular visits to prostitutes. Perhaps not surprisingly, his love life had interfered with his business life, and by 1897 he was on the verge of bankruptcy.

He was also having a strained relationship with his wife, Louise. Neighbours who heard her screaming one day looked into the windows of the Luetgarts' house and saw her husband throttling her; when he realized he was being observed he let her go. A day or two later he chased her down the street with a revolver.

On 11 March 1897, Luetgart unfolded his plan to murder his wife when he purchased 325 lb caustic potash and 50 lb arsenic from the wholesale drug firm of Lor Owen & Company. More than a month later, on 24 April, he ordered an employee nicknamed 'Smokehouse Frank' to take the metal drums of potash to the basement of the factory and crush them up with an axe. Then Luetgart and the employee placed the small pieces of potash in a vat used for sausage meat, turning up the steam until the vat was soon full of boiling caustic potash, a liquid strong enough to dissolve flesh on contact.

At about 10.30 on the night of Friday, 1 May, a young German girl, Emma Schiemicke, saw Luetgart leading his wife down an alley to the back of the factory. The factory's nightwatchman, Bialk, was sent on an errand, and when he came back the main door was closed. Luetgart then sent him to the engine room, which was separate from the factory. Later that same evening, Bialk was sent on another errand. The next morning the watchman asked if he should put out the fire under the vat, but Luetgart replied 'Bank the fires at fifty pounds of steam pressure.' Bialk did so, and was surprised to find a gluey substance on the floor, with flakes of bone in it. Smokehouse Frank also noticed the slime, and was ordered by Luetgart to scrape it off the floor and flush it down the sewer. Larger chunks were scattered on the railway lines.

On 4 May, Mrs Luetgart's brother, Diedrich Bicknese, came to visit her and was surprised not to find her at home. Luetgart said that she had simply walked out of the door a few days before with $18 in her purse. 'Why didn't you go to the police?' Bicknese demanded. 'I don't want a scandal,' Luetgart replied.

Bicknese spent the next two days looking for his sister; then he contacted Captain Herman Schluetter of the Police Department. Schluetter called Luetgart in for questioning, but Luetgart again insisted that he had not called in the police because he was trying to avoid a scandal. A few days later, Captain Schluetter visited the factory to question the nightwatchman and Smokehouse Frank, and heard from them about the slimy substance they had found on the floor.

His interest aroused, Schluetter examined the vats in the basement, finding the middle one half-full of a brown liquid. Using a sack as a filter, the police trapped all the solid matter from the vat. Adolph Luetgart had been correct in his belief that boiling caustic potash would turn a body into soap. He had, however, forgotten to remove his wife's rings. Two of these were found in the filter, one with the initials 'LL' engraved on it.

Even so, the outcome of Luetgart's trial for murder was far from certain. The prosecution evidence, was largely circumstantial, though convincing. Experts testified that fragments of bone found in the basement and in the drain pipes leading from the vat were human. An artificial tooth was also recovered, and Mrs Luetgart had false teeth. Forensic experts Dr Charles Gibson and Professor de la Fontaine identified the soapy substance as human flesh boiled in caustic soda. Moreover, the prosecution was quick to point out that Luetgart had behaved like a man with something on his conscience. When Mrs Tosch, his mistress, inquired as to the whereabouts of his wife, Luetgart had replied, 'I am innocent as the southern skies.'

Luetgart's defence was simple. He had decided to make a large quantity of soft soap to give his factory a cleaning. But as the prosecution pointed out it was absurd to spend $40 on potash to make soft soap when he could have bought enough soft soap to clean the factory for $1.

The jury, suspicious of scientific experts (as many juries were in the late 19th century), was not convinced of Luetgart's guilt – but nor of his innocence either. When they failed to agree a verdict after three days of debate, the judge discharged them. At Luetgart's second trial, the jury was able to agree a verdict of guilty. He was spared the death penalty just in case Mrs Luetgart really did return. Luetgart died in Joliet State Penitentiary in 1911, still protesting his innocence.

CHLORAL HYDRATE
Better known as 'knock-out drops', chloral hydrate is a sedative chemically similar to CHLOROFORM. A crystalline solid, the drug has the criminal advantage of being soluble in water and is the active ingredient of the legendary 'Mickey Finn'. Thus 'knocked-out' the victim can be kidnapped, robbed or killed. Juanita Spinelli (a.k.a. 'The Duchess') famously applied chloral hydrate to the drink of a wavering member of her gang, then had him thrown into San Francisco's Sacramento river; on 21 November 1941, she became the first woman to be officially executed in California.

If the drug is over-liberally used, however, the victim will pass from unconsciousness into what Californians would be pleased to call the 'Big Sleep'. This is what seems to have happened in the Manchester 'Hackney Carriage Mystery' of 1889, when a petty villain by the name of Charlie Parton rendered an ageing business-man unconscious before relieving him of his wallet and jewellery. Parton failed to account for the fact that the man's age would lower his resistance to the drug. An average fatal dose for a healthy adult, if taken orally, is 120 grains. Death occurs from cardiac and respiratory collapse between six and ten hours later.

CHLOROFORM
Chloroform, discovered in 1831 by the German chemist Baron von Liebig, is the distilled result of adding chlorinated lime to alcohol. A colourless, sweet-tasting, volatile liquid, it gives off a dense vapour. In 1847, Sir James Simpson, Professor of Obstetrics at Glasgow University, recognized the anaesthetic use of this vapour (in a 1–2 per cent concentration), publishing a paper to this effect. However, chloroform was denounced from pulpit and physician's lecture hall, and it was not until after Queen Victoria received it during the delivery of her eighth

child that it passed into common medical usage.

Chloroform is a narcotic which causes feelings of wellbeing before it produces unconsciousness. The drug has been used to assist criminal ventures, although the burglar equipped with chloroform on a pad to 'knock out' the householder owes more to the imagination of the penny dreadful writer than real life. The drug is strongly irritant, and will blister the skin if it touches it. Nonetheless, the murderous New York dentist, Arthur Warren Waite, included chloroform (along with BACTERIAL POISONING) in his 1916 plan to murder his father-in-law, rendering him unconscious before suffocating him with a pillow – after already having given him a fatal dose of arsenic. Another orthodontist, New Orleans' Dr Ettienne Deschamps, used chloroform gas to stupefy women patients so that he could sexually interfere with them. He gave too much of the drug to a twelve-year-old girl and killed her, a crime for which he was hanged in 1892. Dot King, the New York model, was fatally chloroformed in her apartment in the course of a robbery in 1923. The murder was never solved. John Wayne Gacy (1942–94), the Illinois serial-killer, used chloroform to immobilize some of his thirty-three teenage victims and may even have dispatched some of them this way. Prolonged inhalation of the drug results in death through heart paralysis.

There have been numerous instances of the accidental or suicidal swallowing of liquid chloroform, but very few documented instances of murder being committed by this method. In the most celebrated of them, 'The Pimlico Mystery' of 1886 (see Case File), Adelaide Bartlett is alleged to have shut up shop on her grocer husband permanently by poisoning him with chloroform. Such ingestion causes blistering of the mouth and throat, with death resulting from heart failure and liver damage. The lethal dose when swallowed is 1–2 ounces.

CASE FILE: The Pimlico Mystery

The death of Edwin Bartlett in 1886 is one of the classic crimes of the gaslight era. If, indeed, his wife Adelaide did murder him it leaves the enduring mystery of how she managed to administer such a strongly irritant poison as liquid chloroform. As Queen Victoria's surgeon Sir James Paget remarked after Adelaide Bartlett's trial, 'Now she's acquitted she should tell us in the interests of science how she did it.'

Born in France in 1855, Adelaide was the illegitimate daughter of an English nobleman, an aristocratic connection which much impressed wealthy thirty-year-old grocer Edwin Bartlett when they met in 1875 at her maternal aunt's. They married in the same year, with Adelaide's family relieved that an illegitimate child had managed to secure a respectable husband. Adelaide herself was not consulted in the matter. From the outset it was no ordinary marriage: like the Victorian aesthete John Ruskin, Edwin Bartlett had no wish to 'sully' his wife by having sexual intercourse with her. Almost immediately after their honeymoon, Adelaide was sent away to finishing school for two years, before joining her husband in the flat above his shop in Herne Hill. Sharing the home was Edwin's father who intensely disliked Adelaide and accused her of having an affair with his other son.

In 1885, the Bartletts moved to Merton Abbey, near Wimbledon, where Adelaide formed a close, possibly sexual, relationship with Reverend George Dyson, the 27-year-old minister of the local Wesleyan chapel. Far from discouraging the friendship, Edwin Bartlett seems to have actively encouraged it, getting Adelaide and Dyson to kiss each other in his presence. Edwin's own effusively admiring attitude to Dyson was, it has been suggested, indicative of latent homosexuality. It was around this time that Edwin Bartlett made a new will, leaving everything unconditionally to Adelaide, and appointing Dyson co-executor. When the Bartletts moved to 85 Claverton Street, Pimlico, the friendship between Dyson and Adelaide continued, even intensified.

Early in December 1885, Edwin Bartlett was taken ill with gastritis and diarrhoea. He recovered – not least because several of his rotten teeth, a contributory factor to his ill health, were removed – by Christmas Day. On 27 December, Adelaide asked George Dyson to buy a bottle of chloroform, saying that it was the only thing that would ease Edwin's pains. Dyson complied with the request, buying three separate bottles of the drug, telling chemists that he wanted it to remove grease stains. Dyson then poured the contents of the three bottles – around 4 oz of liquid – into one large bottle which he gave to Adelaide.

On the last day of the year, Edwin seemed to be getting better, and informed his father he was planning a trip to the country. At 4 a.m. the next morning, Adelaide knocked on the door of her landlord, Mr Doggett, saying, 'Could you call Dr Leach, please? I think Mr Bartlett is dead.' When Doggett entered Edwin Bartlett's room he noticed a strong smell like ether, and a wine glass near the bed which also smelled of the same substance. The doctor on his arrival questioned Adelaide about the smell of brandy on Bartlett's lips, which Adelaide explained by saying that she had administered the spirit in the hope of reviving him.

The post-mortem was carried out the next day at Charing Cross Hospital. As soon as the dead man's stomach was opened, the dissecting room was filled with the smell of chloroform, which was confirmed by analysis (about $1/16$ of an ounce was found). Perplexingly, however, there was no trace of burning in the victim's mouth or throat from the irritant poison. Told of the result of the autopsy

by Dr Leach, Adelaide confided in him the details of her ménage à
trois, adding that Edwin had recently decided to assert his marital
rights in a most unwelcome manner. Adelaide had decided to
discourage him by sprinkling chloroform – hence the purchases by
Dyson – on her handkerchief and waving it in front of his nose to
make him drowsy.

Adelaide Bartlett was charged with murder, George Dyson as an
accessory. At the outset of their trial at the Old Bailey in April 1886
the case against Dyson, who had earlier claimed that he had been
'duped' by Adelaide, was withdrawn. Sir Charles Russell, the
Attorney General, told the jury that chloroform had definitely been
present in the dead man's stomach – the central question was, how
did it get there? The defence suggested that Edwin had drunk the
chloroform while in a suicidal frame of mind, or perhaps as a
desperate remedy for sleeplessness. The Attorney-General's opinion was that chloroform could only have been swallowed by the
dead man while he was insensible from inhaling the drug or,
alternatively, that Adelaide had added the chloroform to a glass of
brandy, telling Edwin it was medicine which she had made more
palatable. Expert medical opinion from Dr Thomas Stevenson,
Professor of Jurisprudence at Guy's Hospital, allowed that chloroform liquid might be administered to an unconscious or sleeping
person, but pointed out that it would be an extremely delicate
operation. Even if carried out by a doctor, the procedure would
probably result in some fluid entering the windpipe, and there was
no chloroform in Edwin Bartlett's windpipe. In all likelihood it
would also burn the person's mouth and throat.

The jury deliberated for over two hours and when they returned
to the courtroom they announced that 'although we think that grave
suspicion attaches to the prisoner, we do not think there is
sufficient evidence to show how or by whom the chloroform was
administered.' The jury found Adelaide Bartlett not guilty.

In fact, Adelaide Bartlett almost certainly, and literally, got away
with murder. The jury's verdict was as much the result of a clever
defence counsel strategy as it was an expression of the benefit of the
doubt. Dyson's acquittal, after his cowardly attempts to pin all the
blame on Adelaide, was unpopular with the public; the defence
counsel led by Edward Clarke showed how closely Dyson's and
Adelaide's actions were linked, making the jury reluctant 'to send
her to the hangman's cord, while he passed unrebuked to freedom'.
Adelaide also had the motive, in that she was determined not to
change the platonic relationship with her husband to a sexual one.
Divorce was out of the question because of the stigma that it would
bring; more, she needed Edwin's money. At some point in
December 1885 she decided to get rid of him with chloroform. Why
did the liquid not leave traces of burning in Edwin Bartlett's throat?
The most plausible suggestion is that she chloroformed Edwin to

unconsciousness and then poured chloroform down his throat. As Dr Stevenson admitted during his testimony, an ordinary person might, with luck, pour chloroform down a sleeping person's throat, not only without it entering the windpipe, but without it causing burning. Adelaide, who had no idea that chloroform was an irritant, was just plain lucky.

It is certainly interesting that a New York porter Frederick Mors – who had had some medical training – used exactly this method thirty years later to kill no less than seven inmates of an old people's home. He said about his killing technique:

First, I would pour a drop or two of chloroform on a piece of absorbent cotton and hold it to the nostrils of the old person . . . Soon my man would swoon. Then I would close the orifices of the body with cotton, stuffing it in the ears, nostrils etc. Next I would pour a little chloroform down the throat and prevent the fumes escaping the same way. It wasn't long before the heart stopped beating.

CHOKING

Most deaths from choking – the internal obstruction of air passages by foreign material – are accidental, the result of food caught in the windpipe. There are about 2500 such 'food inhalation' deaths each year in the USA alone – more than those due to firearms, aircraft accidents and snakebite. Homicides from choking are unusual, except in two instances: if the victim is very old, or very young. Classic aids to choking are rags or cloths which are forced into the mouth. Such 'gags' are sometimes used on watchmen and witnesses during robberies, and have led to death; initially, the victim may be able to breathe through the nose but swelling and mucus blocks this airway. Choking gives rise to death by ASPHYXIA.

Perhaps the most unusual object used to induce murderous choking is the fungus *Mucor phyconyes* (see FUNGI). In ancient Hindu society this fungus was mixed with water and given to the victim, in whose throat it would attach and grow slowly. In about two weeks, the grown fungus and its poison gas choked the victim as surely as if it was an immovable cloth bung.

CONCRETE

The disposal of a corpse by means of a 'concrete overcoat' or a supporting role in the foundations of a motorway bridge is a habit largely restricted to the American mafia. But not entirely. It was long rumoured that British gangsterdom had imitated the technique, although actual documented cases were almost impossible to find – until, that is, the body of Bristol used-car dealer, Wayne Lomas, was discovered in early October 1993. Lomas had gone

missing from his home in August 1988, and an extensive police
search failed to turn up anything. Privately, the Avon and Somerset
police believed he had been murdered in a gangland feud. Then,
five years later, the police raided a number of homes in Bristol and,
proceeding on 'information received', began digging under the
dining-room floor of a nondescript semi in the Southville district of
the city. Buried under the floor, in a one-ton slab of concrete, were
the remains of Wayne Lomas. It took police and forensic scientists
nearly a week of digging at the 'Coffin House' to free the slab, and
some days with a hammer and chisel to chip away the concrete so
that the remains could be freed.

Meanwhile blocks of concrete – a construction material made
from portland cement, water, sand, and a coarse aggregate such as
gravel – dropped from road bridges have figured in at least two
homicides as the instrument of death. In the pre-dawn darkness of
18 October 1981, Jose Hernandez was asleep in the front seat of his
automobile as his wife drove them home from a wedding reception
in Chicago. As the car drove under a bridge on Interstate 65, a 40 lb
concrete block crashed through the windshield of the vehicle,
instantly killing Hernandez. The killer was seventeen-year-old
Martin Myers, who, with several teenage friends watching, had
dropped the block as a 'prank'. The lethal 'prank' ended with
Myers in jail for five years. Four years later, two striking coal-
miners, Dean Hancock and Russell Shankland, dropped a concrete
block off a bridge in South Wales intending to stop a taxi cab taking
a miner to work. They misjudged the drop and the block went
through the front windscreen, killing the driver of the taxi.

CROSSBOWS

In appearance the crossbow is like a small catapult, with the bow
mounted crossways. In medieval Europe and Asia, the crossbow was
used for hunting and warfare; although it lacked the accuracy and
distance of the longbow – as famously used by Robin Hood, and the
English army at the Battle of Crécy – its main advantage was that it
could be used by relatively weak and unskilled people and still be
effective. This is because it was bent mechanically and was aimed from
the shoulder like a gun, so that its bolts could be delivered fairly
accurately without the skilled longbowman's lifetime of practice. It
might be reasonably supposed that the crossbow passed out of use as a
killing weapon in the 17th century or thereabouts; in fact, it seems to
be enjoying a revival of interest, especially as its modern sporting form
is more powerful and more accurate than its medieval ancestor. Nor,
in most countries, is the crossbow subject to regulation. Anyone can
buy and use one. Even children.

Elaine Witte was well-known in the small town of Trail Creek,
Indiana, where she was the local president of the Pioneers, the retired
employees of the Bell Telephone Company. In fact, the last time any

of her friends had seen the 76-year-old widow was at the Pioneers' Christmas party, 1983. It was now well into the New Year and she had failed to attend the spring meeting. Usually she was so punctilious about Pioneer meetings. Her daughter-in-law, Marie Witte, said she was still in California visiting friends. But some Pioneers members were getting uneasy about their president's absence – why hadn't she sent a postcard even? – and went to see the town marshal.

Marshal Chastain had known Elaine Witte for a number of years, and had been friends with Mrs Witte's son, Paul, a dog breeder who had died in a tragic accident some years before. Paul had met his wife Marie in a Florida nudist camp, and they had married when she was only 16. They had two sons: Butch, 15, and Eric, 18, who was serving in the navy. On Paul's death, Marie and her sons had moved in with Elaine Witte.

After listening to the delegation from the Pioneers, Chastain agreed to make inquiries at the Wittes' house. He found Marie's explanation for Mrs Witte's absence unconvincing and notified the state police of his suspicion. A few weeks later, Marie Witte, apparently having got wind of the state police's investigation, fled Trail Creek. Later she was traced to a mobile home park in San Diego, where her son Eric was stationed. Marie had rented a post office box in Elaine Witte's name so that she could cash her social security cheques. She was arrested as she tried to deposit one of Elaine Witte's cheques at the bank.

At the mobile home the police questioned Butch Witte on the whereabouts of his grandmother. He replied, in a matter-of-fact fashion, that he had killed her. He had been told to do so by his mother, he said, because the old woman had caught Marie cashing cheques on her account. He also said that he had been nominated by his mother as the killer because he was a juvenile, and would therefore be treated more leniently if the crime was discovered. His mother had apparently suggested STRANGULATION to do the deed, but Butch had decided to use his sports crossbow. While his grandmother lay sleeping, he had crept into her bedroom and shot her through the torso with a steel bolt. So great had been the force that the bolt had almost completely disappeared into her. She had died more or less instantly. When asked by the officers how he felt about killing his grandmother, Butch replied, 'I felt neutral about it. I didn't care one way or the other.'

There was more. Butch, in loquacious mood, then related how his grandmother's body had been disposed of: Marie and her two boys had dismembered it with knives, a chisel and a chainsaw. Parts of the body had gone into the trash compactor, others into the waste disposal unit and some had been microwaved and fed to their pet dog. A section of corpse had been stored in the freezer and gradually dispersed of in parcels around the environs of Trail Fork. The District Attorney's office decided to try Butch as an adult, which meant a possible execution if convicted. Understanding that his mother's assurance about his invulnerability was worthless, Butch Witte turned state's evidence. Not only did he give a full account of the killing of his grandmother, but also informed the police that his father too had been murdered. The means that time had been a 'shooting accident' with a gun, with Eric pulling the trigger. His mother had masterminded it. The murder had worked so well, with all the authorities believing that it was a tragic mistake, that Marie Witte had had no compunction about a second killing.

Marie Witte was sentenced to ninety years in jail for the murder of her mother-in-law, with thirty years for conspiracy to commit murder to run consecutively. In a separate trial she was sentenced to a further fifty years for the murder of her husband. In both trials, her sons were the main witnesses to testify against her.

CURARE

A poison derived from jungle vines and widely used by the Indians of South America to toxically tip their hunting arrows, curare was introduced to the West by 16th-century Spanish conquistadores. The most important constituent of curare is tubocurarine – first isolated by Dr Harold King in 1935 – which interferes with the nervous system by blocking the neurotransmitter acetylcholine, resulting in paralysis of the muscles.

This characteristic of tubocurarine greatly interested the medical profession who were looking for some means to keep patients absolutely still during delicate operations, and tubocurarine quickly passed into clinical use as a muscle-relaxant (although, since the drug also relaxes the respiratory system, patients administered tubocurarine have to be artificially ventilated). Typically, a dose of 20–30mg produces a paralysis lasting thirty minutes.

Other toxins have been isolated from curare – the supplies of which still come from the South American jungles – of which C-toxiferine is the most important after tubocurarine. Longer-lasting than tubocurarine, it is also twenty-five times more potent. It is likewise used as a muscle-relaxant in surgery. Larger than recommended injections of C-toxiferine or tubocurarine are almost always fatal within forty seconds, with death due to respiratory failure.

Since, with the exception of steamy, snake-ridden Amazonian forests, curare is only available in hospitals and clinics, homicides featuring this exotic poison have been confined to the precincts of the medical world.

CASE FILE: The Ann Arbor Hospital Killings

In the late afternoon of Friday, 15 August 1975, the FBI received a phone call from the Veterans Administration hospital in Ann Arbor, Michigan. The caller, who identified himself as Dr Duane T. Freier, the acting chief of staff at the hospital, said cautiously that the hospital seemed to have a problem. What problem was that exactly, sir?, asked the FBI agent answering the call. The hospital seemed to have a killer on the loose.

Dr Freier went on to explain that there had been no fewer than fifty-six cases of respiratory arrest – breathing failure – since 1 July. A normal number of breathing failures for this period would have been eight to ten. At first the hospital had tried to convince itself that the rise in respiratory arrests was coincidental, but daily reports showed that the rate was not diminishing. The breathing failures, Dr Freier informed the agent, were so frequent now that nurses on the evening duty – when most of the attacks took place – stood waiting in the hall for the next Code Seven alarm. There had also been several deaths. An internal investigation by the hospital and doctors from the Veterans Administration (VA) HQ in Washington had come to the provisional conclusion that the victims had been injected with a curare-based muscle-relaxant, Pavulon. Possibly it had been added to their intravenous (IV) drips. Not wishing to attract adverse publicity the hospital had refrained from notifying the law enforcement agencies, but now the situation was becoming critical. Could the FBI come?

That evening a dozen FBI agents arrived at the VA hospital at Ann Arbor, where they soon learned that one of the victims who had recovered from a breathing failure had sent a note to a doctor stating that he had seen a Filipino nurse, Filipina Narciso, going out of the door just before his attack. The hospital investigation had ignored the note. Ms Narciso had considerable experience as a registered nurse, both in her native land and in the USA, the hospital pointed out. Nevertheless, the FBI made her a suspect, and she remained so right to the end of their investigation.

After intensive questioning of the 300 hospital employees who worked the night shift, it gradually emerged that Narciso and another Filipino nurse, Mrs Leonora Perez, had invariably been seen near the patients or near the IVs in rooms where breathing failures occurred. Agents, meanwhile, were astonished at the ease with which Pavulon – and other dangerous drugs – were available at the hospital. Often they weren't even locked up.

The FBI sent urine and blood samples from the victims who had survived to its toxicology lab in Washington. Pavulon was present in the specimens, although none of the victims had been officially prescribed the drug. The bodies of three of the five patients who had died in suspicious circumstances were exhumed, and tissues removed from vital organs and other parts of the body for analysis. Tests confirmed the presence of Pavulon. Almost certainly this had been administered via the patients' IVs, since none of the dead bore any trace of needle-marks from injections.

The FBI passed on the results of its investigation to the US Attorney in Detroit. It was of more than passing interest to the Bureau that not one suspicious breathing failure had occurred at the hospital since 15 August – the day their agents had appeared on the scene. A federal grand jury was summoned. The two Filipino nurses, along with other witnesses, were subpoenaed. Filipina Narciso was closely examined by the jurors. But it was eventually decided that there was not enough evidence and the two nurses were not indicted.

The FBI renewed its investigation at the Ann Arbor VA hospital. It even used hypnosis on witnesses in an effort to refresh their memories. This additional information was also passed on to the US Attorney's office.

A second grand jury was called, at which some of the survivors of the respiratory failures testified. On 16 June 1976, the grand jury returned a sixteen-count indictment against nurses Filipina Narciso and Leonora Perez, including five charges of first-degree murder by the introduction of Pavulon into the IV tubes of patients.

But before the trial of Narciso and Perez opened in March 1977, a former supervisor at the Ann Arbor VA hospital, Mrs Betty Jakim, claimed responsibility for the deaths. Mrs Jakim, however, was suffering terminal cancer and was a patient at a mental institution. She committed suicide after writing the letter. It was not admitted as evidence at the trial.

On 13 July 1977, after 100 witnesses had testified and 6500 pages of trial testimony had been typed, the jury reached its verdict on the VA hospital trial. Nurse Leonora Perez was convicted of poisoning and conspiracy to murder. Filipina Narciso was found guilty of one murder and acquitted of two charges of poisoning and one of conspiracy. The nurses were sentenced to imprisonment in a psychiatric institution.

In retrospect, nurses Filipina Narciso and Leonora Perez can be seen to be almost classic sufferers of Munchausen Syndrome by proxy (see page 235), causing the breathing failures – which they then tried to rescue – in order to be centres of attention.

The Narciso and Perez case received world-wide media coverage, and may well have brought the homicidal benefits of curare to the attention of Arnfinn Nesset, the manager of an old people's home in Orkdal, Norway. Between Autumn 1977 and his arrest in March 1981, Nesset killed twenty-one of his charges with curacit, a curare-based muscle relaxant, making him Scandinavia's greatest mass-murderer. His claim at his trial to have only been carrying out mercy killings was not believed – especially when it was proved that he had embezzled money from his victims. The evidence against

Nesset was almost entirely circumstantial (post-mortem examinations of the victims evidenced few traces of the curacit); nevertheless the trial jury found him guilty on twenty-one counts of murder. He was sentenced to the maximum term of imprisonment permissible under Norwegian law – twenty-one years.

CUT-THROAT
Homicidal attacks with KNIVES or other SHARP INSTRUMENTS are usually of the stabbing variety, but a significant band of male murderers – particularly, sex killers – have favoured throat-cutting. Jack the Ripper was, of course, the premier exponent of this art. Dr Bagster Philips, who examined the body of the Ripper's victim Annie Chapman, noted in the *Lancet* that 'The wound in her throat consisted of two distinct cuts, parallel to each other and about half an inch apart.' Peter Kurten, the Dusseldorf admirer of the Ripper and an advocate of CANNIBALISM, Heinrich Pommerencke, who perpetrated ten rape murders in Germany in the 1950s, and Edmund Kemper, the Co-ed Killer of 1970s California, all used throat-cutting on occasion.

In truth, it is a difficult method of homicide since it relies on the victim being either asleep, unprepared or immobilized. The standard signs of its perpetration, however, are copious bleeding from several major slashes, which may be so severe and savage as to involve the spinal column. Defence injuries may be seen on the victim's hands from attempts to hold off the assailant's knife or razor.

As a form of suicide, however, throat-cutting is relatively common. Almost always, 'tentative cuts' are present where hesitant trial incisions have been made. This feature is the classic distinction from the homicidal slashed-throat. A suicidal slash is usually made obliquely across the throat, from high up on the left side (in right-handed victims) tailing down to the bottom left.

The cause of death from a cut throat may be blood loss, especially if a carotid artery is cut, in which case blood may spurt several feet. Bleeding from jugular veins may be substantial. Death may also be caused by blood or cut tissues blocking the air passages, resulting in the CHOKING of the victim, who dies of ASPHYXIA. Another rare, but possible, complication is AIR EMBOLISM if a large neck vein is opened.

It is worth mentioning that the most famous cut-throat of them all, Sweeney Todd, the 'Demon Barber of Fleet Street', was a real character and not a fictional one as usually supposed. In the late 18th century Todd ran an itinerant barber's business in London, slashing the throats of prosperous customers with his razor before robbing them. He is believed to have murdered as many as seven unwary gentlemen in this way.

SOME NOTABLE CUT-THROAT CASES

Name	Date	Implement	Victim(s)
Unknown (UK)	1683	razor	1 (Earl of Essex)
Sweeney Todd (UK)	c1790s	razor	20+ (robbery victims)
John Williams (UK)	1811	sailor's knife	7 ('The Ratcliffe Highway Murders')
Constance Kent (UK)	1860	razor	1 (half brother)
Jack the Ripper (UK)	1884	knife	5 (prostitutes)
Thomas Dudley and Edwin Stephens (UK)	1884	knife	1 (boy, killed for food aboard the yacht *Mignonette*)
Robert Wood (UK)	1907	knife	1 (prostitute)
Peter Kurten (Ger)	1929/30	knife	2 (sex victims; killer murdered another 7 by various means)
Heinrich Pommerencke (Ger)	1959/60	knife	1 (sex victim; killer murdered another 9 by various means)
Edmund Kemper (USA)	1972/73	knife	2 (sex victims; killer murdered another 6 by various means)
Orrin Greenwood (USA)	1974	knife	9 (vagrants)

CYANIDE

Like ARSENIC, cyanide is one of the historic poisons. Among its earliest recorded misuses was the killing of the Roman Emperor Augustus by his wife Livia in AD14. Fifteen centuries later, the famous painter Leonardo da Vinci employed it criminally – if with characteristic precision – to murder a certain Giangaleazzo Sforza. Da Vinci injected large quantities of cyanide into the bark of fruit trees in his garden, where it passed in small quantities into the fruit, small enough not to cause death. The fruit had to be eaten for days before it would be fatal. Da Vinci made gifts of his garden's produce to Sforza who ate the fruit for a week and then 'yielded his soul to God'.

Cyanide is a natural vegetable acid, produced by certain plants to deter animals from eating them. In its isolated natural form it is harmless, but it is usually found in association with the enzyme emulsin, which reacts with it in the presence of water to release deadly hydrocyanic acid (also known as prussic acid and Scheele's acid). The seeds of apples and pears contain cyanide-laden compounds, as do the stones of plums, cherries, apricots and peaches; greater concentrations are to be found in the leaves of the cherry laurel and laurel. It would take several leaves (well chewed) of the latter to kill someone, but as ancient Middle Eastern poisoners discovered, evaporation of laurel leaves which have been crushed in water leaves a lethal concentration of the poison behind. It was figs soaked in such laurel water that Livia used to effect her ageing husband's demise.

Other commonly encountered forms of cyanide are potassium cyanide (the favourite suicidal agent of Nazi war criminals), and sodium cyanide or cyanide gas (used in US execution chambers and Nazi death camps). The toxic action of the cyanides is not always as fast as legend might have one believe. A fatal dose – about four grains – of a cyanide salt can take up to five minutes to deliver death; the stomach's gastric juices have to break down the salt before the deadly hydrocyanic acid is released. A fatal dose of hydrocyanic acid is one grain, and is rather quicker; in one recorded case demise was within ten seconds.

Cyanide poisoning is not a pleasant death. As the poison starves the body of oxygen (by inhibiting the blood's capacity to absorb it) the victim suffers a death like SUFFOCATION. The heart pounds from the increased effort of trying to get blood (thus oxygen) around the system. The chest heaves dramatically as the victim fights for breath. This would be followed by weakening of the pulse, coldness in the extremities, and convulsion. A loss of consciousness would follow, and death in its wake.

Post-mortem, the body would be cyanosed – showing a deep purple colour – and the tongue swollen. As countless 1930s thrillers of the Bulldog Drummond sort noted, a smell of bitter almonds on the lips and breath (and in the stomach at autopsy) is a characteristic sign of poisoning by cyanide.

Cyanides are quickly altered in the body by metabolic activity into sulphocyanides, which are normally present in the body. Consequently, a tardy forensic analysis may not spot them.

Notable killers who have used cyanide include Quaker John Tawell, who added it to the stout of his mistress, Sarah Hadler (also known as Sarah Hart), at her Slough home on New Year's Day, 1845. Writhing on the floor in agony, Hadler managed to tell a neighbour what had happened before she expired. The police used the new telegraph line to warn police at London's Paddington Station that Tawell was on the train. On arrival, Tawell was arrested, the first person to be apprehended courtesy of the telegraph. In court it was shown that Tawell had bought 2 g of Scheele's acid from Mr Hughes, a chemist in Bishopsgate Street. In an ingenious ploy, Tawell's defence counsel tried to blame Hadler's death on pips from apples she had eaten. Medical experts did much distilling of apple pips, coming to the conclusion that Hadler would have to have eaten a whole barrel-full of apples before death would ensue. Tawell was hanged in March 1845.

A New York factory manager, Roland B. Molineaux, sent bottles of Bromo Seltzer containing mercury cyanide to two fellow members of the exclusive Knickerbocker Athletic Club in the 1890s. One had annoyed him by courting a girl on whom he had designs; the other made the mistake of beating him at weightlifting. The former died,

and the second gave his Bromo Seltzer to his landlady for her headache
– and she died. Molineaux was found guilty of murder. At a second
trial in 1902 he was released. Some years later he suffered a nervous
breakdown and died in a mental asylum in 1913.

In 1907, Croydon's Richard Brinkley decided – like Tawell – that
stout with a dash of cyanide was the ideal killer drink, his motive
being the elimination of a witness to a forged will. The witness,
Reginald Parker, didn't sup from the bottle, but his landlord, plus
wife and daughter, did. Only the daughter lived. Brinkley was tried
at Guildford Assizes. The landlady's body was exhumed and
examined for traces of poison – there were none. Nevertheless, Mr
Brinkley found that 13 August 1907 was a very unlucky day for him
for on that day he met the executioner.

In 1912, an Austrian army officer, Lieutenant Adolph Hofrichter,
sent several of his comrades boxes of capsules containing a 'nerve-
strengthening remedy' as anonymous Christmas presents. Most of the
officers threw the capsules in the bin, but Captain Richard Mader
decided to give the remedy a try. Within seconds of swallowing the
capsule he died. Analysis of the remaining capsules showed that they
contained lethal quantities of potassium cyanide. Apparently, Hofrichter had sent the capsules to remove all those who had been promoted
above him to the staff position he desired. Found to be 'morally
abnormal', Hofrichter served twenty years in prison.

Dr Pierre Bougrat was a Marseille doctor; despite his respected
position he was a chronic addict of what the French call *nostalgie de
la boue* – the low life. He much preferred the city's red-light district
to his wife's dinner parties, and when she divorced him he took a
prostitute as his companion. Not surprisingly, Bougrat's neglect of
his practice meant that he was heavily in debt. So when Jacques
Rumebe entered his surgery on 14 March 1925, the doctor saw a
way out of his financial dilemma. Rumebe was carrying in his bag
his firm's bank-roll, 20,000 francs. Rumebe had syphilis and was
due to have the prescribed injection of mercuric chloride, but he
was given a far larger injection than normal, beaten up and finished
off with an injection of cyanide. Bougrat hid the body in a
cupboard, which he then pasted over with wallpaper.

With the arrival of warmer weather, however, the decomposing
body began to smell unpleasantly and eventually gave Bougrat away
to the police. Although sentenced to imprisonment on the notorious
Devil's Island, Bougrat was one of the few to escape. He ended up
in Venezuela, where he was allowed to stay because of his skill as a
doctor. He died in 1962, aged seventy-five.

There are many modern cases of cyanide poisoning for, unlike
arsenic, it has never gone out of fashion in murdering circles. In
Japan in 1948, Sadamichi Hirasawa went to rob a bank armed, not
with the traditional gun, but with doses of cyanide (see Case File).
Panic swept through Pasadena, Texas, in 1974 after a boy, Tim

O'Bryan, died from eating trick-or-treat candy found to be laced with cyanide. It turned out that he had been given it by his optometrist father, Ronald, heavily in debt and desirous of cashing in the insurance policy on his eight-year-old son.

Insurance money was also the motive behind Seattle housewife Stella Nickell's murder of her husband in 1986. She substituted cyanide for the contents of his Excedrin headache capsules. To cover up her crime, she then tampered with other boxes of Excedrin capsules, refilling the capsules with cyanide, and put them on the shelves of three nearby stores. Susan Snow, a forty-year-old bank manager, was found dead after swallowing a tampered-with capsule. Apparently, Nickell got the idea for her crime after reading about the 1984 Tylenol poisonings in Chicago, when seven people died after taking cyanide-laced Tylenol capsules. There was little evidence against Nickell, until her daughter Cynthia came forward as a witness against her mother. Nickell was charged with five violations of the Consumer Tampering Act – passed in response to the Tylenol killings – and two counts of causing death by tampering with consumer products. She was the first person convicted under the new federal law. Sentenced on May 9 1988 for two ninety-year terms and three ten-year terms, Nickell becomes eligible for parole in 2018.

An appalling mass murder-suicide by cyanide, involving about 900 people, occurred in Guyana in 1978. They were members of a religious sect, the People's Temple, founded by the Reverend Jim Jones. Fearing an investigation into the sect's activities, the members – a sad assortment of the naive, the retarded and the maladjusted – were ordered by Jones to drink a cyanide potion prepared by the medical officer of the group, Dr L. Schat. Jones shot himself.

CASE FILE: The Teikoku Bank Job

It was raining in Tokyo on the afternoon of Monday, 26 January 1948, and the staff of the Teikoku Bank huddled around heaters as they did their work. At about 3.10 p.m. there was a knock at the door of the bank, which was answered by a young woman cashier. A man stood at the door wearing an armband which identified him as a representative of the Tokyo Metropolitan Disinfectant Corps. He presented a business card which read 'Jiro Yamaguchi, MD, Welfare Ministry', and said that he needed to speak to the manager urgently. Led to the manager, the doctor informed him that there had been an outbreak of dysentery nearby, and that he had instructions from the American Occupation Force to inoculate the bank's staff against it. Dutifully the manager called the staff over to him, while Dr Yamaguchi took two bottles from his bag, one marked 'First Drug', the other 'Second Drug'.

What happened next is described in a memorandum written by

the Director of Tokyo CID:

All the victims, wholly unsuspicious of the fiendish intention of the offender, whose perfect composure and plausible explanations as well as his armband of Tokyo Metropolitan office having satisfied them to lay full credit to his words, formed a circle around him, poor victims sixteen in all. Then the devil opened his mouth and said: 'This medicine will damage the enamel of your teeth, and so I will show you how you must swallow it. There are two kinds of medicine. Take the second about a minute after you take the first. Be sure to drink it within a minute, or you will get a bad effect.'

After such explanations he poured into the victims' cups some liquid medicine, then he took a cup in his own hand and, saying 'This is how to drink,' gulped its contents by dripping them drop by drop on to his tongue, which he put out in the form of a shovel. So the poor victims, without exception, gulped the fatal water, following the devil's example. The liquid in question had a burning taste . . . After about a minute the tricky villain again showed them how to drink the second medicine, and again the poor innocents followed his example, not suspecting in the least that they were actually killing themselves. The devil had the audacity to advise them to rinse their mouths . . .

Within seconds of drinking the medicine ten of the bank staff died, some of them trying to reach the water fountain to quench the burning in their mouths. Two more died later in hospital. There were four survivors. Picking his way through the bodies, Yamaguchi bundled 164,400 yen and a cheque for 17,400 yen into his bag and calmly walked away.

The alarm was raised by one of the survivors, Miss Murata, crawling out of the bank and crying to passers-by: 'The bank – it's awful, help.'

When the police arrived at the bank, they found that helpful citizens had washed up the sixteen cups in which the poison had been administered. But traces of toxin in the victims' bodies suggested potassium cyanide or prussic acid as the killing agent. It was clear that the killer had some expertise in the matter of toxicology: in demonstrating how to take the 'medicine', he had drunk from the liquid which floated at the top of the bottle, avoiding the poison in suspension below.

Led by Chief Fujita of the Tokyo CID, the police soon discovered that Dr Yamaguchi had carried out a dummy run for his method at the Mitsubishi Bank, without fatal results for the staff. It also transpired that a 'Dr Shigeru Matsui' had 'immunized' the staff of the Yashuda Bank several months previously, causing some of them to become ill, though not fatally.

An artist's impression of the killer was circulated, the first time this technique had been used by the Japanese police. The breakthrough in the case, however, came about because of the old Japanese custom of exchanging business cards. The real Dr Shigeru Matsui approached the police, saying that he believed that he may have met the killer at some time and exchanged cards. As Matsui reasoned it, this must have been how the killer was able to present his card during the dry run at the Yasuda Bank. Dr Matsui had given out ninety-six cards, and although he had no record of whom he had given them to, he did have their cards in return. Among the cards was that of Sadamichi Hirasawa, a middle-aged artist living in a Tokyo suburb.

A police detective who visited Hirasawa noted how closely he resembled the survivor's description of the killer, down to a scar and two moles on his face. It was also discovered that Hirasawa had been spending money freely . . . A search of his home produced a medical bag and clothing similar to those worn by 'Dr Yamaguchi'.

On 26 September 1948, Hirasawa confessed to the crime, after relentless interrogation, and was put on trial in July 1950. In the course of the trial he withdrew his confession, alleging that it had been obtained under duress. Nonetheless, the judges – there was no jury – found him guilty of the murder of twelve people and the attempted murder of four more, and sentenced him to death by hanging. The case went to the Appeal Court, which ruled that he had been fairly convicted. A protracted legal row then ensued, in which Hirasawa's lawyers argued that the sentence violated the Japanese constitution which protected citizens from self-destruction. After all, it was argued, it was the condemned person's weight which made hanging work. Hirasawa spent the rest of his life in prison, dying in 1985.

During his time in prison he painted and wrote an autobiography, *My Will: The Teikoku Bank Case*. Meanwhile, an influential campaign, 'The Save Hirasawa Society', was set up, contending that he was the innocent victim of a government cover-up. The real murderer, according to the campaign, was a member of Unit 731, a germ-warfare group set up by the Japanese Army during the war, which had since been taken over by the Americans, who were anxious that its deadly toxicological secrets should not fall into the hands of the Soviets. Rather than arrest the real murderer and so draw attention to the existence of Unit 731, the Japanese and American authorities had colluded in making Hirasawa a scapegoat. Some weight is led to the campaign by impossibilities in Hirasawa's confession, his apparent lack of toxicological knowledge and the fact that Masako Murata, the girl who crawled from the bank, was adamant that his face shape was completely different to that of the Teikoku Bank killer.

One thing is certain, however; *whoever* the devil was who appeared at the Teikoku Bank on that January afternoon, he committed, as Tokyo's CID Director noted, 'one of the rarest and boldest crimes ever seen in the history of all crimes . . .'

D

DEEP-FREEZING   *See* **REFRIGERATION**

DEFENESTRATION
This is, literally, the action of pushing someone out of a window (Latin, *fenestra*), but can be taken to include all throwings of people off of high places. One of the best-known of such events in European history is the Defenestration of Prague, 21 May 1618, when Bohemian Protestant insurgents threw two Imperial commissioners out of a window of Hrdadshin castle. When a secretary was unwise enough to protest at this barbarity, he too was dropped the 60 ft into the moat.

Accidents and suicides account for the greatest percentage of deaths by defenestration. Certain signs at the scene of the incident point to suicide, such as a suicide note, or signs of hesitation and preparation. 'Jumpers', as they are colloquially known in the USA (which, with its numerous skyscrapers, might be said to be the defenestrator's dream country), often wait for an audience before launching themselves to oblivion. Death is caused by the massive impact injuries sustained when hitting the ground at speeds of up to 60 m.p.h. In most instances the jumper will be conscious until he or she hits the earth.

Did he fall or was he pushed? Unless there are eyewitnesses it is difficult for the authorities to determine whether the defenestrated corpse on the ground was accidental or homicidal. The Italian playwright Dario Fo made much of exactly this dilemma in his drama *The Accidental Death of an Anarchist*, when corrupt policemen push a political opponent out of an upper-storey window of their HQ. Who could prove that his death was not accidental? The cold conclusion is that there may well be more murders from defenestration than the black museums allow. Among the proven homicidal defenestrations of more recent decades was that committed on America's Iris Nina Seagar, pushed off a Baltimore balcony by her husband in the early 1970s. The motive was money. Iris Seagar was insured for $100,000. The husband was caught because he made an elementary mistake. Mrs Seagar's body was found sixteen feet out into the road. A person cannot jump further in free air than on the ground, and the portly 48-year-old Iris could not possibly have jumped such a distance. Faced with this evidence, the husband confessed to throwing her from the balcony in a drunken rage.

A celebrated, and most unusual, defenestration happened to Alfred Loewenstein. Loewenstein was a European financier of immense wealth – and some sharp practices – who lived a life of opulence in the Roaring Twenties. He owned no less than eight villas in Biarritz. On 4 July 1928, a Fokker trimotor AIRCRAFT carrying Loewenstein took off from London, bound for Brussels. Also on board were Loewenstein's valet, male secretary, two female stenographers, a pilot and co-pilot. The plane never reached Brussels, however, but landed instead on the Normandy coast where the crew told French authorities that Loewenstein had accidentally fallen from the plane into the English Channel. A hastily held inquest ruled that Loewenstein's death from 15,000 feet was probably accidental; in any case, it happened over international waters, and was therefore deemed to be nobody's business. But as the journalist William Norris established in his 1987 book, *The Man Who Fell from the Sky*, it would have been virtually impossible for Loewenstein to have fallen from the Fokker accidentally. Loewenstein was murdered by one of the crew, acting for a business rival.

Occasionally, murders by other means are dressed up to look as though the victim accidentally fell from a great height. John Laurie was a 25-year-old pattern-maker from Glasgow who befriended a London clerk, Edwin Rose, on holiday in Scotland. On 15 July 1889, Laurie and Rose left their lodgings on the Isle of Arran to climb Goatfell peak. Rose never returned, and Laurie was seen slipping away from the island the next day. A subsequent search of Goatfell involving 200 islanders discovered Rose's body, hidden under a pile of stones. A large-scale hunt was carried out for Laurie, who was spotted by an alert policeman at Ferniegair. Laurie made a run for it, but was eventually cornered in woodland, where he tried unsuccessfully to cut his throat. He was tried for murder in Edinburgh. His defence counsel contended that Rose had died of injuries sustained by a fall. Laurie's evasive behaviour, his written-on-the-run letters to newspapers bragging 'I smile when I read that my arrest is expected hourly', and his admission to robbing Rose told against him. He was found guilty by majority verdict. A sentence of death was commuted to life imprisonment when he was determined to be of unsound mind.

DIGITALIS

An extract from leaves of the purple foxglove (*Digitalis purpurea*), digitalis has been used for centuries as a heart stimulant in folk medicine. It was first officially discovered as a medicinal drug by Englishman Dr William Withering in 1775. In tiny quantities the drug extracted from the leaves – digitalis – regulates the rhythm of the heart. In large doses, as the French poisoner de la Pommerais (see Case File) discovered a little under a century later, digitalis causes the heart to slow to the point that it stops. Totally.

A toxic dose is 2 g of dry leaf extract. The symptoms include nausea, delirium and convulsions, usually occurring within three to four hours of receiving the poison. Large doses administered orally are often not fatal, since the victim tends to vomit up the poison.

CASE FILE: The Strange Death of Madame de Pauw

The doctors called to the bedside of the young widow Mme de Pauw were mystified by her symptoms, in particular her irregular heartbeat. They had little chance to come to any proper medical conclusion about her condition however, since she dismissed them in favour of Dr Couty de la Pommerais, a 28-year-old homeopath who happened to be her lover. Unfortunately, Mme de Pauw's faith in de la Pommerais was misplaced; she died on the night of 17 November 1863. De la Pommerais gave cholera as the cause of death, and his mistress – he himself was married to a former Mlle Dubisy – was duly buried in a Parisian cemetery.

And that would have probably been an end to it, save for the anonymous letter sent to Chief Inspector Claude of the Sûreté. The letter suggested that Claude might look into the question of who would benefit financially from Mme de Pauw's death. When he did so, Claude discovered that de la Pommerais had insured the widow's life for 500,000 francs, and that the insurance company was preparing to pay him.

In all probability, the sender of the anonymous letter was Mme de Pauw's sister, Mme Ritter. Certainly, it was Mme Ritter who later called on Chief Inspector Claude and told him about the insurance swindle that de la Pommerais and de Pauw had hatched together. This required persuading the insurance company that Mme de Pauw's health was poor, so that when she proposed that her life insurance should be exchanged for a small annuity they would be only too glad to do so. Mme de Pauw had then, at de la Pommerais' instigation, made a will in his favour. Shortly afterwards, she had died.

It seemed to Chief Inspector Claude that de la Pommerais had given Mme de Pauw some drug which produced cholera-like symptoms, and he quickly arranged to have her corpse exhumed. Tests for metallic poisons like ARSENIC and ANTIMONY were carried out by Professor Ambroise Tardieu, Professor of Forensic Medicine at Paris University, but no traces were found. A vegetable poison seemed the likely alternative. Painstakingly, Tardieu applied the method pioneered by Jean Stas in determining poisoning by NICOTINE several years before to the dead woman's stomach contents but without result.

Desperate, Tardieu decided to find out if the stomach juices did at least contain a poison. He injected some into a dog. The dog vomited and after six hours its heartbeat slowed dramatically. The liquid from Mme de Pauw's stomach contained a poison, certainly. But what was the poison?

A clue came from one of de la Pommerais' letters, now in the possession of the police, which mentioned the drug digitalis. Furthermore, a new bottle of digitalis in de la Pommerais' homeopathic surgery was almost empty. Digitalis injected into a dog caused its heartbeat to become wildly erratic. The dog died a few hours later.

Tardieu then injected some of its stomach extract into a frog, opening its chest so that he could observe the heart rate, which slowed, then ceased. Digitalis produced exactly the same effect.

It was then decided to exhume the body of de la Pommerais' mother-in-law, the wealthy Mme Dubisy, who had died the previous year from 'Asiatic cholera'. The body had been buried too long to reveal vegetable poisoning, but the symptoms of her illness were those of digitalis poisoning, and there was little doubt that de la Pommerais had murdered her so that he could gain access to the Dubisy assets through his wife, the principal beneficiary.

In June 1864, de la Pommerais was convicted of the murder of Mme de Pauw, thanks in no small part to the skill of Professor Tardieu. The case is a landmark in the history of forensic medicine, and Tardieu's test for digitalis – complete with frog – was used for many years after.

It was, for instance, used to trap the Belgian poisoner Marie Becker, the middle-aged wife of a cabinet-maker who decided to recapture her youth by murdering her husband with digitalis and spending the insurance money on the high life. She became an habituée of nightclubs, where she picked up young men and paid them to have sex with her. She administered digitalis to one boyfriend who overstayed his welcome, and then started adding the drug to the tea of the female patrons of her dress shop. Taken unwell, the patrons were escorted home by the apparently concerned Marie Becker, poisoned some more and robbed. Becker used the proceeds to pay her string of gigolos. Ten known homicides were committed by Becker – making her the worst digitalis poisoner in history – before she drew suspicion to herself, by telling a friend that she knew a poison powder that 'left no trace'. The exhumed bodies of her husband and some of her customers proved her a liar and tested positive for digitalis. Becker was convicted of murder at her trial in 1934, and sent to prison for life, where she died during World War II.

DISMEMBERMENT

New York's Fred Thorn set something of a trend when he chopped the corpse of a rival in love, Willie Guldensupper, into five pieces and distributed them around the Harlem river in June 1897.

Disassembled bodies, or 'jig-saw murders' as the press likes to dub them, have become a periodic fixture on the slabs of the world's path laboratories ever since. Not, of course, that Thorn was the first to try and defeat the identification of his victim by judicious carvery; it was just that before him killers had been content to merely lop off a cadaver's head.

Presumably, carving the victim into five lumps seemed a rather modest total to Dr Buck Ruxton; in 1935, he cut his wife Isabella and maid Mary into seventy pieces (see Case File). Among the few who have since threatened Ruxton's record in human carvery is another doctor, Yorkshire's Samuel Perera, who dissected his adopted daughter Nilanthe in 1983. After combing eight sites in the Wakefield area, forensic scientists were able to identify a total of 106 bony fragments which, in their opinion, came from 77 individual bones or parts of bone from Nilanthe Perera. Included in Perera's disposal sites were the geranium pots at his modern detached home, which gave off an unpleasant sickly smell to police officers when they came to search for Nilanthe at the instigation of worried neighbours. One of the pots was upturned. 'I don't think I shall ever forget,' said Chief Superintendent Walter Cowman later, 'the sight of a virtually complete human spine curled around the roots of a plant.'

Rendering the victim unidentifiable is not the only reason for dismemberment. In some horrific murders, the victim has been carved apart while alive, dying from shock or blood loss. To perpetrate such a death, the killer must desire the infliction of pain upon the victim. Hence, in centuries past, the judicial dismemberment or 'quartering' of those the state wanted to punish most, traitors. Even by the barbaric standards of medieval judicial punishment, this was a brutal death. The prisoner was 'drawn' to the gallows on a sled, hung until nearly dead, taken down, disembowelled, and castrated. The victim was finally put out of his misery by decapitation. The corpse was then cut into four quarters and displayed around the city as a deterrent.

More often than not, dismemberment is the result of simple necessity, the need to make a large corpse more manageable. Hacked into pieces the corpse can then be prepared for final disposal, be it by BURNING, or being dumped in hedges, dustbins, TRUNKS, WATER, or wherever. Naturally, a surgeon like Ruxton achieved dismembering with a minimum of time, energy and mess. Likewise, trained butcher Louis Voisin had little difficulty in reducing Emilienne Gerard to torso, head and hands in World War I London, after she discovered him *in flagrante* with his new girlfriend. Yet even someone without medical or butchery skills, like Ohio home-improvements salesman Ronald Allen, managed to dismember the corpse of his landlady in 1988 with nothing more specialized than a carving knife and a hacksaw. It took twenty-four hours. Another amateur, Moenchengladbach's Martina Zimmermann, adherent of CANNIBALISM, accomplished the dismembering task in rather quicker time, but had the advantage of an electric knife. Dennis Nilsen started as an amateur dismemberer; but after dealing with sixteen corpses between 1978 and 1983, he could probably be considered an expert human butcher. In one of his many prison journals, Britain's most prolific serial-killer described his method in elaborate and chilling detail:

> I got ready a small bowl of water, a kitchen knife, some paper tissues and plastic bags. I had to have a couple of drinks before I could start. I removed the vest and underpants from the body. With the knife I cut the head from the body. There was very little blood. I put the head in the kitchen sink, washed it and put it in a carrier bag. I then cut off the hands and then the feet. I washed them in the sink and dried them . . .

CASE FILE: The Dumfries Jigsaw Murder

Bukhtyar Rustomji Ratanji Hakim was born in 1899 to a Parsee family living in Bombay. He qualified as a doctor of medicine at the university in that city, before moving to Britain to continue his studies. The British found his given name funny and unpronounceable, so Bukhtyar decided to anglicize it by deed poll. Thus, in 1927, Bukhtyar Rustomji became Buck Ruxton.

Ruxton's medical studies at Edinburgh did not go as he hoped, and he failed the examination for fellowship of the Royal College of Surgeons. Probably his failure was due to his infatuation with Isabella Van Ess, a waitress separated from her Dutch husband. If Ruxton failed to net a fellowship, he did at least net Isabella. The couple do not seem to have married officially, but when they moved to a practice at 2 Dalton Square, Lancaster, it was as Mr and Mrs Ruxton. There Isabella bore three children, and for a while the couple seemed to be happy. A young nursemaid, Mary Rogerson, made up the rest of the household.

Domestic bliss was steadily darkened by Buck Ruxton's unfounded suspicion that his wife was committing infidelities. In particular, he was suspicious of a friend of Isabella's, a young man called Bobby Edmondson who worked in Lancaster town hall. Ruxton became insanely jealous, and the subsequent quarrels were violent enough for Mrs Ruxton to seek police protection in spring 1935. On 14 September, Isabella Ruxton drove her husband's car to meet her sisters for a day out in Blackpool, an annual event. Ruxton believed she had gone to meet a lover. Isabella left her sisters at 11.30 p.m. to return home to 2 Dalton Square. She was never seen again. And nor was nursemaid Mary Rogerson.

On the bright, cold afternoon of Sunday, 29 September 1935, Susan Johnson, a young woman on holiday in southern Scotland, walked over the bridge which crossed the Gardenholme Linn stream, a mile or so north of the village of Moffat. Glancing over the stone parapet she saw something which stopped her in her tracks: a human arm was protruding from some wrapping at the bottom of the gully. Johnson ran back to her hotel to tell her brother of her grisly discovery, and he ran and contacted the police. By the time darkness descended that afternoon, Sergeant Sloan of the Dumfriesshire Constabulary, whose bad luck it was to be the duty man sent to investigate, had found four parcels of human remains. Over the following week more human portions were discovered along the banks of the Linn.

Summoned to make some sense of the human remains found at Gardenholme Linn was Professor John Glaister, who had been appointed Professor of Forensic Medicine at Edinburgh University. His inventory of the initial 'bits and pieces', as Glaister quaintly termed them, was as follows:

Four bundles: the first was wrapped in a blouse and contained two upper arms and four pieces of flesh; the second comprised two thigh bones, two legs from which most of the flesh had been stripped, and nine pieces of flesh, all wrapped in a pillow-case; the third was a piece of cotton sheeting containing seventeen pieces of flesh; the fourth bundle was also wrapped in cotton sheeting and consisted of a human trunk, two legs with the feet tied with the hem of a cotton sheet and some wisps of straw and cotton wool.

In addition, other parcels opened to reveal two heads, one of which was wrapped in child's rompers; a quantity of cotton wool and sections from the *Daily Herald* of 6 August 1935; one thigh; two forearms with hands attached but minus the top joints of the fingers and thumbs; and several pieces of skin and flesh. One part was wrapped in the *Sunday Graphic* dated 15 September and was to provide an important clue.

The maggoty, decomposing remains were taken to the anatomy department at Edinburgh University, where they were augmented by other parcels of remains found in the Moffat area. One parcel, containing a left foot, was discovered some nine miles from the village. In all, seventy pieces of what appeared to be two human beings were assembled. The heads had been carefully denuded of their eyes, skin, lips and nose, and some teeth had been extracted. Ends of fingers had been cut off. The extensive and deliberate nature of the dismemberment suggested that it had been done to frustrate identification. Yet if the case was to stand much chance of a successful outcome, the medical experts would have to solve the

Dapper but deadly: arsenic poisoner Major Herbert Rowse Armstrong. (*Syndication International*)

The drum used by 'acid bath' murderer John George Haigh. (*Popperfoto*)

The Lizzie Borden case: the murder axe. (*Topham*)

An array of the tools used by serial-killer and amateur dissectionist Dennis Nilsen, including the copper pot in which he boiled victims' heads. (*Press Association*)

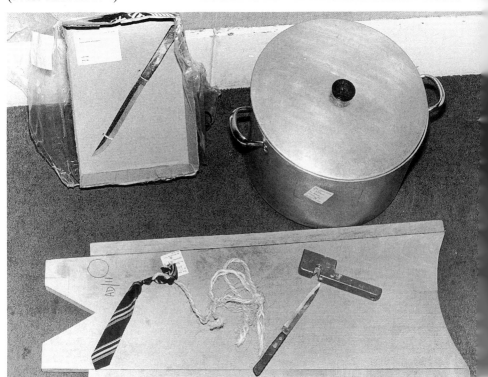

Self-confessed murderer Donald Hume throwing Setty's torso into the sea in a reconstruction of the crime. The aircraft is the actual one Hume used. (*Syndication International*)

No. 63 Tollington Park, home of Frederick Seddon. (*Hulton Deutsch Collection*

A court official displaying boxes of poison at the trial of Marie Besnard, the 'Black Widow of Loudon'. (*Popperfoto*)

The burnt-out car of Alfred Arthur Rouse. (*Topham*)

Sex-killer Jack the Ripper cuts the throat of another victim.
(*Mary Evans Picture Library*)

erman cannibal murderer Peter
urten. (*Popperfoto*)

George Smith, the 'Brides in the Bath'
murderer. (*Syndication International*)

The trial of Adelaide Bartlett (inset, left) for the murder of her husband by
liquid chloroform. (*Mansell Collection*)

The bucket in which Denise Labbé ritually drowned her daughter. (*Popperfoto*)

A policeman holds the .22 Anschutz rifle and silencer used by Jeremy Bamber. (*Press Association*)

two human 'jigsaw puzzles', and find physical features and marks which would identify the victims. It seemed an impossible task.

Meanwhile, as Professor Glaister and his team of pathologists, anatomists and dentists tried to reconstruct the victims, the police found their first major clue. A piece of the *Sunday Graphic* which wrapped one of parcels was found to come from a special 'slip' edition, printed exclusively for Morecambe and Lancaster. And by coincidence, on the very day the Chief Constable of Dumfries telephoned the Lancaster police to inquire about missing local persons, he happened to notice an article in Glasgow's *Daily Record* about a missing girl, Mary Jane Rogerson, who worked for a family called Ruxton in . . . Lancaster. Inquiries soon revealed that Mrs Ruxton was also missing.

When the blouse used to wrap one of the Moffat parcels was shown to Mary Rogerson's stepmother she recognized it at once, having given it to Mary herself. The romper suit was identified by a Mrs Holme, a boarding-house landlady who had donated it to the Ruxtons when they had boarded with her the previous summer. With the leads centring on Lancaster, the responsibility for the case was passed over to the city's Chief Constable, Captain Henry Vann. Vann brought Ruxton in for questioning. The doctor denied that the two bodies were those of Isabella and Mary Rogerson, and stated that his wife was not dead but had run off with another man.

But as much as Ruxton protested his innocence, more and more evidence was beginning to build up against him. Some of the most damning of it came from one of Ruxton's patients, Mrs Hampshire, who had been asked to 2 Dalton Square on Sunday, 15 September to help the doctor 'prepare for the decorators'. The house was in more of a mess than Mrs Hampshire bargained for. Many of the carpets had been taken up and were in the back yard, covered in blood. There were also bloodstains on the bath, towels, clothing and on a man's blue suit, which Ruxton tried to press on Mr Hampshire when he later came to collect his wife. Mrs Hampshire, a somewhat naïve soul, had not asked Dr Ruxton why bloody straw was protruding from under the doors to two of the bedrooms.

Another piece of evidence against Ruxton came from a cyclist he had knocked over on Tuesday, 17 September on a road leading to Moffat. The doctor had not stopped but was caught by a policeman, who had noticed his nervousness.

But all this evidence might have come to nought in court if the scientists in Edinburgh had been unable to prove that the lumps of bone, flesh and gristle on their slabs were those of Isabella Ruxton and Mary Rogerson.

True, there had been successful convictions for murder without a body being found, but juries were far less likely to return a guilty verdict without one. After all, if they sent a man to the gallows for murder, only to find that the report of the victim's death was much exaggerated, the hanging of the innocent could hardly be remedied.

The team at Edinburgh University – Ruxton's old British Alma Mater – had achieved one of the great triumphs of forensic science. At first the miscellaneous body parts from Moffat had been roughly divided into boxes marked Body 1 and Body 2. But a co-opted anatomist, Professor James Brash, had been able to get an exact fit between some of the dismembered remains and, using X-ray and anatomical formulae, sorted out others so that they belonged to one body or the other. After two weeks of painstaking work, Brash had partially reconstructed the two corpses. Both were clearly female, and with the help of odontologist Arthur Hutchinson, Brash had been able to estimate the age of Body No. 1 as 20 (as was Mary Rogerson) and that of No. 2 as between 35 and 45 (Isabella Ruxton was 34).

To make a positive identification of the victims' badly mutilated heads, which had had all their distinguishing features removed, Brash did something never attempted before in a criminal investigation. He obtained photographs of the two women and had them blown up to life size, the measurements precise to the nearest millimetre. Then he cleaned the two decapitated heads of all their tissue, and had them photographed to exact size. The enlarged photographs of the head of Isabella Ruxton and Mary Rogerson were then superimposed on the photographs of the skulls in the laboratory. The resulting 'double exposures' matched remarkably well.

Ironically enough, the dismemberment of the Moffat bodies was so extensively and neatly done that it had proved a sort of clue in itself; it could only have been accomplished by someone with medical knowledge. Moreover, the implement used was a surgical knife.

Dr Buck Ruxton was tried at Manchester Assizes in March 1936 for the murder of Isabella Ruxton and Mary Rogerson. He was defended by the velvet-voiced Norman Birkett KC, one of the great criminal advocates of the time, and known as 'the courtroom magician'. Opening for the Crown, Mr J.C. Jackson KC, gave his account of what happened in the house at 2 Dalton Square, Lancaster, after Mrs Ruxton's trip to Blackpool:

In that house the bedrooms are on the top floor; the back bedroom was occupied by Mary Rogerson, in one of the front slept Mrs Ruxton with her three children, and on the same floor was also the doctor's room. You will hear that Mrs Ruxton had received before her death violent blows in the face and that she was strangled. The suggestion of the prosecution is that her death and that of the girl Mary took place outside these rooms on the landing at the top of the staircase, outside the maid's bedroom, because from that point down the staircase right into the bathroom there are trails of enormous quantities of blood. I suggest that when she went up to bed a violent quarrel took place; that he strangled his wife, and that Mary Rogerson caught him in the act and so had to die also. Mary's skull was fractured: she had some blows on top of the head which would render her unconscious, and then was killed by some other means, probably a knife, because of all the blood that was found down these stairs . . .

Ruxton himself, histrionic and given to verbose, unconvincing answers, made a poor showing in the witness box. To the suggestion that he killed Mary Rogerson he replied, 'That is bunkum, with a capital B, if I may say so.' It was nonetheless the expert scientific testimony of the Edinburgh team, presented with crystal clarity by Professor Glaister, which really sank Ruxton. Even Norman Birkett was powerless against it.

Ruxton was hanged at Strangeways Prison, Manchester, on the morning of Tuesday, 12 May 1936. On the following Sunday, his confession was published in the *News of the World*. Exhibit A from Ruxton's trial, the white enamel bath in which he chopped up his wife and Mary Rogerson, ended up as a drinking trough for police horses.

DROWNING

The infamy of George Joseph Smith, the Edwardian 'Brides in the Bath' murderer (see Case File), has tended to submerge, as it were, the fact that drowning is a highly unusual form of foul play. Most watery deaths are accidental, and between 10 per cent and 30 per cent due to suicide. A goodly number of the accidental drownings occur where the victims have fallen into water under the influence of ALCOHOL.

Drowning is one of the deaths by ASPHYXIA, where air is prevented from entering the air passages and lungs by water. It is also thought that ingested water entering the blood stream disturbs the potassium–sodium balance in tissue fluids leading to a rapid irregular beating of the heart known as ventricular fibrillation. Occasionally, death in the water may be caused by immediate cardiac arrest, a so-called vasovagal attack, due to shock, especially if the water is cold.

In what might be called 'classical drowning', the subject struggles and alternately rises and sinks. Water is gulped into the lungs, water-logging them, the additional weight of the ingested water only ensuring the certainty of sinking. A drowning may take five minutes. Although complete immersion is usual, it is worth pointing out that drowning may occur when only the nostrils and mouth are covered by fluid. Drunks are known to have fallen asleep in puddles and drowned. London serial-killer and mild-mannered civil servant Dennis Nilsen (1944–) dispatched two of his fifteen male-drifter victims by making them insensible with drink and then dunking their heads in a bucket of water.

As for the drowned body, this may exhibit few external signs of its watery fate, save for a fine white froth of mucus, air and water at the mouth and nostrils. If the body has been immersed for several hours or more it will have a wrinkling of the skin on the palms of the hands and the feet, known as 'washerwoman's hands'. A pathologist will also look for the presence of objects such as waterweed, flotsam and stones which have been grabbed during the death struggle and which have become locked into the clenched hand by cadaveric spasm – the origin, incidentally, of the phrase 'clutching at straws'. Where foul play has taken place the corpse may have clutched buttons, fragments of clothing or hair from the killer. Internally, the autopsy of the drowned will show pale, watery distended lungs, and water will be present in the stomach and oesophagus.

It is relatively easy for a pathologist to determine whether a victim has drowned, or was dead before he or she entered the water. Both sea and fresh water are full of microscopic algae with silicon shells called diatoms. In the course of drowning, water containing diatoms is ingested by the subject, going into the lungs, blood-stream and heart. The presence of diatoms in the bloodstream at a post-mortem is clear proof that the victim was alive when entering the water. An already dead body, which has been put into a sea, river, lake or stream as a means of disposal (see WATER), will not have diatoms in the bloodstream or organs. There are over 15,000 species of diatom, many of them peculiar to certain areas, so identification of the diatom type can help locate the place where the drowning took place.

Interestingly, drownings in fresh water are quicker than those in salt water. In fresh-water drowning, the water taken in is quickly drawn from the lungs into the blood stream, causing the upsetting of the sodium–potassium balance already noted, and possibly cardiac arrest. When a person drowns in salt water, the salt water ingested has a higher osmotic pressure than the blood. Consequently, water is not drawn through the breathing membrane into the blood to disturb the sodium–potassium balance.

One of the strangest homicidal drownings was the ritual murder of the French 2½-year-old Catherine Labbé by her mother, Denise. In 1954, Labbé met an officer of the Saint-Cyr military school at Rennes, called Jacques Algarron. She quickly fell under the domination of the handsome Algarron. This was unfortunate, for Algarron, although intelligent, was possessed of the evil belief that women were only on earth to obey his will. He insisted that Labbé sleep with other men so that she could beg his forgiveness. Then he demanded that she prove her love by killing her daughter, the human product of a previous affair. Under Algarron's spell, Denise Labbé drowned her daughter – at the third attempt – in a basin of water, alleging that it was an accident. Friends were suspicious and when the police questioned Denise she admitted: 'Yes, I killed my daughter but it was a ritual murder.' She implicated Algarron, who was arrested. At their May 1955 trial, Labbé was found guilty with extenuating circumstances and sentenced to penal servitude for life. Algarron received a sentence of twenty years' hard labour for provoking the crime.

CASE FILE: **The Brides in the Bath**

George Joseph Smith was a ladykiller in more ways than one. A petty criminal since childhood, in 1898 he married nineteen-year old Beatrice Thornhill – who would turn out to be his only legal wife – quickly setting her to work as a thief. Like the French criminal Henri Désiré Landru (1869–1922), the seducer of no fewer than ten fiancées, Smith recognized his extraordinary power over women and that the female sex would make easy prey. Many bigamous marriages followed as the nomadic Smith, under a variety of aliases, wooed and wed women, relieved them of their savings then suddenly disappeared. On three occasions, however, the Londoner did not simply leave his new bride but murdered her.

In August 1910, Smith – posing as one Henry Williams – married Bessie Mundy, aged thirty-one and with an estate of over £2500. After less than a month of marriage, Smith walked out on Mundy, stealing £150 from her and accusing her of giving him a 'disorder' (VD) in the process, but met her again at Weston-super-Mare eighteen months later. Apparently reconciled, the couple made joint wills and moved to Herne Bay in Kent, where Smith set himself up as an antiques dealer. In July 1912 Smith bought a bath from a local ironmonger. At the same time he took Bessie to the doctor because she was having blackouts and fits. On 13 July the doctor received a note from Smith saying, 'Can you come at once? I am afraid my wife is dead.' The doctor found Bessie lying naked in the bath, face up, mouth and nose submerged. A bar of soap was clutched in her hand. A hastily arranged inquest, marked by terrible sobbing from the apparently grieving Smith, pronounced accidental death. Bessie's assets were handed over to Smith who, with typical parsimony, buried her in a pauper's grave.

Although he had now married at least five women and drowned one, Smith's need for money was by no means diminished. Indeed, his abysmal sense in financial matters only made his need greater. He moved to Southsea in November 1913, where he selected as his next wife, the generously proportioned Alice Burnham. At twenty-five, Alice was some sixteen years younger than Smith. Undoubtedly attracted to him, but also, quite possibly, anxious to avoid the stigma of spinsterhood (many women in Edwardian England were panicked into marriage thinking that any husband was better than none, making it a happy hunting ground for the likes of Smith), Alice agreed to his proposal of union.

On 4 November, Smith 'married' Alice, insured her life for £500 and took her off to Blackpool for a honeymoon. There they trudged the streets looking for suitable accommodation – rooms with a bath. Soon Alice was complaining of headaches, and was taken to see the doctor. In the early evening of 12 December, Smith called out to the landlady 'My wife can't speak to me – go for a doctor!' The doctor found Alice dead in the bath, with her head at the narrow end. Again the inquest recorded death by misadventure. Smith duly collected the insurance money.

Margaret Elizabeth Lofty, the daughter of the late Reverend and Mrs Lofty of Bristol, was the next Mrs Smith, marrying the murderer at, of all grimly ironic places, Bath, on 17 December 1914. Before the marriage, Smith – or 'John Lloyd' as he now was – had taken out a life insurance on Lofty for £700. The couple moved to lodgings in Highgate, London, where there followed the inevitable visits to the doctor. On 18 December, their landlady, Miss Blatch, boiled up a copper kettle of water for the new bride to have a bath. 'I heard someone go upstairs,' she said later. 'I was ironing in the kitchen when I heard the sound of splashing. There was a noise as of someone putting wet hands or arms on the side of the bath . . . Then a sigh.' The next sound the landlady heard was Smith playing 'Nearer My God To Thee' on her sitting-room harmonium. The verdict of the inquest was again misadventure.

Lofty's death was, however, Smith's undoing. The case, because it was committed in the capital rather than some seaside resort, attracted the attention of the national press, particularly the *News of the World*. Reading its account of 'Bride's Tragic Fate On Day After Wedding', was Alice Burnham's father, who was struck by the similarity to the death of his daughter. So too was another reader, a Blackpool landlord called William Haynes, who ran the boarding-house next door to the one in which Lofty had died. Alerted, the police arrested Smith on 1 February 1915 for bigamy and later for murder.

At Smith's trial at the Old Bailey for the murder of Bessie Mundy he was defended by Sir Edward Marshall, who tried unsuccessfully to have evidence of the other two deaths excluded. Consequently, the prosecution was able to show that Smith operated a system of murder. He pleaded not guilty, but the Home Office pathologist Bernard Spilsbury pointed out that the size of the bath did not allow for accidental death. Instead, Spilsbury suggested, Smith had approached his luxuriating bride, placed his right hand on her head as in a gesture of affection, and then slipped his left arm beneath the woman's knees. Then, he quickly lifted her legs out of the water and simultaneously pressed down on her head, causing the whole body to slide down the bath towards the narrow end, submerging her mouth and nostrils.

An Inspector Neil decided to test Spilsbury's hypothesis, and experimented with a policewoman clad in a bathing suit. He asked her to get into a bathtub identical to those used by Smith and, when she was lying down, picked up her legs and pulled. To Neil's horror, as her head slid underwater, she became unconscious almost immediately. It was not until after half an hour's resuscitation that she recovered sufficiently to say that the water, rushing up her nose, had shocked her into unconsciousness. Smith was hanged as a result of this evidence. The execution took place at Maidstone jail in August 1915.

E

ELECTROCUTION

The hairdryer dropped into the bath, the wire worked loose on the electric mower, the tampered-with kitchen appliance. Electrocution is one of the classic modern means of domestic murder, its singular advantage being that the electrocuted spouse can be passed off as an accident. It is not, however, the most reliable of methods, and is frequently more honoured in the trying than in the successful completion.

The effects of an electric shock depend on the strength of the current, its amperage and voltage, the duration of the shock, whether the current is a.c. or d.c. (the former being more dangerous), and the body's resistance. The latter is lowered by moisture, hence the fact that most homicidal electrocutions occur in the bathroom, garden or kitchen. The normal mechanism of death is interruption of the heart beat leading to ventricular fibrillation (a very rapid but ineffective heart beat) or total cardiac arrest. Some people die of respiratory paralysis. Death can be instantaneous but on occasion can be delayed for several hours.

After death, the victim's body is likely to display burn marks, even charred tissue, especially if contact with the conductor was sustained and the person's skin dry. Less destructive burns may be deep but with a noticeable grey-white centre and lilac surrounding edge. Burns may be at both the sight of entry of the current and its site of exit. Quite often, however, electrocution leaves no marks on the body at all.

This was the case with a Mrs Darling, whose husband (a verger at Llandaff Cathedral) threw a plugged-in fan heater into the bath in which his wife sat. She died of the electrical discharge – earthed through the water and drainage piping – after a short period of convulsive shaking. James Darling was convicted largely on a variation in successive statements he made.

More elaborate electrocutions, where baths are wired up to the mains, seem less successful. In an attempted murder in Chelmsford in 1951, a husband was found to have wired the metal soap tray on the bath into the domestic circuit, which he could make live by a switch in his workroom when his wife entered the water. In 1993, Peter Ellis, a 34-year-old Cardiff property developer, also tried to kill his (heavily insured) wife by plugging her bath into the mains. When Ellis flipped the switch a blue flash swept the bath, sending a numbing sensation through Lisa Ellis's legs and melting the plug chain. The flash also bounced her out of the bath and, since she did not touch anything as she left the water, she survived to see her husband jailed for eighteen years for the attempt. If a contact with an electrical conductor is poor or momentary people can survive exposure to very high-tension currents (e.g. 2000 volts). On the other hand, a domestic current of low tension (e.g. 110 volts) may cause death if there is a favourable contact between the skin and the conductor. It is probable that if the heart or brain stem are in the direct path of the current death is much more likely to occur.

In the USA, where electrocution is used by some fifteen states as a form of judicial killing, there has been controversy over its humaneness ever since an 'electric chair' was first switched on in 1890 at Auburn State Prison, New York. The occupant, murderer William Kemmler, took eleven minutes to die. In judicial electrocutions, the prisoner is strapped to a stout wooden chair and has a death cap, containing an electrode, placed on the head. The cap is soaked with a salt-water solution to improve conductivity. Another electrode is placed on the ankle, and the executioner pulls a switch which jolts a three-second charge of 2250 volts through the victim's body. This is repeated four times in two minutes. Despite improvements, judicial electrocution is of questionable efficacy. No less than five charges were needed to kill frail Ethel Rosenberg as late as 1953.

CASE FILE: The Shocking Death of Ingrid Kasper

The dead woman lay face-down on the bed, her arms stretched out on either side of her head and her legs slightly parted. She was wearing a very short baby-doll nightdress and there was a red swollen mark on her exposed left buttock. There were also red burn-like marks on her wrists.

The coroner examining the body of Ingrid Kasper, a 34-year-old farmer's wife from the tiny German village of Rotzel, guessed at once that she had been electrocuted, and his suspicion was confirmed by a post-mortem. Two electrical terminals had been wrapped around her wrists, and another applied to the buttocks. These terminals had then been attached to the house circuit which, in Germany, is 220 volts. Suicide or accidental death were out of the question, because in either case the electrical apparatus would still have been in the bedroom when she was found in the morning of 5 November 1972. Moreover, there were no signs at all that she had tried to defend herself from an attacker. Finishing off his post-mortem report, the coroner could only write: 'The coroner's office is unable to suggest an explanation for Mrs Kasper's failure to defend herself.'

The local police did have a suggestion, however. A search of the farmhouse where Ingrid lived with her husband Karl Kasper, had turned up a library of sex magazines and books, some of which contained instructions for sexual stimulation through the use of electricity. Ingrid Kasper, the police surmised, had been engaged in some dangerous sex game which had gone disastrously wrong. But who was her sex-game partner? As her husband worked long hours on the farm and also did night shifts at a paper mill – which is where he had been on the night his wife had died – it seemed logical that Ingrid had taken a lover. The investigation turned up a likely candidate in the shape of Luigi Antonini, a 32-year-old Italian immigrant labourer seen having intercourse with Ingrid Kasper in the courtyard of a tavern during Karl Kasper's birthday party. The witness to this alfresco sexual encounter was one Erika Jung. A check with the other birthday party-goers confirmed Jung's allegation. It also turned up an another interesting fact: Erika Jung was the mistress of Karl Kasper.

More detective work quickly found out other surprising things about Karl Kasper. Although he claimed poverty, he had recently made a gift of £500 to Erika Jung, and was a regular at the roulette tables in Baden-Baden. A handwriting analysis of the order forms for the sex aids found at the Kasper house revealed that the purchaser was Karl, not Ingrid Kasper.

By now, the police were convinced that Karl Kasper's alibi for the night of his wife's death was false – if difficult to break, since the paper mill's records showed him at work when it occurred – and concentrated on uncovering proof that the man not only had a motive for murdering his wife, but also the knowledge of electricity to carry it out.

Evidence for the latter came from the veterinary inspector of the local abattoir, who confirmed that Kasper killed his own pigs, not by using the standard axe or stock-bolt gun, but by an electrical device he had made himself. This consisted of a pair of large metal tongs connected to a source of electricity; the tongs were placed over the pig's head, the instrument switched on and the charge of electricity went through the pig's brain, killing it. A subsequent search of Kasper's car revealed that his DIY talents not only extended to an electrical pig-killer but a home-made electrical sex-stimulator, which experts from the police lab stated had killed Mrs Kasper.

The motive turned out to be one of the very oldest. Money. The late Mrs Kasper had been insured for £25,000 only six months before she died.

Confronted with the evidence against him, Karl Kasper confessed that he had stolen an hour off work on the night Ingrid Kasper died. He denied murder, however, and maintained that he and his wife had engaged in a sex game which had gone tragically awry when she came into contact with the wrong electrical terminal or, rather, too many terminals at the same time. Afterwards he had become frightened and tried to cover up his part in the crime. There was no way of verifying Kasper's claim, and the jury at his

October 1973 trial decided to give him the benefit of the doubt as to whether he committed the crime with malice aforethought. Karl Kasper was, however, found guilty of unpremeditated murder and sentenced to twelve years in jail.

EMBOLISM See AIR EMBOLISM

EXPLOSIVES

The bomb has long been a favourite weapon of political terror, ever since the black-caped anarchist of capitalist nightmare stalked European capitals at the end of the 19th century, fizzling explosive device in hand. The IRA, Italian fascists, and the Red Brigades have all made a virtue of explosives, whether to kill, damage property or simply cause disruption. Technical advances mean that bombs no longer need to be literally thrown at their target, but can be sited many days beforehand and set off by remote control or timing devices. Small explosive devices can be sent as letters, detonated by a simple spring when opened by the recipient.

Not all explosions are caused by those with political or military motives. A well-known explosives-murder was carried out by Eric Brown, a nineteen-year-old Essex bank clerk in 1943. Brown's father, Archibald, was a hateful man, who incessantly bullied his wife and two sons. Since a motorcycle accident some years before, Archibald Brown had become less mobile and was pushed around in a wheelchair by a nurse, Miss Mitchell. On 23 July, Archibald Brown was taken for his daily perambulation by Miss Mitchell, and when the pair were about a mile from home there was a large explosion. Luckily, Miss Mitchell was unhurt, but Archibald was blown to smithereens. The responsible device was quickly identified as an anti-tank explosive known as a Hawkins No. 75 Grenade Mine, which had been tied to the underside of the wheelchair by Eric Brown, who had simply grown tired of his father's tyranny.

Another unusual case of parent-killing also involved explosives, this being the matricide perpetrated by John Gilbert Graham, who placed a bomb aboard the American AIRCRAFT carrying his heavily insured mother in 1955 (see Case File). This was, in fact, the second case in which someone had blown up an aircraft to obtain insurance, the first being that of Albert Guay, a Canadian jeweller who hid a dynamite bomb in a religious statuette which exploded aboard a Dakota on 7 September 1949. Twenty-three people were killed, including Guay's wife, Rita. Guay's mistress, Marguerite Pitre, was traced as the woman-in-black who delivered the statuette to the airport. Guay, Pitre and her watchmaker brother, who had made the bomb's timing device, were hanged.

A solo bombing campaign was carried out by New York's George Metesky between 1940 and 1956, in which he placed dozens of home-made devices in public places. There were many injuries, but no deaths. The 'Mad Bomber', a sociopath, had a grudge against a firm which dismissed him in 1931, and decided to punish the world for his 'suffering'. Notably, he was caught with the help of a psychological profile – one of the first times this technique was used – drawn up by James Brussel.

In America, organized crime resorted to a crude car bomb to blow up investigative journalist Don Bolles in Phoenix in 1976. After hanging on to life for eleven days, and losing both legs and an arm, Bolles died on 13 June. His last words were: 'Mafia . . . Emprise . . . They finally got me . . . John Adamson, find him'. Hoodlum John Adamson was picked up shortly afterwards and duly convicted of planting the bomb which murdered Bolles.

Like Eric Brown and John Graham, Steven Wayne Benson used a bomb to remove an unwanted parent, his mother Margaret, in 1985. The case became a sensation in the USA because of its high society background, and its story of riches to disaster. The Benson family had made millions in the tobacco industry and the family lived in style. They owned houses in the USA and Canada, and ran ten cars, including a Cadillac and Jaguar. Margaret Benson alone was worth $10 million. Steven craved success in business, but all his schemes only consumed money, not made it. Unfailingly his mother bailed him out; until 1985, that is. Concerned that her fortune was being frittered away by her son, Margaret Benson called her lawyer and discussed excluding Steven from her will and making him pay back the $2 million she had loaned him.

Hearing that his mother intended to stop bank-rolling him, Steven invited Margaret, his sister Carol Lynn and nephew Scott, to accompany him to a property he was considering. As they waited in a Chevrolet Suburban on the drive of Margaret's Florida house on the morning of 9 July 1985, Steven returned inside, ostensibly to fetch a tape-measure. Instead, he activated a remote-control device which detonated two pipe bombs he had planted. Margaret and Scott were killed, Carol Lynn badly injured. On 7 August, Steven Benson was convicted of murder and received a life sentence. 'Money can be a bad thing – and that's what happened in the family's case,' remarked his grandfather. 'Money became bad.'

Explosives are combustible substances which when detonated or ignited create huge quantities of gas and heat energy. Trapped inside a container the gas and heat build up a tremendous pressure, forcing the casing outwards so that it shatters, fragments (shrapnel) flying off at high speed. Released from the bomb's casing, the gases expand massively and push air outwards from the centre of the explosion at up to 7000 m.p.h. – the so-called 'blast effect'. Anyone standing near or over a detonated bomb will literally be blown to bits by the blast. Others, further away, may suffer injuries from the air blast, or, more likely, from shrapnel and flying fragments of glass and building debris. In very large bombs, as, say, of the 400 lb magnitude routinely planted by the IRA in Northern Ireland, anyone in close proximity to its detonation will be disintegrated, with viscera scattered 100 yards or more.

Many substances can be used to make bombs, from petrol to household cleaners to agricultural products (especially fertilizers containing ammonium nitrate and sodium chlorate), and the technical knowledge needed to make a basic device can be gleaned from any school chemistry textbook. In general these kitchen-product bombs are unstable and as likely to blow up in the face of their maker as of their intended victim.

Explosives are classified as either high or low. Low explosives include gas, petrol and the powder used in gun cartridges. High explosives are such well-known – but strictly regulated – substances as TNT, Semtex and dynamite. High explosives, which detonate at rates of between 1000 and 8500 metres per second, need to be triggered by a primary explosion from a detonator or blast cap. These are usually activated by the electrical current from a battery.

CASE FILE: Flight 629

The farmer standing by the barn looked up at the silver aeroplane flying overhead in the darkening sky. It was 7.03 p.m. and the plane, Flight 629, was only eleven minutes out of Denver's Stapleton airport en route to Portland, Oregon. As the farmer watched the plane ascend, it suddenly exploded, showering his beet fields with burning wreckage. He ran for help, but help was useless. All forty-four passengers and crew aboard United Airlines Flight 629, 1 November 1955, were dead.

Within hours, crash investigators were trying to determine the cause of one of the worst air disasters in US history. Mechanical failure and human error seemed the most likely possibilities. Sabotage was considered almost unthinkable, but FBI investigators were detailed to look into the backgrounds of every passenger and crew member anyway. They were amazed to discover that $752,000 in flight insurance had been taken out by eighteen of the passengers, making Flight 629 one of the most heavily insured in aviation history. As these policies were examined, crash investigators collected jagged pieces of the plane until the ill-fated DC-6B's fuselage was completely reassembled. Except, that was, for a section near the tail No. 4 cargo hold, of which nothing remained. The metal near it was bent outwards. Passengers sitting above it had had pieces of metal driven through the soles of their shoes. There was only one possible conclusion: something in the No. 4 hold had exploded.

Then, after the minutest examination of the debris, tiny pieces of metal foreign to the aircraft were discovered with traces of sodium carbonate, and nitrate and sulphur compounds. That added up to dynamite. A bomb had been placed aboard Flight 629.

Among the passengers who boarded at Denver was Daisy King, a woman of considerable wealth. As well as being her principal inheritant, her son Jack Graham, it was discovered, had taken out $37,000 worth of flight insurance on his mother. A check of the remnants of passenger baggage showed that Daisy King's had virtually evaporated, suggesting that the explosion had taken place in or very near her luggage. The handbag she carried, however, was miraculously found intact; inside was a yellowed newspaper clipping detailing her son's arrest for forgery of stolen cheques some years before. Why Daisy King carried the clipping is unknown, but it may have been that she wanted the authorities to find it should she ever meet foul play. In the event, it led the FBI straight to the door of Jack Graham.

While the FBI were at the home of Graham his wife mentioned that he had put a 'Christmas package' in his mother's suitcase shortly before she left home. A search of the Grahams' house revealed a small roll of copper wiring, the type used for detonating dynamite. Under a six-hour interrogation at the local FBI headquarters Graham finally admitted that the 'Christmas present' was a dynamite bomb which he had hidden in his mother's case. In precise detail he told how he had made the bomb from twenty-five sticks of dynamite, amounting to some 14 lb, two electric primer caps, a six-volt battery (the pieces of foreign metal found by crash technicians were from this) and a timer. He bragged how he had worked in an electric shop for more than a week to learn how to make the timer.

Awaiting trial, Graham told psychiatrists and prison officers of his love-hate relationship with his mother, and that she had been 'raising hell' because the drive-in restaurant they co-owned was losing money. When she departed on the fateful flight, it was as if a load had been lifted from his shoulders. 'I felt freer than I have ever felt before in my life,' Graham said. He displayed little remorse, either for the killing of his mother or forty-three other people.

Graham tried to withdraw his confession at his trial, but the jury found no difficulty in declaring him guilty of first-degree murder. The bomber of Flight 629 was executed in the gas chamber at Colorado Penitentiary on 11 January 1957. Nothing in his life acquitted him so well as the leaving of it. As he stepped into the gas chamber, a newspaper man who had particularly irked Graham with his harsh reporting asked if he had any last words. 'Yes', quipped Graham, 'I'd like you to sit on my lap as they close the door in there.'

F

FIRE   *See* **BURNING**

FIREARMS

The history of murder is the history of humankind's search for a more technologically efficient means of killing. After the club came the knife, and after the knife the bow and arrow, each invention deadlier than its predecessor. The most profound revolution in killing, however, came in around AD 1000 with the discovery of gunpowder by the Chinese; within 200 years an Arab inventor had converted the entertaining firecracker into a hand-held device which propelled a bullet. The firearm.

In medieval Britain, the use of guns was largely confined to wealthy sportsmen. But around 1515, a less-expensive and improved version of the firearm reached the shores of the country. It was said to have originated in the Italian town of Pistoia, whence it derived its name. It was the wheel-lock pistol, and it would start a truly modern trend in crime – robbery and murder with a gun. Within a few years of the arrival of the wheel-lock pistol there was a major crime wave on the highways leading into London. 'Evil disposed persons,' wrote King Henry VIII, 'have done detestable murders with little short guns.'

Had good King Hal but known it, the problem of highwaymen would get worse. The various wars of the 17th century would arm the working classes, many of whom showed little inclination to give back their guns – or return to peasant life – when the conflict was over. They much preferred the trade of highwayman.

These early pistols were loaded by pouring gunpowder down a barrel, then a lead ball. A paper wad was then forced down the barrel with a ramrod to keep the charge in place. The pistol was 'primed' by gunpowder poured into the pan at the rear of the barrel, in the centre of which was a 'touch hole'. The powder was ignited either by string soaked in saltpetre, or a spark from flint or pyrites, the resultant flame setting off the main charge. Such guns could only fire one bullet, of course, and then required reloading.

This was a laborious and time-consuming process. In the mid-18th century, a maker of sporting guns realized that it would be simpler to hinge the gun between its stock and its barrel; when the gun was 'broken' – like the modern shotgun – the charge and bullet could be inserted in the exposed end of the barrel. Not only was this an easier process, it made possible the invention of the bullet: a projectile which carried its own gunpowder charge, whereby the metal 'bullet' was shot out of the gun by exploding gases leaving the cartridge case behind.

With the 'breech-loader' the bullet could also be made more of an exact fit, meaning that the exploding gases built up a greater pressure and that the bullet was projected with greater force.

The year 1794 marked the first recorded case of forensic ballistics, the science of firearms identification. A man called Edward Culshaw was found shot in the head at Prescot, Lancashire, and the surgeon who examined him found that the paper wad used to pack the bullet was inside the wound. Flattened out, the paper proved to be a strip torn from a ballad sheet. An acquaintance of Culshaw's, John Toms, was arrested on suspicion of his murder – and found to have the rest of the ballad sheet in his pocket, its frayed edge fitting perfectly that of the paper wad. The evidence was enough to send Toms to the gallows. Later, in 1860, a similar case was proved by matching wads made from the *The Times*, while in France, in 1891, the murder of Charles Guesner was solved by matching a wad torn from the *Lorraine Almanach*.

Meanwhile, gun technology fired resolutely onwards. In 1820, the percussion cap was invented. This contained fulminate of mercury, which exploded when struck with the 'hammer' of the gun, so setting off the main charge. Not long afterwards the young Samuel Colt fashioned a 'revolving chamber', patenting it in 1836. The mass-produced Colt revolver became 'The Gun That Won The West' (it also, in the hands of desperadoes like Billy the Kid, made the West very Wild indeed). The Colt revolver's advertising proclaimed it the weapon which 'Makes All Men Equal'; cheap, easy to use, light to handle, absolutely lethal, it could be used by the weak to kill the big, the poor to shoot the rich.

In 1857, another American gun manufacturer, Smith & Wesson, developed the brass integral cartridge. This was a self-enclosed round of ammunition consisting of a brass case designed to fit the chamber of a particular firearm. The case contained the propellant charge and in its base was a soft metal cap holding the primer charge. When struck by the gun's firing pin it set off the main charge, expelling the lead or metal-jacketed bullet from the gun. The case was left behind. Almost simultaneous with the development of the integral brass cartridge came the widespread introduction of rifling – the cutting of spiral groves into the interior of the gun barrel in order to spin the bullet to give it greater speed and accuracy. This was nothing new, but without breech-loading and a properly fitting bullet it was largely superfluous.

The effect of rifling on the bullet fired from a brass cartridge was crucial to the science of forensic ballistics. Manufacturers differed in the number and width of the grooves and lands (smooth surfaces between the grooves) they cut into their barrels, and whether the 'twist' was to the left or to the right: Colt guns, for instance, had six grooves, narrow lands and left-handed twist; Smith & Wesson firearms, by contrast, had five grooves, with grooves and lands of equal width, and right-handed twist. Because the cartridge fitted tightly into the barrel, the grooves and lands marked the cartridge as it left the gun.

Thus a knowledge of firearms manufacturers' specifications would enable someone to say from which type of gun a particular bullet was fired. The first to realize this was French pathologist Professor Alexandre Lacassagne, during the Echallier case of 1889. Removing a bullet from the victim, he noticed that it had seven longitudinal grooves on its surface – correctly deduced by the professor to be made by the rifling in the barrel of the murder weapon. Eventually a suspect was detained, and a search of his home revealed a gun with seven grooves. The suspect was convicted of murder.

If ballistics was a science, it was not yet an exact science. Undoubtedly, Lacassagne was working on the right lines, but there is a retrospective unease about the court's acceptance of his evidence; after all, all he proved was that the bullet came from *a* seven-grooved gun, not necessarily *the* gun in question. It was only in 1922 that American ballistics expert Charles E. Waite made the discovery which was vital to the perfection of ballistics as an exact science. While in Austria researching a compendium of firearms specifications, he examined the cutting tools which reamed out the grooves in the gun barrels, and found that each one left its individual marks. These imperfections on the interior surface of the gun are imprinted on to the brass casing of the bullet when it is fired. Other machined parts of the gun such as the firing-pin, extractor and breech blocks were also found to carry individual characteristics which became transferred to the cartridge case. As Waite's colleague at the pioneering, New York-based Bureau of Forensic Ballistics Calvin Goddard wrote in 1924, the individuality of a gun barrel leaves on every bullet fired 'the fingerprint of that particular barrel'.

It was, of course, entirely appropriate that the USA should take the lead in forensic ballistics; the country had the greatest problem in firearms crimes. Shooting is the quintessentially American way of homicidal death. After the lawlessness of the frontier came the firearms-backed lawlessness of Prohibition in the 1920s. Today in the USA, gun-ownership runs to 60 million handguns and 100 million shotguns and rifles. The gun is murder weapon No. 1, with 16,000 firearms homicides annually. Over 5 per cent of these deaths occur in Los Angeles, where gang warfare, with its trademark 'drive by' shootings, is rife.

The USA is also the home of 'mass' and 'spree' murder committed with guns. The easy availability of firearms – the Constitution still permits its citizens to bear arms – and a highly competitive, socially divided society produces a lethal result: inadequates, psychopaths and sociopaths who have free access to the 'equalizer'.

On 6 September 1949, ex-GI Howard Unruh strolled out of his house in New Jersey and began shooting his neighbours (see Case File), and ever since then 'crazy gunmen' have become a feature of crime. In January 1958, 28-year-old Charles Starkweather shot dead with a rifle the parents of his fourteen-year-old girlfriend, Caril Ann Fugate; he then choked her two-year-old sister to death by forcing the gun barrel down her throat, before he and Caril went on a murder spree in Nebraska and Wyoming, during which time Starkweather shot seven people. The couple's exploits were later dramatized in the film *Badlands*.

On 31 July 1966, Charles Whitman stabbed his wife and mother to death, climbed a tower at the University of Texas, killing the receptionist en route with a blow from the rifle butt, and then shot nineteen people. After Whitman – who was found to be suffering from a brain tumour – the crazy gunmen came thick and fast: in 1970, deranged hippy John Linley Frazier killed five people in the household of a Santa Cruz eye specialist; in the autumn of 1972, a paranoid schizophrenic called Herb Mullin went on a California murder spree which would last five months, killing thirteen, most of them with a pistol; in 1974, New Orleans' Mark Essex killed nine people; in 1975, James Ruppert killed eleven relatives in Hamilton, Ohio; in the same year, Nazi-sympathizer Frederich Cowan went on a shooting rampage, killing five Jews and blacks at his former New York place of employment; another pro-Nazi, James Herbert, killed twenty-one in a 'gundown' in San Diego; in 1989, 25-year-old racist Patrick Purdy walked into the schoolyard of the Cleveland Elementary School in Stockton, California, and opened fire with a Chinese AK-47 assault rifle on Asian children taking their lunch, killing five. More recently still, unemployed security guard James Swann cruised Washington for eight weeks in 1993 in a battered blue Toyota, shooting pedestrians at random with a pump-action shotgun. He killed four and wounded five. His neighbours had seen him target-shooting in a nearby wood and heard him shouting 'I'm going to get you,' but thought he meant the local squirrels.

The list of United States mass murders by gun goes on yearly. Britain has had only two cases, no doubt due to successive acts restricting gun ownership, beginning with the 1937 Firearms Act. On 19 August 1987, Michael Ryan, a member of a Berkshire gun club, went berserk, killing seventeen people and wounding fourteen others. Among the dead was his own mother, shot when she ran out of the house to plead with him to stop. Ryan, twenty-seven, was armed to the teeth with an AK-47, a pump-action shotgun and a Beretta pistol. Surrounded by police when he took refuge in the John O'Gaunt School, which he had once attended, Ryan shot himself in the head with the Beretta. A sinister 'copycat' shooting spree occurred in 1989, when 22-year-old Robert Sartin opened fire in the town of Monkseaton, Tyne and Wear, killing one and injuring fourteen. Sartin – a psychotic who acted on the instruction of voices – had an obsessive admiration for Ryan, and had made a pilgrimage to Hungerford before embarking on his own rampage.

Tight gun control laws mean that mass shootings are similarly rare in other countries, outside war situations. For example, Canada has only one recent 'gun crazy' case: in December 1989, Mark Lepine walked into a Montreal University classroom with a repeating rifle and massacred fourteen women. His motive was that he hated 'feminists'. And there are two Australian cases: in August 1987, 19-year-old Julian Knight opened fire on a highway in Melbourne, hitting 26 people, of whom 7 died; four years to the month later, Wade Frankum went berserk in a Sydney shopping mall, shooting down seven innocent people before turning the gun on himself.

Contemporary firearms are of two main types – namely, Smooth Bore and Rifled – and thus produce different sorts of wounds.

Smooth Bore Weapons
Apart from antique guns, these consist chiefly of the shotgun, or sporting gun, and have barrels with a smooth inside surface. Such guns fire a mass of lead pellets (shot) to a range of about 50 yards. The plastic or cardboard cartridge is retained inside the gun and removed by hand. The calibre of shotguns is expressed by 'bore', and is gauged by the number of spherical balls of lead, each exactly fitting the bore, which equal 1 lb in weight. Consequently, a twelve-bore shotgun is one in which the bore would need to contain twelve shots in order to make up 1 lb.

Although there are automatic and pump-action repeating shot-guns available, most are single- or double-barrelled, with one cartridge for each barrel. In double-barrelled shotguns the barrels are either arranged 'Side-by-Side' or 'Over-and-Under'.

At point-blank or very close range the shotgun is a devastating weapon, inflicting massive destruction. At ranges of over four feet, the shot begins to spread out, and will 'pepper' the target, causing small perforations without a central wound. A 'sawn-off' variant of the shotgun, whereby the barrel is cut down to about 12 in. and the stock shortened, is much favoured by bank-robbers, its convenience and discretion making up for its reduced accuracy.

A famous forensic case involving a shotgun happened at Whistling Copse, on the estate of Lord Temple near Bath, on the night of 10 October 1927. That night a 35-year-old labourer named Enoch Dix took his .410 single-barrelled shotgun to the copse to 'bag' roosting pheasants. The poacher's shots were heard by Temple's gamekeepers, William Walker and George Rawlings, who hurried to investigate. As the two men arrived Dix spun around and his gun went off; Walker fell dying with a wound in the throat, while Rawlings took a pot shot at the fleeing Dix.

At first Dix denied all knowledge of the crime, but as game-keeper Rawlings insisted that he had hit the poacher with a blast from his gun, Dix was examined for wounds. His back, neck and thighs were peppered with shot-holes. Dix then changed his story, and agreed that he had been in the copse, but that Rawlings had fired at him first.

Who had fired first, and at what range? To solve the question, firearms expert Robert Churchill was called in. Using Rawlings' gun and identical cartridges, he fired at a series of white-washed metal plates, varying the range. By studying these and the pattern of shot-holes on Dix's back, he concluded that Rawlings had hit the poacher at a range of 15 yards. If Dix's gun had discharged accidentally when he was hit, as he claimed, it must have felled Walker at the same range. At 15 yards range, shot from Dix's gun spread to between 27 in. and 30 in., whereas the wound in Walker's throat was 5 in. in diameter. To cause such a wound, Dix must have fired at a range of less than 5 yards, point-blank range. Dix was found guilty of manslaughter, and sentenced to fifteen years' penal servitude.

Airguns, which rely on compressed air for their propellant, can be rifled or smooth-bored. Although not usually as powerful as conventional firearms, they can cause lethal injuries, particu-larly if the head or chest is penetrated by the slug. A type of airgun known as an 'air-cane' was probably implicated in the mysterious shooting of Lancashire small-holder John Dawson in 1934, the projectile being a home-made steel bullet. The bullet entered Dawson's back; the victim refused medication and succumbed to gangrene and blood-poisoning. Investigating the crime the police found a local conspiracy of silence; Detective Chief Superintendent Wilf Blacker remarked afterwards, 'It was like talking to a brick wall.' No one was ever arrested for the shooting of John Dawson.

An airgun also featured in one of the most exotic intended assassinations in British history. A Mrs Wheeldon from Derby and her chemist son-in-law were convicted in 1917 of plotting the killing of Lloyd George, the then Prime Minister. The murder weapon was a powerful air-rifle which was to fire a dart coated in CURARE, a poison used by South American tribes in hunting. Scientific evidence at their trial showed that they could have succeeded. Fortunately for Lloyd George, the man Mrs Wheel-don selected from her small group of conspirators to pull the trigger was an agent for MI5 – who turned her in.

Rifled Weapons
So named because of the spiral 'rifling' inside the barrel, the calibre of these arms in Britain and the United is denoted as a decimal of

one inch, e.g. .22, .303, etc. On the Continent, calibre is measured in millimetres.

Rifled weapons may be long-barrelled rifles (2 feet or more), machine and sub-machine guns, or short-barrelled handguns.

Handguns These are hand-held guns, with low muzzle-velocity (600 to 1000ft per second), intended for use at close range. Handguns are of two principal types: revolvers and pistols.

Revolvers derive their name from their cylindrical magazine containing five or six chambers. The cylinder revolves when the hammer is cocked, bringing each chamber successively into firing position. Revolvers tend to be robust weapons, their few moving parts making them easy to maintain and unlikely to jam. The revolver cartridge case is held in place by a rimmed base. Most police forces in America today are armed with the Smith & Wesson .38 revolver. The gun they most often face is the ubiquitous Colt Frontier (also known as the Colt .45), which was produced continually from 1873 to 1941 and then, after a break, from 1955 to the present. Notable revolver killers include New York's 'Son of Sam', psychopath David Berkowitz, who hunted his human victims between 1976–77 with a .44 Bulldog. Most of his six kills were the female halves of courting couples, shot as they sat in 'made out' cars. After capture, Berkowitz was sentenced to serve 365 years at the Attica Correctional Facility.

Pistols, like revolvers, are short-range handguns. The difference is that pistols have a sealed-in chamber which is an integral part of the barrel. Also, although single-shot pistols can be found, most pistols are what is erroneously and popularly termed 'automatic'. A true automatic weapon is one which will go on firing for as long as the finger is pulling the trigger; pistols require the trigger to be pulled for each shot. They are more accurately described as 'self-loading' or 'semi-automatic'. Pistols generally have a hollow handle into which is fitted a metal magazine containing rounds of ammunition; a spring propels the rounds from the magazine in to the breech, and after firing the spent cartridge is ejected mechanically. Self-loading pistols in common use include the Luger 9mm Automatic, the Walther Automatic and the Mauser 9mm Automatic.

Rifles These are long-barrelled weapons fired from the shoulder. The long barrel of the rifle makes it accurate for ranges of up to 3000 yards and the weapon has a muzzle velocity of 1000 to 4000 feet per second. Fitted with telescopic or infra-red sights, the rifle is the favourite weapon of the assassin and 'hitman', anxious to kill and get away from the scene of crime quickly. John F. Kennedy and Martin Luther King were both assassinated by bullets from a rifle. The Chinese AK-47 military assault rifle, meanwhile, has figured in a worrying number of mass and spree murders, including Michael Ryan's 'Hungerford Massacre'. The fire rate of the AK-47 is 600 rounds per minute. The American Armalite rifle is standard issue with the Provisional IRA, being light and cheap, as well as extremely accurate. It has a muzzle velocity of 3500–4000 feet per second. Some forms of military rifle are truly automatic, firing until either the magazine is empty or pressure on the trigger is released.

It was a .22 semi-automatic Anschutz rifle fitted with a silencer which Jeremy Bamber, twenty-six, used to kill his adoptive father, mother, sister and two nephews at White House Farm, Essex, on 7 August 1985. A notable aspect of the case was the way in which Bamber almost succeeded in disguising the horrific mass killing as the work of his adoptive sister, Sheila 'Bambi' Caffell, who had then supposedly committed suicide. When police entered White House Farm they found 26-year-old Bambi Caffell with a gunshot wound in the throat and another in her jaw. But could she have killed herself with the rifle? Believing Jeremy Bamber's view that his sister was 'a nutter', the Essex police failed to investigate properly. Had they done so, they would have found the silencer the killer used – as two of Caffell's cousins, doubting her guilt, did on searching the farmhouse. With the six-inch silencer attached the rifle was so long that Bambi could not have reached the trigger while the muzzle was pressed under her chin. Nor was it likely that a suicide could have fired a shot into the jugular vein and then another into the brain. The rifle had been reloaded twice, yet Bambi Caffell's nightgown showed no trace of oil residue. Despite all these glaring inconsistencies, the case on the White House Farm murder was closed. Then, five weeks after the massacre the police were obliged to re-open it. Jeremy Bamber made an expensive mistake and finished with his girlfriend, Julie Mugford. Spurned, she went and told the police that Bamber had confessed the crime to her. And so he was eventually arrested. His motive seems to have been resentment that he was not getting his inheritance while he was young enough to enjoy it.

Machine and sub-machine guns Sometimes called 'machine pistols', and usually figuring in crime in their lighter form, as a two-handed firearm of limited range but with a rapid fire rate. (Heavy machine guns need to be fixed to a mounting.) These weapons are capable of being used as semi-automatics or true automatics. With the passing of the Capone era, when American gangsters toted 'Chicago Pianos' – Thompson sub-machine guns – as a matter of course, machine and sub-machine guns have become less common in crime. Although not, of course, entirely extinct. Controversial talk-show host, Alan Berg of Denver's KAO radio station, was gunned down by a .45 MAC10 machine pistol on 18 June 1984. A neo-Nazi group called 'Silent Brotherhood' was responsible. They, apparently, did not like his liberal views.

It is often said that the bullet is the weapon, and the gun is merely the means of getting it there. As already mentioned, bullets have been subjected to their own development process. Modern bullets are designed in a variety of materials, weights and shapes according to their intended use – hunting, military or target. Revolver bullets are usually composed of lead, toughened with tin and ANTIMONY. Most other firearms use metal-jacketed bullets, which have either a lead or steel core with a skin of cupro-nickel (copper and nickel) or some other hard material. Bullets are either cemented into the top of the cartridge case or circumferentially grooved with a 'Cannelure', into which the cartridge case is crimped during assembly. Until the 20th century, the propellant charge in the cartridge was gunpowder or 'Black Powder'. Modern propellants are smokeless, based on compounds of either nitroglycerine or nitrocellulose.

The hitting power of Magnum ammunition has become legendary. It has an additional charge in the cartridge, with a resulting increase in muzzle velocity, approaching that of a rifle. Perhaps the most powerful contemporary handgun is the .44 Magnum Smith & Wesson Model 29, which was produced specifically to chamber the Remington .44 Magnum cartridge. At nearly 3 lb it makes a heavy handgun – with recoil one expert has likened to 'touching off a howitzer single-handed'.

The wounds on the body of the victim will tell much about the nature of the shooting – how close the guilty gun was, and from what direction the shots were fired. The typical appearance of an entry wound is a small circular or oval hole surrounded by an inflamed ring of abraded skin. The blood loss from such wounds is slight. Where a bullet penetrates with sufficient force a larger exit wound is caused. The relationship between entry and exit wounds will generally determine the direction of shooting.

If the muzzle of the gun is placed directly against the surface of the body, the consequent 'contact wound' will be burned by the combustion gases and blackened with soot. Firearms discharged at close range, between 2 and 8 in., cause distinctive powder 'tattooing', consisting of tiny orange burn lesions. Where the firearm is discharged from a longer range, the only marks on the victim's body will be those caused by the entry of the bullet.

As a footnote to bullet wounds, it might be noted that 'tail-wagging' bullets do not create a neat entry wound. Bullets fired from rifled weapons spin at over 2000 revolutions per second, but at the beginning and end of their flight are unstable. The phenomenon might be likened to the wobble of a child's top before it settles into steady motion. A 'tail-wagging' bullet strikes obliquely, creating a ragged entry wound much bigger than the bullet itself. This principle informs the specially designed 'tumbling' bullet, which turns end over end in flight, hitting its target with the impact of a small explosion.

CASE FILE: The First of the Crazy Gunmen

'I'm no psycho. I have a good mind,' Howard Unruh informed the police officers who arrested him on the beautiful late summer morning of 6 September 1949. Unruh had just shot dead thirteen people in twelve minutes on the streets of the small town of Camden, New Jersey. Medical experts disagreed with the 28-year-old gunman as to his mental condition, and found him incurably insane. Not that anyone had noticed beforehand; to those that knew him, Howard Unruh had always seemed a quiet and well-mannered young man.

Unruh had an ordinary childhood in Camden, where his parents were middle-class working people. In High School he decided to become a pharmacist but his career plans, like those of other male teenagers, was interrupted when America entered World War II. As part of a tank command, Unruh fought in Italy and the Battle of the Bulge. Although not unfriendly with his fellow GIs, he kept his own company, spending long hours by himself reading the Bible. The army also introduced Unruh to firearms; somewhat ominously for the future, he became ranked as a sharpshooter.

After the war, Unruh returned home and enrolled at Temple University in Philadelphia to study pharmacy. He found the adjustment to civilian life more difficult than he had anticipated, and complained to his mother that he could not concentrate. He became increasingly withdrawn and stopped attending church. Unruh had become, underneath his benign exterior, a paranoid schizophrenic, viewing the world around him as an alien place, inhabited by enemies. In particular he began to imagine that the neighbours – he was living with his parents – insulted him, and he kept a notebook detailing his grievances. They were petty things like a door slammed late at night, a too-noisy child's bugle, but to Unruh they acquired a deadly significance. Against offenders he wrote the abbreviation 'retal' (retaliation) in his notebook. His mental stability was further undermined by guilt about his discovery that he was homosexual.

For two years Unruh planned his 'retal'. His weapon collection grew from a few pieces brought home from the war as souvenirs into a small armoury. He paid $40 for a 9mm German Luger, which seemed to be his favourite. Relaxation consisted of hours spent practising his markmanship in the basement.

The straw which broke the proverbial camel's back for Unruh

was the stealing of his gate. The Unruhs' back yard was bounded by a high fence, into which Howard had decided to set a gate. He finished in the afternoon of 5 September. When he came back later that day, the gate had been stolen. Although pranksters were responsible, Unruh blamed his neighbours. It was time for 'retal'.

Early the following morning, Unruh loaded his Luger and another pistol, shoved extra clips into his coat pocket, picked up a tear-gas canister and walked out of the back of the house, along an alley, taking him to River Road. One of the deadliest walks in history was about to begin. The time was 9.20 a.m.

First to receive 'retal' was cobbler John Pilcharik, shot twice as he looked up at Unruh entering his shop. He died instantly.

Calmly, Unruh walked out of the shoe-repair shop, and into Clark Hoover's barber shop next-door. Hoover was in the process of giving six-year-old Orris Smith a haircut. The boy was in the way. Unruh shot him in the head, then levelled the gun at Hoover, shooting him in the torso. For good measure he also shot the prostrate barber in the head.

From the barber shop it was only a short stroll to the drugstore. As Unruh was about to go in James Hutton, the Unruhs' insurance agent, came out. Astonished at the sight of Unruh with a gun, he could not move when Unruh said, 'Excuse me'. Unruh shot Hutton twice at contact range. The insurance agent dropped dead to the pavement.

Having removed Hutton from his path, Unruh entered the drugstore to search for those he most wanted to administer 'retal' to: his neighbours the Cohens. Mrs Cohen had once addressed Unruh as 'Hey you'. Seeing the murder of Hutton, Mr Cohen had run upstairs to alert his family. Finding nobody in the store, Unruh too went upstairs. Mrs Cohen was shot by Unruh's Luger as she hid in a bedroom closet; again, a make-double-sure shot was delivered to the head. Mr Cohen's aged mother was shot as she telephoned for help. Cohen himself was picked off as he tried to escape along a sloping roof of the drugstore. The druggist's body fell to the pavement. Taking deliberate aim, Unruh shot down from the upstairs window: the bullet entered Cohen's skull. Of all the Cohen family, only the young son escaped alive.

Not that Unruh had finished killing. Descending to the pavement he shot Alvin Day, a motorist who had stopped to see what was wrong with Hutton. With the smoothness that comes of practice, Hutton then reloaded the Luger and walked across the street to where a car was waiting at the lights. With grim efficiency he shot the woman behind the wheel through the open car window; also her ten-year-old son and her mother.

Unhurriedly, Unruh walked back towards the shoe-repair shop where the shooting had begun. A truck driver was getting out of his cab further down River Road; Unruh took a pot shot at him, hitting him in the leg.

Next-door to the cobbler's was a tailor's shop. The tailor's wife, Mrs Fegrino, was shot as she tried to hide from the gunman. As Unruh fired his customary second shot at Mrs Fegrino, he must have seen a slight movement at a nearby window. It was a difficult shot, but Unruh proved his markmanship. Three-year-old Tommy Hamilton fell down dead.

Unruh left River Road by a side alley, and entered a house on 32 Street. As he sighted the owner, Mrs Harrie, her sixteen-year-old son rushed him; surprised and knocked off balance, Unruh could only wound Mrs Harrie and her son. He was unable to finish the job; he had run out of bullets.

And so Unruh walked back to his home. As he climbed the steps, the first police car arrived outside. The time was 9.32 a.m.

Soon the house was surrounded by armed police. There was an exchange of small-arms fire, but Unruh gave himself up when tear-gas was heaved through the windows.

Howard Unruh was never brought to trial, and was committed instead to an institution for the insane, the New Jersey State mental hospital. He told one psychiatrist there: 'I'd have killed a thousand if I'd had the ammunition.'

CASE FILE: Suicide or Matricide?

In 1927 eighteen-year-old John Donald Merrett stood trial in Edinburgh charged with the murder of his mother by shooting. He maintained that she had taken her own life. The jury returned the peculiarly Scottish verdict of 'Not Proven'. Was 'Donnie', as he was known by all, innocent? Or was he so lucky to get away with murder that he thought he could do it again?

Born in 1908 at Levin in New Zealand, Merrett moved with his mother to England in 1924, where he was educated at Malvern College. Although academically bright, Merrett's main interests were extra-curricular: an unpleasant episode involving a local girl necessitated Mrs Bertha Merrett removing her son and herself to Edinburgh, where Donnie attended university under her surveillance. This, however, was none too strict, and Merrett spent his days in more amusing places than the lecture hall. At night his mother locked him in his bedroom at their Palmerston Place flat, from which he escaped via a rope into the street to spend the late hours at the Dunedin Palais de Danse. Here he studied the fox-trot in the company of the hostesses, on whom he lavished jade and opal rings. He also purchased a motor cycle for £28 and a semi-automatic pistol for £1 17s 6d ('for shooting rabbits'). This free-spending was supported by forging the signature of Bertha

Merrett on sundry cheques, totalling £427, drawn against his mother's bank accounts.

On 17 March 1926 Mrs Merrett's bank sent her a notice informing her that her account was overdrawn. At 9.40 that morning the Merretts' daily maid, Mrs Henrietta Sutherland, who was in the kitchen clearing away the breakfast things, heard a shot, followed by a scream and the sound of a thud. A few seconds later Donald Merrett came into the kitchen and told her, 'Rita, my mother has shot herself.' He added that he had been wasting his mother's money and that they had been quarrelling about it. Together, Henrietta and Donald went to the sitting room where Mrs Merrett was lying insensible on the floor by the desk, bleeding from a bullet wound by the right ear. On top of the desk lay a pistol.

The police were summoned, and Mrs Merrett was taken to the Edinburgh Royal Infirmary. From the first the case was accepted as one of suicide, and this was seemingly supported by a changed story from Henrietta Sutherland, who now informed the police that she 'saw Mrs Merrett fall off the chair, and a revolver or pistol fall out of her hand'. Meanwhile, Mrs Merrett regained consciousness sufficiently to tell a hospital doctor that: 'I was sitting down writing letters, and my son, Donald, was standing beside me. I said, "Go away, Donald, and don't annoy me," and the next I heard was a kind of explosion, and I do not remember anything more.' On 1 April Mrs Merrett died.

His mother's death did nothing to halt Donnie's pursuit of hedonism, and he continued to draw heavily on her accounts. Soon, though, Donald's forgeries came to light, which caused Detective Inspector Fleming of Edinburgh CID to see Mrs Merrett's demise as suspicious and eventually to see the charge of murder preferred against Donald Merrett. On 1 February 1927 Merrett was arraigned before the Lord Justice Clerk, Lord Alness, within the High Court of Justiciary at Edinburgh.

It was essentially a case about ballistics, with everything turning on the question of whether or not Mrs Merrett could have shot herself as Donald claimed. Dr Richard Bell, who had examined Mrs Merrett at the Edinburgh Royal Infirmary, stated that he found no trace of blackening or tattooing round the wound, nor any sign or smell of singeing – as is usually seen in cases of near discharge, that is, in most suicides. The evidence of Professor Harvey Littlejohn, Professor of Forensic Medicine at Edinburgh University, who had examined the wound after death, was of vital importance because it supplied the facts upon which were based the theories of both prosecution and defence. He stated that the bullet had entered Bertha Merrett's head through the right ear, at an angle of approximately 120 degrees to a line drawn longitudinally through the middle of the skull.

He gave as his opinion that 'the direction of the bullet wound, the position of the wound, the distance at which the discharge took place, all point to the weapon being discharged by another party'.

For Mrs Merrett to have produced the wound, said Professor Littlejohn, her arm would have had to be drawn back, bent at the elbow and held in a strained position. It was an unlikely way to commit suicide, or to have a firearms accident. Professor John Glaister, Professor of Forensic Medicine at the University of Glasgow, also appearing for the prosecution, was definite that 'the head injury which caused the death of Mrs Merrett was not self-inflicted'.

With this weight of expert opinion against him, Donald Merrett was fortunate to have retained the offices of the eminent pathologist Sir Bernard Spilsbury who, making one of his rare appearances for the defence, said that he saw nothing in the position of the wound, the track of the bullet, or the distance at which it had been fired which was inconsistent with suicide or with an accident. He demonstrated in the witness box how he imagined an accident might have happened, suggesting that Mrs Merrett, with a pistol in her hand, might have tilted her chair, lost her balance, and jerked her elbow on the ledge of the bureau behind her. The name of Spilsbury – who had given evidence at the trials of Crippen, Seddon and George Smith – was crushing in its authority. The jury gave an indeterminate verdict of 'Not Proven' by a majority of ten to five. Donald did not go free entirely because the jury found no difficulty in convicting him of 'uttering' forged cheques. He received a year's imprisonment.

Within a few weeks of his release he eloped with a seventeen-year-old ward in Chancery named Vera Bonner. He changed his name to Ronald Chesney, and began a career of blackmail and fraud. He served with the Royal Navy Volunteer Reserve during the Second World War, before becoming a black-marketeer in occupied Germany.

In 1954 Merrett decided to rob his wife Vera, who with her mother (Lady Menzies) ran an old people's home in Ealing, London. In February of that year he made his wife drunk on gin and drowned her in the bath, using the technique made famous by George Smith (see DROWNING). Lady Menzies saw him, so he had to kill her too. Her battered and strangled body was found in the house, and what had been planned as an 'accident' became a double murder. Merrett fled the country and an international alert was put out for him. On 16 February his body was found in a wood near Cologne in Germany. He had committed suicide by shooting himself in the head.

This was an entirely appropriate ending, for he had certainly faked the suicide of his mother twenty-eight years before. He got away with it because there is often a greater element of doubt in gun-shooting cases. That and the fact that he happened to have Sir Bernard Spilsbury on his side.

SOME NOTABLE CASES OF MURDER BY FIREARMS

Name	Dates	Victim(s)
Jeremy Bamber (UK)	1985	5 (adoptive family)
John Bellingham (UK)	1812	1 (Prime Minister Spencer Perceval)
Derek Bentley and Christopher Craig (UK)	1952	1 (PC Sidney Miles)
David Berkowitz (USA)	1976/77	6
Werner Boost (Ger)	1950s	5
Frederick Browne and William Kennedy (UK)	1927	1 (PC George Gutteridge)
Pauline Dubuisson (Fra)	1951	1 (lover, in 'crime passionel')
Ruth Ellis (UK)	1955	1 (lover)
Marguerite Fahmy (Fra)	1923	1 (husband, Prince Fahmy)
Samuel Furnace (UK)	1933	1 (a 'pseudocide')
Gary Gilmore (USA)	1976	2 (robbery victims)
John George Haigh (UK)	1949	1
James Hanratty (UK)	1961	1 (the 'A6 Murder')
Anthony Harris et al (USA)	1973/74	15 (strangers; the 'Zebra Killings')
Karl Hulten and Elizabeth Jones (UK)	1944	1 (the 'Cleft-Chin Murder')
Charles Jenkins and Christopher Geraghty (UK)	1947	1 (Alec de Antiquis)
George Kelly (UK)	1949	2 (the 'Cameo Cinema Shooting', Liverpool)
Reginald and Ronald Kray (UK)	1966	1 (George Cornell)
David Lane and Bruce Pierce (USA)	1984	1 (Alan Berg)
Lock Ah Tam (UK)	1925	3 (relatives)
Peter Manuel (UK)	1950s	7+ (robbery victims)
John Merrett (UK)	1924	1 (mother; not proven)
Donald Neilson (UK)	1971/75	3 (robbery victims)
Lee Harvey Oswald? (USA)	1963	1 (President J.F. Kennedy)
Bonnie Parker and Clyde Barrow (USA)	1930s	13+

James Earl Ray? (USA)	1968	1 (Martin Luther King)
Michael Ryan (UK)	1987	17 (strangers; the 'Hungerford Massacre')
Nicola Sacco and Bartolemo Vanzetti? (USA)	1920	2
Saint Valentine's Day Massacre (USA)	1929	5 (Chicago; unsolved)
Paul Snider (USA)	1973	1 (wife and pin-up, Dorothy Stratten)
Charles Starkweather (USA)	1957	9
Richard 'Dick' Turpin (UK)	1735	1
Howard Unruh (USA)	1949	13 (strangers)
'Zodiac Murderer' (USA)	1969	5 (unsolved)

FUNGI

In Ancient Greece and Rome, mushroom poisoning was as common a means of homicide as the gun is in the modern USA. The Greek dramatist Euripedes noted a case of murder by mushroom as early as 450BC. Emperor Claudius of Rome is widely believed to have been killed in AD54 by a mushroom poison applied inside his mouth with a feather on the order of his wife, Agrippina, so that her son Nero could succeed the throne.

Since then deliberate mushroom poisoning has gone out of fashion, although several hundred fatalities are reported each year in Europe from accidental or suicidal mushroom ingestion. There are only about a dozen poisonous species of fungi in Britain (out of a total of about 6000). Most fatalities are due to ingestion of the genus *Amanita*.

These include the *Amanita verna* (Destroying Angel), *Amanita muscaria* (Fly Agaric), *Amanita pantherina* (Panther Cap), and *Amanita phalloides* (Death Cap). The Death Cap is the most deadly mushroom in the world, and was almost certainly the one employed in the murder of Claudius. The ingestion of one mushroom causes very serious illness and three (about 40 g) almost certain death.

Like many other mushrooms, the Death Cap, common in deciduous woods in autumn, contains several toxic compounds. One is called phalloidin, which is four times as toxic as CYANIDE. It is a slow-acting poison which causes vomiting, diarrhoea and severe abdominal pain about eight hours after the mushroom is eaten. If the victim survives phalloidin, there is a period of well-being lasting two to three days. Then, cruelly, just as the Death Cap victim believes he or she may be about to recover, another toxin, alpha-amanitine, kicks in. Alpha-amanitine is 100 times as strong as cyanide. A two-millionth of a gram has been sufficient to kill a laboratory mouse. Alpha-amanitine and other less potent poisons cause renal and hepatic failure. There may be a period of hallucination before the brain finally dies. It is a death beyond adequate description.

Fly Agaric is well-known for its bright-red cap spotted with white, frequently depicted in children's books as a home for little people. Its name refers to its former use as a fly-poison, the responsible toxin being idotenic acid. Amongst the other toxins yielded by Fly Agaric is muscarine, an hallucinogen used in small proportions by people the world over in religious and magical rituals. Fly Agaric is particularly prized by the Koryaks of Siberia. An early Western traveller to Siberia, Von Strahlenberg, noted in his journals of the Koryaks that:

> those who are rich amongst them lay up large provisions of these mushrooms for the winter. When they make a feast they pour water upon some of these mushrooms and boil them. They then drink the liquor, which intoxicates them; the poorer sort, who cannot afford to lay in a store of these mushrooms, post themselves on these occasions round the huts of the rich and watch the opportunity of guests coming down to make water; and then hold a wooden bowl to receive the urine, which they drink greedily as having still some virtue of the mushroom in it and by this way they also get drunk.

The intoxicating effect of urine appeared to be retained even after 'passage' through as many as five persons. Other travellers estimated that a moderate hallucinogenic dose of Fly Agaric was three to four mushrooms.

Certainly, a dose of 120 mg or over of muscarine will kill. It is a fast-acting poison, which produces symptoms of sweating, irregular breathing and heart action almost as soon as ingested.

Outside the *Amanita* genus, the parasitic fungus Ergot, which grows on cereal crops, contains a poison, ergotamine, which is closely related to LSD. Its other attributes include a capacity to cause gangrenous ergotism, a swelling of the limbs necessitating amputation. In less serious cases, ergot poisoning produces a pins-and-needles tingling known as 'St Anthony's fire'.

Other poisonous fungi to be found in Britain include *Paxillus involutus*, *Agaricus xanthoderma* (Yellow-Staining Mushroom), and *Helleva crispa*. A Far Eastern fungus, *Mucor phyconyes*, has the interesting property of CHOKING the victim to death by growing in the throat.

G

GASSING *See* **CARBON MONOXIDE**

GLASS

The allegedly deadly properties of swallowed ground or powdered glass owe more to the fetid imagination of detective story writers than fact. After some searching of dusty volumes, not one documented case of death by powdered glass could be found. Certainly, some murderers have included it in their armoury, adding it to the victim's food or drink, but to little ill effect. Wicked stepmother Pearl O'Laughlin administered it to ten-year-old Leona O'Laughlin in 1930; it failed to kill her, so the misnamed Pearl bludgeoned the child and then drowned her in a Colorado lake. Pearl O'Laughlin also gave ground glass, mixed in with the household sugar, to her husband, Leo, and father-in-law, Dennis. They survived, although the ground glass did cause Leo O'Laughlin some discomfort. Their deaths would have made Pearl very rich indeed.

Edith Thompson, in a letter to her lover Frederick Bywaters, wrote of an attempt on her husband's life: 'I'm going to try the glass again occasionally – when it is safe. I've got an electric light globe this time.' Some weeks later, she reported to Frederick: 'I used the light bulb three times but the third time he found a piece – so I've given up . . .'

To be of any real murderousness glass would need to be in shards big enough to cut the lining of the stomach and intestines. But as Mrs Thompson found, such pieces are difficult to administer surreptitiously.

For glass as a tool of external wounding, see SHARP INSTRUMENTS.

GUNS *See* **FIREARMS**

H

HANGING

The killing of Monsieur Gouffe was by no means a classic; it was a shabby little murder committed in a Paris backstreet by a 22-year-old prostitute, Gabrielle Bompard, and her middle-aged lover, Michael Eyraud. Its great distinction was the unusual, almost unique, way it was done.

In the spring of 1889 Bompard picked up a customer called Gouffe, a bailiff, who bragged about the amount of money he kept in his office. Unwittingly, Gouffe not only set himself up to be robbed, but signed his own death warrant. For several weeks afterwards Gabrielle Bompard courted Gouffe, fussed over him, and cooed in his ear that she was unhappy with Eyraud. When Gouffe was won over, she invited him back to a studio apartment she – and Eyraud – had rented especially.

The one-roomed apartment had been chosen after much searching. Behind the bed there was an alcove, which was completely hidden by a curtain. Inside the alcove Eyraud rigged up a rope and pulley system, with a hook hanging down the side of the curtain where it could not be seen.

When Gabrielle Bompard and Gouffe arrived at the apartment, Eyraud was already there, hiding in the alcove. Bompard plied Gouffe with champagne, led him to the bed and took off her dress belt, letting Gouffe get a good look at her naked body underneath. Apparently in playful mood, Bompard then dropped the belt around Gouffe's neck, knotting it. And then the end came for Monsieur Gouffe. As he lunged for Bompard, Eyraud reached from behind the curtain, attached the hook to the belt around Gouffe's neck – and then hauled on the other end of the rope. Monsieur Gouffe was jerked into the air and hanged.

Hanging is sometimes accidental, usually suicidal and almost never homicidal, which makes Bompard and Eyraud among the true eccentrics of crime. They failed, unfortunately for them, to bring the same flair to the rest of the killing and robbery of Gouffe, however; Eyraud could not open Gouffe's office safe, and they disposed of the cadaver in a TRUNK, which was soon found. At their subsequent trial, Michael Eyraud was sent to the guillotine, and Gabrielle Bompard was sentenced to twenty years' imprisonment. 'Why not the woman too?' Eyraud cried when he heard the sentence.

Hanging is one of the deaths by ASPHYXIA, due to the compression of the neck by a ligature, the constricting force being the suspended weight of the human body itself. In what might be termed the 'typical' hanging, where the victim's feet are clear of the ground, the body weight causes the ligature around the neck to tighten, closing the carotid artery and the windpipe. Stoppage of the blood supply to the brain causes unconsciousness; death results within several minutes. If the victim has fallen a long way, for instance down a stairwell at the end of a rope, the sudden jerk when his fall is arrested may fracture the upper cervical spine or dislocate the head upon the top of the spine.

The body does not need to be totally suspended for a hanging. It can be achieved, if more slowly, when the bulk of the victim's weight is supported by the ground. Many suicides are found suspended from door handles and bedsteads, slumped or crouched down with buckled knees and feet on the ground.

As a form of judicial execution, hanging is believed to have originated in the Middle East, entering Britain with the Anglo-Saxons. Until the 18th century, judicial hanging was a slow, barbaric affair, often taking hours, carried out as a public entertainment. Not unusually, the hanging felon was subjected to some additional torture such as disembowelling. The first humane improvement was the invention in 1760 of a gallows designed to fracture the neck (specifically to dislocate the cervical vertebrae, severing the spinal cord close to the base of the brain) and procure a quick death. This was effected by the victim dropping through a trap-door, opened by the executioner's lever.

Over a century later, in 1868, following a campaign led by the writer Charles Dickens, public execution was abolished, and in the private confines of the prison the search for a more humane type of hanging was speeded up. It was discovered that a metal ring woven into one end of the hangman's rope, with the other passed through it to form a noose, resulted in a faster death in the 'drop'.

When Yorkshire executioner James Berry, who held office between 1884 and 1892, devised a scale which related the prisoner's weight to the length of drop, hanging became almost a science. Giving evidence before a Royal Commission on capital punishment in 1949, the Official Executioner Albert Pierrepoint felt able to say that of all methods of judicial execution, hanging 'is the fastest and quickest in the world bar nothing. It is quicker than shooting and cleaner.' (It might be pointed out that Pierrepoint eventually became an opponent of capital punishment, remarking in his autobiography, *Executioner* (1974), that 'I have come to the conclusion that executions solve nothing, and are only an antiquated relic of a primitive desire for revenge which takes the easy way and hands over the responsibility for revenge to other people.' Parliament agreed with him, and execution was abolished in Britain in 1964.)

Lynching is a form of extra-legal vigilante execution usually, although not exclusively, effected by the 'hang 'em high' method of a rope thrown over a tree branch to form an impromptu gallows.

Named after an American Quaker, Charles Lynch, lynching flourished in the Wild West in the years before organized law enforcement, but it took firmest hold in the ten Southernmost states of the USA. Many of the victims were blacks, especially black males alleged to have raped white girls, but other victims of the white lynch mob included Jews, Catholics and trade union organizers. A lynching was reported in the USA as late as 1954.

A significant number of accidental hangings are the result of a masochistic sexual practice known as auto-erotic asphyxia, which is described by the Kinsey Institute's *New Report on Sex* as 'the deliberate reduction of oxygen to the brain . . . The belief is that it enhances orgasm, but no research has ever verified this.' The means by which the asphyxia is induced varies from self-STRANGULATION to self-SUFFOCATION (as seen with the auto-erotic death of the Conservative MP Steven Milligan in February 1994), but self-hanging is the most common. Even those practitioners who have constructed elaborate self-rescue devices, such as a chair beneath the noose, die because the restriction of the oxygen supply causes them to lose consciousness before they can release the pressure on their necks. Also, pressure on the vagus nerve in the neck can slow down the heart beat, even instantly stop it. An analysis by the FBI of the average 500–1000 per annum auto-erotic deaths in the USA found the victims to be overwhelmingly male, with an average age of twenty-six. Typically, the auto-erotic hanger is found naked or dressed in women's clothing or fetishistic, bondage gear. The ligature around his neck is very often padded with a shirt or scarf to prevent chafing and bruising. Pornography and sexual aids are usually to be found close by.

If homicidal hanging is uncommon, the phenomenon of murderers trying to pass off homicide as suicidal hanging is well-established. They include the KARATE killer Frederick Emmett-Dunne and, most celebrated of all, poultry farmer Norman Thorne (see Case File).

CASE FILE: The Wesley Poultry Farm Murder

Norman Thorne was a failing chicken farmer, who lived in some squalor in one of the huts of his grandly named smallholding, the Wesley Poultry Farm, at Blackness in Surrey. In 1922, when Thorne was twenty, he met Elsie Emily Cameron, a neurotic London typist; she, at least, fell madly in love and determined to marry. Although she lived in London, she travelled down to see Norman at weekends, engaging in heavy petting with him in the converted chicken shed. As Norman later told police, 'we became on intimate terms, that is feeling one another's person and from that it went that I put my person against hers, but in my opinion I did not put it into her. This practice continued on almost all the occasions when Miss Cameron came to the hut.'

Not putting 'it into her' seems to have left Elsie in a somewhat aroused and frustrated state; her letters to 'Lovey' became increasingly passionate and clamorous in their desire for marriage. Elsie was quite prepared to live in the shack; love, after all, is love, whether it is in a hut or a palace. Norman, meanwhile, was casting around for ways to cool Elsie's ardour, even persuading her to sign up with Alliance for Honour, a moral crusade of those pledged to be pure in deed.

Little did Elsie realize it, but Norman had found a brighter and closer attraction in the shape of local dressmaker Elizabeth Coldicott, whom he saw every night between 8.30 p.m. and 10.30 p.m. No doubt sensing Norman's waning interest, Elsie became desperate, writing to Norman that she was pregnant – and that he would have to marry her now. Norman, quite correctly, believed that Elsie's pregnancy was invented, and decided to confess to her in a letter of 25 November that: 'There are one or two things I haven't told you . . . It concerns someone else . . . I'm afraid I am between two fires.'

Elsie, still living with her parents in London, was furious and demanded details. Thorne refused to name his new girlfriend, but explained that 'I have a strong feeling for her.'

His ham-fistedly insensitive letter caused Elsie much grief. She wrote back on 28 November:

> You have absolutely broken my heart. I never thought you were capable of such deception. You have deceived me, and I gave you myself and all my love . . . It's a poor thing for a man to let himself go because his girl has her nerves bad . . . Well, Norman, I expect you to marry me, and finish with the other girl, and as soon as possible . . . For ever and always, your own loving Elsie.

Determined not to be thwarted, on Friday, 5 December Elsie had her hair done in a new style and, wearing a new green knitted dress, set off for Blackness. She was last seen marching towards Thorne's gate at nightfall.

Five days later, Elsie's father sent a telegraph to Thorne. 'Elsie left Friday – have heard no news – has she arrived reply'. Thorne answered back by return. 'Not here – cannot understand.' Mr Cameron contacted the police, who shortly afterwards visited the farm, and seemed satisfied that Thorne was as mystified by Elsie's disappearance as everyone else. The press came too, and Norman ('I want to help all I can'), talked freely, posing for photographs. For one photograph he stood, smiling, in the very chicken-run under which Elsie was buried.

For a month the police pursued their inquiries with little result. Then, at the beginning of January, they made a routine call on Thorne's neighbour, Mrs Annie Price. She had seen Elsie walk through the gate of the chicken farm at about 5.15 p.m. on 5 December.

At 3.30 p.m. on 14 January 1925, Thorne was picked up on suspicion of having something to do with Elsie's disappearance. While he was in the police station, the farm buildings were searched and several items of Elsie's clothing and belongings were found. Other policemen, armed with shovels and pick-axes, began to dig.

Early the very next morning PC Philpott unearthed Elsie's attaché case. It contained her glasses, the lenses broken. Informed of this, Thorne decided to make a statement. He said that he hadn't killed Elsie. After a furious row he had left her in the shack to keep his date with Elizabeth Coldicott. Later, when he returned, he found 'Miss Cameron hanging from a beam by a piece of cord as used for washing-line. I cut the cord and laid her on the bed. She was dead.' Realizing that people would think he had murdered her, he had burned her clothes, cut up her body with a hacksaw and buried the corpse in the run in which he kept his Leghorns.

Thus directed, the police dug up two bundles of sacking containing Elsie's legs and torso, and a biscuit tin containing her head. Thorne was charged with murder.

At Thorne's trial at Lewes Assizes in March 1925, his defence insisted that Elsie had committed suicide, and that creases found on her neck might have been made from a rope. The jury, however, accepted the evidence of the prosecution pathologist, Sir Bernard Spilsbury, who suggested that the marks on the victim's neck were merely natural folds in the skin and that there was no evidence that she had hanged herself; on the contrary, judging from the extensive bruising, there was very good reason to suggest that she had been battered to death. The guilty instrument was probably one of the Indian clubs found outside the shack. Thorne's insistence that Elsie had been the instrument of her own death was further undermined when the police pointed out that the beam in the hut had no rope-marks on it, and the thick layer of dust atop it had not been disturbed for a very long time.

Norman Thorne was executed at Wandsworth Prison on 22 April 1925, on what would have been Elsie's twenty-seventh birthday.

HEMLOCK

Although hemlock is rarely encountered, no reference work that deals with poisons can ignore it, beloved as it was by ancient poisoners. Most famously, it was used in the legalized murder of the Greek philosopher Socrates in 399BC. His crime, according to the Athenian State, was that of 'impiety', and 'corrupting the youth' by encouraging them to think cynically. The seventy-year-old philosopher rejected the option of merely paying a fine, and was therefore sentenced to die by drinking a cup of hemlock, the Athenian method of execution. Those attending Socrates' execution included his pupil, Plato, who later wrote an eloquent account of the event in his *Phaedo*; it remains the classic description of hemlock poisoning, of the way the poison blocks both the sensory and motor neurons, with death ultimately due to respiratory failure:

When the fatal cup was brought he [Socrates] asked what it was necessary for him to do. 'Nothing more,' replied the servant of the judges, 'than as soon as you have drunk the draught, to walk about until you find your legs become weary and afterwards lie down upon your bed.'

He took the cup without any emotion or change in his countenance and, looking at him in a steady and assured manner, 'Well!', said he, 'what say you of this drink? May a libation be made of it?'

Upon being told that there was only enough for one dose, 'At least,' said he, 'we may pray to the gods as is our duty and implore them to make our exit from this world and our last stage happy, which is what I most ardently beg of them'.

Having spoken these words he remained silent for some time and then drank off the whole draught.

After reproving his friends for indulging in loud lamentations, he continued to walk about as he had been directed until he found his legs grow weary. Then he lay down upon his back and the person who had administered the poison went up to him and examined for a little time his feet and legs, and then squeezing his foot strongly, asked whether he felt him? Socrates replied that he did not. He then did the same to his legs, and proceeding upwards in this way, showed us that he was cold and stiff, and he afterwards approached him and said to us that when the effect of the poison reached the heart Socrates would depart. And now the lower parts of his body were cold, when he uncovered himself and said, which were his last words, 'Crito, we owe Aesculapius a cock. Pay the debt and do not forget it.'

'It shall be done', replied Crito. 'But consider whether you have anything else to say.'

Socrates answered in the negative, but was in a short time convulsed. The man then uncovered him; his eyes were fixed and when Crito observed this he closed his eyelids and his mouth.

The account of Socrates' death shows plainly that poison hemlock, *Conium maculatum*, produces a painless demise. It is interesting that, despite the bodily numbness, Socrates' mind is clear until the very end, which occurs moments after he asks about the sacrifice to Aesculapius, the god of the medical arts.

The chief toxic ingredient in poison hemlock is coniine, a pale oily liquid extracted from the leaves and seeds of the plant. Poison hemlock grows wild in many parts of Europe and North America, and is easily mistaken for ordinary parsley. A related species, water hemlock, *Cicuta maculatum*, produces different symptoms, including violent convulsions.

HEROIN   *See* MORPHINE

HIT-AND-RUN
The invention of the motor car transformed the nature of homicide. It gave the murderer a greatly expanded killing range, and a highly efficient means – the boot – of secretly transporting the corpse to a final resting place. It could even be, as demonstrated by Alfred Rouse, a disposal site in itself, a four-wheeled crematorium (see BURNING). Inhaling CARBON MONOXIDE fumes from the exhaust system of the automobile is a suicidal standard. And of course, the car itself can be used as a lethal weapon, a homicidal blunt instrument on four wheels.

Most 'hit-and-run' deaths are accidents where the driver fails to stop, but deliberate murder by motor car dates back to 1935 at least, when Charles Mortimer (see Case File) went for a spin in his Morris with the ultimate crime on his mind.

As a means of murder, hit-and-run has several variants on the classic swerving car aimed at the unsuspecting victim as seen in gangster films. The Texan doctor John Hill tried to kill his second wife in 1969, according to her testimony, by deliberately crashing the passenger side of the car – where she was sitting – into a concrete bridge pillar (see BACTERIAL POISONING for more about Dr Hill).

Late in 1944 Ronald Hedley, a member of a south London gang called the 'Elephant Boys', ran over a Captain Binney RN who had tried to stop his car after a raid on a jewellers. Binney was knocked down, and the car wheels passed over his chest, leaving him motionless on the road. With the road ahead blocked, Hedley backed his car, running over Binney for a second time, and when he drove away Binney was dragged under the car for more than a mile. Both his lungs were crushed and penetrated by the ends of his broken ribs when the wheels of the car ran over him, and he died within hours of being rushed to hospital.

In 1950, a Glasgow policeman, James Ronald Robertson, No. 138D, was convicted of – and later executed at Barlinnie Prison for – running over forty-year-old Catherine McCluskey, after 'striking her on the head with a rubber truncheon or rendering her insensible by other means'. To make sure that McCluskey – who was the

mother of his illegitimate child – was dead after he knocked her
down in his Austin, PC Robertson reversed over her body. A road
traffic officer attending the scene described McCluskey's injuries
'as the worst injuries I've ever seen in a road accident'.

Twenty-five years later, the great Italian film director, Pier Paolo
Pasolini, was killed in a similar manner to Binney and McCluskey
by seventeen-year-old Giuseppe Pelosi (a.k.a Pino the Frog). On 2
November 1975, the violence Pasolini portrayed in such films as
Beggar became a terrible reality, when he picked up Pelosi at
Rome's railway station and the two drove to the outskirts of the
city. According to Pelosi's later testimony, Pasolini made sexual
advances which the teenager refused. Whatever, Pelosi and unidentified accomplices then beat the director senseless with a board
lined with nails before running him over with his own car.

South African killer Carolyn Laurens effected one of the most
daring car murders when, in 1980, she plied her husband with
ALCOHOL until he was inebriated, then drove their car at a ravine
– jumping clear just before it started its descent. The unfortunate
spouse was too drunk to move, and perished. The crime only came
to light when Laurens later killed her sister with poisonous
SPIDERS and confessed to the earlier homicide.

Of course, hit-and-run can be carried out by vehicles other than
the motor car. When Pennsylvanian farm boy Alexander Meyer
decided to kill sixteen-year-old neighbour Helen Moyer in 1937 he
took the farm truck, running Moyer over at an estimated speed of
45 m.p.h. She survived: the impact from the hick juggernaut threw
her clear. (She did not escape Meyer's evil clutches, however;
injured, she was taken to an abandoned farmhouse, raped and
thrown down a well, which Meyer then demolished with two sticks
of dynamite.) Nor, by a long skid mark, is Moyer the only intended
hit-and-run victim to be 'bounced', rather than crushed, by a
speeding vehicle. In fact, hit-and-run is very much a hit-and-miss
method of murder. Where it is fatal, it is usually when the victim is
caught under the vehicle's body or wheels, or where the impact
causes injury to a major organ, especially the brain. Head-wounds
in hit-and-run cases are often of the so-called *contre-coup* type,
where instead of the injury to the brain occurring at the site of
impact, the damage occurs at a point on the opposite side of the
brain. For instance, the skull may be fractured at the rear, but the
force of impact damages the frontal lobes of the brain. The
workings of *contre-coup* injuries are not fully understood, but they
are, in the words of pathologist Dr Milton Helpern, 'a cardinal sign
of damage to a moving head by impact against a hard stationary
surface'.

Homicidal drivers are often inclined to pass off the hit-and-run
deed as a traffic 'accident'. Forensic science has had some success in
distinguishing between intentional and accidental killings by car,

by analysis of such scene-of-crime evidence as the position of the victim's body, the injuries sustained and tyre and skid marks. Usually in hit-and-run killings the difficulty is in identifying the offending vehicle. But the forensic maxim that 'all contact leaves a trace' is truest of all in hit-and-run; the victim's body may bear tyre-tracks from the killer car, while the car itself will have traces of tissue, hair or blood from the victim. It may even bear an imprint of the victim's clothing or body; in 1959, a Metropolitan Officer found, during the routine fingerprint dusting of a suspect car, a near-photographic image of a hit-and-run victim on the wind-screen. Invariably, the model of car can be established by paint chips detached by the force of impact. Because motor manufacturers keep very precise records of the colours and layers of paints used in production, a single paint flake found at the scene of the crime may not only identify the model of car, but its make and year. Comparison of samples is usually done with a microscope, but if identification is difficult spectographic and chromatographic analysis is used.

CASE FILE: Charles Mortimer

On 7 August 1935, Charles Arthur Mortimer, a lance corporal in the Welch Regiment, stole a Morris motorcar and entertained himself by driving around the back lanes of Hampshire, and knocking down female bicyclists.

Mrs Alice Series was the first to be hit, when Mortimer's car forced her bicycle off the road and into a ditch. Mortimer informed her that his steering wheel had jammed, but when she looked into the car he punched her in the mouth, continued punching her as she lay on the ground, and then drove off. In the evening, Mortimer ran cyclist Nellie Boyes off the road. She remembered his number plate, and reported the incident to the police.

The next day, Mortimer resumed his violent antics, this time with an Austin motor car stolen from Farnborough. Outside the village of Winchfield, Mortimer came across two girls cycling along. He drove at them, sweeping twenty-year-old Phyllis Oakes on to the bonnet of the car, carrying her along until she slid over the parapet of a railway bridge. She sustained fatal injuries. Her sister, Betty Oakes, and a pedestrian nearby saw Oakes get hit, and the pedestrian memorized the number plate, AGJJ 825. The car was later found abandoned at Ash Common, with two of its tyres flat. That same day, Lilian Harwood was knocked unconscious by Mortimer when he ran her down as she bicycled near Knaphill in Surrey. A neighbour wrote down the licence plate number.

The police spotted Mortimer on the road to Guildford, and there followed a dramatic car chase, which ended when Mortimer crashed into a parked van. 'I had a drink or two last week,' Mortimer informed police officers upon his arrest, 'and if I have knocked women about it is through drink and heat.' He added that he had fallen into a quarry when young, and had suffered fits ever since. 'I sometimes do things', he said, 'but why I do them I don't know. I can't say I did not hit the women, but I cannot remember.'

Mortimer was tried at Monmouth Assizes three months later, and claimed that the fatality was an accident. The prosecution, however, brought in evidence of the other attacks, showing that Mortimer had deliberately set about running people down. Despite a history of mental disorders and epilepsy, Mortimer was sentenced to hang. On appeal, following a medical inquiry under the Criminal Lunatics Act of 1884, the sentence was commuted to life in prison.

HYOSCINE

Although known to ancient poisoners, hyoscine was reintroduced to the world as a means of murder by Dr Crippen (see Case File). A vegetable drug, it is derived from the seeds and leaves of henbane (*Hyocymaus niger*), a botanical relative of the deadly nightshade, and is also found in jimson weed (*Datura stramonium*). Hyoscine is chemically similar to ATROPINE, and depresses the central nervous system, causing slowed reflexes and impaired judgement – hence its use as a 'truth drug'. Another name for it is scopolamine. It has a medical use in very tiny amounts in the treatment of anxiety-related problems; in large doses it not only causes loss of judgement, but hallucinations. A fatal dose, which is between a quarter and half a grain, causes death through respiratory failure. Like atropine, it can be absorbed through the skin.

CASE FILE: Dr Crippen

Hawley Harvey Crippen was an American born in Coldwater, Michigan, in 1862. Although he never, strictly speaking, qualified as a doctor, he obtained a medical degree from the Cleveland Homeopathic Hospital and practised as an eye specialist. In 1887, young Crippen married Charlotte Bell, who bore him a son, Otto. Charlotte died in Salt Lake City in 1890.

After Charlotte's death, Crippen moved to New York where he met a striking seventeen-year-old, who called herself Cora Turner (her real name was Kunigunde Mackamotzki) and who was the mistress of a stove manufacturer. A doctor, Cora Turner decided, was a better social bet than a stove manufacturer, and in September 1892 she bustled Crippen to the altar. Presumably it was a case of opposites attract; she was a sexual dominatrix, loud, vulgar and stout; he was thin, meek, bulging-eyed and balding.

It was in 1900 that the Crippens came to England, after Hawley secured a position as the London manager of an American patent medicine firm, Munyon's. The couple took a lease on a flat in Shore Street, Bloomsbury. Luckily for Cora, Bloomsbury was the centre of the music hall world, and Cora cherished ambitions to be an artiste, billing herself under the name 'Belle Ellmore'. Unfortunately, her singing voice was not as pretty as her name. Only once did 'Belle Ellmore' tread the London stage – an engagement at the Bedford & Euston Palace when the other music hall artistes were on strike. As she crossed the picket line outside, several strikers tried to stop her until diva Marie Lloyd pointed out 'Let her in and she'll empty the house.'

In September 1905, the Crippens – who had by now come to loathe the sight of each other – moved to 39 Hilldrop Crescent, where Cora made up for her disappointing stage career by surrounding herself with bohemian friends, and holding drunken parties. Although Crippen, who had changed jobs to work for a dubious patent-medicine company, was earning well, Cora took in lodgers, taking all the rent money for herself. One day, in December 1906, Crippen came home to find Cora in bed with a German lodger.

Not that he minded. For some years Crippen himself had been having a relationship with a typist at work, Ethel LeNeve. When Crippen told Ethel about finding Cora *in flagrante*, Ethel took it as sufficient proof that Crippen's marriage was over – and surrendered her virginity to him the very next day.

Over the next three years Crippen continued to live at Hilldrop Crescent, though life with Cora became increasingly unbearable. Mrs Crippen, aware of her husband's association with his typist, threatened to leave with one of her 'gentlemen' friends and take all of their money, £600, which was deposited in a joint account. In the meantime she took little revenges on Crippen, mocking him in public and suggesting he was only one of Ethel LeNeve's many lovers. It may have been at one such moment that Crippen's patience finally came to an end.

On 1 January 1910, Crippen bought five grains of hyoscine hydrobromide, which came in the form of soluble crystals, from a New Oxford Street chemist's, Lewis and Burrows. He told the chemist that he required it for a preparation made by Munyon's. By the 19th he had the poison in the house. He then suggested to his wife that they throw a dinner party for two of Cora's closest music-hall friends, the Martinettis. The dinner was arranged for 1 February, and the Martinettis later recalled it as 'quite a nice evening and Belle was very jolly'. They left at 1.30 a.m., saying goodbye on the gaslit front doorstep. They would never see Mrs Crippen again.

After the Martinettis had left, Cora picked an argument with Crippen over his failure to escort the frail Mr Martinetti to the lavatory. Again she threatened to leave him. It is unlikely that Crippen would have worried overmuch about this, except for one thing: he had lost his job and was in bad financial straits. If Cora took the money from their joint account he would be nearly destitute.

Some time in the morning of 1 February, Crippen poisoned Cora with hyoscine, probably adding it to her coffee. He then dragged her body to the bathroom, where he dissected it, before burying it in the cellar. The task must have taken a day or two, interrupted as it was by an expedition to pawn some of his wife's jewellery on 2 February. Another lot was pawned on 9 February in Oxford Street. Together the two lots gave Crippen £195, more than he used to earn from Munyon's in a year. He told friends of Cora's from the Music Hall Ladies Guild, a charitable organization of which she was treasurer, that she had gone to the USA to look after a sick relative.

On 24 March, Crippen sent a telegram to the Martinettis reading: 'Belle died yesterday at six o'clock. Please phone Annie. Shall be away for a week.' As a sort of secret 'honeymoon' Crippen went to Dieppe with Ethel, who had been openly living with the doctor since 12 March and who had taken to wearing Cora's jewels and furs. On the crossing to France, it is thought that Crippen dropped Cora's head overboard in a weighted handbag.

As the weeks went by, Crippen must have felt that he and Ethel were secure. He underestimated the loyalty of Cora's music hall friends, however, many of whom were suspicious about her disappearance. Their suspicions only deepened by seeing Ethel LeNeve wearing one of Mrs Crippen's brooches as she hung on the doctor's arm. A Miss Lil Hawthorne called on Crippen and questioned him about his wife's demise. His answers left her fearing the worst and she persuaded her husband, John Nash, to contact an acquaintance of his at Scotland Yard. Chief Inspector Walter Dew of the newly formed Serious Crimes Squad visited Crippen at his office – he had set up as a dentist – on 8 July 1910. On hearing the reason for Dew's visit Crippen showed great presence of mind and told the detective that 'The stories I have told about her death are untrue. As far as I know, she is still alive.' She had, he went on to explain, left him to go and live with a man in Chicago, an old prize-fighter lover. Crippen claimed that he had made up the story about her death to 'cover up her absence without any scandal'. The house at Hilldrop Crescent was searched, but nothing suspicious was found. Chief Inspector Dew left satisfied.

And then Crippen's nerve suddenly failed him. He panicked and decided to flee. After putting his affairs carefully (and unnecessarily) in order, Crippen and LeNeve took the boat to Rotterdam on the night of 9 July. From there they made their way to Antwerp, where they embarked on the SS *Montrose*, bound for Quebec. They travelled as Mr and Master Robinson – Ethel was dressed as a boy, with her hair cropped. In London, meanwhile, Dew had returned to ask Crippen about some minor, routine point – to find that the doctor had bolted. Now extremely suspicious, Dew had 39 Hill-drop Crescent searched thoroughly. On 14 July, after three days of inch-by-inch searching, Dew prodded the coal-cellar floor with a poker. As he later reported:

> I found that the poker went in somewhat easily between the crevices in the bricks, and I managed to get one or two up and then several others came up pretty easily. I then produced a spade from the garden and dug the clay that was immediately beneath the bricks. After digging down to a depth of about four spadefuls, I came across what appeared to be human remains . . .

Covering them was a modest amount of QUICKLIME, intended to speed up the decomposition process.

When the 'mass of flesh' was given a preliminary examination by the police surgeon Dr Marshall, it was found to be a human torso from which the neck and head, arms and legs had been severed. Additionally, all the bones had been removed; the remains, in effect, had been filleted. The vagina and uterus had been mutilated extensively. Such DISMEMBERMENT and mutilation, bordering on the psychopathic, is somewhat at odds with the usual picture of Crippen as the 'mildest mannered murderer that ever lived', the pathetic victim of the bullying Belle and of his love for Ethel.

On 16 July the Yard issued a warrant for the arrest of Crippen and LeNeve, wanted for 'murder and mutilation'. The police bill, written by Dew, gives an interesting portrait of Crippen:

> Age 50, height 5ft 4in; complexion fresh; hair light brown, inclined sandy, scanty, bald on top; rather long scanty mous-tache, somewhat straggly; eyes grey; false teeth; medium build; throws feet outwards when walking . . . very plausible and quiet spoken; remarkably cool and collected demeanour.

The *Daily Mail* carried the description of Crippen, together with a photograph, and Captain Kendall of the SS *Montrose* recognized his passengers 'Mr and Master Robinson' as the wanted couple. His suspicions had been aroused by the way 'Master Robinson' squeezed his father's hand 'immoderately'. Kendall radioed London that he believed that he was carrying Crippen on board, and Inspector Dew took a faster ship to Quebec, the SS *Laurentic*. Disguised as a pilot, Dew arrested Crippen on 31 July, 1910, as Crippen's ship entered the St Lawrence river towards Quebec. Amongst Crippen's first words to Dew were, 'I am not sorry – the anxiety has been too much.' He was the first murderer to be arrested by wireless. At the sight of Inspector Dew, Ethel LeNeve screamed once and fainted.

Back in London, pathologist Bernard Spilsbury – in what would be his first major murder case – had conducted a full autopsy on the remains from 39 Hilldrop Crescent. Since the head, limbs and bones were never found, all he had to work with was the torso and internal organs. It was important for the prosecution to establish that the remains were those of Cora Crippen, and an important clue was given by a piece of abdominal flesh which bore a scar consistent with an operation Cora had undergone before marriage. At Crippen's Old Bailey trial in October 1910 the defence tried to claim that the 'abdominal scar' was actually a fold in the skin from a thigh. Spilsbury pointed out that part of the rectus muscle of the abdominal wall was still attached to the portion of flesh. The jury was allowed to make up its own mind when the specimen was passed around the courtroom in a soup-plate. If the identity of the remains was questionable, there was little doubt about what had caused death. The toxicologist Dr William Willcox demonstrated that hyoscine had been the agent involved by dropping an extract of the juices from the internal organs into a cat's eye: the pupil widened dramatically. Exactly the same result was obtained from a drop of hyoscine. It was estimated that half a grain had been administered.

At the trial of Dr Crippen, held before the Lord Chief Justice, Lord Alverstone, his defence was that there was no proof that the remains found in his cellar were those of a woman, let alone of Cora, and had probably been left by a previous tenant. The prosecution's evidence to the contrary was reinforced by the fact that a piece of material used to wrap some of the remains was bought by Crippen himself from Jones Brothers of Holloway in 1909. It took the jury twenty-seven minutes to bring in a guilty verdict.

Ethel LeNeve was tried separately as an accessory after the fact. The trial lasted one day. There was no proof against her and she was acquitted. Crippen himself had been vigorous in protesting her innocence.

While awaiting his execution at Pentonville Prison, Crippen wrote Ethel a number of touching letters; to his credit, his only thoughts in his cell concerned her welfare. Before his execution on 23 November 1910, he asked the Governor that a photograph and two letters from Ethel LeNeve be buried with him. They were.

If Crippen is dead, his name lives on. He is surely the only murderer whose name has passed into the English language as an exclamation of horror. Cripes.

As for Ethel, she emigrated to Canada and then returned to Britain, working as a clerk in an office in Trafalgar Square, and marrying a man who is said to have looked exactly like the doctor. In 1954, Ethel confided her identity to the writer Ursula Bloom, who had just written a novel called *The Girl Who Loved Crippen*. Ethel revealed that she had never ceased to love Crippen. She died in 1967, at the age of eighty-four.

I

INSECTICIDE   *See* **POISONING**

INSULIN
Insulin is a life-saving drug commonly used in medicine in the
treatment of diabetes; if given in overdose, however, it can cause
death. In normal people the pancreas secretes insulin, a hormone
which controls the level of sugar in the blood. Most people produce
twenty to forty units of insulin a day. Sufferers of diabetes have a
faulty pancreas, which produces little or no insulin, which allows
their blood sugar levels to rise. Until it was discovered how to
process insulin from natural sources in 1921, diabetics simply
deteriorated and then died.

For many years, insulin was extracted from human corpses, but
it is now taken from cattle and pig sources. It is dangerous in
overdose because it produces low blood sugar levels, followed by
hypoglycaemia ('insulin shock') and death.

The first person who used insulin to kill was Kenneth Barlow in
1957 (see Case File). There have been a number of cases in Europe
since, one of them involving a Belgian lesbian drug-addict nun,
Sister Godfrida. A medical commission concluded that Godfrida
murdered by insulin as many as thirty patients at the Wetteren old
people's home she worked at in the mid 1970s. Which makes her
one of the most prolific murderers of all time. She was subsequently
committed to a mental institution.

CASE FILE: Kenneth Barlow

One of the duties of male nurse Kenneth Barlow at Huddersfield
Hospital was to inject diabetic patients with insulin. He was quite
aware of its homicidal potential and even used to refer to it as the
perfect murder drug. 'Anybody gets a dose of this,' he once joked
with a patient, 'and it's the quickest way out.' On the night of 3
May 1957, Barlow decided to put the theory into practice. The
guinea pig was Mrs Barlow.

Towards midnight Barlow phoned for a doctor to come urgently
to his home, saying his wife had drowned in the bath while he had
been asleep. He added that he had tried artificial respiration, to no
avail.

The evidence pointed to a different death than that of DROWN-
ING. Barlow's pyjamas were dry and the arms of the deceased were
folded over her chest (trapping water in the inner creases of her

elbow), both unlikely eventualities if he had tried artificial respiration as he claimed. The doctor noted that the deceased's eyes were oddly dilated. More damning still, in the Barlows' kitchen the police found a syringe and needles.

The autopsy, though, revealed no signs of foul play and indicated that the woman had indeed drowned in the bath as Barlow claimed. Elizabeth Barlow was duly buried. The matter might well have rested there except for the persistence of the head of Bradford CID, Detective Chief Superintendent Philip Cheshire. He questioned Barlow again, and this time Barlow conceded that he had given his wife, at her insistence, several injections of ergometrine to induce a miscarriage.

A second examination of Elizabeth Barlow's corpse, exhumed for the occasion, revealed with the aid of a magnifying glass four tiny puncture marks just below the buttocks. An incision into the left buttock showed up inflammation, suggesting that the injection had only been administered a short time before death. But what had been injected? Was it ergometrine or something else? Forensic analysis ruled out an abortifacient and the common poisons; increasingly the team of pathologists on the case came to favour insulin as the murder drug. This hope seemed dashed when an examination of Elizabeth Barlow's heart-blood showed a high level of sugar – the opposite of what could be expected to happen if insulin had been injected. Matters were further complicated by the fact that no test for insulin then existed. The solution came after a massive trawl of the available medical literature on insulin which turned up evidence that in the case of violent death the liver, to try and aid survival, could discharge a massive quantity of sugar into the bloodstream seconds before death. This reached the heart before circulation stopped. As a result, the heart blood was high in sugar.

Elizabeth Barlow could have been given insulin. Tests on 1000 mice injected with tissue from her buttocks caused them to suffer convulsions, coma and then death. Exactly the same happened with mice that were given insulin.

If Barlow had thought, as many in medicine did at the time, that insulin disappeared quickly from the body after death (making its use unprovable), he was mistaken: the formation of lactic acid in Elizabeth Barlow's buttock muscles on her expiration had actually preserved it.

Proceedings opened at Leeds Assizes on 9 December 1957 before Mr Justice Diplock. Mr Bernard Gillis QC defended Barlow, who pleaded not guilty, and Sir Harry Hilton-Foster stood for the Crown. The defence claimed that there was insufficient proof that Elizabeth Barlow's body contained insulin. But *if* insulin was present, argued the defence's expert witness, Dr Hobson of London's St Luke's Hospital, it could have been produced naturally. Elizabeth Barlow's fear at finding herself accidentally drowning and being unable to get out of the bath would cause her body to pour adrenaline into the bloodstream, which in turn would increase the level of sugar in the blood. This, in turn, would lead to the pancreas secreting insulin.

A biochemist expert for the prosecution dealt briskly with this theory. He reckoned that 15,000 units of insulin had been found in Mrs Barlow's body, a quite impossible amount for her pancreas to produce. The jury was persuaded by the case for the prosecution, and the argument that 1000 laboratory mice cannot be wrong. Barlow was sentenced to life imprisonment, serving twenty-six years before his release in 1984. This made him the second longest serving prisoner in British criminal history. But he was absolutely the first person known to have used insulin to kill.

CASE FILE: Beverley Allitt

Liam Taylor, a mere seven weeks old, was the first to die, losing his life on Ward Four of Grantham and Kesteven Hospital, Lincolnshire, on 23 February 1991. He had been admitted for a minor chest infection; doctors were puzzled by his inexplicable and sudden death, which seemed to be caused by a heart attack – something almost unknown in babies.

If the events on Ward Four had ended there, the real cause of Liam Taylor's death would probably have remained undetected. However, on 5 March another child died. Timothy Hardwick, an eleven-year-old suffering from epilepsy and cerebral palsy, expired just when he seemed to be making a recovery after a minor fit. It was an upsetting interlude for the hospital staff, especially State Enrolled Nurse Beverley Allitt, aged twenty-two, who had had special charge of Timothy. As with Liam Taylor – also 'specialled' by Nurse Allitt – the post-mortem attributed the cause of death to 'natural causes'.

Thereafter the emergencies and deaths on Ward Four came thick and fast. In the space of two months, March and April 1991, the hospital's casualty 'crash team' was called out over twenty times to attend to infant cardiac arrests and respiratory failures on Ward Four. Normally, they would expect to be summoned to one or two life-threatening emergencies every year. Two more children died, three-month-old Becky Phillips and fifteen-month-old Claire Peck. Nine other children, the youngest aged eight weeks and the oldest six years, suffered arrests and fits: Kayley Desmond, Paul Crampton, Bradley Gibson, Henry Chan, Katie Phillips, Michael Davidson, Christopher Peasgood, Christopher King and Patrick Elstone.

It was the death of Claire Peck on 22 April that finally convinced the hospital authorities that events on Ward Four were caused by something other than bad luck or a bug. One doctor, Dr Porter, had recently attended a conference of the British Paediatric Association, where Munchausen Syndrome by proxy, the psychiatric condition where people harm others to receive attention themselves, had been discussed (see page 235). It occurred to Dr Porter that events on Ward Four could be caused by a human agency, and the police, in the person of Detective Superintendent Stuart Clifton, head of Lincolnshire CID, were called in. Although Clifton had few leads, a blood sample from one of the children who had survived several heart failures while on Ward Four, five-month-old Paul Crampton, had been sent to a specialist analysis unit at University of Wales Hospital, Cardiff. This revealed an insulin level 'in excess of 500 milli-units per litre of blood' (a normal level would be 4–5). To find just how far in excess of 500 it was, Clifton arranged for more of Paul Crampton's blood sample to be tested at a laboratory at Guildford: the test showed an insulin level of an incredible *forty-three thousand* milli-units per litre of blood, a figure virtually unknown in the medical world.

Suspicion that Ward Four harboured a killer grew when it was discovered that the key to the drugs fridge was missing, allowing someone unrestricted access to its contents, insulin included. It did not take long for Superintendent Clifton to come up with the likely culprit behind the incidents on Ward Four: when the staff rota lists were examined one name appeared alongside every one of the twenty-four incidents that had occurred. The name was Beverley Gail Allitt, the newly qualified SEN who had joined the ward at the beginning of the year.

On Monday, 3 June 1991 Allitt was taken to Grantham police headquarters for questioning. Although she had never been interviewed or locked up by the police before, her calmness astonished detectives, one of whom said later, 'You would have thought she was on a Sunday School outing.' She denied any misuse of drugs on Ward Four, and she was released on police bail after two days.

Superintendent Clifton was sure, however, that he had got his woman. It was a matter of proving it. A mass of medical evidence was gathered, and the team of detectives was joined by insulin and paediatric experts. Routine blood samples taken from other victims on Ward Four were tracked down, several of which showed high levels of insulin; Becky Phillips' was recorded as 9660. The tests on the blood of Claire Peck and Timothy Hardwick revealed traces of another poison, potassium chloride. Potassium chloride is naturally present in the human body at a level of around three millimoles per litre of blood; Claire Peck's blood was found to contain in excess of 16 millimoles per litre. Potassium chloride, like insulin, was kept in the drugs refrigerator on Ward Four.

Steadily, the evidence against Allitt began to mount. It was discovered that the medical records on Ward Four had been tampered with, and some were found in Allitt's flat. She could offer no convincing explanation as to how they had got there. A background investigation into Allitt's life, from her childhood in the village of Corby Glen, revealed a history of histrionics, hypochondria and self-mutilation as a way of attracting attention. During her training to be a nurse she had admitted herself to hospital twenty-nine times with cuts, sprains and other 'illnesses'. One boyfriend told police that she had once deliberately slammed her finger in a car door to get his sympathy. It was but a short step, the psychiatrists explained, from injuring herself to get attention to injuring others so that she could be at the centre of the ensuing drama. In all probability this was Allitt's motive for murder. (See also the case of the Ann Arbor Hospital Killings on page 74 and the Texas Baby Murders on page 234.) But it was a visit to an old people's home in the Lincolnshire village of Waltham on the Wolds, where Allitt did some 'moonlighting' work in her hours off from Ward Four, that sealed the case against her. There she had actually been observed giving an insulin overdose to a resident, 79-year-old Dorothy Lowe, who had miraculously survived.

Superintendent Clifton's file on the Beverley Allitt case, 118 pages long, was sent to the Director of Public Prosecutions in London in September 1991. Two months later, on 20 November 1991, the DPP decided that there was enough evidence to charge Beverley Allitt with four murders – those of Liam Taylor, Timothy Hardwick, Becky Phillips, Claire Peck – and twenty other offences, ranging from attempted to murder to grievous bodily harm. When Allitt was arrested her only comment was 'Thank you'.

On Monday, 15 February, two years after Liam Taylor's death on Ward Four, the trial of Beverley Allitt began at Nottingham Crown Court. The prosecution alleged a 'chilling pattern' to the incidents on Ward Four, and that Beverley Allitt was the instigator of them. Her main weapon was insulin, injected or added to intravenous drips, though she had also used potassium chloride and, on occasion, SUFFOCATION, by placing her hand over the mouth and nose of her infant patients. Beverley Allitt strenuously denied the charges against her. The judge, Mr Justice Latham, would not allow evidence of Munchausen Syndrome to be given to the jury, fearing that it would make it impossible for Allitt to have a fair trial. After forty-four days, the jury retired to consider their verdicts. These took almost a week to deliver. Beverley Allitt was found guilty on all four charges of murder. The jury found her guilty too of all other charges preferred against her save two. She was sentenced to life imprisonment. The court resounded with the sound of cheering and clapping. The murder and injury of children, no matter the mental state of the killer, is not easily forgiven.

INTERRING

The burial, or interring, of the corpse is the disposal method which suggests itself most readily to the murderer. Quite apart from its literal covering up of the crime, interring satisfies some deeply atavistic urge. Humanity has practised the burial of its dead for thousands of years. A murderer might even persuade him or herself that by returning 'earth to earth, dust to dust' they are doing the decent thing.

Interring does, however, present difficulties. Many city-dwellers do not have a garden, and those that do are often boarded by inquisitive neighbours who are likely to notice furtive digging in the night. Such was the ill luck of Edgar Edwards, who was seen digging the massive hole needed for the bodies of the Darby family he murdered for gain in 1902. Then, what does one do with all the spare earth? It is an iron law of grave-digging that it is impossible to fit all the soil back into the hole, not least because of the mass of the corpse. Also, interring disturbs surface vegetation and brings up subsoils, leaving an all-too-visible sign that digging has been done. The too shallow grave dug in haste is easily exposed by the elements and animals.

Moreover, few murderers who opt for burial realize that any vegetation they plant atop the grave to disguise it may not grow normally. When the Trinidadian Fire Brigade attended the house of gangster Malcolm de Freitas (a.k.a. Michael X) in 1972 (see Case File), an inspector noticed that a patch of lettuces in his garden was growing 'too tall and yellow'. His men dug up the lettuces and found the body of one of de Freitas' victims, a henchman executed for not obeying orders.

It was, on the other hand, the sheer lusciousness of serial-killer Dorothea Puente's fruit, roses, and tomatoes that aroused the suspicions of a visiting social worker – that and the way that her aged lodgers tended to disappear without adequate explanation. When police officers dug up Puente's Sacramento backyard in 1993, they discovered that the frail 64-year-old grandmother's 'special fertilizer' was made from seven erstwhile tenants, killed so that she could steal their pension cheques.

The murderer may be tempted to bury the victim away from prying urban eyes, in woods or in farmland. But the transportation of the corpse to a more suitable location is a task fraught with the danger of discovery. East London brush-manufacturer Henry Wainwright was caught blood red-handed in 1875 as he unloaded the bits of his dismembered mistress Harriet Lane from a horse-and-cab. No doubt it was an awareness of such dangers that prompted Dr Crippen to opt for an in-the-house burial of his wife

Cora, after he murdered her with HYOSCINE. She was interred under the cellar floor. John Christie interred one of his victims under the kitchen floor of 10 Rillington Place. Prostitute Lofie Peete thought she had made doubly sure that millionaire boyfriend Jacob Denton was safely buried in 1947, by hiding his corpse in the basement of his mansion and covering it with a ton of topsoil. She told his gardener that she was growing mushrooms. Denton's worried family hired a private detective who eventually found the businessman's rotting remains.

The speed with which the buried corpse putrefies is partially dependent on soil type. A body buried in light porous soil will decay faster than one buried in dense, heavy soil. Similarly, a naked body will decay faster than a clothed one. The reason is that air generally encourages decomposition, allowing bacteria and insects to develop and multiply. Certain types of acid, peaty soil will even preserve corpses; archaeologists in north European countries, including Britain, have discovered almost perfectly preserved Iron Age 'Bog People', some of whom died 5000 years ago. A side effect of some poisons like ARSENIC, ANTIMONY and zinc chloride is that they slow down decomposition. Sometimes the corpse is treated with amounts of QUICKLIME in the belief that it will advance putrefaction; it rarely does. As a general rule of thumb corpses interred in earth putrefy eight times less quickly than those left in open air.

It would be criminally negligent to fail to mention that interring can be a method of dispatch as well as disposal. 'Buried alive' is the stuff of nightmare and occasionally of true crime. One of the female entourage of the aforementioned Trinidadian gangster de Freitas was subjected to such a death.

CASE FILE: The Burial of Gale Benson

Born in Trinidad, the son of a Portuguese planter and a Port of Spain black girl, de Freitas moved to London in the late 1950s, where he became a pimp and sometime hired thug for the slumlord Rachman. De Freitas then became fascinated with the Muslim-influenced black nationalist movement in the USA and in 1963 adopted the Islamic faith, changing his name to Abdul Malik. Soon after he founded the 'Racial Advancement and Action Society', a black political pressure group. Much taken with the American Black Power leader Malcolm X – though sharing none of his principle – de Freitas insisted that his followers call him 'Michael X'. In 1967 he served a jail sentence for advocating the shooting of any white man seen with a black girl. Three years later, after being convicted on a robbery charge, he fled to Trinidad.

Undoubtedly, de Freitas had a certain charisma, and had gathered around him a circle of the adoring. Among those who fell for him was an English girl, Gale Benson, daughter of the former MP for Chatham, Captain Leonard Plugge. Gale Benson was utterly slave-like in her devotion to de Freitas, while he exercised a Svengali-like hold over her. He later recalled that he had 'done all manner of evil things to her and she never complained; but I didn't love her for this, I hated her. Once I tied her spreadeagled on a bed and beat her until I was tired.'

Benson and her lover, another of de Freitas' followers, Hakim Jamal, followed the leader to Trinidad when he fled in 1970. Initially, de Freitas had some political success on his home turf, and his Black Power movement enjoyed a brief puff of influence. After an army mutiny in which de Freitas was implicated was put down, however, his popularity waned and he returned to being a gangster-man, pure and simple, organizing armed robberies and prostitution. And the murder of anybody who disobeyed him.

On 19 February 1972, de Freitas' bungalow commune, La Chance, was set alight, while the boss was in Guyana on a 'lecture tour'. When de Freitas heard about the fire, he wired his lawyer to get an injunction barring anybody from setting foot on the premises. It was too late. The Fire Brigade had entered, and an inspector had noticed the etiolated lettuce which signalled the grave of Joseph Skerritt. Skerritt, it transpired, had been personally decapitated by de Freitas for refusing to fall in with a plan for an armed robbery. Further digging in the de Freitas garden unearthed another grave, this time of a white woman wearing a print frock. Professor Keith Simpson, the British pathologist, was called in to examine the bodies, which were identified by dental and fingerprint evidence.

Gale Benson had been subjected to murderous violence. There were slashed cuts on her chest, and a single stab wound which penetrated 6½ in. down into her chest from entry at the root of the neck. This injury in itself would have been fatal, but it was not the only cause of death. In the back of Benson's throat, in her windpipe, air passages and stomach, Simpson found earth, identical to that of her grave. The fact that she had inhaled and swallowed soil particles showed that she must have been buried alive, and that the consequent obstruction to her breathing caused, or at least accelerated, her death.

After extradition from Guyana, de Freitas was tried in August 1972 for the murder of Skerritt. He was convicted. Two other men, Stanley Abbott and Edward Cheddi, were convicted along with de Freitas in the following year for the murder of Gale Benson. Adolphus Parmesser, a Crown witness who had taken part in Gale Benson's murder, said that she had been lured to the scene of the crime by gang member Steve Yates, and shown the pit that had been dug. When she asked what it was for, Yates answered 'To put fresh matter to be decomposed', and pushed her in. The stab to her neck was effected by a cutlass. Apparently, de Freitas ordered Benson's killing because she caused mental upset to another of his followers.

The de Freitas gang might almost be held up as a 'Crime Doesn't Pay' advert. At least four members were murdered by de Freitas, and two were hanged by the Trinidadian authorities – as was the leader himself on 16 May 1975, after his last appeal was turned down.

K

KARATE

The maxim that the suddenly roused killer uses the nearest thing to hand is particularly true of those who have murdered by karate chopping their victims, using the outside of the hand as a BLUNT INSTRUMENT. The karate chop is most dangerous if directed at the front base of the neck at the level of the larynx, where the carotid arteries have numerous pressure-sensitive areas; indeed, troops trained in unarmed combat are taught precisely to 'chop' at this area. Such chops kill by compressing and over-stimulating the pressure-sensitive areas, which causes a stream of nervous impulses to be sent to the brain, which reacts by depressing the heart to the point of sudden death – so-called vagal inhibition or reflex cardiac arrest. In extreme cases, if the punch or chop is delivered with sufficient force it can kill by crushing the bones in the throat, which causes bleeding into the windpipe. The victim inhales the blood and dies of ASPHYXIA within a few minutes. Murderers who have used this means are invariably martial arts experts, or ex- and serving soldiers, such as William Brittle, who 'chopped' his Gloucestershire money lender in 1965, and Sergeant-Major Frederick Emmett-Dunne, who killed a friend by this method in 1953 (see Case File).

To kill, karate chops do not have to be directed at the throat; other parts of the body will serve. In what must be counted one of the most extraordinary of modern murders, West German karate expert Axel Roeder, aged thirty-three, karate chopped his wife – also a karate champion – to death in a fit of jealousy after she danced at a discotheque with another man. The duel, in which Alex had the advantage because of his 31-year-old wife's inebriated state, took place in the early hours of the morning of 14 May 1977. The subsequent autopsy report by the Darmstadt pathologist revealed that Ute Roeder's ribs had been broken on both sides, her lungs had burst, her liver had been split in half and even her stomach had been ruptured in four places. She had died of internal bleeding.

Karate, of course, is not the only possible use of hands as blunt instruments. Punching with a clenched fist is a common means of homicide. Since the face is a natural target in punching, the action can fracture the skull (with brain damage a result), drive facial bones into the skull (again with brain damage a result), or cause dislodgement of the teeth and tearing of the soft tissues in the mouth. As the mouth is very well supplied with blood vessels, there may then be severe haemorrhaging. Such bleeding may cause asphyxia, particularly if the victim is left unconscious or disabled, lying on their back, allowing the blood to enter the windpipe. But in general the karate chop is more dangerous than the closed-fist punch for a simple reason of physics. Its swinging pendulum action means that a great deal of weight and speed is built up – and then delivered through a proportionately small (and unfeeling) area, the edge of the hand. Such a chop can even break bricks.

CASE FILE: Frederick Emmett-Dunne

Towards the end of 1952, Sergeant-Major Frederick Emmett-Dunne of the Royal Electrical and Mechanical Engineers became infatuated with a German girl called Mia. She lived in Duisberg, the West German town where Emmett-Dunne was based. Unfortunately, Mia was married to Emmett-Dunne's fellow soldier, Reginald Watters.

In the early hours of 1 December 1953, Sergeant Watters was found HANGING from the banisters of the Glamorgan Barracks in Duisberg. He appeared to have committed suicide. A post-mortem concluded that death was the result of shock brought on by self-strangulation. Although there was no apparent reason why Watters, a popular and likeable NCO, should take his own life, the army court accepted that this is what he had done.

The matter was forgotten until Emmett-Dunne married Mia Watters six months later, which fuelled old rumours amongst Sergeant Watters' friends. The rumours reached the army's Special Investigation Branch, which decided to reinvestigate the case. This, in turn, passed on its findings to Scotland Yard, and the Yard ordered Watters' remains to be disinterred.

Undertaking the second post-mortem was the percipient Francis Camps, who announced that Watters had not died of hanging but from a blow across the throat, such as a Commando-style karate chop. Emmett-Dunne was an ex-Commando. Shortly afterwards, Emmett-Dunne's half-brother, a private in the same barracks, stepped forward and informed the police that Emmett-Dunne had told him that he had killed someone accidentally, and had tried to make it look like a suicide, hanging the dead man from the banister, and leaving a bucket overturned nearby.

Frederick Emmett-Dunne was charged with murder on 15 April 1955. His trial began in Dusseldorf on 27 June. The defendant was represented by Mr Curtis-Bennett, who claimed that his client had killed in self-defence, after Watters had threatened Emmett-Dunne with a revolver over his relationship with his wife. In an effort to disarm Watters, Emmett-Dunne had struck him a glancing blow across the neck. He had not intended to kill. Then, fearful of being drummed out of the army, he had staged the suicide. On 7 July, the jury retired and after an hour and a half, they reached a verdict of guilty of murder. Since Emmett-Dunne was tried in Germany, where there was no capital punishment, he was sentenced to life imprisonment. He served ten years and was then released.

KICKING

The third most common method of homicide in Great Britain. Victims of kicking are frequently a mass of lacerated wounds, bruises and abrasions, and suffer considerable crushing and fracturing of bones in the head – the natural target for the shod foot when the victim is 'downed'. Kicks in the neck are especially dangerous. Closely allied to, and often used with, kicking is stamping, though the force – and danger – from the swinging foot is far greater. In stamping, the imprint of the sole of the shoe may be imprinted on the soft tissues of the victim's body. Conversely, the victim's blood may be left on the offending shoe. Such was the tell-tale evidence found by the police on the footwear of Francis 'Flossie' Forsyth, when he was apprehended by the police in June 1960. With a gang of three others, Forsyth had attacked Alan Jee in a secluded alley in Hounslow with the intention of robbing him. To 'shut him up', Forsyth kicked Jee in the head repeatedly. The match of blood from Jee with that on Forsyth's shoe led the eighteen-year-old to the gallows. Along with gang member Norman Harris, Francis Forsyth was hanged on 10 November 1960.

Night, alcohol, a cityscape, male youths and innocent victims are the typical ingredients in a death from kicking. All were to be found in the killing of Les Reed (see Case File).

CASE FILE: The Killing of Les Reed

The Ely housing estate lies on the western edge of Cardiff. It has a certain local infamy, and even briefly attracted the attention of the national media when a dispute over an Asian shopkeeper on the estate erupted into a riot in the summer of 1992. The riot shocked the people of Ely, many of whom afterwards tried to make it a better place. Which somehow made the killing of Les Reed all the more difficult to bear.

Les Reed, a 46-year-old retired steelworker, spent the evening of Friday, 11 June 1993 as he spent most Friday evenings, at the West End Social Club, chatting over a few pints of beer with Philip Tull, a friend he had known since his schooldays. When the club closed they began walking home along the estate's Grand Avenue. As they neared a pedestrian crossing they saw a gang of nine male youths smashing traffic bollards. The gang had spent the evening drinking cans of lager and roaming the estate. By the time Les Reed and Philip Tull reached the pedestrian crossing, most of the youths had moved off, but 20-year-old Michael Mundell and Stephen James stayed. As he crossed, Tull told the two youths that kicking the traffic cones 'was a stupid thing to do'. The youths then began following Reed and Tull, until Reed turned and told them 'to go home and give the neighbours some peace'. And that was all it took.

Mundell and James shouted for reinforcement from the rest of their gang, one of them calling 'Come on boys, we've got trouble. Come on boys, we'll have some blows.' After being dragged to the ground, Les Reed and Philip Tull were kicked over and over again. Les Reed – who was at the time only yards from his house – died shortly after being taken to hospital. Philip Tull, who suffered serious head injuries, including a broken jaw, was lucky enough to survive.

When pathologists examined Les Reed's body they found injuries so extensive that it was as if he had been in a car crash – there were fifty-five separate wounds to the body. One kick to his head was so severe that it stretched his spinal cord.

Four youths from Ely – Mundell, James, Shane Hutchinson and Andrew Thomas – were tried for the murder of Les Reed and of causing grievous bodily harm to Philip Tull in February 1994. After three weeks of trial James, Hutchinson and Thomas (the latter two both aged seventeen) were found guilty of the murder of Les Reed and detained at Her Majesty's pleasure. Michael Mundell was found guilty of manslaughter. James, Hutchinson and Thomas also received eight-year current convictions for causing grievous bodily harm to Philip Tull.

KIDNAPPING

'No police £50,000 ransom to be ready to deliver wait for phone call at Swan shopping centre telephone box 6 p.m. to 1 a.m. . . . you must follow instructions without argument from the time you answer you are on a time limit if police or tricks death.' Such was part of the ransom note received by Mrs Dorothy Whittle in January 1975. Her daughter, Lesley Whittle, had been abducted from the family's Shropshire home during the night by a masked intruder brandishing a shotgun. The kidnapper of the seventeen-year-old heiress was Donald Neilson. Although nobody knew it yet, he was also the infamous post-office raider known as the 'Black Panther'.

Despite the warning in the note, Mrs Whittle immediately contacted the police, who advised paying the ransom. While the Whittle family raised the £50,000, Neilson laid out an elaborate trail of Dymo-tape instructions for its delivery around various Midlands telephone boxes. It was while checking the route for the payment of the ransom that Neilson was interrupted by Gerald Smith, a security officer at the Freightliner depot in Dudley. Smith was shot several times by a .22 pistol. A green Morris car parked nearby was later found to contain Dymo-tape messages, clearly part of the ransom trail.

At 11.45 p.m. on the night of 16 January, the third day of the kidnap, the Whittle family received a telephone call. On the other end of the line was Lesley Whittle's recorded voice, instructing the courier to take the ransom money to a phone box at Kidsgrove.

The courier, Lesley's brother, reached the Kidsgrove telephone box, and was directed by a Dymo-tape message to drive to nearby Bathpool Park. And there the trail ran cold.

Following extensive publicity, a local headmaster remembered a torch one of his pupils had found in Bathpool Park with a strip of Dymo-tape bearing the message 'Drop Suitcase into Hole'. Police and tracker dogs then began to search the park's underground culverts, and it was during this operation that Lesley Whittle's naked body was found in an access shaft. She had been hung by a wire noose around her neck.

A further nine months passed before Britain's most wanted man was caught. By chance. In December 1975, two policemen noticed a man loitering outside a Nottingham public house, and when they questioned him he produced a sawn-off shotgun from under his coat. A scuffle ensued, in which the gun-man was overpowered. Under questioning, Neilson (born Donald Nappey) admitted the abduction and murder of Lesley Whittle. He also confessed to the murders of three Post Office officials during armed raids between 1971 and 1975.

His defence during his trial at Oxford in June 1976 was that all his murders were due to his clumsiness: in the case of Lesley Whittle he had accidentally knocked her off the tiny platform on which she lay, and the wire around her neck had only been used to tether her. However, to claim four accidental deaths was to stretch the credulity of the jury, who convicted the diminutive former National Serviceman on four counts of murder. It seems certain that Neilson killed Lesley Whittle in a fit of fury when he suspected – rightly – that the ransom delivery by Ronald Whittle was part of a heavy-footed police trap to ensnare him.

Gerald Smith, the freightliner security officer shot by Neilson, died in March 1976 as a result of his gunshot wounds. Under English law, however, if a charge of murder is to be brought the victim must die within a year and one day of the incident which caused death. For this crime, at least, Neilson escaped justice.

Kidnapping, the unlawful seizure and detention of a person or persons, is a long established crime. And often a prelude to murder. One of the first appearances of the word 'kidnap' in the English language is to be found in John Bunyan's *The Pilgrim's Progress* (1684). There are four main motives for kidnapping:

1) *Slavery and forced labour* Originally 'kidnapping' referred exclusively to the practice of abducting children and sending them to plantations in America. Another early form of kidnapping was the 'press-ganging' of sailors. Women have often been abducted for

prostitution or concubinage. Or even, as with the victims of Philadelphian 'Baby Farmer' Gary Heidnik in the 1980s, forced motherhood (see Case File).

2) *Raising ransom money* A form of kidnapping which arose in the late 19th century, becoming widespread in the USA in the 1920s and 1930s. The underworld saw that easy pickings were to be had by taking rich businessmen or members of their family hostage. The most famous of these kidnappings was the abduction of Charles Lindbergh Jnr, the nineteen-month-old son of aviator Charles Lindbergh, on 1 March 1932. A ransom note left on a windowsill at the Lindberghs' New Jersey mansion demanded $50,000 for the child's return. A nationwide hunt for the kidnapper – who raised the ante to $70,000 – began, and the first lead came when a friend of the Lindbergh family, Dr Condon, made a public appeal to the abductor's humanity. A man called 'John' responded, sending some of the missing child's clothes to prove his authenticity.

At a secret meeting Condon handed over $50,000 to 'John' who in turn told him that the missing child would be found on a boat called *Nellie*, moored near Martha's Vineyard. Lindbergh and Condon rushed there – only to find themselves the victims of a bitter hoax. The badly decomposed body of the kidnapped child was found in May 1932 only miles from the Lindbergh home. It had been killed by a blow to the head on the day of the kidnap.

The kidnapper was caught after an alert filling-station attendant took a note which had come from the ransom, the details of which had been circulated by the police. The driver was traced through his car registration number – and found to be Bruno Hauptmann, a 36-year-old German soldier. Over $11,000 of the ransom money was found in Hauptmann's garage. He was sent to the electric chair at Trenton State Prison, New Jersey, on 3 April 1936.

With the decline of the Prohibition mobster the frequency of kidnapping for ransom also declined – until 1974, when it began a rising curve. That same year saw the infamous abduction of Patti Hearst, daughter of multi-millionaire newspaper magnate Randolph Hearst.

3) *Torture or murder* Most homicides take place 'on the spot', but occasionally circumstances oblige the killer(s) to abduct the victim first. For instance, if the victim is to be tortured, either for the extraction of information, for revenge, or for pleasure.

Notable amongst such kidnappings was that of American student Mark Kilroy in 1987. Enjoying an end of term holiday with friends in the Mexican town of Matamoros, Kilroy was bundled at knife point into a car by a gang of Mexicans and driven to a shack on the Santa Elena ranch. The kidnappers were members of a drug-smuggling gang led by 37-year-old Adolfo de Jesus Constanzo, considered by his underlings to be a 'high priest' in a Satanist cult based on the Cuban religion of Santeria. Constanzo needed an 'Anglo' human sacrifice. Mark Kilroy was it.

On the afternoon following his abduction, Kilroy was taken to a makeshift temple on the Santa Elena ranch, and forced to kneel over an orange tarpaulin, where he was purified by rum poured over the head. Constanzo then cut off the back of Kilroy's head with a machete. 'The sound', a gang member David Valdez later told the police, was 'like a ripe coconut being split open'. Constanzo then scooped Kilroy's brains out and added them to a stew bubbling in an African cauldron called an *n'ganga*. After the 'cannibal feast', Kilroy's body was mutilated and dismembered.

A raid on the remote Rancho Santa Elena by drug-squad Federales, after a gang member had incautiously led them to the hideout, revealed that Mark Kilroy was not the Constanzo cult's only victim. Detainees showed the Federales the graves of fourteen other men. Although Constanzo escaped the raid, police caught up with him in Mexico City on 5 May 1989. Besieged, Constanzo ordered his followers to shoot him as he enjoyed a last embrace with his homosexual lover in a walk-in wardrobe. He died in a hail of bullets from an AK-47.

4) *Political* Like kidnapping for ransom, a type of abduction which increased in the 1970s, as groups like the Red Army Faction in Germany stepped up their war on the state. The most sensational of the politically motivated kidnappings was that of Signor Aldo Moro by the Red Brigade in 1978. The Italian Government refused to negotiate with the Brigade and Moro was murdered.

These are the main categories of kidnapping although, of course, the categories can overlap: political kidnappers often show an interest in raising funds, for instance. A common problem facing all kidnappers is where to incarcerate the victim, and how to prevent the abductee escaping. Michael Sams had the facility of a private workshop and some engineering knowledge in his kidnapping of his two victims.

Posing as a client, the one-legged Sams picked up his first victim, Leeds prostitute Julie Dart, in the summer of 1991. After tying her up and gagging her, 51-year-old Sams drove Dart to his isolated, rundown workshop in Newark, where the eighteen-year-old was kept in a wooden coffin-shaped box behind a curtained area. Sams then wrote a note to the police in Leeds demanding £140,000 for Miss Dart's safe return. Before the ransom could be paid, he murdered Dart by bludgeoning her over the head – probably because she tried to escape and saw his face.

Undeterred, Sams, an ex-heating and lift engineer, then tried to blackmail British Rail for £200,000 by threatening to derail an express train. To show he meant business, he suspended a block of sandstone from a bridge in Staffordshire. However, he abandoned the plan, and switched his efforts instead to the kidnapping of Stephanie Slater, an estate agent. Pretending to be a buyer, he abducted her in January 1992 as she showed him around a house in Great Barr, Birmingham. Armed with a knife and a chisel, Sams knocked her into the bath, bound, gagged and blindfolded her and then bundled her into his waiting car. On arrival at the Newark workshop, she was manacled around her wrists and ankles, her legs were chained, and then she was imprisoned in the same wooden box that he had used for Julie Dart. An infra-red detector was focused on the box in case Slater tried to escape. It was connected to the redial button on the workshop telephone, which would dial Sams' home number seven miles away in the village of Sutton-on-Trent.

Sams made a ransom demand of £175,000 on Slater's employers, Shipways Estate Agents. However, he was arrested before he could collect. The first of his three wives heard a tape of his voice and saw an artist's drawing of the Slater kidnapper on the BBC's *Crimewatch UK* programme. At Sams' trial in July 1993, Stephanie Slater told how she thought she would die of cold as she lay inside the wooden box. On the seventh day, only hours before her release, she considered suicide by SUFFOCATION, by putting blankets over her face. Described by Mr Justice Judge as 'an extremely dangerous and evil man', Sams was sentenced to four life terms for the kidnapping and murder of Julie Dart, the kidnapping of Stephanie Slater, two attempts to blackmail police and an extortion demand against British Rail.

CASE FILE: The Baby Farmer

It ended on the evening of 24 March 1987. That night, after long weeks of incarceration Josefina Riviera persuaded her abductor to allow her to visit her children. So sure was Gary Heidnik of his power over the black street walker, that he agreed. Besides, she had promised to bring him another woman for his Philadelphia-based 'United Church of the Ministers of God'.

Riviera did not go and see her children (they had been adopted some years before), but ran to the house of a former boyfriend, Vincent Nelson.

> She was . . . you know, [recalled Nelson] talking real fast about this guy having three girls chained up in the basement of this house and she was held hostage for four months . . . She said that he was beating them up, raping them, had them eating dead people just like he was a cold blooded nut . . . I thought she was crazy.

But just in case she was not, Vincent telephoned the police. A brief examination of Riviera's body, which bore the marks of shackles, persuaded them she was telling the truth. Gary Heidnik was picked up as he waited for Riviera to return in his grey and white Cadillac Coupe de Ville. He did not resist arrest.

At 4.40 a.m. on 25 March, a squad of officers broke into Heidnik's heavily fortified house, 3520 North Marshall Street. What they found was, if anything, worse than what Riviera had led them to believe. In the dim squalor of the basement, they discovered two black women, Lisa Thomas (captured by Heidnik on 22 December 1986) and Agnes Adams (captured 23 March 1987) huddled together on a mattress on the floor. They were shackled and chained to heating pipes. Initially they believed that the police officers were an execution squad sent by Heidnik. Then, reassured, they indicated a pit in the floor, hidden under a board. Inside was another black girl, Jacquelyn Askins (captured 18 January 1987) also chained. The catalogue of Heidnik's house of horrors did not end there; in the kitchen officers found bits of human body, some cooked, some refrigerated.

In their statements to the police, the women explained that Heidnik had intended to start a 'baby farm' in his basement. He claimed that God had told him to 'make some babies', so he had 'collected' women and imprisoned them. The abductions had been easy enough to accomplish; with one exception, the women were all prostitutes who had willingly gone to Heidnik's house, and because they led irregular lives nobody showed any interest when they disappeared. Once imprisoned he had starved them, beaten them and every day he compelled them into having sex with him and each other.

It also transpired that there had been two other inmates of the 'baby farm', Sandra Lindsay, a mentally-retarded friend of Heidnik's, and Deborah Dudley (both captured 29 November 1986). Heidnik had killed both of then after they had irritated him. Sandra Lindsey had been strapped by her wrists to an overhead beam, and force fed bread. After a week of this, the weakened girl choked on a piece of bread and died. She was dismembered with a chain saw, and parts of her body were cooked. These were fed to the other inmates, mixed in with dog food. Deborah Dudley consistently fought her gaoler. She was accordingly placed in the basement pit, which was filled with water. Josefina Riviera was then commanded by Heidnik to poke a live electric wire into the pit and touch Dudley's chains with it. The ELECTROCUTION killed her. Her body was dumped by Heidnik in a remote spot in New Jersey.

Predictably – for most abnormal behaviour originates in childhood trauma – Gary Heidnik suffered much as a child. He was born on 21 November 1943 in Cleveland, Ohio, and his parents divorced when he was a baby. Heidnik did not like his stepmother, and his father was a ferocious disciplinarian. When Heidnik messed the bed, his father displayed the soiled sheet in the windows for the neighbours to see. Heidnik's mother, an alcoholic, committed suicide. Gary Heidnik was also tormented unmercifully at school by being called 'football head', because a fall out of a tree had altered the shape of his skull. He joined the army in 1961, where he 'scored exceptionally fine marks'. However, he suffered mental health problems, and was admitted to army hospital no less than twenty times for psychiatric treatment.

Heidnik was honourably discharged in 1963, and used his army pension to speculate on the American stock exchange with great success. Above everything, however, he wanted children. He fathered several by mentally retarded black prostitutes, but these were taken away by the authorities for fostering. The mothers were deemed incapable. It never seems to have occurred to Heidnik to choose a more suitable would-be mother or create a stable home environment. Instead he set up the 'United Church of the Ministers of God', with himself as Bishop (his brother, Terry, was also on the board). The church made a lot of money for Heidnik; eventually, it would also give him the justification that 'collecting' women to have his children was 'God's work'.

At his trial in June 1988, Heidnik was charged with murder, kidnapping, rape, aggravated assault, involuntary deviate sexual intercourse, indecent exposure, false imprisonment, unlawful restraint, simple assault, making terroristic threats, recklessly endangering another person, indecent assault, criminal solicitation, possession, and abuse of a corpse. Heidnik's defence lawyer, A. Charles Peruto Jnr, portrayed his client as insane, and much court time was taken up with definitions of insanity, mental illness, and proofs thereof. After retiring for two and a half days, the jury decided that Heidnik was sane, and found him guilty of the first-degree murder of Sandra Lindsay, of the first-degree murder of Deborah Dudley and guilty of most of all the other charges, save involuntary deviate sexual intercourse. Heidnik was sentenced to death on the two main charges – although the death penalty is in abeyance in Philadelphia – and 120 years' imprisonment on the rest. Heidnik was, said Judge Lynne Abrahams, possessed 'not of an illness in his head, but a malignancy in his heart. I don't want any parole order to put Mr Heidnik back on the streets as long as he's breathing.'

KNIVES

In the genealogy of murder weapons, the knife succeeded the axe and the club, bringing ease of concealment – and thus the element of surprise – to the act of killing. The technical advantages of the knife were obvious in the assassination of Julius Caesar in 55BC. The conspirators, with knives hidden under togas and robes, approached the unsuspecting Emperor – and stabbed him twenty-three times. (It is of some forensic interest that the subsequent post-mortem examination, carried out by the physician Anstitius, is the first recorded where the subject was a murder victim.) The lethal subtlety of the knife was also evidenced in the homicide of another royal personage, England's King Edward in AD978. A monk in Edward's entourage described the slaying in his *Life of Oswald*:

> Soldiers were therefore holding him, one drew him [the King] to the right towards himself as though to give him a kiss [of welcome] another seized his left hand violently and wounded him, but he cried as loud as he could 'What are you doing, breaking my right arm?' and he fell from his horse and died.

His right arm – which was also his sword arm – was held by the one soldier, his other arm was twisted away from his body by the second soldier, who drew out a knife and stabbed Edward in the torso.

Over 800 years later, in 1793, Charlotte Corday proved the usefulness of the knife as an assassin's tool in the murder of the French revolutionary Jean Paul Marat. She bluffed her way into his house at No. 20 Rue des Cordeliers, Paris, where he gave her an audience from his medicinal bath (he had a painful skin complaint). As they talked, she suddenly drew out a kitchen knife and plunged it into his breast. His scream brought members of his household running, but Marat was dead by the time they lifted him from the bath. When asked how she had managed to kill Marat with a single thrust, Corday answered: 'The anger in my own heart showed me the way to his.'

Unlike some other murder weapons the knife has never gone out of fashion. It is as popular today as it has always been. The carrying of knives is part of the culture of inner city youth (especially flick knives, switchblades and chef's knives), football hooligans (whose tool of the trade is the Stanley knife) and small-time gangsters. Jack Henry Abbott, hoodlum and author, catches something of such violence in his book *In the Belly of the Beast* (1982): 'You've pumped the knife in several times without even being aware of it. You go to the floor with him to finish him. It is like cutting into hot butter, no resistance at all.'

The knife, however, is possibly unique in the sheer range of people who wield it homicidally. It is just as likely to be used in a domestic fracas as it is in a street brawl. The reason is its ubiquity, especially in the home, where it has a deadly tendency to be lying there waiting to be snatched up in a moment of rage. As murderer Margaret Williams put it, after killing spouse Sergeant Major Williams in 1949, 'If the knife hadn't been on the table my husband wouldn't be dead.' The knife is not usually a weapon of dispassionate killing, like the gun or poison, both of which allow a certain distance between killer and victim. It is a 'close quarters' weapon, invariably used in anger or in hate. In Great Britain the great majority of the 600 or so annual murders are committed with knives. In the USA, knives are the second most common method of murder after FIREARMS.

Wounds made with a knife are of two main types: incise wounds, or cuts made with the edge of the knife, and stab wounds, where the point and length of the blade are plunged into the body. Incise wounds, although often spectacularly bloody, are generally not as dangerous as stabbing. The exception is a quite specialized form of murder, where the throat and windpipe are severed by a knife or razor – the CUT-THROAT.

Stab wounds may be singular or multiple, usually with a trivial-looking entry slit under which great damage has been done. As the famous forensic scientist, Professor Keith Simpson, observed, 'It is the penetrating character of stab wounds that makes them so dangerous.' Stab wounds can damage internal organs, causing internal bleeding or AIR EMBOLISM. The lethal effect of stabbing varies with the direction and depth of penetration; if the aorta is penetrated death may rapidly supervene. In other cases, death may be delayed for hours, even days.

Stabbing, of course, can be accomplished with weapons other than a knife; such other SHARP INSTRUMENTS are discussed elsewhere. The force used to cause a stab wound with a knife is often less than imagined. Jack Abbott's 'like cutting into butter' description of knifing is no exaggeration: once the skin is penetrated the weapon slips easily through underlying tissues and viscera; even the sternum and ribs do not require great force for their penetration, especially if the knife is sharp.

In cases of multiple stabbing, many of the wounds in the skin may be irregular, the skin being torn as the victim struggles under the knife. Less distorted wounds may give clues to the type and shape of the knife used, although matching wounds and weapons is something of an inexact science. Not the least reason for this is that when a blade penetrates the skin there is a certain amount of stretching – and when the blade is withdrawn, the skin springs back to its original position. Nevertheless, the wound-shape sometimes gives the weapon away. A clean-cut wound with two sharp ends is indicative of a double-edged knife such as a dagger. A wound with one sharp end and one blunt suggests an ordinary blade, such as a kitchen knife.

In the 'Wig Wam Murder Case' of 1942, Keith Simpson was able not only to identify the BLUNT INSTRUMENT which actually killed Joan Wolfe but also to make an important deduction from the disabling wounds on Joan Wolfe's body: 'A fragment of muscle had been drawn out of the wound in the right forearms, and a tendon had been similarly hooked out from a wound on the palm of the hand. The point of the weapon must have been something like a parrot's beak.' There were three similarly shaped wounds in the skull. A massive hunt began for a knife with a hook-shaped end. The trail ended at Witley Army Camp, where August Sangret, a Canadian soldier stationed in Britain, was found to have hidden just such a knife. It fitted the wounds in the skull of Joan Wolfe perfectly, as Simpson demonstrated to the satisfaction of the jury in Sangret's trial for murder.

In addition to its shape, the angle of the wound may be revealing. A Mrs Swift of Stockton-on-Tees insisted to the police that her husband Patrick had stabbed himself following a quarrel. Sir Bernard Spilsbury, the eminent pathologist, was able to prove a quite different account of the fatal injury. Patrick Swift was right-handed, and the angle of the wound was such that he could not have stabbed himself with that hand; nor could he have found sufficient force in his left hand. In other words, he had been murdered.

A common undoing of the murderer who tries to disguise his or her deed as a suicide by knife is the plunging of the knife into the 'wrong' part of the victim's body. The suicide who chooses the knife – and they are more common than might be supposed – usually elects to inflict the wound through the lower middle chest where he believes the heart to be. Often the clothing is pulled up to expose the 'target area'.

The 'target area' in a homicide by knife, meanwhile, is usually the upper chest, with the knife penetrating through clothing. The victim may well have defensive injuries on the hands and arms from trying to fend off the blade. A corpse with multiple stab wounds is a fairly sure sign that the victim did not kill himself.

Of course, a knife is not only a murder weapon; it is an instrument of DISMEMBERMENT and mutilation. Its suitability for the latter goes some way to explaining its popularity with those who want to brand their victims (as in the carving of 'S' – probably standing for *spic*, or double agent – in each cheek of Polish Jew Leon Beron in the Clapham Common murder of 1911) and sex murderers, although of course the symbolic 'penetration' the knife allows the sex killer should not be underestimated. The corpses of some victims of sex murderers have recorded sixty or more stab wounds. The list of knife-wielding serial and sex murderers is a who's who of evil, headed naturally by Jack the Ripper, but including Peter Kurten, Heinrich Pommerencke ('The Beast of the Black Forest'), William Heirens, Ed Kemper, The Manson Gang, William McDonald ('The Sidney Mutilator'), Coral Watts ('The Sunday Morning Slasher'), Peter Sutcliffe ('The Yorkshire Ripper') – and a thousand others.

It might be pointed out that knifings committed by women are often of a frenzied nature, manifesting a great deal of pent-up anger. Nancy Lee Kantarian, the thirty-year-old daughter of American media tycoon John Heselden, stabbed her six-year-old daughter thirty-two times at the family home outside Washington DC in May 1984. The demands of motherhood had simply become too much and she 'got mad', and became uncontrollably murderous. Kantarian is far from an isolated example.

If in modern murder the knife tends to be used more in the heat of the moment than in premeditation, it continues to figure in planned murders on a 'needs must' basis. It is at least efficient – certainly more efficient than most of the killing means dreamed up by Edith Thompson and Frederick Bywaters (see Case File).

CASE FILE: Bywaters and Thompson

Just before midnight on the misty evening of 3 October 1922, the quiet gas-lit length of Belgrave Road in East London was pierced by a woman screaming. There was then a clatter of high-heeled shoes as the woman ran along the road to catch up with two startled pedestrians. Reaching them she gasped: 'Will you help me? My husband is ill. He is bleeding!'

The couple followed the woman as she hurried back along the street to the prostrate form of her husband. A doctor was summoned but by the time he arrived, the husband, Percy Thompson, was dead. Asked what had happened, the woman cried, 'Oh don't ask me. I don't know. Somebody flew past and when I turned to speak to him blood was pouring from his mouth.'

In fact, Edith Thompson knew very well who the assailant was and what had happened. Her lover, Frederick Bywaters, had just stabbed her husband to death.

Edith Thompson (née Graydon) was born in 1893, to a middle class family. From an early age she exhibited a head for figures, and before she was twenty she had become chief buyer for the City firm of Carlton and Prior, fabric importers, based within walking distance of the Old Bailey. She earned as much as £6 a week, a small fortune when the average white-collar wage was £3 10s. In January 1915 she married Percy Thompson, a shipping clerk in Eastcheap. It was an unsuitable match, for Edith was a thorough-going vivacious romantic, an avid reader of bodice-rippers, while he was dull and pedestrian. No doubt the fact that most of his peers were away fighting in World War I – he cheated service by making his heart race unnaturally through smoking fifty cigarettes a day before his call-up medical – helped his chances. Despite this, their marriage jogged along uneventfully until 1921.

In the summer of 1921 the Thompsons invited young Frederick ('Freddy') Edward Francis Bywaters to join them on their annual holiday on the Isle of Wight. Freddy, then aged eighteen, was a merchant seaman, the ship's clerk on the SS *Morea*. He was to be company for Edith's younger sister. But by the end of the holiday, he and Edith had become obsessed with each other. On 14 June they exchanged their first kiss. For her, Freddy was everything dull, routine Percy was not: virile, exciting, and the heroic survivor of several U-boat attacks.

Percy, unaware of the growing attraction between his 28-year-old spouse and young Freddy, invited the likeable merchant seaman to lodge with them at the Thompson home, 41 Kensington Gardens, Ilford. It was a three-cornered argument on 1 August which brought things out into the open. A disagreement between Percy and his wife about who should fetch a pin developed into a full-blown row, during which Percy threw his wife bodily across the room. It was Freddy who comforted the sobbing Edith. He also entreated Thompson to grant his wife a divorce. Thompson responded by asking him to leave the house. Freddy Bywaters moved into his mother's home four days later. Some time before he did so, the lovers consummated their affair, as may be inferred from one of Bywaters' letters to Edith:

> I do remember you coming to me in the little room and I think I understand what it cost you – alot more darlin[ges]t than it could ever now. When I think about that I think how nearly we came to be parted for ever. If you had not forfeited your pride darlint I don't think there would ever have been yesterday or tomorrow.

The little room was the one in which Bywaters lodged in the Kensington Gardens house.

For the next month, before Bywaters rejoined his ship, he met Edith every day, with parks, railway carriages and empty buildings doing the duty of 'the little room'.

During the next year Bywaters spent a total of eighty-four days in England in the intervals between his voyages in the SS *Morea*. When he was on leave they managed to see a great deal of each other, and while he was at sea 'Peidi' [his nickname for Edith] and Freddy kept up a copious correspondence – a correspondence which would eventually condemn them.

From the extant letters – all but two of which are from Edith to Freddy – it seems pretty certain that Percy knew of his wife's adulterous relationship. This, if anything, made him insist more frequently on his 'rights'. For her part she seems to have yielded, rather than cause a complete break.

In early 1922, however, Edith changed her mind about a complete break with her husband, and conceived a plan to murder him. Divorce was out of the question; not only would Percy not grant one, the scandal might cause her – and Bywaters – to lose their jobs. And she was determined to bind Freddy to her by marriage; which left, in her eyes, murder as the only viable option. Failing this, they were to commit suicide together. She began to correspond with Freddy about possible methods. In a letter of 10 February 1922 she writes: 'It would be so easy darlint – if I had things – I do hope I shall . . . Have enclosed cuttings of Dr Wallis's case. It might prove interesting.'

The cuttings, from the *Daily Sketch*, referred to a curate being poisoned by HYOSCINE.

Other letters indicate that she tried to poison Percy with ground GLASS, as well as slipping something 'with a bitter taste' into his tea. She tried to encourage Bywaters in her plan by sending him examples of characters in fiction who had got rid of an unwanted spouse. Sending Freddy a copy of the romantic novel *Bella Donna*, she carefully copied out the headnote to the novel: 'It must be remembered that digitalin [DIGITALIS] is a cumulative poison, and that the same dose, harmless if taken once, yet frequently repeated, becomes deadly.'

At the end of September 1922, Bywaters returned from a voyage to Australasia. He would never go to sea again. Matters were quickly moving to their climax. Freddy met Edith on a Friday evening, and they made love before she went home to Percy for the weekend. On the Sunday she wrote to Freddy, finishing the letter by informing him that her husband had insisted on sex; at least so she told Bywaters, perhaps to goad him into decisive action. Certainly, something happened that weekend which unleashed murder.

On Tuesday, 3 October Freddy and Edith met in a teashop, after which she went to the theatre with Percy. Freddy went to Edith's parents' home, where he was not only tolerated, but where his relationship with Edith was tacitly approved of.

Freddy left Edith's parents at about 11 p.m. and walked out into the mist towards his mother's house. He decided instead to intercept the Thompsons on their way home from the theatre, an idea which he said 'came across him all of a sudden'. It may have been an impulse, but what is certain is that in his pocket he carried a seaman's sheath knife and by about 11.40 p.m. he was hidden behind a privet hedge just off Belgrave Road.

When the Thompsons approached he jumped out, and pushed Edith out of the way. Bywaters then slashed and stabbed Thompson with the seaman's knife. Percy Thompson was cut slightly in four places on his left side below the ribs; there were also two superficial cuts on his chin, two deeper cuts on the right of his lower jaw, one on the inner right arm by the elbow, and two 2-in. stab-wounds in the back of the neck, one of which severed the carotid artery. Percy Thompson died, drowning in his own blood from ASPHYXIA.

Bywaters then fled, dumping the knife in a drain in Seymour Gardens.

Edith Thompson named her lover to the police next day, and both were charged with the murder of Percy Thompson.

They were tried at the Old Bailey in December 1922. Freddy's defence was a feeble one of self-defence, that Percy had threatened to shoot him, and that thinking he had a gun Freddy pulled out his knife. It was an unconvincing story. As the judge, Mr Justice Shearman, pointed out, Bywaters had gone out of his way at a very late hour to intercept the Thompsons; it was hardly an impulse. A seaman's sheath knife is moreover a largeish, non-folding knife, not easy to carry about in the everyday civilian run of things. There was no evidence that Bywaters carried it as a matter of course. Most telling of all was that Bywaters had stabbed Thompson in the *back* of the neck *twice*.

The case against Edith Thompson was that it was she who had incited Bywaters to commit the deed. Bywaters denied that she had done so, as did Edith herself. Edith also tried to explain the talk in her letters of poisoning her husband as mere fancy, a claim borne out to a degree by the evidence of pathologist Bernard Spilsbury, who found no trace of glass or poisonous substance in Percy Thompson's body. Whether or not Edith was a guilty party in her husband's murder remains a controversial question. The letters, though, read out in court were damning. More damning still was Edith herself, who decided against the advice of her counsel, Sir Henry Curtis-Bennett, to take the witness stand. Her vanity and sexuality were obvious, and she made the tactical mistake of throwing Freddy – who had done the decent thing in trying to shield her – to the wolves. The judge, who made little secret of his dislike of the adulterous Edith, reminded the jury they were 'trying a vulgar, common crime', and dismissed the letters as 'full of the outpourings of a silly but at the same time wicked affection'.

On Monday, 11 December both the accused were found guilty. After sentence was passed Mrs Thompson cried: 'I'm not guilty! Oh, God, I'm not guilty.'

Despite many protests, the verdict was upheld. On 9 January 1923, Edith Thompson was dragged from her cell in Holloway Prison in a drugged stupor and hanged by John Ellis. At the same time, Frederick Bywaters was hanged by Thomas Pierrepoint at Pentonville.

CASE FILE: The Foxes in the Wood

The exposure of private lives and suburban adultery in the Thompson & Bywaters case made it a source of fascination to the public in the 1920s. A whiff of similar sexual scandal emanated from the so-called 'Foxes in the Wood' murder in 1992, another occasion on which a knife would be used to end a marriage.

As Sandra Quartermaine would later acknowledge, marrying Robert Wignall was the biggest mistake of her life. The two of them met in the autumn of 1990, while they were walking their dogs in woods near Addlestone, in suburban Surrey. By a nasty twist of fate – and a knife – Robert Wignall would meet his end in those very same woods on 5 September 1992.

At the time of their marriage on Christmas Eve 1991, Sandra Wignall, as she now was, was forty-six, Robert was fifty-three. Apart from a mutual like of dog-walking, the couple were ill matched. She found that he restricted her freedom, and that their 'sex life was not so active because of his asthma'. Within nine days of her marriage to Robert, Sandra Wignall had resumed an affair with Terry Bewley, a 41-year-old chauffeur. In fact, Sandra Wignall, it might fairly be said, was obsessed with Terry Bewley. They regularly had sex in the back of Rolls Royce cars in garages where he worked; at his behest she also had sex with other men in his presence.

At some point in the late summer of 1992 Mrs Wignall decided that her husband had to go. If one motive was lust for Terry Bewley, the other was greed. Robert Wignall had taken out a life insurance worth £21,000 to his widow. Mr Bewley – by now out of work – had debts of £21,500.

On 5 September 1992, after just nine months of marriage, Sandra Wignall lured her husband into the woods behind their home on the pretext of 'watching the foxes'. Once there, she lulled him into a false sense of security by performing oral sex on him. As oral sex took place, Terry Bewley and a friend, Harold Moult, came up upon Robert and stabbed him three times in the torso with a kitchen knife. Two of the stab wounds penetrated his heart, killing him. One of the men also hit Robert Wignall around the head with a bough of wood.

Sandra Wignall later claimed that the killing was perpetrated by three youths, who had pounced on her husband in an unprovoked attack. In fact, three youths had witnessed two men – Bewley and Moult – hurrying away from the scene of the crime. Mrs Wignall's story was further undermined by her unwidowly post-murder happiness, and her incautious – and excited – talking to neighbours about how she was going to spend her husband's insurance.

The choice of murder weapon in the 'Foxes in the Wood' case was not only dictated by its availability. If Bewley and Sandra Wignall were to successfully pass off the killing of Robert Wignall as the work of delinquent youths, they had to use the staple weapon of delinquent youth: the knife. It was unfortunate for them that some of the youth they were trying to incriminate were there to witness their bloody work.

M

MERCURY

Sometimes called 'quicksilver', mercury was known to the Egyptians as early as 1550BC. Roman alchemists named the liquid natural element after their most wily and fleet-footed of gods, and in the 17th century it was carried by the vial as a guard against rheumatism. The English writer Woodal described it well when he wrote of mercury in 1639: 'It is the hottest, the coldest, a true healer, a wicked murderer, a precious medicine and a deadly poison . . .'

In its liquid metal form, mercury is relatively harmless if ingested, although its vapour is poisonous. In 1515, when the Margrave of Brandenburg 'overheated on his marriage night with love and wine and, rising to quench his thirst, drank by mistake a large draught of quicksilver' he suffered no harm. But the various soluble compounds of mercury are extremely dangerous. The most commonly encountered of them is mercuric chloride or corrosive submilate. About fifteen grains will cause severe burning and swelling of the mouth, and death from heart failure in as little as an hour. When it was freely accessible to the public it was sometimes the choice of suicide. In 1941, for instance, there were 130 British suicides by mercuric chloride.

Homicidal poisoning by mercuric chloride was commonplace in bygone centuries. It was, for instance, used in the murder of homosexual poet Sir Thomas Overbury in 1613. Overbury had been thrown into the Tower as the victim of a plot between his former lover Robert Carr, and Carr's mistress, Lady Frances Howard. Not content with the imprisonment of her old rival, Lady Frances thought Overbury should die, preferably from some wasting illness which could be blamed on the dampness of the dungeons. Through an intermediary, Lady Frances and Carr approached apothecary James Franklin, who in turn handed over vials of mercuric chloride, ARSENIC, powdered GLASS and CANTHARIDIN. To administer these poisons to Overbury was easy; the murderous duo used their influence to get a personal retainer, Richard Weston, appointed as Overbury's personal attendant. For three months Overbury was given these poisons in his food, until he died, severely emaciated and weakened, in September. A jury declared that his death was due to natural causes – chronic mercury poisoning leads to anaemia, kidney failure and palsy – and he was buried with haste.

Lady Frances and Robert Carr married soon after. Unfortunately for them, however, the apothecary's assistant who made up the poisons confessed to a priest. King James I ordered the arrest of everyone involved and their execution. Robert Carr – a sometime lover of the King – and Lady Frances were spared their lives, serving six years in the Tower instead. Afterwards, the couple, who had by now come to hate each other, were obliged to retire to their country home.

Other homicidal employers of mercury salts include France's Marquise de Brinvilliers, who poisoned her way through 100 family members, friends and total strangers from c1650 to 1676 (although her preferred toxin was ARSENIC). In 1898, Roland B. Molineaux of New York's Knickerbocker Club doctored Bromo Selzer with mercuric cyanide, killing two, while in a rare 20th century mercury poisoning case, Marseilles' Dr Bougrat injected a wealthy patient with an overdose of Novarsurol, an anti-syphilitic drug based on mercuric chloride, before polishing him off with CYANIDE.

MORPHINE
The most powerful of the narcotics derived from opium, the dried juice of the white Indian poppy, *Papapaver somniferum*. It was first isolated by the German chemist Friedrich Sertuner in 1806. Just seventeen years later, morphine was used in a murder, the killing of Hippolyte and Auguste Ballet by Parisian doctor Edme Castaing.

A fatal dose of the drug varies from person to person, but about three grains usually cause the respiratory system to fail within a few hours. The symptoms are drowsiness and a drop in body temperature before the victim enters coma. Convulsions may occur before death. One of the most distinctive characteristics of morphine poisoning is the pin-point contraction of the pupils of the eyes.

Naturally, the symptoms of opium poisoning are the same, though raw opium has never been popular in poisonous circles even though it was readily available – it could after all be found in any 'den' frequented by Chinese sailors, who smoked it as a soporific. Moreover, the Victorian Age's favourite panacea, laudanum, was composed of opium dissolved in alcohol. The draw-back to opium as a killing-agent seems to have been its distinctive smell and slow action. The only opium murder of any note took place in Edinburgh in 1877, when alcoholic teacher Eugene Marie Chantrelle poisoned his wife with the drug, and tried to make the death appear accidental by filling the bedroom with coal gas. A trace of opium in the dead woman's vomit gave him away.

Morphine, a white crystalline powder, easily soluble and quickly lethal, was altogether more suitable as a means to murder. Nor was it a coincidence that it was first used homicidally by a doctor. In mild doses the drug has a beneficial use as an analgesic (it would be widely used on the battlefields of World War I), and physicians soon carried it around in their bags as a matter of course. The medical profession's easy access to morphine doubtless explains their dominance on the list of morphine killers.

In 1890, Carlyle Harris was a New York medical student, the grandson of a famous professor of medicine. He had sexual designs on nineteen-year-old Helen Potts, and married her secretly on 8 February. Her mother, horrified to find her daughter married, insisted that Harris make a proper announcement. This Harris did not want to do, fearing his grandfather's wrath. Instead he paid particular attention to three lectures by toxicologist Dr George L. Peabody on morphine overdose, and how it was – supposedly – impossible to detect.

Harris then stole enough morphine from his college dispensary to kill his wife. He also made out a prescription to a chemist for six sleeping capsules. As a matter of course, these contained a small amount – one-sixth of a grain – of morphine, together with several grains of quinine. Harris doctored one of the capsules, removing its contents and filling it with five grains of morphine. He gave the capsules to his wife, instructing her to take one before retiring each night. On 31 January 1891, the girl complained of feeling ill, and she died the next day. The doctor called in noticed a contraction of the pupils of her eyes. At the inquest, the coroner ruled that Helen had died accidentally; either the pharmacy had made a mistake in the prescription, or the girl had taken too many of the prescribed capsules. Harris's method showed some ingenuity; he had even kept back a couple of capsules, to show that there was nothing wrong with them, making an overdose seem the most likely cause of death.

Two months later, the *New York World* newspaper published an exposé of Harris's gambling and sexual behaviour. As a result, Helen Potts' body was exhumed, and the toxicologist Dr Rudolph Witthaus found morphine in all the organs. Carlyle Harris was charged with murder.

His trial became a battle between medical experts over the degree to which morphine poisoning could be proved. An acquittal was widely expected. Instead, the jury – swayed mostly by circumstantial evidence – found Harris guilty. He died in the electric chair at Sing Sing on 8 May 1893.

At around the very moment Harris was being electrocuted in 'Old Sparky' at Sing Sing, another New Yorker, Dr Robert Buchanan, was boasting to a saloon full of people that *he* could perpetrate a murder by morphine and it would be undetectable (see Case File). Harris, he said, was a 'stupid amateur'.

CASE FILE: Dr Robert Buchanan

Robert Buchanan was a successful physician with a wealthy practice. Like a later murdering doctor, Dr Bougrat of Marseilles, Buchanan tired of his middle class wife and looked for excitement in the local red-light district. In 1890 he fell for an obese madame called Anna Sutherland, and divorced his wife so that he could marry her. It was probably not just sex that attracted him. Anna Sutherland was rumoured to have made a fortune from her bordellos. In the spring of 1892 the new Mrs Buchanan fell ill, and when she died shortly afterwards, the cause was certified as a brain haemorrhage. Buchanan became richer by $50,000, and sailed off to Europe.

In Buchanan's absence, friends of Anna Sutherland – among them a financially disappointed former suitor – started voicing suspicions about her death. Initially the medical examiner refused to reopen the case, pointing out that morphine poisoning could not have been responsible for Anna Sutherland's demise as there was no pin-pointing of the eyes. But then the *New York World* started campaigning for a reconsidered verdict, even persuading the New York coroner to write a column in favour of a fresh investigation; reluctantly, the medical examiner agreed to an exhumation and a second post-mortem. This was carried out by Professor Witthaus, who had also been brought in to the Harris case, and he found that the body contained $1/110$ of a grain of morphine in the remains, which he estimated was the residue of a fatal dose of five or six grains.

But why had there been no tell-tale pin-pointing of the victim's eyes? The answer came out in court. Witnesses for the prosecution said that when Buchanan had referred to Harris as a 'stupid amateur' he had gone on to claim that a few drops of belladonna, the active constituent of which is ATROPINE, would permanently halt the pin-point symptoms. The nurse who had attended Mrs Buchanan confirmed that the doctor had put drops into his wife's eyes for no apparent reason. The prosecution then conducted a bizarre experiment in court, in which a cat was administered a fatal dose of morphine, and as it lay dying drops of belladonna were applied to its eyes to prove its effectiveness in stopping the pin-point process. In turn the defence showed that the colour reaction tests used by Dr Witthaus to identify the presence of morphine were not infallible. At this point, Dr Buchanan elected to enter the witness box in his own defence. Arrogant and evasive, he made a poor impression. And so ended up in the chair at Sing Sing, so recently occupied by the 'bungler' Carlyle Harris.

Not that the line of medical morphine-killers ended with Buchanan. In England, Dr Robert Clements found morphine the best agent for an inexpensive divorce from his fourth wife in 1947. When his crime was discovered he took his own life with a morphine overdose. Ten years later, Dr John Bodkin Adams of Eastbourne 'eased the passing' of a number of his elderly patients by judicious use of morphine and heroin (another narcotic derived from opium, introduced by Dresser in 1874 as a means of treating morphine addiction). Though Adams benefited much from the wills of the deceased (including receiving two Rolls Royces), and the policeman leading the case thought him 'guilty as hell', he was acquitted of murder at his Old Bailey trial. The outcome was widely seen as a personal triumph for the defence lawyer, Geoffrey Lawrence QC. John Bodkin Adams died in 1983, aged eighty-four. His estate was valued at over £400,000.

An equally celebrated English morphine poisoning case took place some years before, in 1935, and for a change it did not involve a male doctor. That time the killer descended in the guise of a female nurse, an angel of death (see Case File).

CASE FILE: Death's Angel

The entry of Dorothy Waddingham into the world was as unprepossessing as her departure from it would be. She was born in 1899 to a poor farming family in Hucknall, a village north of Nottingham, and attended the village school without distinction. Afterwards she worked in a local factory, before swopping this drudgery for the job of a ward maid at the Burton-on-Trent Infirmary. While Dorothea – as she now called herself – was working there she met and married Thomas Leech, a man almost twice her age. In 1930, with their three young children, the Leeches moved to Nottingham, where Thomas Leech succumbed to cancer of the throat three years later. Before he died, Dorothy had decided that she would make her way in the world by opening the Waddingham Nursing Home. She also styled herself 'Nurse' though she was not entitled to. Her partner in this venture was Ronald Sullivan, Tom Leech's friend, and a man closer to Dorothea's age.

The first Waddingham Nursing Home for the Elderly was the Leeches' house in Haydn Road, Sherwood. When Thomas Leech died in June 1933, 'Nurse' Waddingham and Ronald Sullivan moved to 32 Devon Drive, Nottingham. Before long there was another mouth to feed – baby Ronald, for Dorothea Waddingham and Ronald Sullivan had become lovers. To drum up business for the nursing home, Waddingham advertised for patients in the local newspaper.

Among those who saw the advertisement was Miss Winifred Blagg, the honorary secretary of the County Nursing Association. On the afternoon of 5 January 1935 Miss Blagg knocked on the door of the Waddingham Nursing Home. As Dorothea was out, it was the handyman-lover Ronald who answered. The Home had come to the favourable attention of the Association, Miss Blagg was pleased to say (that is to say, it was cheap), and she wondered if there was room for two new patients, ninety-year-old Mrs Louisa Baguley and her crippled fifty-year-old daughter, Ada. There was.

For some months everything went well. Then Dorothea decided that the £3 a week the Baguleys paid for their care was not enough. She was frequently heard grumbling about such little return for looking after two infirm patients: 'They would have to pay five guineas for no better treatment in hospital; which is really the place for them.' Dorothea's moaning became worse when her only other patient, a Miss Kemp, died; Dorothea, Ronald Sullivan and four children now had to exist on the £3 a week income from the Baguleys alone. Dorothea decided something drastic had to be done.

She began to threaten the Baguleys with eviction unless they made over their savings to her. These, as Dorothea well knew, comprised a £500 conversion loan, £120 in the bank, and £1000 which Ada had inherited from her father. The Baguleys were desperate to avoid an upheaval which might well lead to the workhouse. So, on 7 May 1935 Ada Baguley compromised and made out a new will, by which all her property was settled on Nurse Waddingham and Sullivan, in return for the 'consideration they have undertaken to look after me and my mother for and during our joint lives'.

Within a week Mrs Louisa Baguley was dead. 'Cardiac muscular degeneration', wrote Dr George Herbert Manfield on the death certificate. She was laid to rest in the earth of Caunton churchyard.

For the first time in her life, Ada was alone. Not that Nurse Waddingham intended to let her suffer for long. On 10 September, Ada had a visit from Mrs Briggs, an old friend. They sat in the garden at the Waddingham Nursing Home, enjoying the last of the summer sun and eating chocolate drops that Mrs Briggs had brought from her little confectioner's shop in Alfred Street. At 4 p.m., with fond farewells, Mrs Briggs left.

At 2 a.m. the next morning Ada Baguley went into a coma. By 10 a.m. she was dead. Dr Manfield carried out an external examination and wrote on the death certificate: 'Cerebral haemorrhage due to cardio-vascular degeneration.' In other words, a stroke.

Nurse Waddingham wasted no time in arranging for Ada's body to be cremated, showing Dr Manfield a letter purportedly written by the dead woman, claiming: 'I desire to be cremated at my death for health's sake, and it is my wish to remain with the nurse, and my last wish is my relatives shall not know of my death.' In fact the note had been penned by Ronald Sullivan who had also witnessed it.

Cremation in the 1930s was unusual; less than 1 per cent of deaths received them. Although kindly and trusting Dr Manfield signed the cremation certificate without a scintilla of suspicion, it caused a considerable flicker of doubt when it landed up on the desk of Dr Cyril Banks, Medical Officer for Nottingham and the crematorium referee. Quite apart from the letter's strange wording

– 'my last wish is my relatives shall not know of my death' – Dr Banks happened to know that the address on the letter was not, as it said, a 'registered' nursing home.

Dr Banks informed Wilfred Rothera, the Nottingham City Coroner, who ordered an immediate post-mortem examination. After ten days' investigation, 2.59 grains of morphine were found in Ada Baguley's stomach, 0.37 grains in the spleen and kidneys, 0.14 grains in the liver, and 0.092 grains in the heart. A quite lethal dose of 3.192 grains in total. Since the body breaks morphine down relatively quickly, the Home Office analyst, Dr Roche Lynch was able to state that the original dose, administered by mouth, must have been much higher.

Ada Baguley had died of morphine poisoning. Inevitably, this led to suspicion that her mother had died from the same cause. Mrs Baguley's remains were exhumed on 30 September, and the autopsy was carried out by Dr Lynch – who found that Mrs Baguley too had died of morphine poisoning.

On 14 February 1936, Dorothea Waddingham and Ronald Sullivan were put on trial before Mr Justice Goddard. In an unusual departure from his role as defender, Norman Birkett KC led for the prosecution. On 26 February, Mr Justice Goddard instructed the jury to formally acquit Ronald Sullivan, as there was no direct evidence against him, leaving Dorothea Waddingham alone in the dock. In the proceeding against her a conflict of testimony soon became apparent: her defence was that she had only given her patients morphine tablets as prescribed by Dr Manfield. Manfield was adamant that 'I never gave them, I never prescribed them.' There was little doubt as to whom the jury would believe. And by admitting administering morphine – no matter who prescribed it – Waddingham incriminated herself. If she had said nothing, it would almost certainly have been impossible to prove who was responsible for the administration of the morphine. As it was, and despite a strong recommendation for mercy from the jury which found her guilty, Nurse Waddingham walked to the gallows at Birmingham's Winsom Green Prison on the morning of 16 April 1936.

MUMMIFICATION

Knowledge of mummification dates back to ancient Egypt, where it was found that the INTERRING of bodies in the hot desert sands caused them to become dried out and preserved in a 'life-like' state. Such an arrestation of the natural process of putrefaction can also occur in temperate climes with the right environmental conditions.

The commonest instances of mummification are those of unwanted babies, hidden in drawers or at the back of airing cupboards. It is not only their small size which makes babies suitable for the process; a new-born baby's alimentary system contains few bacteria to initiate decomposition.

Adult mummification is invariably by accident and not design, and examples of it are few and far between. In 1935, pathologist Sir Bernard Spilsbury was called into to examine a mummified body, wrapped up in a curtain and tied with electric flex, found in the coal-cellar of a Southwark public house. Seven years later, while examining the shallow-buried corpse of Joan Wolfe in the 'Wig Wam Murder Case' at Hankley Common, Home Office pathologist Keith Simpson noted that parts of her body were undergoing mummification. More celebrated than either of these cases, though, was the desiccated corpse found in a cupboard at an address in Rhyl, North Wales, in 1960.

While his mother was in hospital, Leslie Harvey decided to redecorate her house as a 'welcome home' surprise. The surprise was on Leslie Harvey when he prised open the landing cupboard, which had been locked and out of bounds since he was a boy. To his horror, Leslie Harvey was confronted with a human mummy . . .

The authorities were called in, and the pathologist who examined the doubled-up leathery body described it as hard as stone – the whole corpse had been preserved naturally by the warm air circulating around the cupboard, gradually drying out its human contents. Because the mummification conditions were so perfect, there had been no tell-tale odour of decomposition.

Mrs Sarah Harvey, the police decided, needed to do some explaining, especially when the post-mortem revealed a suspicious-looking groove on the side of the corpse's neck. According to Mrs Harvey, the body in the cupboard belonged to a Mrs Knight, a semi-invalid who had boarded with her in 1939. During the autumn of that year, Mrs Knight had dropped down dead and Mrs Harvey, not knowing what to do, had hidden the body in the cupboard. And there it had stayed, mummifying nicely.

Mrs Harvey's trial for murder was a half-hearted affair, in which the prosecution could give no substantial evidence of STRANGU-LATION. Neither the thyroid cartilage nor the hyoid bone of the corpse appeared to have been fractured as would be expected in such a death. Mrs Harvey was acquitted of murder. However, she was found guilty of fraud, because for twenty years she had been drawing the dead woman's pension. She was sentenced to fifteen months' imprisonment.

The only other well-known British mummification occurred seventeen years later at Rochdale in Yorkshire (see Case File) . . .

CASE FILE: The Rochdale Mummy

Most killers who murder at home like to remove the body as

quickly as possible after the act. Sometimes this is done bit by bit following DISMEMBERMENT; more usually, the body is sneaked out whole at night. Occasionally – as with Mrs Harvey – those finding a body on their hands decide to dispose of it in a cupboard as a long-term solution. John Reginald Christie, after gassing Hectorina MacLennan, Kathleen Maloney and Rita Nelson with CARBON MONOXIDE, fitted all three of them into a wall cupboard in the kitchen at 10 Rillington Place. New tenant Mr Beresford Brown uncovered the corpses by following his nose. A fainter but equally vile smell from under the floorboards in the front room revealed the remains of Mrs Christie.

The CYANIDE crime of Marseilles' Dr Bougrat was also betrayed by its stench, which refused to be contained by the papered-over cavity in his waiting-room. Although London serial-killer Dennis Nilsen eventually disposed of most of his victims by BURNING, some he kept under floorboards for up to seven months. Terrified of loneliness, Nilsen needed the corpses handy so that they would provide him with company. But any longer than seven months and the smell of decomposition became too overpowering, the bodies too far putrefied to be propped up in the armchair of an evening.

More successful at keeping the corpse around the house was a Mrs Eileen Finlay. The courts may not have viewed her actions as homicide, but the case of the Rochdale Mummy does highlight the problems of home disposal, as well as provide an insight into the means by which forensic science can identify the desiccated deceased.

On 8 March 1977, a woman and her two daughters noticed a wire shopping trolley containing a large bundle in the refuse area behind a block of flats in Ashfield Valley, Rochdale. A male resident saw the trolley on 10 March, but avoided going near it because of its vile smell. Three days later, the caretaker, noticing the trolley, poked the sack-like bundle on it. It seemed to be a mixture of sand and cement. He arranged for the Cleansing Department to take the trolley away, and the refuse cart arrived on the 14th. The two council workers detailed for the job gave the trolley a hefty push across the concrete floor towards their collection vehicle . . . at which point the trolley struck a piece of wood and toppled over, revealing a partially mummified body.

The corpse's head was covered by a plastic bag enclosing millions of maggots and mites (the caretaker's 'sand and cement'), which had picked the face clean, rendering facial identification impossible. However, the skin of the trunk and legs had mummified, as had the internal organs. From the preserved liver it was discovered that the corpse had died of BARBITURATE poisoning; specifically, an overdose of Amytal.

Having discovered how he had died, the police needed to know who the Rochdale Mummy was. The hands, which, like the feet, had been bound together, were in an advanced stage of decay. This would have ruled out fingerprint identification, except for some clever work by Inspector Tony Fletcher of the Manchester fingerprint bureau. Not long before the Rochdale Mummy was discovered, Fletcher had taken part in an experiment at Manchester Museum's Egyptology Department to find a way of fingerprinting archaeological mummies. The traditional roll-and-ink method was impossible because of the fragility of the ancient fingers. Fletcher solved the problem by gently applying a fine-grain, quick-drying dental cement to the fingertips, which was left to set. The 'mould' was then taken off and given several coats of black acrylic paint. When the acrylic paint had dried it gave a cast which could be inked and printed in the usual manner.

Inspector Fletcher now applied the same technique to the one digit – the right middle finger – on the Rochdale corpse which might possibly yield a print.

It did. Furthermore it showed a sixteen-point similarity with prints already on file. Those of James Edward Finlay.

Finlay, the police soon established, had been born in Southport in 1943. He had married for the first time at the age of twenty, but had divorced six years later. Not long afterwards, he met Eileen Willan, who bore him a daughter in 1971, just before the couple moved to Rochdale, where Finlay had taken a job with R & T Howarth, a local builders. Finlay and Eileen married in 1974, shortly after which Eileen had given birth to a son. In February 1975, the Finlays were granted the tenancy of a council flat at 28 Buttermere, in the Ashfield Valley area of Rochdale.

When police officers spoke to Finlay's employers they found he had last collected his wages on 29 August 1975. A check with the local council revealed that Mrs Finlay had been served with an order to quit the flat at No 28 Buttermere because of rent arrears. She had handed in the keys on 1 March 1977.

Eileen Finlay was interviewed. She insisted that the body found in the refuse area of the flats adjacent to Buttermere was not her husband, because he had left her nearly two years previously. Informed that the body definitely was that of James Finlay, she changed her story . . .

Some time towards the end of August 1975 she and James Finlay had been arguing. During the altercation he had hit her, and then, in a fit of remorse and desperation, had threatened to kill himself. Tired of his violence, Eileen had thrown him a bottle of sodium amytal tablets and shouted 'Bloody well get on with it then.' After which, she had stormed out of the flat, returning some three hours later, to find James Finlay dead.

There was the small matter of what she had done with the corpse. For some reason that was never properly explained, she had then bound the hands and feet of the corpse together (difficult to achieve alone), before putting a carrier bag over his head so that she would not have to look at his face. She had then pushed the body into the airing cupboard, where it had remained until the March 1977 eviction order had made it necessary for it to be moved elsewhere. Namely, the refuse area at the neighbouring block of flats.

Although there was some doubt as to whether Eileen Finlay was a totally innocent party in her husband's death, there was no real evidence on which to bring a serious charge. Instead she was tried on and convicted of two obscure and medieval charges: concealing a body which had died from unnatural causes and so preventing a coroner from doing his statutory duty; and not giving a corpse a decent Christian burial. She was sentenced to two two-year prison sentences.

MUSHROOMS   *See* **FUNGI**

N

NICOTINE

The tobacco plant, *Nicotiana tabacum*, was introduced into Europe in 1561 by the Spanish, who had observed the Red Indians of the New World smoking it. The new import was first landed at Lisbon, where the French ambassador, Jean Nicot, took an interest in the discovery and introduced it to France, where its medicinal uses in the treatment of eczema and palsy became associated with his name. When the active poison in tobacco was isolated in 1823, it was likewise called after the ambassador.

Nicotine is a violently powerful alkaloid poison, a pale yellowish oil at room temperature, which can kill within minutes if ingested. Perhaps only hydrocyanic acid (CYANIDE) and some animal toxins act more rapidly. Less than one grain can induce a fatal paralysis of the respiratory system. It is also soluble in water and is readily absorbed by the skin.

The initial effect of nicotine on the human body is that of a stimulant, but taken in oral overdose it produces a burning sensation in the mouth, oesophagus and stomach respectively. Vomiting and nausea follow, then convulsions, unconsciousness and death. The amount of nicotine – which, in addition to its other qualities, is addictive – in a cigarette is enough to kill an adult if injected. The smoker, however, only absorbs enough of the drug to become slightly stimulated, as most of the nicotine goes up in smoke. Children have died from sucking at the brown deposits left in old tobacco pipes.

For some years nicotine was used in agricultural insecticides. Accidental skin contact with, or inhalation of, the nicotine-based spray resulted in the deaths of scores of farmworkers. Suicides drank the insecticide. It has now been withdrawn from use.

CASE FILE: Hippolyte de Bocarme

Homicidal nicotine poisoning is a rare occurrence. An early and ingenious case took place in Belgium in the middle of the 19th century, the outcome of which was not only a corpse but the first successful detection of a vegetable poison.

The marriage of Comte Hippolyte de Bocarme and Lydie Fougnies was a match made in hell. Alleged by the local peasants to have been suckled by a lioness, de Bocarme had been a wild child, and on succeeding to his father's title in 1843 had done nothing to modify his behaviour. A drunk, gambler, crook and inveterate womanizer, he married Lydie Fougnies in the belief that her father, a Mons apothecary, was wealthy enough to bail him out of trouble. Lydie Fougnies, who only married the Comte for his title, also hoped for a substantial inheritance from her father. They were both disappointed when the old man died, for what little he left went to Lydie's brother, Gustave.

There was still some hope, however. Gustave was wealthy and unmarried, and if he died childless Lydie would be the beneficiary. Even better, a recent leg amputation seemed as though it might hasten Gustave's end.

But the de Bocarmes saw their future crumble when Gustave suddenly announced that he was about to marry. They decided that he had to be prevented from such a disastrous – for them – course of action.

On 20 November 1850, the de Bocarmes invited Gustave to dine with them at their chateau. In the middle of the meal, the kitchen servants were summoned to the dining-room to be told by Lydie 'Gustave has fallen ill – I think he is dead . . .' Extraordinary scenes then followed as the Comte ordered vinegar to be brought, which he poured down the throat of the prostrate Gustave through a funnel. When this failed to revive him, as it was allegedly intended to do, de Bocarme ordered a servant to strip off all Gustave's clothes and wash the body in vinegar. The Comtess herself took the washing to the laundry, and put it in boiling water. Later in the night, the servants could hear their master and mistress scrubbing and scraping the dining-room floor.

News of Gustave Fougnies' strange death reached the authorities, who arrived at the chateau in the form of an Examining Magistrate and three doctors. Despite de Bocarme's insistence that his brother-in-law had died of apoplexy, the doctors were suspicious of the signs of corrosive burning in the dead man's mouth and throat. After a post-mortem the doctors decided that he had swallowed a caustic substance, most probably ACID. The magistrate placed the de Bocarmes under arrest, and the contents of Gustave Fougnies' stomach were sent to Jean Servais Stas, Professor of Chemistry at the Ecole Royale Militaire in Brussels.

Stas immediately noted the smell of vinegar in the stomach contents. When told that vinegar had been poured down the dead man's throat, he became convinced that this had been done to mask some other smell. To determine what, Stas set about mixing some of the stomach contents – which had been preserved in alcohol – with water, and filtering and distilling the result. Body substances are soluble in water or alcohol, but not in both. Therefore, he reasoned, any body substances which passed through the filter with alcohol would be caught by water, and vice versa. The result would be a near pure solution of the poison used.

After repeated distillation the professor's keen nose thought it could detect the mousey smell of coniine, the HEMLOCK derivative. But more distillation produced a stronger smell: tobacco.

The problem Stas now faced was how to separate the poison from the liquid distillate. Acting on a hunch, he treated the distillate with ether. After a while the ether, being lighter than water, separated out on top of the water, taking with it the brownish colouring which smelled of tobacco. Stas carefully poured off the excess ether, leaving the remainder in a dish to evaporate away. He was left with a quantity of a pale, oily liquid which smelled of tobacco. A series of chemical tests confirmed that the oil was nicotine. Stas reported the result to the police.

Subsequent investigation by the Belgian police revealed the truly elaborate nature of de Bocarme's murder plot. A keen student of agricultural sciences, he had heard that nicotine was deadly and knew that vegetable poisons were undetectable. So he had grown tobacco leaves in a corner of the chateau garden, and then distilled from them a quantity of nicotine. The coachman divulged that his master had visited a professor of chemistry in Ghent, with whom de Bocarme (having given a pseudonym) had discussed the problems of nicotine extraction. De Bocarme's laboratory apparatus was discovered hidden behind some wall panelling in the wash-house. Buried in the garden were the remains of various dead animals which de Bocarme had tested his concoction on.

Gustave Fougnies, the police reasoned from the evidence, must have been seized from behind and thrown to the floor; then as he was held down by de Bocarme, his sister – de Bocarme's wife – must have poured the poison down his throat, until he lost consciousness. Some of the liquid must have splashed on to the floor, hence the de Bocarmes' frantic scrubbing of it. (Even so, Stas was able to later find traces of the poison there.)

The Comte, the amateur chemist, then made the mistake which cost him his life. To disguise the smell of the nicotine he poured vinegar into the dead man's mouth. Vinegar (acetic acid) combines with nicotine to form a powerful corrosive, causing the burns which had made the doctors and magistrate suspicious. To prove the point Stas carried out experiments with two dogs, poisoning them both with nicotine, but only putting vinegar into the mouth of one. Only this dog developed acid burns.

At the de Bocarmes' trial, the Comtess insisted that she had been forced into the murder by her husband; she was acquitted. Her husband went to the guillotine at Mons on 19 July 1851. 'I hope the blade is sharp,' he said as he put his head on the block.

The method of detecting vegetable poisons in which he unintentionally assisted Jean Servais Stas is still in use.

P

PARAQUAT

Paraquat is a modern weedkiller which is composed of dimethyl bipyridilium, and is available as a concentrate (Gramoxone) or as a weaker granulated preparation (Weedol). Although the fashion for homicidal poisoning is in decline, a number of those intent on this method have opted for paraquat, despite restrictions on its use to those professionally engaged in farming or horticulture. Meanwhile, suicidal ingestion of the poison has increased appreciably since the 1960s.

Death has occurred from a dose as low as 5 ml of Gramoxone concentrate. Symptoms include convulsions, painful inflammation and ulceration of the mouth and mucous membranes, followed by renal and hepatic failure. The poison is then taken up by the lung tissue, causing haemorrhaging, oedema and fibrosis. It is the consequent respiratory failure which kills the victim. The quickest paraquat death on record occurred in a victim who died two hours after swallowing a pint of Gramoxone; the longest surviving victim was a man who lived for 104 days after taking the poison.

CASE FILE: Steak and Kidney Pie

It was a classic scene of marital betrayal that greeted Michael Barber when he returned home unexpectedly from a fishing trip on Saturday, 31 May 1981. His wife Susan was naked in the bedroom with his fellow darts-team member, Richard Collins. Barber beat his 28-year-old wife across the side of the head, and threw Collins out. In fact, Susan and Richard had been lovers for nearly two years before they were so rudely interrupted, with Richard Collins – who lived with his parents three doors away – entering the Barbers' bed every weekday morning after Michel Barber left for his job as a packer in the Rothmans cigarette factory at Basildon, Essex.

The following Tuesday the Barbers consulted their GP about the painful bruise on Susan's ear, and confessed their marital problems. Susan said that she was willing to try and preserve the marriage. The doctor suggested counselling. Although he did not know it, Michael Barber would not need counselling for very long.

On 4 June 1981, while at the factory, Michael Barber developed a severe headache, then throat and stomach pains. By 16 June, he was having difficulty in breathing and was taken by ambulance to Southend General Hospital, where the following day, gravely ill, he was admitted to the intensive care unit. Doctors first diagnosed pneumonia and then a rare nervous condition known as Goodpasture's Syndrome. On Wednesday, 17 June he was transmitted to the Hammersmith Hospital in West London, where he died on 27 June. A death certificate was issued giving the causes of 35-year-old Barber's demise as cardiac arrest, renal failure and bilateral pneumonia.

But his illness and death had puzzled the staff at Hammersmith Hospital, one of whom suspected poisoning and ordered specimens of Barber's blood and urine to be tested for paraquat at the National Poisons Unit at New Cross Hospital. An autopsy was carried out and the pathologist, Professor David Evans, was uncomfortable about the apparent cause of death and preserved the major organs in a bucket of formalin, which was placed in the mortuary ante-room. However, when doctors asked for the results of the tests for paraquat from the National Poisons Hospital, they were informed that these had excluded the presence of paraquat. And there the matter of Michael Barber's demise rested.

Meanwhile, life looked good for Susan Barber. Michael's employers granted her a death benefit of £15,000, an £800 refund of her husband's pension contributions and £300 a year for each of her three children. Richard Collins had moved in with her the night of Michael Barber's funeral, but had since been usurped by a number of lovers. Susan Barber spent part of the death benefit on a CB radio, and used the call-sign 'Nympho' to contact additional paramours, becoming something of a local celebrity.

But, unknown to Susan Barber, the mystery of her husband's death had been resurrected. In September 1981, Professor Evans examined the histology slides, became convinced that they indicated an ingested toxin, and suggested that the doctors involved in the case met for a 'clinical conference' in January 1982. Samples of blood were sent again to the National Poisons Unit, while samples of tissue from Barber's main organs – still in the bucket in the mortuary ante-room – were sent to ICI, the makers of paraquat. When the results came back, both reported the presence of paraquat, and the situation was reported to the police.

But why the earlier negative result? In preparing for Professor Evans' clinical conference, a doctor discovered that Michael Barber's samples had never been sent to the National Poisons Unit. It was all a mistake.

A small team of Essex CID, directed by Detective Chief Inspector John Clark, began making softly-softly inquiries as to whether the death had been accidental, suicidal or something more sinister. (A particular problem was that Richard Collins' sister was a WPC in Essex.) One mystery was where the paraquat, a restricted substance, had come from? This was solved when it was discovered that Michael Barber had worked as a landscape gardener in the late

1960s, and had kept some back for his own personal use. It had been stored in his garden shed. By 5 April 1982 – nine months after Michael Barber's death – the police decided that they had enough evidence to arrest an astonished Susan Barber. Richard Collins was taken into custody the same day.

'There is no doubt that the two [Susan Barber and Richard Collins] had lived for months in the belief that the perfect crime had been committed,' Clark later wrote in the *Police Review*:

> However, after a short time, both admitted the part they had played. The truth of the poisoning will never be known as Susan, well practised in the art of deception, gave, altogether, three different versions of her actions. One thing is certain: either just before or just after the assault on her by her husband, she had taken some paraquat from the garden shed into the kitchen of her house . . . One evening . . . she had put some in her husband's dinner and watched him eat his meal which, she remembered, was steak and kidney pie. When nothing happened immediately, she followed this with a further dose administered by the same method. Whilst it could never positively be established, it was strongly believed by the investigators that she administered yet a third dose, this time in the medicine Michael had been prescribed for his sore throat, which was in fact the result of the first poisoning.

The trial, at Chelmsford Crown Court, opened on 1 November 1982. Barber was accused of murder, Collins of conspiracy to murder. Throughout her trial, Susan Barber insisted that she had only meant to make her husband ill. The jury did not believe her and the judge told her: 'I cannot think of a more evil way to dispose of a human being.' She was gaoled for life, though in July 1983 she was allowed to marry a CB enthusiast. Richard Collins was gaoled for two years for conspiracy.

The liquid paraquat (Gramoxone) used to kill Michael Barber was manufactured in the 1960s. Paraquat of such vintage did not contain the 'stink' agent added by the manufacturers in 1977 to guard against its unlawful use. If Susan Barber had used a 1981 Gramoxone her job would have been infinitely more difficult.

PHOSPHORUS
Mrs Sarah Ricketts died at home at 3.15 a.m. on 14 April 1953. Keeping her company in her last hours at the bungalow in Blackpool's Devonshire Road was her housekeeper, Mrs Louisa Merrifield. It is more than probable that as Mrs Ricketts died she realized that matronly-looking Mrs Merrifield was more than just a house-keeper; she was a poisoner.

The murder had begun a little over a month before, on 12 March 1953, when 46-year-old Louisa and her third husband Alfred, seventy-one, took up an appointment as live-in housekeepers to Mrs Sarah Ricketts, an eighty-year-old widow. Naturally, Mrs Merrifield had not apprised her new employer of the fact that this was her twentieth job in three years, or that she had served a prison sentence for ration book fraud. But she must have acted as the perfect 'treasure' to begin with, because Mrs Ricketts thought herself very fortunate in her employee; so fortunate that, as an incentive to make Louisa and Alfred stay as long as she might need them, she changed her will. She left her bungalow to the Merrifields.

Friction developed almost immediately thereafter, with Mrs Ricketts complaining that she did not get enough to eat and Louisa Merrifield boasting to friends that she worked for an old woman who had died and left her a bungalow worth £3000. 'Actually, she's not dead yet', confided Louisa to one friend, 'but she soon will be.'

And so on 14 April 1953 Mrs Ricketts died. The doctor, who had not been called until some hours after expiration, was puzzled by the cause of death and Louisa Merrifield's haste in wishing to cremate her employer. He declined to issue a death certificate. At the subsequent autopsy 0.141 grains of phosphorus was found in Mrs Ricketts' body, and death was put down to poisoning.

Soon police were searching the bungalow for clues to support their suspicion that Mrs Ricketts had been murdered, while outside, at Louisa Merrifield's request, the Salvation Army Band played 'Abide With Me'. No trace of phosphorus was found until the police looked in Louisa's handbag; there they discovered a spoon bearing traces of a phosphorus-based rat poison and rum.

The Merrifields were tried for murder at Manchester; both pleaded not guilty. The prosecution maintained that Mrs Ricketts had died of phosphorus poisoning and that the poison was unlikely to have entered the body by suicide or accident; therefore it must have been deliberately administered. A prosecution witness, a Blackpool chemist's assistant, identified Mr Merrifield as the customer to whom she sold a tin of Rodine, a proprietary rat poison containing phosphorus. The defence maintained that the old lady had died of cirrhosis of the liver. Louisa Merrifield was convicted of murder, and executed at Strangeways on 18 September 1953. The jury failed to agree a verdict on her husband. Later, the Attorney-General issued a *nolle prosequi* declaring the Crown's unwillingness to prosecute Alfred Merrifield in a retrial.

Phosphorus is a waxy yellow non-metallic irritant poison which is kept under water since it ignites when exposed to air. It is highly toxic. Acute poisoning has been caused by as little as one grain, resulting in damage to the liver, vomiting, a burning in the throat, convulsions and death, often delayed by several days. An interesting aspect is that the vomit and faeces of the phosphorus victim will glow in the dark. One of the characteristics of chronic phosphorus poisoning – common among industrial workers in the days when phosphorus was used in the manufacture of matches and animal poisons – was 'phossy jaw', a necrosis of the upper and lower jaw which caused the teeth to fall out. If ingested in small quantities over a long period it was virtually undetectable, becoming oxidized in the bloodstream into phosphate, a chemical which is naturally present in the body. It was not until relatively recently that the rate of oxidization of phosphorus in the blood became known, which made it difficult to say with certainty when, and how much, phosphorus had been ingested.

The first person known to have used phosphorus to kill was Dr J. Milton Bowers of Chicago, who married three times in fifteen years, each wife dying suddenly and unexpectedly. After the demise of his third spouse, Cecilia, an anonymous letter to the insurance company alerted the police, who had the body of Cecilia Bowers exhumed. Phosphorus was found in the remains.

Tried in March 1886, Bowers was found guilty of first-degree murder. There was then a dramatic development in the case; while Bowers petitioned for an appeal from his jail cell, Cecilia Bowers' brother, Henry Benhayon, was found dead. Next to his body was a bottle of potassium CYANIDE and a suicide note, in which he confessed to killing his sister. The police suspected John Dimmig, a shady acquaintance of Dr Bowers, of having murdered Benhayon at Bowers' behest, and fabricating the 'suicide' confession in an effort to get Bowers' body out of the electric chair. Charged with Benhayon's murder, Dimmig was tried in December 1887, but the jury failed to agree a verdict. At a second trial he was acquitted. Not long after, Bowers himself was released from prison. After all, 'suicide' Henry Benhayon had admitted poisoning his sister, thus exonerating Bowers.

Almost certainly, Bowers administered phosphorus to Cecilia Bowers in her food or drink, and this has been the standard vehicle for the poison. But not the only one; there are records from the Victorian era of match heads – which then contained phosphorus – being inserted into the rectum of a fifteen-year-old boy by his mother to deadly effect; another woman mixed match heads in her husband's tobacco.

A German case of 1954 is noteworthy, because it introduced the killing public to E-605, an especially lethal phosphorus compound. On 12 February of that year, Christa Lehmann of Worms sent 75-year-old Eva Ruh, the mother of her best friend, Anni, a box of chocolates with poisoned centres. Not wanting to eat the chocolates straight away, Frau Ruh put them in the fridge. Noticing the tempting sweets on her return home from work, Anni took a bite, grimaced and spat most of the chocolate out on to the floor, where the family dog wolfed it down. Shortly afterwards, Anni doubled up in pain; she died some hours later. The dog, too, went into convulsions and died. A university scientist identified the responsible toxin as E-605, a phosphorus compound which had been developed as an insecticide. Christa Lehmann had intended to poison Frau Ruh because she suspected her of trying to break up her friendship with Anni. The case prompted natural suspicions about the recent sudden deaths of Christa Lehmann's husband and father-in-law; the bodies of both men, when exhumed, were found to contain substantial traces of phosphorus. Publicity surrounding the case led to a spate of 'copy-cat' murders, and more than seventy suicides, using the insecticide containing E-605.

In England, meanwhile, it was a phosphorus-based rat poison called Rodine which was being used as a means to murder by Mary Wilson, the so-called 'Widow of Windy Nook' (see Case File).

CASE FILE: The Widow of Windy Nook

Some killers start young in life. Mary Elizabeth Wilson, however, was not one; it was not until she was in her mid-sixties that she produced her first corpse. But she quickly made up for her late start, killing three more times in a matter of months.

Born in 1893 in the industrial north, Mary Wilson, like many girls in that Edwardian age, went into service at fourteen. It was a good position, with a builder's family. In 1914, she married the eldest son of the house, John Knowles. At the time Mary must have thought she had bettered herself considerably but unfortunately John Knowles never rose higher than labouring work. Although the couple stayed together for more than forty years, they ceased to share a bed, or even to talk to each other. They took in a lodger, chimney-sweep John Russell, who became Mary's lover. In July 1955, the previously healthy John Knowles was taken ill. Within a fortnight he was dead.

No sooner was Mr Knowles in the ground than Mary Wilson moved to a larger, more modern house in Windy Nook, Felling-on-Tyne. The lodger went with her. It was fated not to last; just before Christmas 1955, John Russell fell ill with stomach cramps, his condition deteriorating until he died in January. John Russell left Mary Wilson £46 in his will.

In the spring Mary met Oliver James Leonard, a retired estate agent living in lodgings. As with Mary's previous 'loves', it was his money she loved most, a fact she made little secret of with Mr Leonard's landlady, inquiring of her: 'Has the bugger any money?' The answer must have been affirmative, for in the twinkling of a wedding she became Mrs Leonard, the marriage ceremony taking place on 21 September. Thirteen days later, a neighbour, Mrs Russell, was called and found Mr Leonard doubled up in agony on the bedroom floor. Mrs Russell felt obliged to point out that Mr Leonard might be dying. 'I think so too,' Mrs Wilson replied. She waited, though, until the next morning – by which time Mr Leonard was dead – to fetch the doctor. After a cursory examination, he signed the death certificate, blaming the demise on myocardial degeneration and chronic nephritis. Mrs Mary Wilson was £50 better off.

It was a year before Mary decided to marry again. This time she set her sights on a 75-year-old retired engineer, Ernest Wilson. Doubtless his eligibility was improved by his not only having £100 in savings, but a fully paid up insurance policy on his life. Within two weeks of her moving into Mr Wilson's council bungalow, the bridegroom was dead – due to 'cardiac muscular failure'.

Like Frederick Seddon (see ARSENIC), parsimonious Mary Wilson decided to try and save a few pennies by asking the undertaker to provide a cut-price funeral. After all, she joked with him, she had put so much business his way that she should be entitled to 'trade rates'. This was not her first 'joke' in bad taste; at the reception after her marriage to Wilson she told the caterer: 'Save the leftover cakes – they'll come in handy for the funeral.'

Talk about the merry widow of Windy Nook reached the ears of the local constabulary, who decided that the bodies of Messrs Wilson and Leonard might bear examination. The conclusion reached by pathologists Dr William Stewart and Dr David Price was that both men had died of phosphorus poisoning. It did not require great toxicological work to determine this; the exhumed corpses contained so much phosphorus that they glowed like neon.

Traces of wheatgerm alongside the phosphorus suggested that Rodine, a popular rat poison, was Mary Wilson's 'inheritance potion'. There was considerable discussion about the means by which Rodine could have been administered to the victims as, like all phosphorus substances, it has a strong garlicky taste (it could not, for instance, be disguised in jam or cups of tea, although a highly flavoured soup would do). The consensus was that it was added to the men's cough mixture.

Mary Wilson was defended at her trial for the murders of Oliver Leonard and Ernest Wilson by Miss Rose Heilbron QC, who advanced the suggestion that both men had died of an accidental overdose of aphrodisiac pills containing phosphorus, freely available over the chemist's counter. 'What more natural,' she said, 'that these old men, finding a wife in the evening of their lives, should purchase these pills?'

Miss Heilbron also pointed out to the court that at the time phosphorus poisoning was little known to forensic toxicology – and because the rate of oxidization of phosphorus was then unknown, there was no accurate means of assessing how much of the poison had been ingested. Miss Heilbron had also been astute enough to secure the services of Dr Francis Camps, soon to become one of Britain's foremost forensic pathologists, who gave his opinion that phosphorus poisoning was not necessarily the direct cause of death in the cases of Leonard and Wilson. This was a rash observation, since Camps had not examined their remains personally. The prosecution, for its part, maintained that phosphorus poisoning was most certainly the cause of the demise of Messrs Leonard and Wilson; a prosecution expert noted that for the men to have obtained a lethal dose of phosphorus from the sex-stimulant pills they would have been obliged to have swallowed three whole bottles each. Moreover, there was no evidence of the men buying such love aids.

On the advice of Miss Heilbron, Mary Wilson did not give evidence on her own behalf, which prompted Mr Justice Hinch-cliffe to remark: 'Has she helped us all she could?' Found guilty as charged, Mrs Wilson was sentenced to hang, although in recognition of her advanced years the Home Secretary reprieved her. She died in Holloway prison at the age of seventy.

It should be added that, in light of the fate of Mr Leonard and Mr Wilson, the bodies of the other men in Mary Wilson's life were exhumed for pathological examination. Both the late Mr Knowles and the late Mr Russell were found to contain appreciable amounts of phosphorus.

POISONING

It takes no great imagination to realize that primitive man must have learned through, literally, bitter experience which berries and fungi he could eat, and which he could not. The inedible, though, had their purpose; they could be used to extend man's power to kill animals for food. And his fellow man. For more than 3000 years poison was the favourite agent of the murdering public. The reason was simple: it could be administered by stealth, often little by little over a long period, without drawing suspicion. Moreover, most poisons were virtually undetectable. No doctor in Ancient Egypt, Rome, or even 18th-century Britain could distinguish with absolute certainty between a death due to poison or sudden death due to heart attack or some other natural cause.

The first famous poisoning was that of Socrates in 399BC. The hideously ugly philosopher was found guilty by the Athenian state of corrupting the minds of the nation's youth; in reality, a scapegoat for Athens' defeat in the Peloponnesian war, Socrates was executed by being forced to drink a cup of HEMLOCK. This was just one of a variety of poisons in circulation in Greece at the time, which numbered among them ARSENIC, ANTIMONY, MERCURY, gold, silver, copper, ACONITINE, and colchium. But it was the Ancient Romans, the succeeding 'classic' civilization, who developed the cult of the poisoner. In Rome, at the time of Caligula, death from poisonous FUNGI, ATROPINE, arsenic, and lead was as common as death from bullet wounds in Prohibition Chicago.

By the time of the Borgias, Rome was at the height of her Renaissance glory. Originally, the Borgias came from Spain ('Borgia' being the Latin version of 'Borja'), and were an intensely ambitious family, in 1455 succeeding in getting Alonso Borgia elected Pope Calixtus III who spared no effort in elevating his own family. Among those so helped was the licentious Roderigo Borgia, made a cardinal in the church. In 1492, Roderigo became Pope Alexander VI, and, together with his three illegitimate children – Cesare, Lucrezia, and Juan – schemed homicidally against all rivals (they also all schemed with each other; the psychopathic Cesare almost certainly killed his brother, Juan). Allegedly, the Borgias' favourite murderous means was *cantarella*, a white powder resembling sugar, but tasteless in itself, which would suggest that it was in fact arsenic. They may also have used a poison called *aqua Toffana*, an arsenic solution developed by a Neapolitan woman called Toffana for removing skin blemishes; it also removed spouses and rich relatives. Some 600 deaths were attributed to *aqua Toffana* before it was banned.

Someone who claimed to know the secret of *cantarella* was Exili, a 17th-century poisoner whose reputation alone was enough to get him imprisoned in the Bastille when he washed up in Paris. Exili had apparently learned his craft in Italy – one chronicler states that he was a student of La Toffana – and had been employed by Queen Christina of Sweden. In 1654, Exili found himself sharing his Bastille cell with Chevalier Godin de Sainte-Croix, a nobleman arrested because he was the lover of the married Marquise de Brinvilliers, a liaison which her powerful father found unacceptable, inducing the King to end it by incarcerating the Chevalier. Recognizing that the young aristocrat might make a valuable patron, Exili proceeded to teach Ste-Croix the fundamentals of the art of making poison; the Chevalier was only too eager to learn, since he was planning revenge on de Brinvilliers' father, the Viscomte d'Aubray, for his present incarceration. Among the poisons Exili is supposed to have taught Ste-Croix to prepare is *venin de crapaud* – toad venom, made by injecting a toad with arsenic, and distilling the putrefied flesh. More probably, Exili taught the administering of arsenic and mercury in quantities which did not arouse suspicion of foul play. After three months, Ste-Croix was released and found that Marie de Brinvilliers – having decimated her husband's fortune – was short of money. Between them they plotted to poison her father, so that Ste-Croix might be avenged, and she might inherit. In Whitsun 1666, the Viscount d'Aubray, believing that his daughter had broken off relations with Ste-Croix, invited her to his estate at Offément. There, after eating

Hyoscine murderer Dr Crippen and Ethel LeNeve in the dock at the Old Bailey. (*Syndication International*)

Poultry farmer Norman Thorne poses for the press only yards from where his girlfriend is buried. (*Hulton Deutsch Collection*)

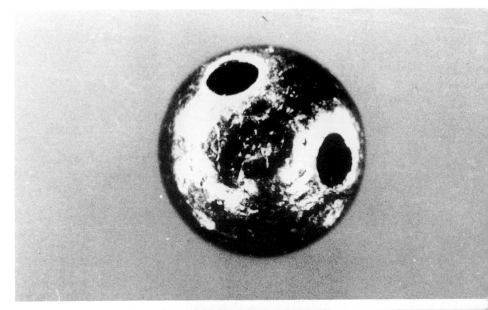

The microscopic pellet used in the assassination of Georgi Markov. (*Press Association*)

The wire noose that killed teenage kidnap victim Lesley Whittle. (*Hulton Deutsch Collection*)

Louisa Merrifield. (*Popperfoto*)

Dr Marcel Petiot. (*Popperfoto*)

Petiot's charnel house at 21 Rue Lesueur, Paris. The quicklime pits were at the rear in the stables and garage. (*Popperfoto*)

TRIANGULAR ROOM

FALSE DOOR

FAKE BELL PUSH

WAITING ROOM

RÉCEPTION DE LA FUTURE VICTIME

MUR CONSTRUIT PAR PETIOT

CABINET TRIANGULAIRE

INCINE

SPY HOLE

RESTES DE INCINERATION

RUE DU BOIS DE BOULOGNE

BELL PUSH

DOUBLE DOOR

RUE

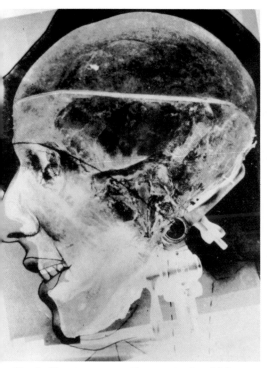

e Buck Ruxton case: the portrait of Mrs
uxton with her skull superimposed.
opham)

Crotalus atrox, the rattlesnake
with which Robert James
attempted the murder of his wife.
(*NHPA*)

The hands of a strangler: Harold Loughans writes his confession to murder
with his fingerless right hand. (*Syndication International*)

Strychnine killer Dr Neill Cream.
(*Mansell Collection*)

Police search the garden at 10 Rillington
Place, residence of John Christie.
(*Popperfoto*)

The trunk in which Tony Mancini deposited the corpse of Violette Kaye. (*Syndication International*)

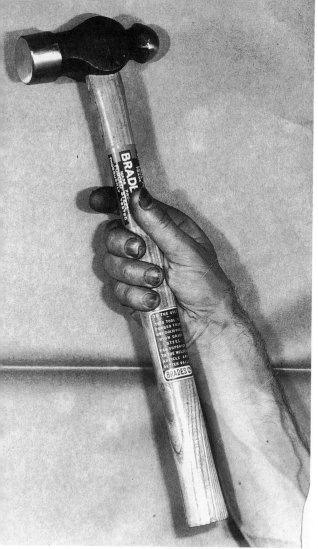

The hammer with which Violette Kaye was battered. (*Syndication International*)

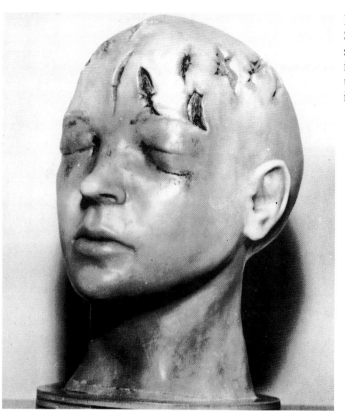

Model of Marilyn
Sheppard's head
showing the wounds
inflicted by the
unidentified blunt
instrument. (*Topham*)

Thallium poisoner
Graham Young: his
favourite photograph.
(*Hulton Deutsch
Collection*)

a bowl of soup, he died. The post-mortem report on d'Aubray's
death noted:

> That for the last three days which Monsieur the Lieutenant-Civil
> lived, he grew very lean, very dry, lost his appetite, vomited
> often, and had a burning in his stomach. And having been
> opened . . . they found his stomach all black, the liver
> gangreen'd and burnt, etc., which must have been occasioned by
> poison, or a humour which sometimes is so corrupted as to have
> the same effects as poison.

Within four years the Marquise had spent her inheritance, and was
urgently in need of money. The greater part of her father's fortune
had been inherited by her brothers. If they died . . . It was,
however, necessary to be cautious, since too many deaths in the
same family would arouse suspicion. To make sure the poison was
undetectable, the Marquise tried it out on the patients of the Hotel
Dieu, Paris's public hospital, where she charitably volunteered her
services. The doctors were puzzled by the wasting disease which
caused fifty patients to die over the next months. As a result of her
tests, the Marquise now knew the exact dosage needed and that, for
all practical purposes, the poison was not detectable. The two
brothers were quickly dispatched.

By now the Marquise had developed the poisoning habit. Her
motives were no longer confined to financial advancement, and she
began killing indiscriminately – one woman died just for spilling
coffee on her dress. Then in July 1672, Ste-Croix, who had been
dutifully making the Marquise's poisons in his laboratory in the
Rue des Bernadins, died. He had left instructions that a small
leather-bound box, about a foot in length, should be handed over to
the Marquise de Brinvilliers. But Ste-Croix's wife insisted that the
box be opened in the presence of officials; it contained documents
which incriminated the Marquise in murder together with various
packets of poison, listed as corrosive sublimate (mercury), opium,
Roman vitriol, powdered vitriol, antimony, as well as a phial of a
clear liquid which could not be identified. Marie Marguerite de
Brinvilliers was arraigned in 1676. She was found guilty and
sentenced

> to be beheaded on a scaffold which shall be erected for that
> purpose; her body shall be burnt and her ashes thrown in the air.
> But before her execution she shall be put to torture, both
> ordinary and extraordinary, to make her confess her accomplices.

It was nearly a century and half before the free reign of poisoners
like Marie de Brinvilliers was brought to an end. Forensic toxicology – the scientific investigation of poisoning – was born in the

1800s with the work of Mathieu Orfila, the Spanish emigrant to France who published the *Treatise on Poison, or General Toxicology* (1814), a catalogue of poisons and their effects. Orfila's studies ushered in a period of rapid achievements in the detection of poison. In 1836, Englishman James Marsh devised his Marsh Test for arsenic, a test that proved reliable and sensitive enough for its results to be accepted in a court of law. His paper in the *Edinburgh New Philosophical Journal* detailed a method for converting arsenic traces into arsine gas, which itself was revealed as a metallic 'mirror' on a piece of glass. With the test, amounts of arsenic as small as one-fiftieth of a milligram could be detected. In a case which became a *cause célèbre* throughout Europe, Orfila used the Marsh Test in 1840 to prove that Marie Lafarge had arsenically poisoned her husband. This should have signalled the end of arsenic as the murderer's favourite, but attachment to the poison proved stubborn.

Although most metallic poisons could be detected, there were many vegetable poisons like aconitine, atropine and strychnine which could not. As late as 1847, Orfila suggested that vegetable poisons would remain forever unidentifiable. In fact, it was only three years before a pupil of his, Jean Servais Stas, pioneered a test for NICOTINE, which proved its presence in a cadaver. Few could now hope to get away with a murder with venom.

Since the gaslight era, the number of homicidal poisonings has dwindled and dwindled. Although poisoning holds an especially sinister place in the annals of murder, in practice it is now one of the least used methods of homicide. Less than 6 per cent of homicides are caused by poisoning. In 1989, there were just seven confirmed cases in England and Wales.

The decline of the poisoning murder is partially explained by progressive restrictions on the sale of toxic substances; in Victorian or even Edwardian Britain there was nothing easier for those about to go a-murdering than to stop at the corner ironmonger's for some poison; insecticides were commonly made up of potassium arsenate or THALLIUM; weedkiller contained acetate of lead, while other gardening and household substances usually provided something deadly. Rat-poisons might contain anything from arsenic, to phosphorus to cyanide, or a combination thereof.

And if the ironmonger's was closed, there was always the chemist's, where such proprietary medicines as Fowler's Solution (arsenic) and Easton's Syrup (strychnine) were there for the buying. Legislation, beginning with the Arsenic Act of 1851 and the Pharmacy Act of 1852, has made poisons progressively more difficult to obtain than ever, while the rise and rise of forensic toxicology has made detection ever more likely. There are now, for instance, over thirty different tests for morphine alone.

Ironically, the decline of poisoning has occurred as the number of poisons – thanks mainly to the synthetic products of the chemical and pharmaceutical industry (notably BARBITURATES) – has mushroomed. In the 1940s, there were sixty possible poisons the murderer could use; today, there are over 5000.

Poisoning has often been called the coward's weapon, relying as it does on stealth and deceit, and sometimes the woman's weapon, but if any group has evidenced a tendency to dabble in the toxic arts it is doctors and members of the medical profession. The temptation is great; doctors have ready access to poisons and drugs, while the administration of an overdose can always be passed off as a tragic accident.

Medical murderers have also been prone to the belief that their specialist knowledge of esoteric toxins will enable them to commit the perfect poisoning, the one which leaves no trace. It is a belief, it seems, which dies hard, and many of the most notable modern poisonings have been committed by medics on a quest for the undetectable poison; Navy Sick Berth Attendant John Armstrong's murder of his son with Seconal in 1955; the killing by INSULIN of Mrs Barlow by male nurse husband Kenneth Barlow in 1957; Dr Carl Coppolino's administration of the drug SUCCINYLCHOLINE CHLORIDE to his wife in 1967; the 1978 (failed) attempt by a German technician to inject his wife with cancer cells; the killing of seventeen patients by Michaela Rosa, the nurse nicknamed 'the Angel of Death', in 1989 with Catrapresan, a blood pressure drug.

Of course, if anybody is going to get away with a murder by poison it is likely to be a nurse or a doctor. In 1979, Paul Vickers, a Newcastle surgeon, injected his wife with CCNU, an anti-cancer drug, which had the attributes of potential undetectability: it was esoteric, and there was no known way of tracing it in the human body. Vickers had ambitions of a political career and a mistress, and considered his invalid wife an encumbrance to both. Vickers administered the drug in her food, and she developed a rare blood disease called aplastic anaemia, from which she died in June 1979. Unfortunately for Vickers, however, his mistress had a fit of conscience and informed the police that he had obtained the drug by making out false prescriptions. The police investigated, and Vickers was charged with murder. If it had not been for the conscience of the mistress Vickers would never have been caught.

The term 'poison' is notoriously hard to define since many poisons, like Vickers' CCNU, if used correctly, can be beneficial, not harmful. As the German Romantic writer Goethe observed, 'There is no such thing as poison; it all depends on the dose.' Even Sir Robert Christison, the famous 19th-century toxicologist, was obliged to write that 'although the most skilful have tried to define a poison, everyone has hitherto failed.' Whether a substance is a poison depends on its dose, the way it is administered, and the constitution of the victim or patient it is given to. But as a working definition, a poison is any compound which in relatively small quantities and by its chemical actions can cause death or disability.

There is no standard system of classifying poisons, but many forensic toxicologists group poisons by their chemical nature, the main types being:

1) *Gases*, including CARBON MONOXIDE.
2) *Corrosives*: ACIDS; Alkalis, including CAUSTIC POTASH (potassium hydroxide), caustic soda (sodium hydroxide), and ammonia.

If taken orally, corrosives cause death through shock, or ASPHYXIA from the dissolving of the larynx, from damage to the stomach (thus prohibiting gastric functions), or perforation of the stomach, or from the breathing of dead material into the lungs. In very rare cases, corrosives are applied externally, burning the victim to death. The flesh-destroying nature of corrosives has attracted a number of killers wishing to remove the cadaverous evidence of their deed.

3) *Synthetic Organic Substances*, including acetylsalicylic acid (aspirin, a common suicidal agent), BARBITURATES, CHLORO-FORM, CHLORAL HYDRATE, hydrocyanic Acid (CYANIDE), nitrobenzene (Oil of Mirbane), lysol, and oxalic acid.

4) *Alkaloids*, essentially plant and animal poisons, which number ACONITINE, ATROPINE, HYOSCINE, Hysocyamine (similar to hyoscine and atropine, and derived from henbane), cocaine, colchine, gelsemium, coniine (HEMLOCK), MORPHINE, NICOTINE, ersine, STRYCHNINE, and brucine (derived, like strychnine, from the shrub *Strychnos nux vomica*, but with only some 15 per cent of its potency; once upon a time it was used by brewers to make bitter beer more bitter).

5) *Metallic and Inorganic Poisons*, including ANTIMONY, ARSENIC, barium, MERCURY, PHOSPHORUS, and THAL-LIUM.

Lead and copper were frequently pressed into criminal service in the ancient past, but their modern homicidal incidence is scarce. Notable instances include the poisonings of both the first and second Mesdames Moreau by money-hungry spouse Pierre-Desirée Moreau, a Parisian herbalist; unwisely, Moreau had underlined the passage on copper sulphate in one of his pharmacy books, a carelessness which cost him his head on the guillotine on 14 October 1874. In 1926, one Antoinette Scieri of France was sentenced to life for a double homicide of two neighbours by dosing their food with acetate of lead, a constituent in numerous weedkillers.

6) *Alcohol* (see pages 15–16).

7) *Animal Toxins*, including the venom of SNAKES and SPIDERS and poisonous fish, the latter detailed in the entry on ANIMALS.
8) *FUNGI* (see pages 120–21).

Essentially, all poisons with the exception of the corrosives work by attacking the body's enzymes and/or by affecting the nervous system.

An enzyme is a chemical catalyst manufactured by living cells, one which enables the body to function. For example, thrombin is an enzyme in the blood which causes coagulation, while maltase manufactures glucose. Some enzymes, the so-called 'key' enzymes, are important and others less so. A poison which attacks a 'key' enzyme is particularly destructive; and if sufficient molecules of the poison are present the enzyme is destroyed. Cyanide, for example, immobilizes a vital blood enzyme, cytochrome, which helps the cell take oxygen from the blood. Because this process is prevented, the victim of cyanide poisoning has blood so loaded with untaken oxygen that his or her face appears pink.

As for the poisons which affect the nervous system, some influence the central nervous system, the brain and the spinal column, by depressing it (Seconal, for example) or over-exciting it (strychnine). Others work more indirectly by interfering with the electro-chemical switches between the nerve endings and the muscles. At the end of each nerve are tiny clusters of acetylcholine – a fluid which, when activated, bridges the gap between nerve and muscle, allowing the impulse travelling from the nerve to reach the muscle. After the impulse has crossed, another chemical, cholinesterase, is released which annihilates the acetylcholine, breaking the connection to prevent over stimulation of the muscle. The whole process takes only $1/5000$ of a second. It is, however, very delicate – and very vulnerable to the effects of poison. BACTERIAL POISONING from botulism prevents the release of acetylcholine, meaning no impulses reach the muscles, which relax, or completely collapse. CURARE also produces over-relaxed muscles, although it does so by forming a barrier between the nerve ending and muscle, blocking the action of acetylcholine. Still other poisons, among them neostigmine, dampen down the action of the enzyme cholinesterase, leading to over-excitation of the muscles, among them the heart.

It is the suffering that most poisons inflict on their hapless victim that have earned the poisoner the special opprobrium of society. Even many years after their deeds, names like Seddon, Armstrong, and Crippen have a special chill to them. More sinister than the gunman or the knife-wielder, it is the poisoner's dark blend of stealth and calculation as he or she administers death, drip by drip, which causes such unease. This is only added to by the fact that poisoners so often come in the guise of angel – doctor, nurse, but

especially spouse – and administer the agent of death via things
which are innocuous, even beneficial – Susan Barber's
PARAQUAT-flavoured steak-and-kidney pie, Major Armstrong's
ARSENIC-laced scones, Dorothea Waddingham's MORPHINE
injections, the allegedly poisoned suppository given to Marilyn
Monroe, and Graham Young's THALLIUM-added 'nice cup of
tea'.

Q

QUICKLIME
The popular belief in the flesh-eating property of quicklime when sprinkled on the superfluous corpse is nowhere better illustrated than in Oscar Wilde's lines concerning the lime pit at Reading Gaol, into which the bodies of hanged murderers were thrown:

> And all the while the burning lime
> Eats flesh and bone away,
> It eats the brittle bone by night,
> And the soft flesh by day,
> It eats the flesh and bones by turns
> But it eats the heart alway.
> (*The Ballad of Reading Gaol*, 1898)

In truth, quicklime is not such a dramatic decomposer, and often has the opposite of its intended effect: it preserves the remains by arresting putrefaction.

Murderers have tended to favour three types of lime (CaO):

Quicklime Irregularly shaped white lumps of calcium oxide, produced by strongly heating limestone.
Slaked lime Calcium hydroxide, a white powder produced by adding water to quicklime.
Chlorinated lime Produced by the action of chlorine gas on slaked lime. Once common as a disinfectant.

When a body is buried in quicklime and then slaked with water, only a superficial degree of burning results; the main effect is to dry out the tissues, thus preserving the body in a state of MUMMIFI-CATION. Quicklime is also an efficient insecticide, killing the very wildlife – maggots and beetles – which would otherwise aid the murderer by eating the cadaver.

Not that any of this has deterred murderers from reaching for a sack of quicklime when the need to dispose of the victim has arisen. In the case of the 1847 'Bermondsey Horror', Frederick and Maria Manning achieved a modicum of success in speeding-up the decomposition of unfortunate Patrick O'Connor, when they buried him in five bushels of quicklime; the quicklime worked 'so rapidly that its [the corpse's] identity was only established by the remarkable and less perishable features of an extremely prominent chin and a set of false teeth'. The Mannings were clever enough to throw their victim naked into the pit, where the moisture from the surrounding soil slaked the lime and burned the exterior of O'Connor's body. Brought to trial, they indulged in noisy mutual recriminations, and were hanged before a crowd of 50,000 in November 1847.

Dr Crippen made a small use of lime in burying Cora Crippen beneath the cellar floor at 39 Hilldrop Crescent; probably its only useful purpose was – by arresting decomposition – to prevent the tell-tale smell of death wafting out. Another Londoner, Harry Dobkin, buried the late Mrs Dobkin with a shroud of quicklime. In 1942, when Mrs Dobkin was discovered by wartime workmen under a slab in the cellar of the bombed-out baptist church in Vauxhall Road, forensic pathologist Keith Simpson was able to prove that she died unlawfully. 'Thanks to the lime,' wrote Simpson later, 'certain injuries to the throat, in part to the voice box, had been preserved . . .' These mummified injuries showed she had died from STRANGULATION. Dobkin's success was further confounded by his victim's teeth, and forensic work similar to that pioneered by Glaister in the Ruxton case (see DISMEMBERMENT) which proved her identity beyond doubt. On 27 January 1943, 49-year-old fire-watcher Harry Dobkin was hanged at Wandsworth Prison for 'The Skeleton in the Cellar' murder.

Yet all these British lime users are mere dilettantes when compared with Monsieur Petiot of Paris (see Case File).

CASE FILE: 21 Rue Lesueur

The households on Rue Lesueur, a dignified street near the Arc de Triomphe in Paris, first noticed the acrid black fumes coming from the chimneys of No. 21 on 6 March 1944. Initially, no one complained; in comparison to the horrors of the Nazi occupation and the course of the war, a smoking chimney seemed trivial. But by 11 March the smoke was so nauseating that M. Jacques Marcais, who lived next door to the objectionable property, could tolerate it no longer, and called the police.

Two gendarmes arrived almost immediately. Nobody appeared to live at the offending address, but a card fixed to the door invited inquirers to call at 66 Rue Caumartin. The telephone number was Pigalle 77-11. A Mme Petiot answered, and fetched her husband, Dr Marcel Petiot, who was informed that the smoke billowing from his property at Rue Lesueur was a public nuisance. He asked whether the police had broken into the house, and on being reassured that they had not, said he would present himself there in a quarter of an hour.

It took him longer than that and the police, fearing a conflagration, called the fire brigade. The fireman in charge, Corporal

Boudringlin, was later to give the following evidence in court:

> After I had broken a window-pane, I entered the house and, guided by the smell, went down to the basement. Near the boiler, I saw human remains. The boiler was drawing rather noisily. It was burning human flesh. I saw a hand, at the end of a skeleton arm. It looked like a woman's hand. I made haste upstairs. I opened the street door for the police and said to them: 'You'd better come and look, there's a job for you.'

The following Monday's *Le Matin* recounted the episode somewhat more dramatically, stating that the fireman had come out of No. 21 shouting 'This is no job for us! The place is full of corpses!'

Not quite full, perhaps, but certainly well stocked. The basement contained the dismembered remains of seventeen people waiting to fuel the furnace. The premises also accommodated a large lime-heap in the garage and a 12-foot-deep lime pit in the stables. In these lime sinks were the shapeless viscera and body parts of another ten human beings.

While the police were trying to comprehend the sights before them in the charnel house at Rue Lesueur, Dr Petiot himself arrived. When called upon to explain the carnage, he pompously told the police that he was 'a patriot – risking his head – on business for *la Patrie*'. The house, he whispered, was an execution chamber of the Resistance movement.

The police, being patriots themselves, let Dr Petiot go – long enough for him, together with his wife and son, to escape from Paris. Marcel André Henri Felix Petiot, however, was no patriot; he was in the business of murder for profit.

Petiot was born on 17 January 1897, the son of a postal employee. Like a number of other mass murderers, he exhibited in childhood a sadism towards animals and a penchant for petty thieving; after being caught stealing mail in 1914, he was found abnormal by a psychiatrist. During World War I he had an undistinguished career in the army, being discharged in 1918 with a 100 per cent (mental) disability pension. Despite this he qualified three years later as a Doctor of Medicine from the University of Paris (there was some suspicion that he cheated in his finals). In 1927 he was elected the Socialist mayor of his home town of Villeneuve-sur-Yonne. There were rumours that he knew more about the disappearance of a pregnant girlfriend than he told the police; this, together with convictions for fraud and for robbing his electric light meter, hastened his removal to Paris, where he was arrested in 1936 for shoplifting. As always, when caught, Petiot invoked mental illness and was confined to a sanatorium instead of a prison. By 1941, with the war creating a huge black market in France, Petiot was involved in all manner of profiteering, much of it involving drugs. More lucrative, however, was his trade in people.

Towards the end of 1941, a wealthy Jew called M. Joachim Gusbinov asked Petiot to help him and his family escape from the Nazi occupation of France. Petiot agreed to do so for a handsome fee. Gusbinov was never seen again. Nor were a number of other wealthy Jews who approached Petiot, or 'Dr Eugene' as he called himself, about his 'escape line'. Other customers included prostitutes and pimps, people with colourful names like Jo le Boxeur and Paulette la Chinoise. All were murdered by Petiot. No doubt he would have gone on killing desperate refugees if his enterprise had not set fire to the chimney at 21 Rue Lesueur.

To operate such a death factory required more than just the labour of Petiot. He was assisted by his younger brother, Maurice, whose duties included delivering the quicklime to the house, a lorry load of it in February 1944. His explanation that it was required to kill cockroaches and to whitewash the buildings was not taken too seriously. He was charged with conspiracy to murder.

The elusive Petiot himself was captured in November 1944, posing as Captain Henri Valery of the Free French Army. During his period in custody, Petiot confessed to killing sixty-three people – all of whom, he claimed, were collaborators or enemies of France – but it was for the twenty-seven murders that were pieced together from the Rue Lesueur that he was tried. The task of compiling the 'human jig-saws' fell to Dr Albert Paul, a distinguished forensic expert and Paris coroner. To sift the massive heaps of quicklime he was obliged to hire four grave-diggers. Most of the dismembered fragments retrieved were quite well preserved, the quicklime taking up their moisture. A forensic toxicologist called in to examine them described the quicklimed viscera as emitting 'a piquant and extremely disagreeable odour'.

Unsurprisingly, the court at the Seine Assizes was packed for 'Dr Satan's' trial in 1946. Stacked behind the dock was a pitiful wall of forty-seven suitcases – luggage containing clothing and valuables that Petiot stole from his victims. Petiot himself was, by turns, abusive, witty and violently angry, all the while proclaiming that he had only killed 'for the glory of France'. A singular weakness in the case of the prosecution, not that it affected the outcome of the trial, was that it was unable to prove how Petiot killed his victims in the strange sound-proofed triangular room with a peep-hole in the door at 21 Rue Lesueur:

PRESIDENT: Dr Paul, you examined all the remains that were found two years ago in the Rue Lesueur. In your view, how did those people die?
DR PAUL: It cannot be established. It was not by a bullet or a blow on the head, that is certain. Asphyxiation, strangling, poison, a knife-wound – all those are possible.

PRESIDENT: Injections?

DR PAUL: It is possible, but I must not theorize.

PRESIDENT: Might gas have been used?

DR PAUL: Again, it is possible. Not coal gas, however. The discoloration produced by carbon monoxide poisoning would have been apparent in the fragments of skin which remained.

PRESIDENT: The bodies had been skilfully dissected?

DR PAUL: The man had a knowledge of anatomy. I said to M. Goletty, 'A doctor has done this. Pray God it was not one of my pupils.'

(For the Defence) MAÎTRE FLORIOT: Mr President . . . I don't know whether Dr Paul is aware of the fact that, during his medical training, my client never followed any course in dissection.

DR PAUL: That surprises me. It's a pity, too. He dissects very well.

The jury, bearing in mind the sinister apparatus of disposal at 21 Rue Lesueur and the accusing contents of the forty-seven suitcases, did not seem to care that Petiot's killing method was not established and did not believe his patriotic defence. He was found guilty on twenty-four counts of murder, and sentenced to death. Before he walked out on the morning of 26 May 1946, to face Madame la Guillotine, Petiot was asked one more time to answer some of the mysteries still surrounding those vanished refugees. He replied flippantly, 'When one sets out on a voyage, one takes all one's luggage with one.'

It is estimated that the business Petiot ran from the charnel house at 21 Rue Lesueur brought him in profits of over a million pounds.

R

RAT POISON *See* **POISONING**

RAZORS *See* **CUT-THROAT**

REFRIGERATION

Refrigeration by means of natural ice has been employed for thousands of years. The ancient *Shih Ching* (Book of Odes) reveals that ice cellars were in use in China as early as 1000BC. However, it was not until AD1834 that the Anglo-American inventor Jacob Perkins secured a British patent for a machine which produced artificial ice, and initially 'refrigerators' were limited to meat-packing plants and food industries. As late as 1920, sales of domestic refrigerators in the USA reached only 75,000. But in the 1930s the number of home refrigerators began to grow, and only rarely are homes today without some mechanical refrigeration unit.

Few inventions have proved so useful to the murderer, especially the murderer with a taste for CANNIBALISM. The arrest of a 'vampire killer' is invariably attended by a police officer opening the perpetrator's fridge door to reveal a display of delicacies fit for eating, or maybe preserved for some form of sexual perversion. On 24 July 1991 a search of the refrigerator in the flat at 213 Oxford Apartments, Milwaukee, owned by 31-year-old serial-killer Jeffrey L. Dahmer, found two severed heads, plus assorted other human parts. Unfortunately, the sixteen-plus victims, who were drugged, strangled and dismembered – some while they were still alive – were so prolific that Jeffrey was obliged in addition to use much less suitable storage facilities, including a barrel, a pot, saucepans and any available surface. It was presumably of cold comfort to the predominantly black and Hispanic victims and their families that Dahmer, remembered by one school friend as a 'generally weird dude', only ate the victims he liked most.

Martina Zimmermann, the Moenchengladbach cannibal, was a step more advanced than Dahmer, in that she made full use of her deep freeze, with the 'best cuts' of the late Josef Wirtz neatly packaged inside it. She explained to the police who arrested her that meat was beyond her budget, and by freezing Wirtz she could ensure a long-term supply. The 'eat by' period of human flesh (uncooked) in a domestic refrigerator is somewhere in the region of six to seven days. After that, it will go off, and become injurious to health. Flesh put in a deep freeze will keep almost indefinitely; it will certainly be edible for eighteen months. And even if the flesh is not to be eaten, because freezing prevents putrefaction it means no

tell-tale smells of decomposition. Other cannibal killers who have
kept victims' parts in the fridge include the Japanese student Issei
Sagawa (see CANNIBALISM), CROSSBOW killer Marie Witte,
and Ed Gein, the unassuming Wisconsin farmer who provided the
inspiration for *The Silence of the Lambs* and Hitchcock's *Psycho*.
Gein, who was arrested in 1957, kept some of his victims' edible
organs in the kitchen refrigerator, although other parts of theirs
were dried and preserved to make covers for chairs and for Gein to
drape himself with for sexual arousal.

Another noteworthy sex killer who made a use of Mr Jacob
Perkins' refrigerator outside anything the latter might have envis-
aged for his invention was Oregon's Jerry Brudos. An example of
the sub-species of serial-killer that forensic psychiatrists call a
'lust-killer', Jerry began exhibiting a shoe fetish at the age of five.
In adolescence he became sexually aroused by women wearing
black stiletto-heeled shoes. In adulthood, Jerry bludgeoned to
death Linda Slawson, an encyclopedia saleswomen who knocked at
his door by mistake one day in 1968, and cut off her left foot. The
rest of her body he dumped in the local river. Jerry kept the foot in
the freezer in the garage, to be taken out on special occasions and
dressed in one of Jerry's collection of high-heeled black shoes.

Refrigeration is not the special preserve of the cannibal and sex
killer. Several 'ordinary' killers have given the victim a temporary
berth in a large deep freeze, while musing on the right time and
place for final disposal. But one of the most original users of a deep
freeze for nefarious purposes is Richard Crafts, the perpetrator of
the 'Woodchipper Murder' (see Case File).

CASE FILE: The Woodchipper Murder

American airline pilot Richard Crafts, an ex-Marine, married his
Danish-born wife, Helle, in 1975. Eleven years later Helle, tired of
her husband's infidelity, hired a private eye to spy on him, so that
the evidence could be used for a divorce. The private eye, Keith
Mayo, had no difficulty in proving Richard Crafts' adultery, and
got some nice photographs of Crafts with mistress Nancy Dodd,
who, like Helle, was an air stewardess. That Crafts was unhappy
about this turn of events was indicated by the fact that Helle told
friends 'If something happens to me, don't believe it was an
accident.' On Tuesday, 18 November Helle Crafts disappeared.
When asked where his wife was, Crafts explained to some people
that she had gone home to Denmark because her mother was sick.
To others, he said that she had gone away with an Oriental
boyfriend. Not believing this, Helle's friends hired Keith Mayo to
investigate, and he found a suspicious blood-stained carpet at a
nearby dump. It had nothing to do, in fact, with Helle Crafts'

disappearance, but it did finally rouse the police to begin looking for her.

The Connecticut police interviewed Crafts, and gave him a polygraph (lie-detector) test. He passed every question, including the one 'Did you kill Helle?' (To beat the machine Crafts must have inflicted pain on himself when answering unimportant questions so that his reaction would be no different when he responded to key questions, or used his military training to blank out his mind under interrogation.) The police, however, were interested in Crafts' credit-card transactions: on 13 November he had bought a $375 home freezer and six days later hired a woodchipper, a heavy machine for disposing of tree logs. He could not satisfactorily account for either transaction. Then stories about Crafts operating a woodchipper at a secluded field he owned near a local river began to filter through. When the police examined the spot by the river at Newtown, they found a mass of woodchips on the ground – and an envelope addressed to 'Helle L. Crafts'. Convinced that the chips had a story to tell, the police gathered up thirty bags of them. Sifting through the chips at the station the police found clumps of blonde hair, bits of bone, a metal dental crown and a pink-painted fingernail. They were pieces of Helle Crafts.

How did Crafts carry out his crime? In his book *The Woodchipper Murder* (1989), Arthur Herzog conjectures that Crafts bludgeoned his wife in the bathroom with a heavy torch, and then put her body in the newly acquired deep freeze, which he had on the back of a Toyota pickup and which was plugged into the mains by an extension cord to the garage. The freezer was then transported to the secluded field, where it was kept going by an emergency generator. Why so much effort to refrigerate? If he was to 'woodchip' Helle into thousands of pieces, she had to be frozen hard – otherwise she would have gummed up the woodchipper.

Crafts was clearly a believer in 'no body, no case'. And in the event the few retrievable fragments of Helle were judged sufficiently weak by the prosecution that they concentrated on Crafts' suspicious behaviour to win their case. He was convicted at his second trial, November 1989, of his wife's murder. Judge Martin L. Nigro sentenced him to fifty years in prison.

RICIN

An apparently accidental injury with an umbrella inflicted by a passer-by brought death to Georgi Markov. A defector from Bulgaria who worked for the BBC, Markov left his office at Bush House in central London in the early evening of 7 September 1978. As he stood at Waterloo Bridge waiting for a bus to take him home, Markov felt a pain at the back of his right thigh. Turning round, he saw a man stooping down to pick up an umbrella. The man muttered an apology in a thick accent and hailed a passing cab.

Later that night, Markov was running a temperature of 104; early the next morning his wife Annabella took him to St James Hospital, Balham. Although the staff did everything they could think of, Markov's condition inexorably worsened. At 9.45 on the morning of 11 September his heart stopped. A subsequent analysis of the 49-year-old Bulgarian's blood showed a high white blood cell count – the highest the hospital had ever seen – of 33,000 per cubic millimetre (the normal count is 5,000–10,000). Death was attributed to toxaemia (blood poisoning).

It was only now that anybody, save for his wife, took Markov's claim that he had been assassinated seriously. Scotland Yard sent the dead man's wounded leg to Porton Down, the government's secret microbiological research establishment, where an extensive pathological examination found a microscopic pellet, 1.52mm in diameter, in the thigh. Bored into the platinum-iridium pellet were two holes which, where they met in the centre of the pellet, formed a reservoir for a poison. As the reservoir could contain no more than 500 micrograms, the list of sufficiently toxic poisons was quite modest. Animal poisons would have produced different clinical symptoms, which left two plant toxins, ricin and abrin. The most likely, it was decided, was ricin, a protein derived from the castor oil seed. A test, the Porton Down pathologists decided, was necessary on an animal about the same weight as a man. An unfortunate pig was chosen and an appropriate amount of the poison injected. The pig died, just over twenty-four hours later. Its post-mortem appearance showed a white cell count and haemorrhaging of internal organs similar to those suffered by Markov.

The coroner's verdict was that Georgi Markov had been 'unlawfully killed'; the 'Case of the Umbrella Murder', however, has never been fully put to rest. Annabella Markov and others, believing the Bulgarian secret service to be responsible for her husband's death (and for an attack on another Bulgarian defector in Paris, who died after feeling a stinging pain in the back), have since visited Bulgaria several times in an effort to establish the identity of the killer. In June 1991, the Bulgarian Interior Minister, Kristo Danov, admitted the culpability of the Bulgarian secret police in the affair. Later, other senior officials laid the blame for the assassination on ex-president Todor Zhivkov. A key figure in the investigation, Stoyan Savov, the 'Black General', a former head of the Bulgarian secret police, committed suicide in February 1992 while awaiting trial for destroying files relating to the Markov affair.

Alongside botulism (see BACTERIAL POISONING), ricin is one of the deadliest substances known; as little as 21-millionths of a gram can kill an individual. One gram would be enough to kill 36,000 people. The poison, which kills by agglutination of the red corpuscles of the blood, was first isolated during World War II, when it was considered as a chemical warfare agent. Its present status as a potential weapon of war is unknown, although the Markov murder does at least suggest that the now vanished Stalinist countries of Eastern Europe developed ricin as an agent of assassination. According to KGB defector Oleg Gordievesky, the umbrella and tiny poisoned sphere were provided by the KGB. Bulgaria only provided the hand that pulled the umbrella's trigger.

Four years after the Markov murder some direct clinical evidence of the effects of human ingestion came from a would-be ricin suicide. The director of the Mid America Poison Centre in Kansas City, Dr Snodgrass, received an irate telephone call from a suicidal 32-year-old man. He was telephoning to complain that he was still alive having taken fifty or more castor bean seeds, which was between ten and fifty times the lethal dose according to a book he had read in a public library. Snodgrass kept him talking long enough for the call to be traced and for an ambulance to pick him up.

A stomach pump retrieved a number of whole and partially decomposed beans, and he was given activated charcoal as a binding agent. About seven hours after swallowing the beans, the patient developed pain in the throat, abdomen and kidney, and virtually ceased his output of urine. His blood pressure dropped and his pulse rate increased. There was an improvement after he received large quantities of fluids, but this was followed by a severe setback with breathing problems that required four days of assistance from a respiratory ventilator. In his report on the case Dr Snodgrass concluded that 'The general public should be made more aware of the toxicity of castor bean seeds.'

S

SHARP INSTRUMENTS

Although most stabbing and CUT-THROAT injuries are inflicted by KNIVES and razors, a miscellany of other pronged and cutting instruments have been wielded murderously. Many of these sharp instruments, like BLUNT INSTRUMENTS, are snatched up in a moment of murderous rage, merely happening to be the nearest thing to hand: the screwdriver, the scissors, the knitting needle and, in many a drunken street fight, the smashed glass bottle.

However, sharp instruments, more so than blunt instruments, are carried by those with premeditated murder in mind. Chisels have featured in a number of celebrated crimes, including that of Nathan Leopold and Richard Loeb, scions of prominent Chicago families who murdered 14-year-old Bobbie Franks on 21 May 1924 in an attempt to prove their Nietzschean superiority to traditional ethics and mores. Bobbie Franks had his skull fractured four times with a chisel after accepting a ride from the duo; later his head was held under water to ensure death.

The vicious chisel murder of Mrs Anne Louisa Kempson in August 1931 was notable for the police work and the circumstantial evidence which enabled the apprehension of vacuum-cleaner salesman Henry Seymour (see Case File, Henry Daniel Seymour). Another prominent chisel user was British serial-killer Peter Sutcliffe ('The Yorkshire Ripper') who, on his 'just cleaning up the streets' mission between 1975 and 1980, disfigured the corpses of many of his thirteen victims with a wood chisel, after killing them by blows to the head with a hammer. In a somewhat vigorous self-killing in 1959, a Missouri handyman named Jackson gripped a wood chisel in his hands and plunged it into his own neck with such force that he almost severed the vertebrae.

A spectacular assassination by sharp instrument was carried out in Mexico City on 20 August 1940, when Ramon Mercader swung an ice-pick into the head of the exiled Russian revolutionary, Leon Trotsky. The crime was ordered by Josef Stalin, who, despite having banished Trotsky, was troubled that the latter's brand of democratic communism would become an opposition to his own tyrannical sort. (There was also more than a shade of personal envy and hatred involved.) Mercader later gave this account of Trotsky's murder, which takes up the story with him entering Trotsky's study:

I put the raincoat on the table on purpose so that I could take out the ice axe which I had in the pocket . . . I took the piolet out of

my raincoat, took it in my fist and, closing my eyes, I gave him a
tremendous blow on the head. The man screamed in such a way
that I will never forget [it] as long as I live. His scream was . . .
very long, infinitely long, and it still seems to me as if that scream
was piercing my brains.

Mercader tried to swing the ice-pick a second time, but evidencing
a tremendous will power, Trotsky overwhelmed him. He died the
next day, though, of the injury sustained to his brain.

Occasionally the gross circumstances of a murder by sharp
instruments are enlivened by the peculiar motive. One such case
was the 'Murder by Request' involving William Adams of London
and a shoemaker's awl in 1919 (see Case File); another was the
murder of Charles Walton in 1945. On 14 February of that year,
74-year-old Walton, a hedgecutter, was found impaled to the
ground by a pitchfork in a field near his Warwickshire home. The
two prongs of the pitchfork had been driven through his neck with
such force that they had gone 6in. into the ground. On the old
man's cheeks, throat and body, the sign of the cross had been
etched with Walton's own slash-hook. Close to the body lay his
walking stick, bloody from the blow to the head which felled him.
The superstitious (or canny?) locals blamed the murder on the
Warwickshire Witches and Robert Fabian of Scotland Yard, called
in by the local CID, was unable to make any headway against a wall
of silent fear. Fabian later wrote in his autobiography, apropros of
'The Mystery of Lower Quinton':

I advise anybody who is tempted at any time to venture into
Black Magic, witchcraft, Satanism – call it what you will – to
remember Charles Walton and to think of his death, which was
so clearly the ghastly climax of a pagan rite. There is no stronger
argument for keeping as far away as possible from the villains
with their swords, incense and mumbo jumbo. It is prudence on
which your future peace of mind and even your life could
depend.

More prosaically, Fabian was inclined to blame Walton's death on a
local man called Alfred Potter who owed Walton a large sum of
money. Walton had apparently been asking for repayment just
before he died.

The catalogue of murder by sharp instrument is vast, and most
cases, if terrible, are unremarkable. But some are noteworthy for
the sheer eccentricity of the instrument. For example, Wisconsin
sex-oriented serial-killer Jeffrey Dahmer murdered a number of his
victims by boring into their brains with an electric drill (see
CANNIBALISM). Lodger Henry Perry, an ex-serviceman made
mentally unstable by his war experience, smote a whole family –

Walter and Alice Cornish and their two daughters – at Forest Gate, London, on one day in 1919 with 'a carving fork from the drawer' and a pick-axe. In June 1972 Norbert Splett of the Austrian Tyrol stabbed holidaying Kurt Rheiners with an ornamental wooden spear, after discovering him engaged in intercourse with his girlfriend, Petra Schumacher. Sally Potterton, meanwhile, blamed the suicide of her daughter Penny on the teenager's boyfriend Maurice Searle and decided to take revenge. In August 1979 she accosted Searle in a Glasgow street and, at the point of her husband's Luger pistol (a souvenir from the war), forced Searle to her house and bound him to the bed. Then Sally Potterton, an ex-nurse, stuck a needle into his arm and attached it to a blood transfusion machine she had borrowed from the hospital. She literally drained the blood out of Searle, drop by drop. It took several hours.

CASE FILE: Murder by Request

William Nelson Adams, a 17-year-old market porter, was sentenced to death at Guildford Assizes in July 1919 for a murder he claimed he had only committed to oblige his victim. This was a man named George Jones, aged sixty, who, according to Adams, was 'worried out of his life' by a large income tax demand. Adams gave the story the sort of detail that seemed to make it ring true. He had met George Jones one evening on the Thames Embankment and Jones, discovering that he was homeless, invited him to share his lodgings. Some days later, Jones, an habitual thief, confided to Adams that he could not pay his income tax bill, and could see no way out of his dilemma save death. As a special service for the kindness that he had shown Adams, he asked the youth to kill him. 'I've done you a good turn. Now you do me one. Will you kill me?' Adams replied he would, if he could 'find the pluck'. He waited a week and then met Jones for a drink on 19 June 1919. Adams had with him a friend (who later proved untraceable) called Charlie Smith. All three had gone by tram to Tooting, where they had some more drinks at a public house. Then they had walked towards Sutton, Jones all the while asking Adams to kill him. 'God help me,' Jones said, 'will you kill me?' at the same time forcing a shoemaker's awl into Adams' hand. Adams replied, 'I will try.' At length the trio had reached a field adjoining the houses in Ridgeway Road, Sutton, where Jones prepared himself for his end, taking off his coat, waistcoat and shirt, and lying down on the grass. 'The best way is to stab me on the left side of the neck,' Jones told Adams. Adams hesitated, but Jones kept pleading with him. The indecision lasted for fifteen minutes, Charlie Smith all the while standing there silent. Finally, Adams decided to do it: '. . . temptation overcame me. I stabbed him, three times in the neck and three times in the

stomach. But I was not able to kill him.' Desperate, he tried to drag
Jones to a pond to drown him. However, the older man was too
heavy to move. Smith, as ever, was silent and of no help. So they
simply left Jones lying on the grass, after having first divested him
of the money he had on him. Jones was found early the next
morning, with his shirt tied around his stomach in an attempt to
staunch the bleeding.

He lived for three days, during which he told the police that he
was puzzled why Adams had stabbed him. 'I had done nothing to
him,' said Jones. He mentioned that Charlie Smith had been
present, but gave no explanation as to what the three of them were
doing in a field in Sutton in the middle of the night. The jury,
listening to Adams' odd story of the 'murder by request', was
disinclined to believe him when he said that he was 'only trying to
oblige the old gentleman', and found him guilty. Through the
intervention of the Home Secretary, Edward Shortt, the death
sentence on Adams was commuted to one of life imprisonment.

CASE FILE: Henry Daniel Seymour

On August Bank Holiday Monday 1931 Mrs Louisa Kempson,
aged fifty-eight, was found dead in her semi-detached house in St
Clements Street, Oxford. She had been beaten about the head with
a blunt instrument, such as a hammer, and in her throat was a
clean-cut wound 3 in. deep – it might have been made with a chisel,
it was thought. The wound had severed her carotid artery. The
house had been ransacked, but the murderer had got little for Mrs
Kempson's pain – as little as £3, stolen from her purse. Pathologist
Sir Bernard Spilsbury's analysis of the dead woman's stomach
contents suggested that she had been killed just after breakfast on
the Saturday. A man had been seen at the Kempson front door on
that day, and he was later found to be Henry Seymour, an habitual
thief turned vacuum-cleaner salesman. Mrs Andrews of Heading-
ton Hill, a former customer of Seymour's, was also able to tell the
police a curious story about Seymour: he had called on her the day
before Mrs Kempson was murdered, and said that his money had
been stolen from him while he was swimming. She gave him some
4s 6d for his bus fare, but he had returned later in the day saying he
had missed the last bus. He had persuaded her to put him up for the
night. The next morning, before Seymour left, she had noticed a
parcel on the hall-stand. It had been open at both ends, and she had
been able to see what was inside it – a brand new hammer and a
brand-new chisel with 3/4 in. blade. (Later it was proved that he had
bought these implements from a nearby ironmonger's with the
money that Mrs Andrews had lent him.) Mrs Kempson's house was
a mere ten minutes away.

The police on the case were also approached by an Aylesbury hotelier, who reported that he had retained the luggage of a customer who had failed to meet his bill. The suitcase belonged to Seymour, and upon examination by the police disgorged a hammer and chisel, both washed clean. Minute fragments of paper in the bottom of the suitcase, when sprinkled with water, unfolded to reveal the maker's name and were identifiable as the tools Seymour had bought at the ironmonger's. The hammer was too small to have caused the injuries to Mrs Kempson's head, but Spilsbury discovered under the microscope tiny traces of cloth, which suggested that the hammer's head had been wrapped in layers of cloth when being wielded. Seymour was apprehended in Brighton. He was staying in a lodging house run by a widow, and the hoover-salesman had purchased another chisel and bored two spy-holes in the floor of his room (which was above that of the landlady), so that he could keep watch on her to ascertain where she kept her valuables. Seymour was evasive in the witness box during his trial at Oxford Assizes, and his guilt was easily proved, even though the evidence was purely circumstantial. He was duly executed at Oxford Prison.

SNAKES

One of the first recorded intentional deaths from snake venom was Queen Cleopatra's suicide in 30BC. In order to discover the most efficient and painless passage to the other world she experimented with various poisons, using her slaves for acute toxicity tests. Extracts of HYOSCINE from henbane and ATROPINE from belladonna were rapid but painful; STRYCHNINE was also quick, but left the face contorted in agony, the so-called *risus sardonicus*. However, the venom of the asp allowed a swift and tranquil death. Her self-killing is immortalized in Shakespeare's *Antony and Cleopatra*, in which the Bard has her say of the asp: 'His biting is immortal; those that do die of it seldom or never recover.'

Venomous snakes fall into three main types: elapids (the cobra family), sea-snakes and vipers. Most inject a cocktail of poisons into their victims, which may have twenty-five or more active ingredients. But essentially, all snake venoms contain degrees and types of neurotoxins, anti-coagulants, vasculo-toxins (which stimulate cardiac arrest) and ingredients which destroy tissue. How the victim of a snake bite will die depends upon the species of snake which bit him. Rattlesnake venom, for example, contains a high proportion of anti-coagulant and vasculo-toxin, which results in the victim bleeding to death while having a heart attack. Venom of the Australasian taipan (*Oxyuranus scutellatus*), on the other hand, has a virulent neurotoxin which paralyses the central nervous system, causing breathing to stop. There has never been a definite case of taipan bite which has not been fatal to the human victim.

Meanwhile, something of the relative toxicity of the neurotoxin in the venom of the African cobra (*Naja Naja*) can be gathered from the following data which details the minimum lethal dose per kilogram of body for the mouse of various poisons:

POISON	LETHAL DOSE (micrograms)
Botulinus toxin	0.03
Cobra neurotoxin	0.3
Strychnine	500
Sodium cyanide	100000

Around two million people are bitten each year by poisonous snakes, of which 100,000 die. Few of these cases are homicidal, for outside of crime fiction (Sherlock Holmes 'The Speckled Band') and various thriller movies, the murderous use of the snake is extremely uncommon and fraught with difficulty.

Still, some have tried.

CASE FILE:　The Rattlesnake Murderer

When Mary James was found dead in the lily-pond outside her Los Angeles bungalow in 1935, it was thought she had died accidentally. Her grief-stricken husband Robert James (alias Raymond Lisemba) said so, and the police were inclined to believe him. Until, that is, three months later, when a Los Angeles captain of detectives, Jack Southard, saw a report that James had been arrested for propositioning a woman and considered it unsuitable behaviour for so recently a widowed man.

Southard learned that an employee of James (who ran a barber shop) called Charlie 'Chuck' Hope had been around the James bungalow at the time of the tragedy, and had since been phoning James constantly. Southard searched Hope's apartment and found a receipt for two rattlesnakes. Hope was arrested on suspicion of murder, and once inside the police station wasted little time in unburdening himself of the whole story.

Robert James had taken out a large insurance on his 25-year-old wife only months after their marriage – an insurance policy which he intended to cash as soon as possible. He persuaded Chuck Hope that a friend of his wanted to kill his wife, and that Chuck would receive $100 if he secured a 'hot pair' of rattlesnakes. The obliging Chuck (who claimed afterwards to have been hypnotized by James) visited various dealers, but the rattlesnakes he brought back were poor specimens. James tried them out on rabbits and chickens, none of which seemed the least prone to die from the snakes' attentions. Eventually, James told Chuck to go to a Pasadena dealer called 'Snake Joe' Houtenbrink, where Chuck procured two *Crotalus atrox* rattlers which were very hot indeed. (James tested them on chickens, which positively keeled over.) At this point, James let Chuck in on his real intention, which was to murder Mrs James, and promised him part of the insurance money. 'I was helpless and couldn't resist the look in his eyes,' said Chuck later.

James took Chuck Hope home with him one evening, passing him off as an 'eminent physician'. James persuaded his pregnant wife to let Hope perform an abortion on her that very night. She was encouraged to drink copious quantities of whiskey as an anaesthetic, and, once she passed out, was tied to a table. James then brought the snakes into the house in a specially designed box, which was constructed so that her leg could be inserted into it without letting the snakes escape. Mary James was left for several hours with her leg in the box, and was bitten numerous times by the rattlers. Chuck and James retired to the garage to eat sandwiches and drink rye. She was still alive, however, on their return and complained about the terrible pain in her leg, which had swelled to twice its normal size. Impatient with the snake method, James persuaded his wife to have a bath to soothe the leg, and while she was in the tub pushed her head down under the water and lifted her legs high (a method of DROWNING made infamous by 'Brides in the Bath Murderer' George Smith). When she was dead, James dressed her and placed her body in the lily-pond to make it look as though she had accidentally drowned.

The unlawful nature of Mary James' death encouraged the police to examine the fates of the four previous Mrs James. The first Mrs James had filed for divorce because she could no longer tolerate her husband's requirements for sado-masochistic sex. The second Mrs James was deserted when James left Emporia town, Kansas, pursued by the irate father of young girl he had made pregnant. His third wife, Winona, was badly injured in a car accident on the couple's honeymoon; she survived, only to die in a drowning accident in the bath. James collected $14,000 in life insurance – a policy he had taken out on the eve of their wedding. His fourth wife, Helen, complained that James was sexually impotent unless she whipped him, and became suspicious when he told her he wanted to insure her life. She refused, and quit the marital home saying that 'people who have it [insurance] always die of something strange'. As if to prove the truth of her words James' nephew, Cornelius Wright, who was insured by James for $10,000 drove the car his uncle had loaned him over a cliff near Santa Rosa. It was only now, in the course of the investigation into Mary James' demise, that the mechanic who towed the car away told the police that the car's steering had been sabotaged.

Why did Mary James not die from the bite of the rattlesnakes?

The answer is that she might well have done, if she had been left longer. Death from rattlesnake venom takes approximately fifteen hours, and James moved her while she was only suffering the initial symptoms. The other explanation is that the confines of the box and the thickness of Mrs James' leg prevented the snakes from injecting a full bite.

Robert James, who, despite his failure, became known as 'The Rattlesnake Murderer', was hanged at San Quentin in 1943, the last man to receive this form of the death penalty in California, the state thereafter switching to gas.

The moral of the James case might be that murderers, like actors, should never work with animals. A murder which, in its way, was perfect was committed by a German killer who used snake venom but no snake (see Case File).

CASE FILE: Aschaffenburg Mamba

Unlike most murder victims, Frau Christine Albert was able to name the person who murdered her, and how and when it happened. As she left her home at 9 Haselmuehl Way in Aschaffenburg, West Germany, to attend mass on the morning of 13 November 1984, she was approached by her estranged son-in-law, Heinrich Birzer. His complaint was a familiar one: 'It's all your fault!' he shouted, 'you're the one who destroyed my marriage.' He had then taken her by the shoulders, and shaken her violently. As Birzer shook her, Frau Albert felt a sharp, pricking sensation in her right shoulder. Birzer then ran off. When she examined her shoulder in the bathroom mirror she found a tiny puncture wound, as though from a large pin. She bathed it in disinfectant and went off to church.

At the church she met her daughter, Helga, and told her what had happened. By the end of the service, Frau Albert had become nauseous, and decided to see the doctor. The doctor listened to her account of the assault, and examined the wound. He said that it was not serious, and prescribed camomile tea.

Resting on the sofa that afternoon, Frau Albert's face became paralysed. Her daughter summoned an emergency ambulance, and rushed her to hospital. Despite the effort of the doctors her condition worsened rapidly, and she died just before midnight.

Although she had been under observation for nearly seven hours, the doctors were unable to diagnose the cause of death. Accordingly a death certificate was not issued and permission for burial was not granted. The case was passed to the local police, who ordered an autopsy.

The pathologist at the police morgue, Dr Milton Berger, was startled to find that she had died from the effects of the venom of a black mamba, with the venom presumably entering via the wound on her right shoulder.

It was the first time that the Aschaffenburg CID had ever encountered murder by an African serpent.

Having ascertained that Frau Albert herself had never been to darkest Africa, nor was an amateur herpetologist, the local CID arrested the person she said had murdered her, 55-year-old bus driver, Heinrich Birzer. Birzer said that he was delighted that his mother-in-law had died (he hoped that it had been painful) and admitted to having scuffled with her. He denied that he had killed her. 'What's a black mamba?' he asked when told the cause of death.

At his lodgings a small bottle of North African origin and a hypodermic syringe were found. Birzer explained that the bottle was a souvenir from a holiday to Tunisia the previous year, and that he had found the syringe under a seat in his bus. He had removed it so that no one would be injured. Neither bottle nor syringe bore traces of any substance. If there ever had been any substance in them, they had been very thoroughly washed since.

Friends of Birzer, who had holidayed with him to Tunisia, confirmed that the bottle was a souvenir, and that it had been empty on purchase. Nor had they ever left the resort of Gabes, which was hardly a black market for snake venom. The Tunisian police were unable to find any evidence of black mamba venom ever having entered the country. Where, then, had the poison come from? As the police investigation soon discovered, there was no uncontrolled source of black mamba poison in Germany and probably not in the whole of Europe. Germany had one snake farm near Munich where black mamba venom was produced for scientific and medical purposes. It was produced in very small amounts and every drop was registered and accounted for. Every shipment for the last three years was traced to its destination.

The investigation continued for a year, during which time a steady troop of medical experts examined and re-examined the remains of Frau Albert, the majority finding, like Dr Berger, that she had died from a dose of black mamba venom.

Almost exactly a year after Frau Albert died, Heinrich Birzer was tried for her murder. The prosecution was able to establish motive (Birzer not only blamed Frau Albert for breaking up his marriage to Helga, but of breaking a promise to him that she would leave half her villa to him, a villa on which he had spent thirty years' work), and placed Birzer at the incident which seemed to have set her death in train. However, the prosecution was unable to furnish any proof that Birzer had ever possessed black mamba venom.

He was acquitted.

SPIDERS

The motive which prompted Carolyn Laurens (née Fichardt) to murder her husband, and then her sister, was a standard one of obsessive love. The means she employed, however, demonstrated a quite original talent for the fine art of murder.

Ever since she was a girl in the Cape Province of South Africa, Carolyn had harboured an unrequited love for Adrian Dreyer. He, however, determined to marry Carolyn's sister, Georgina. On the night of Adrian and Georgina's engagement, Carolyn, in a sort of revenge, lost her virginity to neighbour Daniel Laurens, and agreed to marry him. The two couples were married in a double ceremony on 16 February 1975.

The passage of time did nothing to lessen Carolyn's desire for the man who was now her brother-in-law. She determined to marry him.

On 28 February 1980, as she later confessed, Carolyn murdered her husband in a daring car 'accident'. She plied him with drink at a restaurant and agreed to let him drive home. As the Toyota car wound along a mountain road, she suddenly wrenched the wheel, opened the door and jumped. Taken by surprise, and sluggish from ALCOHOL, Daniel Laurens was unable to stop the car from going over the cliff. A tragic accident, was the opinion of the police.

Carolyn's murder of her sister was no less inventive. Late in the evening of 19 February 1982 Adrian Dreyer, watching TV, heard a series of terrible moans from the bedroom where his wife was asleep, having taken a soporific. He rushed in to find her being bitten by a small, pea-sized red button spider, *Lostrodectus indistinctus*. Dreyer killed the spider, but his wife died even before the ambulance could reach their Worcester home.

The local coroner, Dr Morris Vander Houten, had little difficulty in establishing the cause of death, since Dreyer was able to give him the squashed remains of the arachnid. However, although Vander Houten wrote 'spider bite' on the death certificate he was not altogether satisfied and passed a report to the offices of the criminal police in Cape Town. The reason for his dissatisfaction was that the red button spider was an uncommon species, found only around the town of Malmesbury, which was fifty miles away from Worcester. He had been unable to find any previous reports of the species in Worcester.

An investigation was begun by Inspector Johann Groote of the Cape Town CID, who was informed by an academic entomologist that the chances of the Malmesbury red button spider making its way to Georgina Dryer's bed in Worcester by accident was one in a million. It also transpired that a centre for research on the red button spider at Malmesbury agricultural college had recently given three spiders to a blonde-haired Dr Helena Dippenser from the University of Witwatersrand. No such person existed.

The police were about to give up their investigation and search for Dippenser when they learned, from one of Dreyer's servants, that he had been having intercourse on a regular basis with Carolyn Laurens for a number of years. A possible motive of spouse-removal began to suggest itself. They could find no proof, however, that dark-haired Carolyn Laurens was a be-wigged 'Dr Helena Dippenser' or, indeed, that the red button spider which bit Georgina Dreyer had come from the Malmesbury laboratory. A search of Carolyn's house revealed nothing more incriminating than a remarkably complete set of reference works on spiders, snakes and other poisonous creatures, together with a number of true crime books. In desperation, the police decided to confront Carolyn Laurens, in the hope of startling her into an incriminating action. They found her sipping tea on Adrian Dreyer's veranda. When told that police were searching her house for evidence that she was implicated in the murder of her sister, Carolyn Laurens excused herself and retired into Dreyer's house. After about half an hour, there was the sound of a twelve-bore shotgun going off. Carolyn Laurens had killed herself. She left behind a detailed two-page confession, both to the murder of Georgina and her husband, Daniel. Adrian Dreyer was completely innocent of her plan to free both of them so that they could marry. As the Cape Town police was later obliged to admit, if Carolyn Laurens had kept her nerve at the very end she would have got away with murder. Twice.

There are some fifty species of poisonous spider which are dangerous to humankind. Most dangerous, apart from the red button spider, are the southern black widow spider (*Latrodectus mactans*), the Australian red back spider, the funnel-web spider, and the New Zealand katpio. There are an average of 1000 fatalities each year worldwide from spider bite, most of which are children. Virtually all of these are accidental deaths (although, as the Carolyn Laurens case demonstrates, homicidal spider use is difficult to prove), with the widespread black widow being a prime culprit, since it interprets any touching of its web as a fly to be eaten. The venom of the black widow has four main poisons, composed essentially of protein compounds, three of which are concerned with stunning and killing its insect prey. However, the fourth poison, alpha-latrotoxin, is a nerve poison which is effective against humans. It damages the nerve endings by keeping the nerve transmission fluid acetylcholine flowing until its supply is exhausted (see POISONING for more on the workings of toxins and the nervous system). Eventually, this causes paralysis of the muscles. A bite from a black widow is rarely fatal, but where it is death will take two to three days. Something of a devotee of poisonous animals, America's Robert James tried to kill his fifth wife with a black widow, as well as SNAKES, making him one of the select few known to have attempted, let alone achieve, murder with a venomous arachnid.

STARVATION

Mass homicidal starvation is commonplace in war. Of the six million who died in the Nazi death camps, many did so from privation, not CYANIDE gas. Likewise, many Allied prisoners of the Japanese during World War II expired from malnutrition, particularly those set to work on the infamous Burma–Siam railway.

Individuals may also be deliberately starved. Adults most at risk are political prisoners held in jail or some other confinement. A fit adult may survive some six to ten days if he or she is denied food and water. (If fluid is given, survival may be extended for many weeks.) Outside this context the homicidal starvation of individual adults is unusual. Perhaps the most celebrated British case is the starvation of Harriet Staunton, by her husband and others in 1875 (see Case File).

Elizabeth Brownrigg, a London woman who would have not been out of place as a guard in a concentration camp, starved her fourteen-year-old servant girl Mary Clifford between 1765 and 1766. Whether this was the direct cause of Clifford's death is difficult to know, however; when she was eventually rescued by parish officials she was a bleeding mass of cuts and sores, the result of Brownrigg's daily beatings and whippings.

Much the most frequently encountered form of individual homicidal starvation is that of children, where it is, inevitably, accompanied by other forms of neglect, such as hypothermia. Starvation may present itself as a mass vitamin defect, or malnutrition with some superimposed infection, as well as gross (no food) starvation. The body of the starvation victim will be emaciated, the skin dry and drawn like parchment over the bony prominences, the cheeks hollow, eyes sunken and legs and arms 'like broomsticks'. Pigmentation may vary from sallowness to melanosis. The external emaciation is mirrored in the internal organs, which are often atrophied.

The law provides special enactments to discourage the neglect of children. Under the Children and Young Persons Acts of 1933 to 1963, and the similarly titled (Scotland) Act of 1937:

> A parent or other person liable to maintain a child or young person shall be deemed to have neglected him in a manner likely to cause injury to his health if he has failed to provide adequate food, or clothing, medical aid or lodging, for him, or if, having been unable otherwise to provide such food, clothing, medical aid or lodging, he has failed to take steps to procure it to be provided.

Despite this law a sad procession of child starvation cases goes through the courts each year.

CASE FILE: The Emaciation of Harriet Staunton

In 1875, auctioneer's clerk Louis Staunton married left-on-the-shelf Harriet; at thirty-six she was ten years older, plain and not very bright. Her most attractive attribute, as far as Louis was concerned, was her £3000 endowment. Harriet's mother was intuitively opposed to the marriage and visited the newly weds at their home in Loughborough Road, Brixton. Upon being asked how she was, Harriet replied 'Middling well, Mama.' Her mother was only allowed to stay ten minutes, and on the following day received letters from both Harriet and Louis informing her that it would be best if she never called again.

Soon after, Harriet produced a son, and was persuaded in the summer of 1876 to move to Cudham, Kent, where Louis' artist brother Patrick and his wife Elizabeth had a cottage. Louis paid Patrick £1 a week (out of Harriet's inheritance) to look after her. Louis, meanwhile, moved into a nearby farmhouse, where he lived with Elizabeth Staunton's younger sister, Alice Rhodes. In February 1877, Harriet's mother met Alice Rhodes (they were distantly related) in London, and noticed that she was wearing one of her daughter's brooches. She was also conspicuously unforthcoming concerning Harriet's welfare. Alarmed, Harriet's mother searched out Louis' farmhouse retreat, and called on him on 5 March, only to have the door slammed in her face. Just over a month later, Patrick and Elizabeth Staunton left Harriet's child at a London hospital, where it died as a result of its starved condition. On 12 April Louis and Elizabeth booked lodgings at 34 Forbes Road, Penge, in South London for 'an invalid lady'. Harriet was installed later that evening, only to die next day. The doctor who attended her, Mr Dean Longrigg, initially gave the cause of death as 'cerebral disease and apoplexy'.

Quite by chance Harriet's brother-in-law overheard someone in a Penge post office inquiring about the registering of Harriet's death, and informed the police. At the inquest on Harriet Staunton it was found that there was not an ounce of fat on her body (which weighed 5 stone 4lb), and that it had been in a filthy and verminous condition. Pathologists examining the remains decided that the cause of death was neglect and starvation, a conclusion that Dr Longrigg himself now concurred with. The three Stauntons and Alice Rhodes were arrested on a charge of murder.

Their trial at the Old Bailey in September 1877 was dominated by medical evidence. Defending Patrick Staunton, Mr Edward Clarke suggested that Harriet's death might have been caused by diabetes, phthisis, Addison's disease or tuberculosis, with several eminent expert witnesses testifying to this effect. According to Dr Longrigg, however, 'the amount of tubercle was very, very slight' and had no bearing on her demise.

Mr Justice Hawkins, too, was brusquely intolerant of the medical evidence. Manifestly biased against the defendants, he summed up heavily against them. On 26 September they were found guilty and sentenced to death.

The sentence was greeted with protest by some in the medical fraternity, who believed that Harriet Staunton had died of TB. The *Lancet* observed that before murder by starvation was proved it was necessary to prove death by starvation. Some 700 doctors, headed by Sir William Jenner, signed a petition of protest, and forwarded it to the Home Secretary, who reprieved the accused. Alice Rhodes was released, while the others were given varying terms of imprisonment.

STRANGULATION

'I began to tie the nylons around her neck. She came to a little and she was putting up a fight now. I stuck the gag in her mouth. Now she was looking at me, right at me and I had the nylons around her neck, but she kept struggling so I had to pull them tight . . .' Thus did Albert DeSalvo, the Boston Strangler (see Case File), recall the killing of one of his victims. Strangling is one of the most commonly encountered forms of killing (about ten per cent of the 708 homicides recorded in Britain in 1991 were by this method), and is invariably committed by men against women. It is a virtual occupational hazard amongst women prostitutes.

Strangulation is one of the several deaths from ASPHYXIA and is caused by constriction of the neck, either by some form of ligature or the hands. In manual strangulation, or 'throttling', the victim's throat is compressed by the hands and fingers of the assailant, and this impedes respiration, the flow of blood to the brain and may cause almost immediate death from pressure on the carotid nervous plexuses, leading to reflex cardiac arrest ('vagal inhibition'). The attacker's fingers, pressing deeply into the flesh, will leave external bruising, usually at the level of the voice box, and there may well be multiple scratch marks on the strangled corpse caused by the victim herself trying to claw away the compressing hand. Death from manual strangulation is probably in the order of fifteen to thirty seconds, although it varies with the age and fitness of both the assailant and the victim. According to some authorities, children can survive the oxygen deprivation caused by strangling for as long as six minutes. It is physically impossible for a person to strangle himself manually because as he begins to lose consciousness he will relax his grip and begin to recover.

Ligature strangulation involves the use of some pliable strip which is put around the victim's neck and the ends crossed over and pulled tight (variations on the theme include knots and running nooses). Stockings, tights, scarves and belts are common ligatures.

Herbert John Bennett, the Yarmouth beach murderer of 1897, strangled his unwanted wife with a bootlace. America's Ruth Snyder ('Granite Woman') and her paramour Henry Judd Gray ('Lover Boy') killed Snyder's corset-salesman husband in the early hours of 20 March 1927 by attacking him with a sash-weight; when he continued to struggle they knocked him out with CHLORO-FORM and then garotted him with picture wire.

Some ninety years later John Duffy, the 'Railway Killer' who murdered and raped three women in the vicinity of London train stations between 29 December 1985 and 17 May 1986, killed two of his victims with a device known as a Spanish windlass. This consisted of a strip of material looped around the victim's neck and tightened by winding a stick. In the case of 19-year-old Alison Day, the diminutive acne-ridden Duffy used a strip of her own shirt for the garotte. (Pathologist Peter Vanesis reported that the tightening of the ligature knot at the front of Alison's neck had affected the voice box, and was taken as a sign that the killer was acquainted with martial arts or had been in the forces; Duffy was a Kung Fu freak.) Duffy strangled fifteen-year-old Maartje Tamboezer, the daughter of a Shell Oil executive living in West Horsley, with her own scarf, tightened by a branch.

The marks left by a ligature consist of a groove around the neck, usually at the level of the thyroid cartilage or 'Adam's Apple'. The line of constriction will often be patterned, corresponding with the surface pattern of the material used for the ligature. Self-strangulation with a ligature is possible, although uncommon. Pathologist Keith Simpson found only three such cases in his first twenty-five years of medical-legal practice (out of 40,000 cases of all kinds). Strangulation by ligature may occur accidentally, when someone's clothes get caught in a machine or moving object. Such a fate famously befell the flamboyant American dancer Isadora Duncan, who was accidentally strangled in 1927 when her scarf got caught in the wheels of her car.

However strangulation is caused, the victim is, in the under-stated words of Sir Sydney Smith, 'not a pretty sight'. He or she will have: 'Bluish or purple lips and ears, change of colour of the nails, froth and possibly blood-staining about the nose or mouth, the tongue forced outward, the hands clenched – these are the typical signs of asphyxial death.' With homicidal strangling, espe-cially of the manual sort, the hyoid bone, a delicate structure in the throat above the Adam's Apple, is often fractured. Suicidal and accidental strangulation almost never causes it to be broken. If great force is used in homicidal strangling, damage may be caused to the thyroid and cricoid cartilages.

To be counted amongst the most unusual motives for strangula-tion was that offered by Edward Leonski, an American GI based in Australia during World War II. In May 1942 Melbourne was shocked by three murders by strangulation (manual) in three days; the victims were all women – Ivy Mcleod, Pauline Thompson and Gladys Hosking – and all killed in the street. On the night of the last killing an observant sentryman at the local US Army base challenged a dishevelled soldier trying to sneak into the camp. A Melbourne woman also reported that a GI had threatened to strangle her on a date. Both the sentry and the 'date' identified burly Texan Edward Joseph Leonski, a man who had recently confided to his tent mate that 'I'm a Dr Jekyll and Mr Hyde! I killed! I killed!' Leonski readily confessed to the killings. The reason, he explained, was that he liked women with soft voices: 'That's why I choked these ladies. It was to get their voices.' He recalled with particular affection that Pauline Thompson had had an especially mellifluous voice: 'I could feel myself going mad about it.' Despite a family history of insanity, Leonski, 'The Singing Strangler', was executed.

In Spain and the Spanish empire, strangulation was the official form of execution, the means employed being only a slightly more sophisticated version of the windlass used by John Duffy above. 'Garotting' involved tying the victim into a special chair and a metal collar being placed around the neck. A heavy lever at the back of the chair was used to pull the collar tight. The device was used as capital punishment in Spain as late as 1963.

Stranglings are invariably one-to-one affairs. It is an unusual method of serial-killing, although Pasadena youth duo Dean Allen Corll and Elmer Wayne Henley seem to have strangled most of their thirty-two vagrant and hitch-hiker victims, after KIDNAPPING them and subjecting them to sodomy and other indignities while they were strapped to a 'torture board'. Eventually sickened by the gruesome twosome's hobby, Henley shot Corll on 8 August 1973 and gave himself up to the Texan police. Serial-killers Jeffrey Dahmer and Dennis Nilsen also dispatched at least some of their victims by this method, as did Frenchwoman Jeanne Weber, the baby-sitter from hell. Between 1905 and 1907, Weber – an alcoholic prostitute, as well as an unofficial minder of children – killed five children in her care. Acquitted twice of murder, she was finally caught literally red-handed; not only did she strangle her final victim, she maniacally tore at his limbs and continued to do so until restrained by police. Interned in an asylum at Mareville, she proved to be so keen on manual strangulation that she tried to kill herself by this method. She failed, but seems to have died in the attempt, probably from choking on her own vomit.

Presumably the attraction of strangulation for serial-killers is that it allows the exercising of domination and control: the process of extinguishing life can be prolonged almost at will by a slight lessening of the pressure to allow a temporary remission.

And of course, the archetypal serial-killer to adopt this method of murder was 'The Boston Strangler' himself.

CASE FILE: The Boston Strangler

It began on 14 June 1962 and ended on 4 January 1964. During the intervening eighteen months Boston was subjected to a one-man reign of terror that left thirteen women sexually assaulted and murdered, and the city with a criminal legend to rival that of London's Jack the Ripper. No one was ever charged for the crimes of 'The Boston Strangler', but he was almost certainly Albert Henry DeSalvo, a sexual psychopath who was also known to the police as a fraudster ('The Measuring Man)' and a rapist ('The Green Man').

Born in Chelsea, Massachusetts, in 1931, DeSalvo was one of six children fathered by a tyrannical brute who beat them and their mother ceaselessly. On one notable occasion he broke the mother's fingers one by one. Frequently he brought home a prostitute and had sex with her in front of the children. The mother, for her part, was preoccupied and had little time for her offspring. Albert DeSalvo developed a taste for sadism early, but the real key to his criminal development was sex, for which he had an insatiable need. By the age of eight he had experienced sexual intercourse and oral sex. In his teens, like his father, he turned to petty crime and was arrested several times for breaking and entering. After serving with the US army of occupation in Germany, he returned to the US with his German wife, Irmgard, and was stationed at Fort Dix, New Jersey, where in January 1955 he was charged with his first sex offence, the molestation of a nine-year-old girl. But the mother of the girl, fearing what the publicity would do to her daughter, dropped the case. Later, DeSalvo was released from the army with an honourable discharge, and moved with his wife to Boston, where he worked as a handyman.

In 1958 DeSalvo began his 'Measuring Man' con-trick, where he approached attractive young women in their apartments, telling them that he represented a modelling agency, and that they would make ideal models. Clipboard and measuring tape in hand, DeSalvo would then measure the woman's vital statistics. On these occasions, he made no molestations, although he did seduce a number of the 'models'. In 1960 he was caught in the act of breaking and entering a premises in Cambridge, Massachusetts, and admitted to the police that he was the 'Measuring Man'. He received a two year prison sentence for burglary.

After his release, he graduated almost immediately from caressing girls as he measured them to violent sexual assault, breaking into women's apartments and raping them. He was described by his victims as the 'Green Man' since he wore green work trousers and shirt. According to his own count, DeSalvo raped more than 1000 women.

In the summer of 1962 he began to strangle to death, as well as rape. His first victim was 55-year-old divorcee Anna Slesers, whom he knocked unconscious with a BLUNT INSTRUMENT and then strangled with the belt of her housecoat, afterwards tying the ends in a bow beneath her chin – a technique which would become his trademark. (In a remarkably accurate psychological profile of the Strangler, psychiatrist Dr James A. Brussel suggested to the police that the killer was of Spanish or Italian descent, since garotting is a method used by bandits in both countries.) The body was left lying on its back with the legs apart. After killing Slesers, he ransacked her apartment, although he stole nothing.

Within a fortnight DeSalvo had assaulted and murdered 85-year-old Mary Mullen, an attack he would later prove reticent about, since she reminded him of his grandmother. On 30 June DeSalvo murdered for the third time, strangling 68-year-old Nina Nichols with a stocking. Medical examination showed that her assailant had bitten her and assaulted her with a wine bottle.

Two days later, on Monday 2 July, neighbours of a 65-year-old retired nurse named Helen Blake, who lived in Lynn, north of Boston, became anxious at not having seen her for two days and called the police. She was found face down on her bed; she had been strangled with a pair of stockings. As well as the stockings, a brassiere was tied around her neck, and fastened under the chin in a clumsy bow. The medical examiner estimated that she had been dead for two or three days.

On 21 August Mrs Ida Irga, aged seventy-five, was found dead in her apartment. This time death was due to manual strangulation, after which a pillow case had been tied around the neck. She had been sexually assaulted and bitten.

Ten days later DeSalvo struck again. This time his victim was Jane Sullivan, a 67-year-old Irish nurse. She was found in a kneeling position in the bathtub, her face in 6 in. of water. A powerful woman, she had evidently put up a great deal of resistance. Two stockings were knotted around her neck.

Boston was now in a state of near-hysteria, with the police apparently incapable of catching the Strangler. They rounded up scores of sexual deviants – but not Albert DeSalvo, since they had him entered in their files as a burglar. DeSalvo refrained from making more attacks until 5 December. He later claimed that on that day, as on the days of his other attacks, he became so obsessed with the image of violent sex that the top of his head 'was so hot that I thought it would explode'. On that evening DeSalvo knocked on the door of an apartment and, employing his usual ruse, pretended to be a repairman sent by the landlord to check the pipes and toilet. The girl refused to let him inside, so he went to another apartment, where he persuaded twenty-year-old Sophie Clark, an attractive black student, to open the door. Inside the apartment, Clark turned her back on DeSalvo who later said that he was overwhelmed by her curvacious body. He grabbed her from behind, subdued her and strangled her with nylon stockings. Medical examination established that she had been raped, and a semen stain on the carpet beside the body indicated that her killer had later masturbated over her. This was the first case in which rape was unquestionably established, and it led to speculation that her killer was a second Boston Strangler, one who preferred younger women.

In fact, it was Albert DeSalvo simply altering his victim 'type'. Three weeks later, on the last day of 1962, a businessman stopped his car outside the apartment of his secretary at 515 Park Drive and blew his horn. When she failed to come down, he assumed that she had already left, and went on to work. Finding that she was not at the office, he asked the superintendent of her apartment block to check on her. Patricia Bisette, aged twenty-three and white, was lying on the bed strangled with her own nylons. DeSalvo had visited Bisette several years earlier in his Measuring Man guise.

On 16 February DeSalvo gained admittance to the apartment of a German girl named Gertrude Gruen, who was at home with flu. The man removed his coat and told her that she was pretty enough to be a model. He then informed her that there was dust on the back on her housecoat collar; she turned away to let him brush it off; instead, he hooked his arm around her neck and began to strangle her. However, Gruen fought so frantically, sinking her teeth into his hand until she bit the bone, that he turned and fled. The police were disappointed to find that the shock of the encounter had wiped all memory of the Strangler's face from her memory.

On 9 March 1963 the Strangler murdered another elderly woman, Mary Brown, aged sixty-nine, this time with unchecked violence. He took with him a brass pipe, which he used to smash the victim's head, and drove a fork into her breast several times. He also manually throttled her – although she was already dead – and then committed necrophilia.

On 6 May 1963 Oliver Chamberlin, a friend of 23-year-old graduate student Beverly Samans, was puzzled when she failed to answer the phone in her Cambridge apartment. He borrowed the key from the building supervisor. Beverly Samans had been stabbed in the throat, and a stocking knotted around her neck, along with two handkerchiefs. She was naked, and her legs were tied to the bedposts. The autopsy reported 22 stab wounds. De Salvo later said he stabbed the girl before leaving the apartment: 'Once I stabbed her, I couldn't stop. I kept hitting her and hitting

her with that knife . . . She kept bleeding from the throat . . . I hit
her and hit her and hit her . . .'

The eleventh victim of the Boston Strangler was 58-year-old
Evelyn Corbin. She was found almost naked on the bed, nylon
stockings tied in a bow around her ankles. She had been manually
strangled.

On 23 November 1963, the day after President Kennedy was
assassinated, the Strangler killed his next victim, 23-year-old Joann
Graff, a dress designer and Sunday School teacher. He killed her
with her own black leotard, afterwards knotted into the trademark
bow, and left her nude body on a day bed in her apartment. Later
that day, DeSalvo watched a TV news report on Joann Graff's
murder with his wife and two children. He later said: 'I knew it was
me who did it but why I did it and everything else, I don't
know . . . I wasn't excited. I didn't think about it. I sat down to
dinner and didn't think about it at all.'

The final victim was strangled on 4 January 1964. She was
nineteen-year-old Mary Sullivan, whom he manually strangled after
gaining admittance to her apartment. Her dead body was found by
her flatmates on their return home from work. In the words of the
police report, Mary Sullivan's body was 'on the bed in a propped
position, buttocks on pillow, back against headboard, head on right
shoulder, knees up, eyes closed, viscous liquid dripping from
mouth to right breast, breasts and lower extremities exposed,
broomstick handle inserted in vagina . . .' Knotted around her
neck were a stocking and a silk scarf tied together in a huge comic
bow. A bright greetings card which read 'Happy New Year' was
propped against her foot.

The public were incensed, and the special 'Strangler Task Force'
set up by the police worked tirelessly to find the culprit. However,
the murders themselves ceased.

On 27 October 1964 a young woman phoned the police to say
that she had been sexually assaulted in her apartment by a man who
had pretended to be a police detective. He had pinned her to the
bed and threatened her with a knife, and bound her hand and foot.
After molesting her he had made off saying 'I'm sorry.' The girl
described the assailant in such detail that a police artist was able to
make a sketch of the face. Looking at it, one detective commented
'This looks like the Measuring Man'. DeSalvo was arrested on 5
November 1964 and was identified by some of his rape victims. On
4 February 1965 he was committed to the Bridgewater State
Hospital, a mental institution in Massachusetts, where he was
diagnosed as schizophrenic. It never occurred to the police that the
Measuring Man and the Green Man rapist were also the Boston
Strangler.

This was left to an inmate of Bridgewater Hospital, a murderer
named George Nassar, to find out. Listening to DeSalvo talk about

sex and violence, and some of his exploits, he became convinced that DeSalvo was the Strangler. Nassar, hopeful of securing the $110,000 reward on the Strangler's head, informed his lawyer, F. Lee Bailey, and Bailey interviewed DeSalvo, recording the conversations. DeSalvo admitted to being the Strangler and even to two killings not yet attributed to the Strangler (taking his count to fifteen). His knowledge of the murders and the victims' apartments was such that little doubt could be entertained as to the truth of the confession. Nevertheless, there was not one single piece of direct evidence to support the claim, and DeSalvo's attorney managed, in a phenomenal piece of plea bargaining, to have his client stand trial only for the 'Green Man' rapes and a series of robberies.

On 26 November 1973, Albert DeSalvo was found dead in his cell at Walpole State Prison, stabbed through the heart; he was forty-two years old. He never stood trial for the crimes of the Boston Strangler.

CASE FILE: The John Barleycorn Strangling

An unusual British case of strangulation was that of pub landlady Mrs Rose Robinson at the John Barleycorn public house in Portsmouth. On the night of Sunday, 28 November 1943 Welch the barman left at about 10.35 p.m., and heard his 63-year-old employer bolt the door behind him. The next morning, Rose Robinson was found strangled in her ransacked bedroom; her handbag had been emptied. Pathologist Dr Keith Simpson concluded that Mrs Robinson had been strangled as the killer sat astride her:

> The fingermarks told a clear story – a deep bruise on the right side of the voice box, presumably made by a thumb, and three lighter bruises in a line on the other side. Right-handed, four inches across. There were no curved fingernail impressions immediately related to these marks, but there were several scratches on the neck that could have been made by Mrs Robinson as she struggled to prise away her attacker's hands.

A month later, two London policemen on the lookout for thieves spotted a shabby, furtive man, one Harold Loughans, trying to sell a pair of new shoes in a cafe in Waterloo Road. Taken in for questioning, Loughans told his captors: 'I'm wanted for things more serious than this. The Yard wants me. It's the trapdoor for me now.' He then made a statement in which he confessed to a string of burglaries, among them breaking into the John Barleycorn public house, Portsmouth, and assaulting Mrs Robinson. Forensic examination of Loughans' clothes backed up his confession. The one problem seemed to be that Loughans had no fingers on his right hand, a fact the police passed on to Simpson with some anxiety. Simpson was undaunted: Loughans still had a thumb and four half-fingers and if he was sitting astride the victim his body weight behind the hand would have been sufficient for the purpose he intended. Loughans' missing finger ends also explained why there had been no fingernail impressions on the corpse.

By the time of his trial at Winchester Assizes, Loughans had changed his mind about the advisability of admitting to murdering the landlady of the John Barleycorn (a crime for which he would surely 'swing'), and declared that he was innocent, and that the police had put words into his mouth. The jury at Winchester Assizes failed to agree a verdict, after Loughans produced an alibi sworn to by four independent witnesses, which placed him in a London bomb shelter on the night of the murder. The case was retried at the Old Bailey.

Here Loughans' defence produced a masterstroke: they had retained the services of the eminent pathologist Bernard Spilsbury. Although Spilsbury had not examined the corpse, he had visited Loughans in prison, where he had been impressed by his weak handshake. Spilsbury told the court: 'I do not believe he could strangle anyone with that hand'. Spilsbury's evidence won Loughans a not guilty verdict.

In 1960 *The People* newspaper published the memoirs of J.D. Caswell, who had prosecuted Loughans. Caswell intimated that Loughans was very lucky to have got off. Loughans reacted by starting libel proceedings from prison, where he was serving a sentence for burglary, and the case was heard in 1963. The jury found for the paper and against Loughans. Effectively, he was proved guilty of a murder charge after being found not guilty. Three months later Loughans, knowing he could not be tried for the same crime twice, wrote a confession for *The People*: 'I want to say I done that job. I did kill the woman in the public house in Portsmouth.'

He used his 'bad' hand to write the confession.

STRYCHNINE
The berries of the Indian shrub *Strychnos nux vomica* are mentioned in a number of Western textbooks of 17th-century medicine, which recommend powdered berries for the poisoning of vermin, dogs and birds. It was perhaps this practice which gave others more sinister ideas; by the 19th century strychnine was one of the most popular homicidal poisons.

The active principle of the berry *Strychnos nux vomica* and its near, but less common relative, *Strychnos ignatii* ('St Ignatius' Bean'), was isolated in 1818 by the chemists Pelletier and Carenton as a white crystalline alkaloid which they named 'strychnine'. Extracted from the dried disc-shaped seeds of the *Strychnos nux vomica* berry, strychnine had a medicinal application in very low concentration as a stimulant, and Tincture of Nux Vomica and Easton's Syrup were popular tonics for the convalescent. In anything other than medicinal doses, strychnine is a ruthless and especially violent poison. One and a half grains taken orally is usually considered to constitute a fatal dose, but doses as low as one third of a grain have resulted in death.

The symptoms of strychnine poisoning are notable. In the words of Professor Glaister, whose *Medical Jurisprudence and Forensic Toxicology* is the 'bible' of most forensic pathologists: 'There is no set of phenomena, from disease or poison, which is exactly comparable to that which follows the absorption of strychnine into the body.' Reaction to the administration of strychnine is swift, producing a sense of suffocation, and breathing difficulties. When the drug reaches the motor areas of the spinal cord, it causes the back to arch in a condition known as 'opisthotonos', so that only the head and heels touch the ground. Such spasms can last for up to two minutes, the victim being conscious and in extreme pain throughout, before the muscles relax prior to the onset of another spasm. This pattern may be repeated several times, producing a tetanic spasm in which the chest is fixed, the neck stiffens and the face is set in a macabre grin, the *risus sardonicus*, which is accompanied by a wild-eyed staring expression. Death is usually after four or five spasms, with the intervals between the spasms lasting between ten and fifteen minutes. The victim dies of suffocation, due to paralysis of the respiratory muscles. Alternatively, the poison acts on the medulla area of the brain which is responsible for such reflex actions as the heartbeat, resulting in death from cardiac arrest.

Until the mid 19th century there was no reliable test for strychnine poisoning, which meant that London's Thomas Wainewright, writer and dandy, could only be suspected in the matter of the unpleasant convulsive death of his grandfather in 1829. However, Wainewright inherited the old man's fortune, which nearly all went to his creditors. Wainewright's next move was to invite his wife's mother, Mrs Abercromby, and her two youngest daughters, Helen and Madeleine, to live at Linden House, his Turnham Green home. Mrs Abercromby died in great pain in August 1830. Four months later Helen, whom Wainewright had insured for £18,000, died suddenly from a 'fit'. By now the insurance company was suspicious about the number of people insured by Wainewright who encountered unexpected death and refused to pay. Wainewright sued them for payment. The decision went against him, however, and he fled to France in 1831, where his girlfriend's father, whom Wainewright had benevolently insured for £3000, died from a mysterious illness. On returning to England in 1837, Wainewright was recognized as 'Wainewright the Poisoner' and was put on trial at the Old Bailey, but only for forgery. He pleaded guilty, and was sentenced to transportation for life to Van Diemen's Land. Before he was shipped out, various of his literary and artistic acquaintances – who included Dickens – visited him in Newgate, and when one of them asked why he had poisoned Helen, he replied: 'Yes, it was a dreadful thing to do, but she had very thick ankles.' Wilde immortalized Wainewright in his essay 'Pen, Pencil and Poison', which suggests that murder may be acceptable on aesthetic grounds.

If Dr William Palmer, the infamous 'Rugeley Poisoner', had paid more attention to developments in his profession rather than those on the horse-racing track, he would not have chosen strychnine as well as ANTIMONY. For shortly before Palmer poisoned his friend John Parsons in 1856, and helped himself to his winnings from Shrewsbury Race Track, an absolutely accurate test for detecting alkaloid poisons had been developed by Belgium's Jean Servais Stas. More latterly, suspected residues are treated with sulphuric acid and go into solution, and the edge of the solution is touched with a crystal of potassium chromate. Where strychnine is present the solution turns purple, then crimson, before fading completely.

The prime difficulty in administering strychnine to the victim is its exceptionally bitter taste. Palmer added it to his victim's brandy. Another Victorian doctor, Neill Cream, disguised it as medicine (see Case File), while Ethel Lillie Major, a Lincolnshire gamekeeper's daughter, gave it to her violent and unfaithful husband in his corned beef. Arthur Major died on 22 May 1934, a death which the unsuspicious hospital staff certified as status epilepticus. An anonymous letter from someone who signed himself 'Fairplay' to the police alleged that a neighbour's dog had died after eating scraps put out by Ethel Major, and suggested that she had poisoned her husband. The letter ended: 'In the name of the law, I beg you to analyse the contents of his [Arthur Major's] stomach.' They did. And she had. Ethel Major was executed at Hull Prison on 19 December 1934.

Sweet, rather than savoury, foodstuffs and beverages have also been pressed into strychnine-administering service. George Hersey of Boston, USA, poisoned his pregnant fiancée Betsy Frances on 3 May 1860 after showing a friend a vial containing white powder, and remarking: 'There is something to kill the little one.' Betsy died screaming. A search of her room revealed that Mr Hersey had spoon-fed her strychnine mixed with jam; he had left the spoon, which bore traces of the mixture, behind. An ex-medical student, Hersey was convicted of first-degree murder.

Grape juice was the medium for strychnine selected by Mark Shank, an Ohio lawyer who wished to silence an honest employee who had knowledge of his swindling. Shank invited Alvin Colley and his family to a woodland picnic on 10 August 1933, poisoned them and then hot-footed it. An observant sheriff who visited the crime scene noticed that the picnic cake had been cut into six pieces, and since there were only five in the Colley family, surmised that the sixth, and absent, member of the party was the poisoner. The sheriff called out the men with the bloodhounds, who tracked down an exhausted Mark Shank. He was executed in 1937.

Excuses offered by killers for buying strychnine have tended to concentrate on its quality as a rodenticide. Evan Rablen told the chemist that she needed it to kill gophers, though much of her purchase ended up in her husband's coffee during the weekly dance at Tuttletown, California, 26 April 1929. He died in great distress, complaining about the bitter taste of the drink. Dr Bennett Clarke Hyde, who cunningly administered both strychnine and CYANIDE to his father-in-law, Mr Swope, and the Swope family executor, James Hunton, in an effort to confuse the diagnosis told the chemist he needed the poison to get rid of wild dogs who had been 'howling near my house and causing me no end of sleepless nights'. An otherwise inventive murderer, Hyde included BACTERIAL POISONING amongst his repertoire of death.

Jean-Pierre Vaquier, the perpetrator of Surrey's 1924 'Blue Anchor Hotel' murder, offered the most implausible excuse to purchase strychnine, namely that he needed it for 'wireless experiments'. The wonder of it is that the chemist's in London allowed him to purchase .12 of a gram of the poison, plus 20 grams of perchloride of mercury. Vaquier signed the poison book in the name of Wanker. Needless to say, the strychnine did not go to further the cause of Marconi. Instead, it ended up in the Bromo Seltzer of Vaquier's mistress' husband, Mr Jones, landlord of the Blue Anchor. Drinking the Bromo Seltzer to cure a hangover, Mr Jones let out a cry of 'My God! They are bitter,' and fell to the floor, dying in agony. A post-mortem disclosed strychnine poisoning. Although Vaquier tried to blame the death on the postman, Mrs Jones' solicitor and anybody else he could think of, he was hanged on 12 August 1924. He failed adequately to clean the Bromo Seltzer bottle, which still contained traces of the poison he had administered.

Being a doctor, Neill Cream had no need to invent a reason to purchase strychnine. It was a perk of the job (see Case File).

CASE FILE: Dr Cream

At about 7.30 p.m. on 13 October 1891 a young prostitute called

Ellen Donworth, who was plying her trade along Waterloo Road, London, collapsed and fell to the pavement. A man called James Styles, waiting outside The Wellington pub, rushed to her aid, and managed to carry her to her lodgings at 8 Duke Street. On the way she managed to tell Styles that 'a tall gentleman with cross eyes, a silk hat and bushy whiskers' she had met in the York Hotel had given her a couple of draughts from a bottle of 'white stuff'. She thought that this was responsible for her present condition. She died on the way to hospital. A post-mortem revealed strychnine in her stomach.

The killing of Ellen Donworth caused a great sensation in the neighbourhood, and was called 'The Lambeth Poisoning'. Detective Inspector Harvey had the task of investigating her murder, but his inquiries made little progress. The coroner officiating at Donworth's inquest, George Wyatt, however, did get a letter of some interest. It read:

I am writing to say that if you and your satellites fail to bring the murderer of Ellen Donworth, alias Linell . . . to justice, I am willing to give you such assistance as will bring the murderer to justice, provided your government is willing to pay me £300,000 for my services. No pay if not successful.

The sender signed himself 'A. O'Brien, detective'.

Another letter, from 'H. Bayne, Barrister', dated 6 November, was received by Mr W.E.D. Smith, of the newsagent family W.H. Smith. This letter informed Mr Smith that, found among Ellen Donworth's possessions, were 'two letters [in] incriminating you, which if they ever become public property will surely convict you of the crime'. The letter offered to save Mr Smith if he retained the writer as a barrister.

A week after the murder of Ellen Donworth, the occupants of a brothel in Lambeth Road were woken at 3 a.m. by the screams of 26-year-old prostitute Matilda Clover. Writhing in agony she managed, before she died, to say that a man called 'Fred' had given her some white 'long pills'. A maid working in the house, named Lucy Rose, remembered seeing him arrive, although in the dimly lit hall she had only been able to make out that he was tall and wore a high silk top hat and a cape. Matilda Clover's death was attributed to delirium tremens as a result of alcoholism.

A month later the distinguished physician, Dr Broadbent of Portman Square, received a letter signed 'M. Malone'. The author accused the doctor of having murdered Matilda Clover with strychnine, and demanded £2500 to keep his mouth shut. If the doctor wanted to do a deal, he was to put a personal advertisement in the *Daily Chronicle*. The doctor informed the police about the letter, and the advertisement was published. 'Mr Malone' failed to keep the rendezvous. In December, the Countess Russell, living at the Savoy, received a letter in which Lord Russell was accused of the murder of Matilda Clover.

Then the murders and poison-pen letters ceased. The killer had found other things to do. He had fallen in love with a girl called Lucy Sabbatini.

On 12 April 1892 the brief respite came to an end. In particular it ended for 21-year-old Alice Marsh and 18-year-old Emma Shrivell, two prostitutes up from Brighton, and currently residing at a house of ill repute at 118 Stamford Street. Before they died, in the agonizing pain of strychnine poisoning, the girls told Police Constable George Cumley that they had been entertaining a man called 'Fred', who represented himself as a doctor. Before leaving he gave each girl 'three, long thin pills'. As capsules were a novelty in Britain at the time, and 'Fred' had hinted that they were good for menstrual pain, the girls swallowed the pills. PC Cumley himself had seen 'Fred' leave the building as he walked by on his beat. By the light of a street-gas lamp the policeman noted the reflected glint of the spectacles worn by the well-dressed gentleman.

It was now obvious to both police and public that a systematic murderer was at large. A sergeant from Scotland Yard recalled that Matilda Clover had exhibited the same symptoms as Marsh, Shrivell and Donworth. An order was issued for the exhumation of her body – fourteen coffins had to be moved to reach hers – and an autopsy revealed strychnine poisoning. Detective Chief Inspector John Tunbridge was put in charge of the case.

The man for whom Tunbridge searched, Dr Neill (as Dr Thomas Neill Cream called himself), was as apparently concerned as everyone else that the 'Lambeth Poisoning Mystery' be solved. 'What a cold-blooded murder!' he exclaimed to his landlady, Miss Sleaper, at 103 Lambeth Palace Road, when he read the inquest details on Marsh and Shrivell in his newspaper. And then, confidentially, he told Miss Sleaper that another resident, Walter Harper, a medical student at St Thomas' Hospital, was the killer of Stamford Street. Closer to the truth than she realized, Miss Sleaper replied that he must be mad. This notwithstanding, Cream wrote to Harper's father, accusing his son of the murders and offering to exchange the evidence he had for a sum of £1500. Cream wrote: 'The publication of the evidence will ruin you and your family for ever, so that when you read it you will need no one to tell you that it will convict your son . . . If you do not answer at once, I am going to give evidence to the coroner at once.'

Cream was just as outspoken in denouncing young Harper to a drinking acquaintance called John Haynes, who happened to be a private detective. Cream even took the private inquiry agent on a tour of the murder spots. Haynes was most interested in what Dr Neill had to say, and passed it on, in turn, to a contact of his, Mr

McIntyre. Mr McIntyre found Dr Neill's inside knowledge of special interest because at work he was known as Police Sergeant McIntyre of the CID. Mr McIntyre was also taken into the voluble confidence of Dr Neill, who showed him a letter that had supposedly been received by the Stamford Street victims of the poisoner. The letter warned them about a Dr Harper, lest he serve them as he had done Matilda Clover and Lou Harvey.

This was the first time anybody had heard of Lou Harvey. It was Dr Neill's fatal error. For Lou Harvey was alive and well, and was traced to Brighton. Dr Neill had given her some pills but, being more sensible than her sister professionals, she had only pretended to swallow them.

According to Harvey, she had met Cream on 25 October in Regent Street, having seen him earlier in the evening at the Alhambra Theatre. They had spent the night at a hotel in Berwick Street, and met again the following night on the Embankment. Cream said he was going to give her some pills to cure some spots he had noticed on her forehead. After greeting her on the Embankment with roses, he took her to a nearby pub, the Northumberland, for a glass of wine. They had left the pub and as they walked along the Embankment, Cream produced the 'long pills'. Some instinct warned Lou Harvey of danger, and while pretending to swallow them– he was very insistent– she passed them to her other hand. When he happened to look away, she threw the pills into the Thames.

Harvey described Cream as a 'bald and very hairy man; he had a dark ginger moustache, wore gold-rimmed glasses, was well-dressed, cross-eyed, and spoke with an odd accent'. In fact Cream's 'odd accent' was a result of his transatlantic upbringing. Although he had been born in Scotland, on 27 May 1850, he had emigrated with his parents to Canada when he was thirteen, where his father managed a prosperous shipbuilding business. Cream graduated as a doctor from McGill University, and immediately set his sights on a career as a criminal, beginning with arson insurance fraud. He then performed an abortion on a girlfriend, Miss Flora Brooks, so badly that she almost died; her father insisted on marriage, and Thomas Cream was dragged down the aisle. On the day after the wedding, Cream absconded for England. When Flora died of consumption, Cream demanded $1000 from her father for his 'loss'. Returning to Canada, after rounding off his education with a qualification from the Royal College of Physicians and Surgeons in Edinburgh, Cream practised in Ontario and Chicago as a 'back street' abortionist, one of murderous negligence. Three women died under his care as a doctor.

On the side, Cream ran a business marketing quack remedies. He became enamoured with the wife of one of the customers of his remedies, and decided that the husband, Daniel Stott, was an inconvenience and poisoned him with strychnine. Although the coroner ruled that Stott's death was due to epilepsy, the enigmatic Cream sent letters to the authorities suggesting they investigate for strychnine poisoning. They did, and prisoner 4374 Thomas Neill Cream was sent to the Illinois State Penitentiary at Joilet. He was released after ten years, thanks to the offices of his wealthy family. Stopping in Canada only long enough to collect his inheritance, he had then sailed for London, settling in Lambeth Palace Road, the heart of South London's slums and seedy activities, in October 1891. The month that Ellen Donworth died, and Lou Harvey escaped death.

After Cream showed Sergeant McIntyre the letter which mentioned Lou Harvey, the police began a cautious investigation. His lodgings were put under surveillance, and he himself was tailed. On 12 May Constable Crumley was summoned to observe Cream at a discreet distance; he confirmed that it was the same person he saw leaving the house in Stamford Street. Five days later, another prostitute escaped poisoning when Cream offered her 'an American drink', which she wisely refused. 26 May saw Cream complain to the police, through his solicitors, that his business was being adversely affected by the very heavy-footed police shadow. Inspector Harvey called on Dr Cream and explained that because he was a stranger to the area, he was naturally under suspicion. Harvey asked Cream to confirm the nature of his business. The doctor fetched a sample case, and letters to show that he was acting as an agent for an American company. Apparently satisfied, Harvey left.

Next, Inspector Tunbridge of the CID went to Barnstaple and saw young Harper's father, who showed him the letter he had received from someone signing himself 'W.H. Murray'. By now the police had several poison pen letters associated with the case, one of which, from 'M. Malone', was particularly significant, since it claimed that Matilda Clover was poisoned by strychnine. At the time the letter was written only the killer could have known this. Sergeant McIntyre was instructed to get a sample of Cream's handwriting, then visited Cream at his lodgings, listening sympathetically as the doctor complained about the continuing police surveillance. McIntyre indicated some notepaper on Cream's desk and suggested: 'Just write down the facts about the way you have been bothered. I shall see that it gets into the right hands and puts a stop to any further persecution of your good self.' The handwriting was found to match that on some of the letters (later, it would be discovered that Cream's innocent fiancée, Miss Sabbatini of Berkhampstead, had been duped into writing the others). Furthermore, the watermark on the note Cream wrote for McIntyre and on the letter Harper had received were identical: 'Fairfield Superfine Quality'. Fairfield paper was unobtainable in Britain, and came from the USA. The net was tightening around Dr Cream.

Inspector Tunbridge decided to have another talk with Dr

Cream, ostensibly to answer his complaint about police harassment. In the course of an amiable chat, Cream showed the police detective his sample bag. Looking at the strychnine capsules it contained, Tunbridge remarked how dangerous they would be in the wrong hands. Cream replied: 'It is not intended to sell them to the public direct, but only to druggists and doctors.' The inspector left.

At 5.25 p.m. on 3 June, Inspector Tunbridge returned to Cream's lodgings and arrested him for the blackmailing of Dr Joseph Harper of Barnstaple. 'You've got the wrong man!' exclaimed Cream heartily. 'Fire away!' Cream had just booked a passage to the USA.

While Cream was held at Bow Street for the attempt to extort money from Dr Harper, the inquest on the exhumed Matilda Clover began, and led to the conclusion: 'We are unanimously agreed that Matilda Clover died of strychnine poisoning and that the poison was administered by Thomas Neill [as Cream was still referred to] with intent to destroy life.' Now charged with murder, he was put on trial at the Old Bailey before Mr Justice Hawkins on 17 October 1892. Arrogant and contemptuous, Cream was convinced that he would be acquitted. It took the jury only ten minutes to find him guilty. 'The jury', intoned Mr Justice Hawkins

. . . have felt it their bounden duty to find you guilty of the crime of wilful murder, of a murder so diabolical in its character, fraught with so much cold-blooded cruelty, that one hardly trusts oneself to speak of the details of your wickedness. What motive could have actuated you to take the life of that girl away, and with so much torture to that poor creature who could not have offended you, I know not. But I do know that your cruelty towards her, and the crime that you have committed, are to my mind of unparalleled atrocity. For the crime of which you have been convicted our law knows but one penalty – the penalty of death.

Having escaped capital punishment several times before, Cream seems to have believed that he would escape again. It was not to be. Pale and sweating, Thomas Neill Cream stepped on to the scaffold at Newgate on 15 November 1892 at the age of forty-two. Before the drop opened, he said 'I am Jack the –'

He was not. At the time of the Whitechapel murders, Cream was incarcerated in Joliet. He did leave behind another enigma, however. What was his motive?

SUCCINYLCHOLINE CHLORIDE

Born in Brooklyn in 1933, anaesthesiologist Dr Carl Coppolino was a poor boy made good. He married doctor's daughter Carmela

Musetto and ran a successful practice in New Jersey. In February 1965 he abandoned this and moved to Sarasota in Florida, citing heart problems as the reason for the move. Although the insurance company suspected he was faking the illness, they paid him an annual benefit of $22,000. The Coppolinos lived comfortably on this insurance, plus the money which derived from Carmela's own medical practice. While his wife was at work, Carl Coppolino played doctors and nurses with 38-year-old divorcee Mary Gibson.

In September 1965 Carmela Coppolino died of a heart attack. Three weeks previously her husband had insured her life for $65,000. Less than a month after his bereavement, Coppolino married Mary Gibson.

This provoked a fit of jealousy from 48-year-old Majorie Farber, who had also been having a long-standing affair with the doctor. Piqued, Farber informed the police of her affair with Coppolino, which had begun back in New Jersey, and claimed that Coppolino had injected her suspicious, cuckolded army colonel husband with succinylcholine chloride, and then suffocated him with a pillow. Further, Farber stated that Coppolino had used the same drug to kill his wife. The cause of Colonel Farber's death had been given as coronary thrombosis. Carl Coppolino was indicted for murder in both New Jersey and Florida.

Succinylcholine chloride is a synthetic muscle relaxant that is widely used in anaesthesiology, and was therefore easily available to Dr Coppolino. An overdose of the drug paralyses the muscles of the lungs, causing respiratory failure. It is an especially subtle choice of poison, because once it enters the body it breaks down into succinic acid and choline, both of which are normally present in human tissues.

At his trial for the homicide of Colonel Farber, Coppolino was found not guilty, after the jury was bombarded with conflicting medical evidence. In April 1967 Coppolino was again in court, this time for the homicide of his wife. Here the medical evidence for the prosecution was stronger. The exhumed remains of Carmela Coppolino found that the victim had been in good health, and had not suffered a heart attack as Coppolino alleged. Dr Milton Helpern, the eminent New York Medical Examiner, was called in, and found the unmistakable mark of a hypodermic needle in Mrs Coppolino's body. Dr Joseph Umberger, a toxicologist, conducted six months of intensive research before locating suspicious traces of succinic acid in the system of the corpse, notably in the body organs and around the needle track. On the witness stand, Dr Umberger testified that while succinic acid is naturally present in the human brain in a 'bound' form, the evidence showed that the acid in the victim was 'unbound'. Despite the vociferous efforts of defence attorney F. Lee Bailey, Dr Carl Coppolino was convicted in 1967 of second-degree murder, and sentenced to life imprisonment at the

Avon Park Correctional Institution. He was released on 16 October 1979, for exemplary behaviour.

The publicity given the Coppolino case resulted in succinylcholine being accorded the tag of 'the doctor's poison'; in fact, the next person to use it with malevolence was a killer nurse, Genene Jones.

In 1981 the paediatric unit of Bexar Hospital in San Antonio, Texas, was plagued with a series of unexplained bleedings and cardiac arrests amongst its tiny patients. Some of the babies lived, but many died. An investigation revealed that someone had added an anti-coagulant to intravenous drip bottles. All the evidence pointed to a licensed vocational nurse by the name of Genene Jones, whose 3 p.m.–11 p.m. shift had become known as the 'death shift'. Despite the results of the investigation, however, the hospital authorities decided not take any disciplinary action against Jones for fear of a lawsuit. Instead, they replaced all the licensed vocational nurses on the unit with registered nurses, and rid themselves of the problem that way. Genene Jones was left with a reference saying that she was 'loyal, dependable, and trustworthy'.

Soon Genene Jones got a job at a newly opened baby clinic in Kerrville, run by Dr Kathleen Holland . . . And the inexplicable deaths and illnesses started immediately, always with Genene Jones as the centre of the drama. On one occasion a child with a cold left with Jones while his parents filled in some paperwork had a cardiac arrest, and had to be revived. On another, a seven-year-old went into seizures and was rushed to hospital in San Antonio. On the way a paramedic saw Jones inject something into the child's intravenous drip, and a few minutes later the child stopped breathing. Jones maintained that the child had already been having breathing difficulties and she had injected the drug to help. On yet another occasion a five-month old baby went into cardiac arrest after Jones had taken blood samples.

In September 1982 Chelsea McClellan, seventeen months old, and brought to the Kerrville clinic for routine immunizations, went into seizures after being given two injections by Jones. On the way to hospital with Jones the baby died. By now staff at the Kerrville hospital were expressing concern about the number of babies from Dr Holland's clinic needing emergency treatment. One of the doctors spoke of his worries to a colleague who had recently worked in the paediatric unit at San Antonio. The name of Genene Jones came up. 'You've got a baby-killer on your hands,' he was told.

With Jones under suspicion, Dr Holland began an internal investigation at the Kerrville clinic. She found discrepancies in the records of the drugs she had ordered and that bottles of succinylcholine had been tampered with. One bottle of succinylcholine 'lost' by Jones and then found again had needle-marks in the top. When Holland examined the contents, she found that the drug had been replaced by salt water.

Jones was sacked, and on 25 May 1983 she was arrested and charged with murder. She failed a lie-detector test but a psychiatrist who examined her found that she was convinced of her own innocence. A letter Jones wrote to Dr Holland substantiated this view: 'I have never hurt a child or given a child anything that might hurt them . . .'

The jury did not accept Jones' innocence, and she was sentenced to ninety-nine years' imprisonment for the murder of Chelsea McClellan by administration of succinylcholine. At a second trial, for injuring a child by administering an anti-coagulant drug, she was sentenced to sixty-six years, to run concurrently.

Several witnesses remembered that Jones thrived on the excitement of the emergencies and the sense of self-importance she got from issuing orders and being in command. This suggests that Jones was a classic sufferer of Munchausen Syndrome by proxy, the psychological condition named after Baron Karl Friedrich Hieronymous von Munchausen, an 18th-century mercenary and storyteller, who invented tales to amuse his guests. Munchausen Syndrome was first identified in 1951 by Dr Richard Asher, father of actress Jane Asher, who noticed the bizarre number of hospital patients who dreamt up illnesses in order to get attention. Twenty-five years later, another species of oddballs was identified, those who seek attention for themselves by inducing illnesses in others. Their condition was termed Munchausen Syndrome by proxy.

'The Texas Baby Murders', as the Genene Jones killings became known, were later the subject of a paperback book entitled *The Death Shift* (1987), which sold all over the world, including Britain. There is some suggestion that Nurse Beverley Allitt (see page 139), the 1990s baby-killer of Grantham, may have read the book. Already a latent sufferer of Munchausen Syndrome by proxy, she decided, runs this theory, to perpetrate a 'copy-cat' crime, albeit with somewhat different means, namely INSULIN, SUFFOCATION and a rare homicidal use of potassium chloride.

SUFFOCATION
Variously the obstruction of the nose and mouth to prevent respiration or the incarceration of the victim in an airless environment, suffocation is one of the several deaths from ASPHYXIA. The classic instance of homicidal suffocation is the baby or old person smothered by a pillow. It is estimated by some forensic experts that 10 per cent of 'cot-deaths' are in fact deliberate suffocations, making it the pre-eminent method of contemporary infanticide. Suffocation of infants is notoriously hard to prove. The post-mortem findings of the pathologist are usually confined to a few petechial haemorrhages (see page 34) and pressure whitening around the nose and mouth – findings which are also consistent with accidental suffocation. In the absence of a confession by the

parent or a clear-cut pathological finding, prosecutions for infanticide are difficult to sustain.

It is perhaps no surprise then that serial baby-killers are notable practitioners of smothering. One of the worst examples occurred in New Zealand in 1984, when Lise Jane Turner was convicted of the murder of three babies (two of them her own) by this method. Initially the deaths of eleven-week-old Megan Turner and six-week-old Cheyney Louise Turner had been attributed to cot death syndrome. Michael Clark Tinnion was left in the charge of Lise Turner by his mother on 28 May 1984, and when Mrs Tinnion returned her eight-month-old son was dead, a sticky fluid dribbling out of his nose and mouth. Asphyxia was easily established and in the face of searching questions about the deaths of her own children, Lise Turner was unable to provide convincing answers. The habitual baby-killer was sentenced to life imprisonment for murder and further terms of five years' imprisonment on three counts of the attempted murder of another two babies. Beverley Gail Allitt, the murderer of four children at Grantham's Kesteven Hospital, England, in the 1990s may well have used suffocation as well as INSULIN and potassium chloride. Certainly, some of her attempted murders involved this method.

The homicidal suffocation of the old who, like the very young, are often too weak to resist the pillow held too long over the face, can also cause diagnostic difficulties for the investigating authorities. On 25 September 1950, 76-year-old Mrs Parkinson died at a nursing home in Worthing. Her doctor examined her remains and was told by the matron that the victim had been 'troublesome' shortly before she died, adding that 'We had to hold her hands and get her back to bed.' This explained the small bruises on the dead woman's arms. Seeing no other mark or injury and having no cause for suspicion, the doctor issued a certificate giving the cause of death as 'chronic myocarditis, coronary arteriosclerosis, and senility'.

Arrangements were made for Mrs Parkinson to be buried in the afternoon of 27 September. At about 2.30 p.m., as the funeral cortège started moving, a night nurse from the nursing home called on the doctor and confided her anxieties. Apparently, on the night in question Mrs Parkinson had been very difficult about taking her pills, and had spat at and abused two young nurses. To keep the patient in bed, Matron had to throw herself across the old lady. This did little to subdue Mrs Parkinson, and Matron suddenly lost control. According to the nurse:

> She grabbed the patient's hair with her left hand and pulled her head back on to the bed while she held both hands with her right. Then the patient shouted 'Murder! Murder!' and Matron suddenly leaned over to the pillow on the right side and pulled one of

the pillows over with her teeth . . . Mrs Parkinson's face was completely covered . . . and Matron then buried her own face on the top of it, holding it down. Matron lay there for quite a long time . . . then got off the bed and said 'Take the pillow away'.

According to the nurse, Mrs Parkinson's face was almost black, her tongue was protruding and her eyes half-closed. Her mouth emitted a trickle of blood. She was clearly dead.

The funeral cortège was stopped, and within three hours pathologist Keith Simpson was performing an autopsy on the late Mrs Parkinson. The blue colour had faded from the face because the corpse had been lying in its back, but was well marked in the ears and back. Simpson also found pinhead haemorrhages in the scalp, eye membranes, brain, heart and lungs. He was able to conclude that death was from rapid suffocation, taking no more than twenty to thirty seconds. At the matron's trial the judge, Mr Justice Humphreys, directed the jury that the killing had resulted from provocation, and amounted to manslaughter. This verdict was returned, and because the matron had already served three months in prison awaiting trial, she was allowed to walk free.

An unusual case of the suffocation of a geriatric, that committed by George Russell on Minnie Freeman Lee in 1948, is discussed in the Case File 'Entombment'. Accidental deaths from suffocation occur with sad regularity amongst alcoholics and epileptics who lie face down and incapable in bedding or floor material which can occlude the nose and mouth. Plastic bags placed over the head and neck cause accidental asphyxia amongst young children imitating spacemen, glue-sniffers and adherents of auto-erotic asphyxia (see HANGING). A plastic bag over the head is a common – and rapidly fatal – form of suicide.

The homicidal suffocation of teenagers and healthy adults is not generally achievable, unless they are immobilized first. Notable murderers who have used suffocation include Arthur Beard, a night watchman sentenced to death at Chester Assizes in October 1919 for the murder of a thirteen-year-old girl named Ivy Lydia Wood, whom he suffocated while committing rape upon her. The case is famous in English criminal law as *Rex v Beard*, because Beard was drunk at the time of the crime, a circumstance which induced the Court of Appeal to reduce the finding to one of manslaughter. The ground for the finding was that Beard, being in a state of intoxication, was incapable of forming the *intention* of murder and could not have acted with 'malice aforethought'. The Crown took the matter to the Lords, where the decision of the Court of Appeal was overturned. The Lord Chancellor, Lord Birkenhead, ruled that while Beard might have been too drunk to form the intention to kill, he had not been too drunk to form the intention to rape. As the girl's death was caused by an act of violence in furtherance of a felony, it followed that Beard was guilty of murder. On the advice of the Home Secretary, Beard nonetheless escaped the hangman's noose, and was sentenced to a long term of imprisonment.

John Robinson suffocated prostitute Minnie Bonati in 1927 (see TRUNKS) after first knocking her out with a blow to the head, while Canada's Russell Johnson is unusual in being one of the few mass-murderers of adults to adopt this method. Moreover, Johnson's case demonstrates all too clearly the possibilities of suffocation: he literally got away with murder four times in the cities of Ontario and London.

The first victim was twenty-year-old student Mary Hicks, found dead in her bed on 19 October 1973. A pillow partly covering her face was ignored, and there were no signs of violence. Her death was attributed to suffocation caused by reaction to a prescription drug. A month later Alice Ralston, forty-two years old, was found dead in her apartment; her death was attributed to hardening of the arteries. On 4 March 1974, Eleanor Hartwick died, like Mary Hicks, from a reaction to medicine. In August 49-year-old Doris Brown was found dead. A pathologist noted minor abrasions and some blood in her throat, but the police were not called in. Thereafter, however, Johnson seems to have tired of deaths which could be passed off as natural, employing STRANGULATION to kill, in quick succession, Diane Beitz, Louella Jeanne George and Donna Veldboom. Police investigating the killing of Donna Veldboom compared a list of tenants of the apartment block with records of sexual deviants, and the name of Russell Johnson emerged. At his trial in February 1978, Johnson was charged with the Beitz, George and Veldboom murders, and found not guilty by reason of insanity. After the trial, the police announced that Johnson had admitted to other crimes, including the four 'natural' deaths. If Johnson had not abandoned his suffocation technique he might never have been caught.

No list of 'suffocaters', of course, would be complete without Neville George Clevely Heath (see Case File).

CASE FILE: The Murder of Margery Gardner

It was the misfortune of Margery Aimée Bramwell Gardner, a 32-year-old film extra, to like sado-masochistic sex. For that was the reason that she first struck up a friendship with the man who introduced himself to her as Lieutenant Colonel Heath. In May 1946, after a night on the town, the couple booked into the Pembridge Court Hotel in London's Notting Hill Gate district. There Mrs Gardner was tied up and whipped by her blond, good-looking escort. The couple's activities were interrupted by a hotel detective, who was presumably surprised to find that the screams coming from the room were those of pleasure and pain.

The next woman to be taken to the Pembridge Court Hotel was nineteen-year-old Yvonne Symonds, signed in by the amorous officer as 'Mrs N.G.C. Heath'. She was not interested in flagellation, so the night must have been a touch boring for the man who called himself Lieutenant Colonel Heath. The couple had met at a WRNS dance in Chelsea on Saturday 15 June 1946, and after a day of charm (which the pomaded Heath oozed), the gallant young colonel had proposed marriage; she had accepted, and then consented to a premarital night in the Pembridge's Room 4. Afterwards, she left for her parents' home in Worthing. Heath, bored, decided to telephone Margery Gardner. She agreed to see him on Thursday, 20 June. It would prove a fateful date.

That evening they had dinner at the Normandie Hotel, followed by drinks and dancing at the Panama Club in Cromwell Place, leaving just after midnight. They took a cab to the Pembridge Court Hotel, Heath paying the 1s 9d fare. Heath had a front door key to the hotel, so let himself in and took Mrs Gardner up to Room 4.

At two o'clock the following afternoon a chambermaid knocked on the door of Heath's room and, getting no answer, went in. Lying on one of the two single beds, under some disordered sheets, was an inert body. The chambermaid fetched the assistant manageress. Mrs Alice Wyatt entered the room and drew back the curtains. When she had recovered from the shock of what she saw, she summoned the police, who arrived in the person of Sergeant Fred Averill.

The naked body of Margery Gardner lay on her back under the bedclothes, her right arm underneath her. Her ankles were tied together with a handkerchief; her wrists, judging by the marks, had also been bound, though the ligature had been removed. There were seventeen lash marks on various parts of her body – made with a distinctive diamond-weave whip – and her breasts were almost bitten off. Her face had been bruised, probably from repeated punching. Finally, there was extensive laceration of her vagina; this, said Home Office pathologist Keith Simpson, was 'consistent with a tearing instrument being thrust into her vagina and rotated'. Margery Gardner had been alive while all this savagery had been inflicted on her. Death had come later from suffocation. 'Her blue face indicated asphyxia,' said Simpson, 'and when I continued my post-mortem at Hammersmith Mortuary, I found typical asphyxial changes in the heart and lungs. As there was no sign of strangling she had evidently been suffocated.' A pillow or the scarf used to gag her were the likely instruments. Bound hand and foot for pleasure, Margery Gardner would have been unable to defend herself when Heath decided to change the rules of the game to murder.

That same Friday afternoon Heath went to Worthing to meet his 'fiancée' and her family. Over dinner the next evening at the Blue

Peter Club in Angmering, Heath told Miss Symonds that a terrible
murder had taken place in the very bed at the Pembridge Court
Hotel she had so recently been deflowered in; furthermore, he had
actually lent the deceased the keys to the room. An Inspector
Barrett had taken him to see the body. 'He said Mr Barrett had said
that he thought she had been suffocated . . . that a poker had been
stuck up her,' recalled Miss Symonds later.

The Sunday morning papers were full of the case, and Miss
Symonds' parents were understandably anxious to find that Scotland Yard wished to interview a six-foot man named 'Neville
George Clevely Heath', aged twenty-nine. But they were not as
anxious as Neville Heath himself, who promptly took off for
Bournemouth, where he booked into the Tollard Royal Hotel in the
unlikely name of 'Group-Captain Rupert Brooke'. Ten days passed
without incident. And then on the morning of Wednesday, 3 July
he saw nineteen-year-old Doreen Marshall, who was in Bournemouth recuperating from influenza. He took her to tea at the
Tollard Royal Hotel, and that same evening she dined there with
him. At around 11.30 p.m. she ordered a taxi, but Heath counter-
manded this saying that he would walk her to her hotel. They left
the Royal Tollard together, Heath remarking to the night porter
that he would be back in half an hour. 'No – in a quarter of an
hour,' said Miss Marshall. Two days later the manager of Miss
Marshall's hotel reported her missing.

Exhibiting an extraordinary compulsion to go to the police (as
did Haigh, the ACID-bath murderer), Heath – still posing as
Group-Captain Brooke – trotted along to Bournemouth police
station to ask if they had a photograph of the missing girl? While he
identified the girl in the photograph as the girl who had dined with
him on the previous Wednesday, Detective George Suter thought
that the helpful gent bore an uncanny resemblance to the man
Heath that Scotland Yard were anxious to trace. Eventually, Suter
gave voice to his thought: 'Brooke,' he asked, 'is your real name
Heath?' 'Good Lord no!' he replied. Wisely, Suter did not believe
him. Among the belongings of the detained Heath, left in Bournemouth West Station, were the blue saliva-soiled scarf used to gag
Margery Gardner (and possibly murder her), and the metal-tipped
riding whip which had left such an original pattern on her skin.
Despite washing, there were still traces of blood on the whip.
Several hairs from her head were stuck to the scarf.

Doreen Marshall's body was found on 8 July in Branksome
Chine, lying in some bushes. A CUT-THROAT, courtesy of two
slashes from a knife, was the cause of her death. She had been
extensively mutilated.

The trial of Neville George Clevely Heath opened in the Old
Bailey's No. 1 Court on Tuesday, 24 September. He was charged
only with the murder of Margery Gardner. The question was not

whether Heath had committed the crime, but whether he was insane or not. Mr J.D. Caswell for the defence tried to establish that his client was obviously mad, because only a madman would commit such sadistic crimes. Heath, Caswell maintained, was so 'morally defective' that he did not understand that what he had done was wrong. To support his case he gave a detailed account of Heath's life from his birth in Ilford, Essex, in 1917, through his education at a local Catholic school to his three courts martial (for desertion, fraud and undisciplined conduct) while a serving officer in the RAF and the South African Airforce. The killing of Doreen Marshall, not mentioned by the prosecution, was also dwelt on by the defence, since only a very mad killer, it was claimed, would murder twice. For the Crown, two prison doctors, while agreeing that Heath was a psychopath and a pervert, refused to agree that he was within the scope of the McNaghten Rules – which determine the legal definition of insanity – and was undeniably insane. He was sane, they thought, but sadistic.

The jury resolved the competing claims as to the state of Heath's mind for themselves by bringing in a verdict of guilty. Heath seemed bored by the whole thing.

Awaiting execution in Pentonville he made no appeal or confession. He refused to see his family, but on 15 October, the day before his execution, he wrote two letters to his mother. The first said: 'My only regret at leaving the world is that I have been so damned unworthy of you both.' In the second he wrote: 'I shall probably stay up reading tonight because I'd like to see the dawn again. So much in my memory is associated with the dawn – early morning patrols and coming home from night clubs. Well, it really wasn't a bad life while it lasted . . . Please don't mourn my going – I should hate it – and don't wear black.'

When Heath was offered the traditional nerve-steadying glass of whisky before the walk to the scaffold, he managed to rustle up a grin from somewhere and said 'You might as well make that a double.'

CASE FILE: Entombment

Mrs Minnie Freeman Lee was a widow of ninety-six who lived alone in a seventeen-roomed house in Ray Park Avenue, Maidenhead. When she had moved to the house in 1908 with her barrister husband and three sons, she had been a wealthy woman. The money had gradually disappeared after her husband's death, and she lived on a small grant from a legal benevolent society. Since few people visited her there was nothing to disturb the local belief that she was rich.

On 1 June 1948 the milkman wondered why her milk had not

been taken in for two days. Together with a carpenter working next door he peered through the letterbox and was disquieted by the sight of a large black leather trunk in the middle of the hall, with a lady's court shoe and a bunch of keys lying near it. The police were called and the trunk in the hall opened. Doubled up inside it was the body of Mrs Lee, her arms tied behind her back with a shawl. She had been struck around the head by some blunt object, but it was not the battering which had killed her. Mrs Lee had been placed in the trunk alive, and had been allowed to suffocate, probably over three to four hours.

There seemed to be no clues of any kind, but Chief Superintendent Cherrill of Scotland Yard persisted and eventually found, among the fold of the quilt on her bed, a cardboard box. Under the bed was the lid to the box, and this yielded on its edge two very fragmentary prints – but enough to identify the housebreaker as George Russell, a well-known 'screwsman'. He was arrested at a tramps hostel in St Albans five days later. When confronted by the fingerprint evidence he broke down and wept. He admitted approaching Mrs Lee about some gardening work, and in seeking to clear himself made a remark which gave him away: 'I was told she had a lot of money by another man. Did I murder this poor woman for something she was supposed to have, and had not?' The words made plain to his jury at Berkshire Assizes that he had searched for treasure at Mrs Lee's house and not been able to find it, and in the process had killed Mrs Lee by suffocation. Russell was found guilty and sentenced to death. He was hanged at Oxford Prison on 2 December 1948.

T

THALLIUM

Discovered by Sir William Crookes in 1861, thallium is a heavy metal, closely related to lead and MERCURY, although more poisonous than either. It has some claim to being the almost 'perfect' poison, since its salts are practically tasteless and it dissolves readily in fluids; moreover, the symptoms of thallium poisoning are virtually indistinguishable from those of a number of ordinary illnesses, such as influenza, peripheral neuritis, typhus and encephalitis.

Thallium was once commonly found in ant-bait and rat-poisons. It is still used in some developing nations as a pesticide – in 1987, a number of people in Guyana were affected by drinking milk contaminated by thallium sulphate used to kill sugar-cane rats – but thallium products are outlawed in most developed countries.

Once ingested, thallium interferes with the body's metabolism, affecting the nerve cells and upsetting the calcium balance. The poison is excreted only very slowly, so that repeated doses have a cumulative toxicity. The tell-tale sign of thallium poisoning is alopecia, or hair-loss, and before the dangers of the metal were understood thallium was sold over the counter as a depilatory for women.

Something of an expert on poisons, due to her voluntary work in a hospital dispensary during World War I, Agatha Christie wrote a celebratedly accurate account of thallium poisoning in her novel *The Pale Horse* (1961). Ngaio Marsh, another crime writer, had featured it earlier, in 1947, in *The Final Curtain*; her version lacked veracity, however, with the victims dropping dead instantly, whereas in reality death by thallium is a slow process. A fatal dose is 800 mg.

Although the most famous instance of thallium as an instrument of murder is the 1972 case featuring England's Graham Young (see Case File), two other cases are notable. They may have even given Young inspiration.

Martha Lowenstein was a Viennese orphan who, in 1919, was spotted by a wealthy businessman in the dress shop where she worked and became his ward. She was sent to finishing schools in England and France, and was left a large bequest when he died. In 1924, she met and married Emil Marek, an engineering student, but they quickly spent their way through her inheritance. To get more money they devised an insurance fraud, whereby Emil had himself insured against accident for £10,000. Only weeks later, he had an accident, almost severing his leg with an axe. The leg had to be amputated below the knee, and the surgeon concluded that the injury, which consisted of three separate cuts, had been self-inflicted. Although the Mareks were cleared of a fraud charge, they served a prison sentence for bribing a hospital orderly to say that he had seen a doctor tampering with the wounds.

Thereafter, the couple were reduced to near-poverty. In 1932 Emil died, followed by the Mareks' baby daughter. Martha then became the companion of an elderly relative, Suzanne Lowenstein, who died soon after, leaving her estate to her young woman. For the second time, Martha spent, spent, spent her bequest, and was forced to rent rooms to lodgers. When one of these died mysteriously, Martha was suspected of poisoning her. Thallium was found in the body, which prompted the authorities to exhume the bodies of Emil, baby Marek and Suzanne Lowenstein. All contained thallium, which Martha had bought from a chemist's shop. She was beheaded on 6 December 1938.

Nine years later, in Australia, 62-year-old Caroline Grills, or 'Aunt Carrie' as she was known around her suburban neighbourhood, called in the pest control officer to deal with an infestation of rats. The vermin poison he used was based on thallium, and did the job with supreme efficiency. In case the rats returned he left an extra supply behind. Little of it was used for its intended purpose.

Later in 1947 Caroline Grills' stepmother, Christiana Mickelson, aged eighty-seven, died. This caused Caroline little upset, since she had never liked her father's second wife. Not long afterwards, an 84-year-old family friend, Mrs Angeline Thomas, died, leaving Caroline's husband a cottage. Caroline had never liked her either, so there were few tears of mourning.

The next year saw Caroline's brother-in-law John Lundberg become seriously ill after apparently developing food poisoning while on holiday with the Grills. He died in October 1948. Tragedy struck Caroline's family again that month when Mary Ann Mickelson died, after suffering the same symptoms. Then John Lundberg's widow, Eveline, and daughter Christine Downey began to feel a numbness in their limbs and to lose their hair. Kindly 'Aunt Carrie' was a frequent visitor to the couple, dispensing tea – and thallium. But she was caught in the act by Christine Downey's husband, who saw her take something from her pocket and add it to a cup of tea. When analysed by the police chemist the cup was shown to contain the metal poison.

At the trial of 'Aunt Thally', as Caroline Grills quickly became known, the prosecution contended that she had originally begun poisoning for gain, and continued because she enjoyed the sense of power she gained from controlling the life and death of her victims. Eveline Lundberg, rendered blind and barely able to walk by the effects of thallium poisoning, appeared as the main prosecution witness. 'Aunt Thally' was sentenced to life imprisonment, after being found guilty on four charges of murder and two of attempted murder.

CASE FILE: The Poisoner's Apprentice

Nicknamed 'Pudding' by his family, Graham Frederick Young was born in 1947 – the year his mother died – and was to all outward appearances a normal child as he grew up in drab Neasden, where he lived with his father, sister and step-mother at No. 768 on the North Circular Road. Yet, by the age of eleven he was already a regular borrower of books on poison from the local public library, and had developed a morbid fascination with the gaslight killer William Palmer, of STRYCHNINE infamy. When he was a year or two older he was spending most of his 10s a week pocket money on poisons, telling neighbourhood chemists that he was seventeen (the minimum legal age to buy poison), and signing the register as 'ME Evans'. Among the few things allowed to break into his obsession with toxicology were Black Magic and Nazism. At John Kelly Secondary School – where he was, perhaps unsurprisingly, quite excellent at chemistry – Young regularly wore a swastika in his lapel and treated classmates to readings from *Mein Kampf*.

In 1961, Young seems to have decided that he had had enough of the theory of poisoning, and moved on to the practice. In May of that year, Young's best friend, Chris Williams, suffered an acute attack of cramps and headaches and was taken to hospital. A young intern diagnosed migraine. Meanwhile, members of Young's family were showing signs of the same illness as Williams. His stepmother, Molly, began to suffer stomach pains throughout 1961, though at first she dismissed them. Young's father, Fred, and sister, Winifred, also became violently ill. Even Graham, on occasion, was subject to bouts of sickness. In November, Winifred collapsed on the way to work after drinking a breakfast cup of tea. At the Middlesex Hospital in Goodge Street, London, to which she was taken, the doctor was surprised to find that Winifred had ingested belladonna, a poison extracted from deadly nightshade, the active constituent of which is ATROPINE. At the Youngs' home, meanwhile, Molly's condition deteriorated markedly; she aged rapidly and became bowed over by backache. On Easter Saturday, 21 April 1962, she died after a violent convulsion. The renowned pathologist, Dr Donald Teare, ascribed her death to a misplaced spinal section. While the family was in mourning, Graham nagged his father to have Molly cremated. The distraught father gave in. Then, at the post-funeral reception at the Youngs' home, one of Graham's uncles began vomiting after eating pickle.

It was only a few days later that Fred Young's own stomach pains returned. Tests at the hospital revealed either arsenic or antimony poisoning. The diagnosis caused Graham to sneer: 'How can any doctor not tell the difference between the symptoms of arsenic and antimony?' Graham could. On his father's release Graham sat by his sick bed taking notes.

The suspicion that Graham was a poisoner grew. His Aunt Winnie, who had looked after him in the three years between his mother's death and his father's remarriage, had long suspected him, but he denied everything. An astute science master at Young's school, however, went through the boy's desk, finding bottles of poison, sinister drawings, and essays about murder. The master, Geoffrey Hughes, informed the headmaster and together they arranged for Graham to be interviewed by a psychiatrist posing as a careers guidance counsellor. After the interview, the psychiatrist went straight to the police. On 21 May, Harlesden CID searched Graham's bedroom at 768 North Circular Road while he was at school, finding enough poison to kill 300 people, alongside copies of books such as *A Handbook on Poisons*, *Sixty Famous Trials* and *Poisoner in the Dock*. When Young got home, the police found a phial and two small bottles in his shirt. The phial, which Graham referred to as 'my little friend', contained antimony and the bottles thallium.

The next day, after a night in the cells, Young made a statement. In it he confessed to administering antimony to Williams on a cream biscuit and to 'giving my family members antimony tartrate on prepared foods . . . After my mother died on April 21st, 1962, I started putting antimony tartrate into milk and water my father was drinking.' On occasion, he said, he had accidentally swallowed poison himself (thus accounting for his own bouts of vomiting).

At Ashford Remand Centre, Young underwent tests, where, revealingly, he told a psychiatrist that: 'I am missing my antimony. I am missing the power it gives me.' On 5 July 1962, then aged fourteen, he appeared at the Old Bailey, one of the youngest criminals to ever be tried there. He pleaded guilty to poisoning charges involving Chris Williams, and his father and sister. Mr Justice Melford Stevenson ordered that Young be detained in Broadmoor, the psychiatric hospital for the criminally insane, for a minimum of fifteen years and that he should be released only on the authority of the Home Secretary. He added the warning: 'Such people are always dangerous and are adept at concealing their mad compulsion, which may be never wholly cured.'

The issue of Young's stepmother was not raised in court, but following the trial Young admitted to his Aunt Winnie that he had given antimony to Molly for over a year. She had built up a resistance to the poison, so the evening before her death he had added a massive dose of another poison to her meal: thallium.

Young was released from Broadmoor in 1971, after serving less than ten years of his sentence, apparently 'cured'. The Home Office sent him to a Government Rehabilitation Centre at Slough, from where he joined the Hertfordshire photographic laboratory of John Hadland Limited. Young's employers knew nothing of his Broadmoor sojourn, but were impressed by his application form, in which he informed them that he had 'previously studied chemistry, organic and inorganic, pharmacology and toxicology . . .'

Young began work in Hadland's store-room on 10 May 1972, under the supervision of Bob Egle, a popular man looking forward to retirement. By the end of the month, Egle was suffering from stomach upsets. His condition worsened, and he began to experience a numbness which virtually paralysed him. On Wednesday, 7 July, Bob Egle died. A post-mortem recorded death as the result of broncho-pneumonia and polyneuritis. At Egle's funeral, Hadland's was represented by the managing director and Egle's co-worker, Graham Young.

In the car back to the laboratory, Young informed the MD that peripheral neuritis was just a general term to cover damage to the nervous system. 'The proper name for it,' Young said knowledgeably, 'is the Guillan–Barré Syndrome.'

At Hadland's others were falling ill. More and more of them, and all displaying the same symptoms: diarrhoea and severe vomiting. In the worst cases there was also extreme hair and weight loss, and numbness in the legs. The workers' complaints began to centre on the tea – often fetched for them by the kindly Graham Young – which many thought tasted bitter. A medical team was called in to check the factory. Young asked one of the doctors if he thought the 'bug' might be thallium poisoning?

On 19 November, after an excruciating three-week-long illness, another Hadland's employee, Fred Biggs, died from the 'bug'. With the workforce now close to panic Hadland's summoned the firm's GP, Dr Ian Anderson, to address them in the canteen. He pleaded for calm and suggested a virus as the cause of the outbreak. 'Why has heavy metal poisoning been ruled out?' asked a voice from the back. It was Graham Young. He continued to ask probing questions.

Interested by Young's apparent expert knowledge, the doctor casually questioned him after the meeting, and found him only too keen to show off his toxicological learning. The doctor reported his suspicions to Hadland's management, who reluctantly called the police. Young's record was checked with Scotland Yard. When it came over the teletype line, Hemel Hempstead CID were amazed. They had a psychopathic poisoner on their hands.

Young was immediately arrested, a lethal dose of thallium – 'my "exit" dose', as he referred to it – in his pocket. At his lodgings the police found bottles of thallium, antimony and aconitine. The walls were covered with pictures of Nazi wartime leaders. Under the bed they found Young's poisoner's diary, entitled 'A Student's and

Officer's Case Book'. As well as demonstrating Young's guilt, the diary was a record of his experiments upon the Hadland's workforce, whom he regarded as 'guinea pigs'. On 31 October, an entry referring to Fred Biggs, noted:

> I have administered a fatal dose of the special compound to him and I anticipate a report of his progress on Monday. I gave him three separate doses . . . In a way it seems a shame to condemn such a likeable man to such a horrible end, but I have made my decision and therefore he is doomed to premature decease.

The entry for 1 November: 'A disturbing symptom has occurred in the case of D (David Tilson). He has started losing hair . . .'

3 November: 'D's loss of hair is almost total . . . if it looks like I might be detected I shall have to destroy myself.'

10 November: 'F (Fred Biggs) must have phenomenal strength to fight the special compound.'

Although the diary was damning, the police needed more evidence against Young if they were to clinch the case against him. An initial post-mortem on the body of Fred Biggs, on 22 November at St Pancras Hospital in London, revealed symptoms of thallium poisoning, but no traces of the substance. It took Scotland Yard expert Nigel Fuller a further ten days to locate traces of thallium in Bigg's organs. An examination of the exhumed 1780 remnants of Bob Egle's cremation revealed 9 mg of thallium (the first time in British legal history that the exhumation of cremated ashes had led to a murder charge). The techniques used did not exist in 1962 when Young's stepmother Molly was cremated after he poisoned her with antimony and thallium, a murder Young was now describing to the police as 'perfect'.

At his trial at St Albans Crown Court in 1972, Young denied murdering Biggs and the attempted murder of two of his Hadland's workmates, and the malicious poisoning of four others, dismissing his incriminating diary as 'notes for a novel'. He was subsequently acquitted of the malicious poisoning of two of the Hadland's workers, but the jury found him guilty on the other charges and he was sentenced to life imprisonment. It was the first time in the UK that anybody had been convicted of using thallium for murder.

Young spent most of his sentence in Parkhurst Prison. Early in August 1990 the Home Office announced that he had died after a heart attack at the age of forty-two.

TRAINS

In the November 1862 issue of *Cornhill Magazine*, the novelist and journalist William Makepeace Thackeray wrote: 'Have you ever entered a first-class railway carriage, where an old gentleman sat alone in a sweet sleep, daintily murdered him, taken his pocket-book and got out at the next station?' Just two years later, life imitated art and an old gentleman, Thomas Biggs, *was* robbed and murdered – if not quite daintily – in the way that Thackeray suggested. It was Britain's first murder on a train.

As a scene for homicide the railway carriage would become increasingly familiar over the next decades. The isolation of the passenger in the old-fashioned railway carriage – which had no connecting corridor – and the difficulty in summoning assistance provided the killer with an ideal setting. Once inside a closed compartment passengers carrying money were easy prey, and while the train was on the move the murderer was guaranteed privacy, the murderee no means of escape. Sounds of shots and screams were drowned out by the noise of the train itself. The body could be either left in the carriage or pushed out on to a deserted line. On arrival at any busy station the killer could detrain and simply melt into the crowds. 'It is the considered opinion of past and present chiefs of the Criminal Investigation Department,' wrote Scotland Yard's Chief Inspector William Gough, 'that the train murder forms the most difficult of all the categories of homicide.'

The vintage years of English murder matched almost exactly the Age of Steam, the 1850s to the 1950s, when the train was the pre-eminent mode of mass transport. In addition to providing a killing place, the train was a useful aid in tidying up a crime. It was a means of escape, while corpses in TRUNKS might be disposed of at left-luggage. The American murderess Winnie Ruth Judd (see TRUNKS) even used the train to ship cadavers to their intended resting place.

Although Hollywood in its Silent Era had a penchant for films in which maidens were tied to tracks to be decapitated by an oncoming train, outside the confines of the movie studio this extreme method of homicide is probably unknown. (It did feature, though, as a dramatic end piece to the axe-murder of circus showman 'Lord' George Sanger at his East Finchley home on the evening of 28 November 1911, when the insane culprit Herbert Cooper laid himself down afterwards on the Great Northern line between Crouch End and Highgate to be beheaded and belegged by a locomotive.) Where a train has been used as an actual murder instrument, the victim has always been pushed before its moving wheels – a variation of HIT-AND-RUN and sharing the same pluses and negatives as that method. With the exception of suicide, it is rare, running only to a handful of documented cases. They include an elderly woman who pushed her sister in front of an approaching train one foggy morning at Chingford Railway Station in the 1960s; the murderer was found to be far too senile to justify criminal proceedings.

In 1905, one of the first examples of DEFENESTRATION from

a locomotive occurred, when a young woman by the name of Mary Money was thrown from a train on the Brighton and South Coast Railway. Money's body hit the wall of the Merstham tunnel, and bounced back under the wheels of the train, mutilating her body so badly that identification from it was impossible.

Like killers, writers of crime fiction have frequently utilized the murderous possibilities of the railway, most famously Agatha Christie with her classic *Murder on the Orient Express* (1934). Other writers to set murder-most-foul stories aboard trains include Ethel Lina White's *The Wheel Spins* (1934) (filmed by Alfred Hitchcock as *The Lady Vanishes*) and Sebastian Japrisot's *The 10.30 to Marseille*. George Simenon's novel *The Man Who Watched Trains Go By* (1938) is loosely based on the real-life case of Sylvestre Matushka who, as train murderers go, was in a league of his own, committing a series of train derailments using EXPLOSIVES in central Europe in 1931. The most spectacular of these was the wrecking of the Orient Express on 12 September 1931 as it crossed the viaduct at Bia-Torbagy, Hungary. The dynamite bomb Matushka had planted on the viaduct was triggered by the wheels of the train, and the explosion plunged the engine and nine of the eleven coaches 100 feet into a gorge, killing twenty-two passengers and crew and injuring 120 more. The Fascist Hungarian government promptly blamed 'Communist terrorists' for the Bia-Torbagy tragedy, and were embarrassed to find that Matushka, when apprehended, was an ardent Fascist. But his motive for the derailments was, bizarrely, sexual; a sadist, Matushka admitted to deriving sexual excitement from watching the results of his bombs. Forensic tests on the trousers Matushka had been wearing that September night revealed semen stains. Sentenced to life imprisonment for the Bia-Torbagy bombing, Matushka was released from jail sometime during or just after World War II. Afterwards, he disappeared, and the end of his life is a mystery.

CASE FILE: The First Train Murder

On the evening of Saturday, 9 July 1864, shortly after 10 p.m., two bank clerks boarded a train of the North London Railway at Hackney Station, London. The train had left Fenchurch Street at 9.50 a.m. and had already stopped at Bow and Hackney Wick. The men had only just sat down in their first-class compartment when one of them felt something sticky on his hand. The carriage was only dimly lit, but they could see that it was blood.

Alighting hurriedly, they called the guard, who, with the aid of a lamp from the brake van, discovered the whole carriage, even the windows, to be marked with blood. On the carriage floor the guard found a stick, bag and hat. It was the latter that provided one of the main clues to the identity of the killer, for in his rush to leave the scene of the crime the murderer had mistaken the victim's hat for his own.

The body of the victim was found later that evening lying on the railway line between Bow and Hackney stations. Identified as Thomas Briggs, 69-year-old chief clerk of Roberts & Co. bank, the victim was alive, but completely unconscious. His skull had been fractured by severe blows from a BLUNT INSTRUMENT, probably his own walking stick, which was heavy and stained with blood. Other injuries suggested that Briggs had been thrown from the train after his assault, the motive for which was clearly robbery; Briggs' gold watch and chain and other possessions were missing. He expired the next day.

The original setting for the murder prompted massive public interest. Although there had been murders on trains in France as early as 1860 (when a Russian army doctor was robbed and murdered on a train passing through Alsace), nothing like it had happened in Britain.

Police checks on jewellers' shops found that Briggs' gold chain had been exchanged for another in a Cheapside shop. The jeweller – who went by the not inappropriate name of Death – described a sallow-faced man with a German accent. A description of the hat the murderer left behind brought forward a cab driver who recognized it as belonging to Franz Muller, a German tailor living in London.

When the police arrived at Muller's lodging house, they found that he had sailed to the USA on board the SS *Victoria*. They gave chase in the faster SS *City of Manchester* and arrested Muller on his arrival in New York. In his possession he had Briggs' gold watch and the clerk's hat, which he had cut down to alter its appearance and to suit his own taste.

At his Old Bailey trial Muller pleaded not guilty, but the jury took only fifteen minutes to convict him. Just before his public execution, on 14 November 1864, he confessed 'Ich habe es getan' ('I did it').

As a robber and murderer Muller was a bodger. The total proceeds from his crime amounted to just 30 shillings. He would have been better off as a hatter. Young men were much taken with the Old Bailey descriptions of his cut-down top hat, and a 'Muller' became the height of male fashion in Victorian England.

TRUNKS
The hiding of a body in a trunk is a thoroughly quaint method of disposal, irresistibly linked to the steam age of TRAINS and days when ocean liners graced the waves. It is also invariably useless, since the smell of the putrefying corpse soon seeps out, attracting

attention to the crime the trunk was intended to hide. Also, unless the killer happens to have a very large trunk to hand, the human body does not fit easily into the space, which necessitates the messy business of DISMEMBERMENT.

Such was the task which fell to both England's John Robinson in 1927 (see Case File, The Charing Cross Corpse) and the USA's Winnie Ruth Judd (see Case File, The Phoenix Trunk Murders) four years later, accounts of whose classic trunk crimes follow below. Patrick Herbert Mahon was also obliged to reduce Miss Emily Beilby Kaye to kit-size to fit her into a trunk, after he murdered her at their 'love bungalow' on the Crumbles, near Eastbourne. Having seduced Kaye, a typist at his workplace, the narcissistic, womanizing Mahon had tired of her, and wanted the affair to end. For her part, Kaye had fallen violently in love, and wanted Mahon to leave his wife. This he had no intention of doing, and killed Kaye on the night of 12 April 1924.

It took him a week to pluck up the courage to begin cutting up Kaye with a purpose bought knife and saw, severing the legs and head on the Good Friday, then stuffing the mutilated body into a trunk. He then spent the weekend at the bungalow with another girl whom he had met casually a week before. They were together there from the Friday to the Easter Monday – during all of which time the partially dismembered body of Emily Kaye was lying in the trunk in the spare bedroom. At his later trial, Mahon said: 'The damn place was haunted. I wanted human companionship.'

Having hidden the body while Mahon entertained, the trunk had served its purpose, and the body parts of Emily Kaye were taken out on the Easter Tuesday for more dismemberment, some of them put on the fire for BURNING. Mahon found it a long and laborious business. On the Tuesday evening he went back to his wife, and worked at the office for the rest of the week. On the following Saturday and Sunday he resumed his grisly task at the bungalow, boiling some flesh in a cauldron which, together with the leg bones, he put in a Gladstone bag. This was later thrown out of the window of a train between Waterloo and Richmond.

A left-luggage ticket proved to be his undoing. His wife, concerned by his philandering, found the ticket, which, when she presented it at Waterloo railway station, produced a Gladstone bag containing blood-stained clothing. Mahon was picked up when he went to collect the bag.

Detectives visiting the bungalow at the Crumbles found it to be a butcher's shop, with pieces of Kaye in saucepans, a hat-box, a biscuit tin and bone fragments in the fire. It was one of the great bodged jobs of dismemberment. Some parts of Emily Kaye had even been stuffed back in the trunk. It came as no surprise to anyone that Mahon was hanged for the crime, the sentence being carried out on 2 September 1924.

If Mahon viewed the trunk as a mere temporary expedient, Tony Mancini seems to have viewed it as a long-term solution. In August 1933, having been recently released from prison, Mancini got a job at a cafe not far from Leicester Square, and it was there that he met Violette Kaye, a vaudeville dancer turned prostitute. When the cafe closed down, Kaye persuaded the handsome Mancini – who, despite his Italianate looks and name, was actually an Englishman born Cecil England – to set up house with her in Brighton. Kaye became steadily infatuated with Mancini, and did not approve of him taking a job at the Skylark Cafe. She rarely passed a day without visiting him to ensure that he was not being too familiar with the waitresses. On Thursday, 10 May 1934, Violette was in the Skylark, drunk, and took exception to a joking remark Mancini made to a waitress. A violent and embarrassing scene ensued, before Kaye was persuaded to leave.

The next day, Mancini turned up at the cafe and when a remark was made about Kaye said, 'She's left. Gone to Paris.' That morning, Violette Kaye's sister-in-law received a telegram which read: 'Going abroad good job sail Sunday will write – Vi'. But Vi had not sent it. On Monday, after the cafe closed, Mancini bought a large black trunk second-hand, for which he paid 7s 6d. The following day he left the flat he shared with Violette, taking with him all his belongings, including the trunk – which he trundled on a hand-cart to 52 Kemp Street, where he had taken a room. The trunk was placed in a corner, and there it stayed for two months. Comments were made about the smell which seemed to emanate from it, with one visitor asking Mancini, 'Do you keep rabbits?'

How long Mancini would have been prepared to suffer the odour of decomposition is unguessable, for his crime was about to have its lid lifted on it. By a bizarre coincidence, on 14 June, the body of a woman, minus head and legs, was found in a trunk deposited in left-luggage at Brighton Railway Station. 'The Brighton Trunk Murder' was absolutely nothing to do with Mancini (and, in fact, would never be solved); however, Mancini was one of hundreds routinely interviewed by the police, and became so frightened that he bolted to London.

When the police turned up at Kemp Street on 15 July to ask further questions they found no Mancini, only the trunk he left there. Inside was the decomposing body of Violette. At his subsequent trial at Lewes Assizes, Mancini claimed that he did not murder Violette. On returning home from work, he had found her dead and panicked, telling the court he did not fetch the police because: 'Where the police are concerned, a man who's got convictions never gets a square deal.' A brilliant defence by Norman Birkett KC ended with an exhortation to the jury to 'Stand firm!' The jury took nearly two-and-a-half hours to decide upon their verdict – acquittal. Mancini seemed dazed and kept repeating 'Not guilty, Mr Birkett'.

'I've got away with murder' was the title of Mancini's confession to the killing of Violette Kaye, published in the *News of the World* forty-two years later, on 28 November 1976. Mancini told the newspaper that: 'I honestly didn't mean to kill her – I had just lost control of myself in the heat of the moment . . . Of course I feel ashamed and guilty about what happened [at the trial]. I did what any man would do. I did everything to save my life.' The offending murder instrument seemed to have been a hammer, applied to Violette's head.

Since the 1920s and 1930s, body-in-the-trunk murders have all but gone out of fashion (who has a trunk anymore?), though a few foolish or antiquated souls have persevered with them. Mark Fein, a 32-year-old New York millionaire businessman, shot his bookie on 10 October 1963, the motive seemingly being a reluctance to pay a $7200 debt. Fein stuffed the body of Rubin Markowitz in a cabin trunk, and asked Gloria Kendall, a prostitute of his acquaintance, to arrange its disposal. With two friends she dumped the trunk in the Harlem river, where it was found four months later.

Another trunk murder was consigned to WATER in 1982, and likewise floated to notice, this time near the Sant' Elena pontoon at Venice's Lido. The body inside was that of waitress Emma Giraldo, and packed alongside it were two large dolls and several bags of nails, intended as weights. She had been strangled by a rebuffed admirer, pizza baker Roberto Festinese, who had gone to extraordinary lengths to convey her body from Vitipeno, where the killing took place, to Venice. Since Venice has no cars, Festinese was forced to build a wooden cart to carry the trunk across the city to the lagoon. Obliging Venetians even helped him pull the cart and trunk up some of the more difficult steps.

In the absence of a trunk, a number of murderers have been tempted to use the trunk's descendant, the suitcase. This, however, presents even more problems than a trunk. A particularly gruesome 'suitcase murder' occurred in Britain in 1968. Suchnam Singh Sandhu, a 39-year-old Punjabi Sikh living at Fanshawe Avenue, Barking, found his eldest daughter intolerable and shameful. Nineteen-year-old Sarabjit Kaur had fallen in love with her cousin, a man who was both married and of a lower caste. She became pregnant by him, and was forced to have an abortion by her father.

On the morning of 4 April, as Suchnam Singh would later inform the police, his daughter came downstairs and informed him that she had taken an overdose of BARBITURATES and had written a suicide letter informing the world that she had taken her own life because her father refused to let her live with the man she loved. In a fit of anger or panic, Suchnam Singh grabbed the coal hammer and hit his daughter twice on the head. She dropped to the floor unconscious. Suchnam Sing then went to a local hardware shop, and bought a high tensile hacksaw. On returning home he placed his daughter's body in a large plastic bag, to minimize mess, and then began dismembering her while she was alive. At one stage she seems to have revived, and grabbed the blade, but was overpowered. The grisly job done, Suchnam Singh placed the upper torso into a large green suitcase. The head was wrapped in towelling and an old copy of the *Daily Telegraph*, and placed inside a blue duffle bag. The lower torso was placed in a reddish suitcase. Later that day, Suchnam Singh travelled by public transport to Euston Station, taking with him the green suitcase, which he placed under a table in a train bound for Wolverhampton. That same evening, Singh threw the other suitcase into the River Roding.

On the day after, Singh set off on his moped, carrying the duffle bag containing his daughter's head over his shoulder. He dropped the bag under some bushes on Wanstead Common, only feet from the road.

Meanwhile, the suitcase, complete with its bloody contents, left on the Wolverhampton train had been found. A woman spotted the other suitcase under a bridge at Ilford. From examination of the various body pieces, Professor Robert Warwick of the Anatomy Department at Guy's Hospital Medical School was able to conclude that the victim was an Asian woman of between eighteen and thirty-nine, who had undergone an inexpert abortion. Consultations with experts on India suggested that her unshavenness indicated that she was a Sikh, while the pattern of her clothes was unique to an area around Jullundor in the Punjab. Calluses on her feet led to the conclusion that she had only latterly begun wearing European shoes, and was thus a recent immigrant to Britain. A tedious search through hospital records for an Indian woman with gynaecological problems revealed that one Sarabjit Kaur had attended Barking Hospital, from where the trail led to the front door of Suchnam Singh. He began by denying the crime, and then by saying that his daughter had accidentally struck her head on a sewing machine as she fell over due to the effects of the Phenobarbitone overdose. Among those who did not believe him was the jury at his Old Bailey trial. He was sentenced to life imprisonment in November 1968.

CASE FILE: The Charing Cross Corpse

At about midday on Friday, 6 May 1927, a man drove up to Charing Cross Station and left a large trunk in left-luggage. The trunk had a rounded top, was made of wicker-work, and was encased in black cloth and bound with a wide strap. Urging that the trunk be handled carefully, the owner indicated that he would

return and collect it later in the day. The trunk remained
unclaimed. Four days later, Mr Glass, the head of left-luggage,
noticed a peculiar smell coming from the trunk. A policeman was
sent for and the trunk forced open.

Inside the trunk were four brown-paper parcels, all tied with
string. When opened the parcels revealed a dismembered woman's
body. In the first parcel were the arms, severed at the shoulders;
these were wrapped in towels and a pair of knickers with a tab
bearing the name 'P. Holt'. Parcels two and three contained the
legs, and the last parcel the severed head and torso. The head was
wrapped in a yellow duster, the torso in a blue jumper and some
underclothes. A crude, and failed, attempt, had been made to cut
one of the legs in half. A divisional police surgeon, Dr Rose, was
summoned to certify that the woman was dead.

The trunk and its contents were then transported to Westminster
mortuary, where the remains were examined by the renowned
Home Office pathologist, Sir Bernard Spilsbury. When pieced
together, Spilsbury concluded that the woman had sustained
bruising on her forehead, stomach, back and limbs before she died.
SUFFOCATION was the means of her demise. The woman had
been dead, Spilsbury thought, for about a week. Her age had been
about thirty-five.

As well as the label 'P. Holt' the trunk yielded another significant
clue, laundry marks (581, and 447) on two items of clothing.
Within twenty-four hours, the knicker label and laundry marks led
the police to a Mrs Holt of South Kensington. Mrs Holt herself was
very much alive, which suggested that the dead woman had
purloined her clothing, and had probably been in her service. Mrs
Holt agreed to view the severed head at the mortuary, and
identified the deceased as Mrs Rolls, a cook who had briefly worked
for her.

Mr Rolls was soon found. It transpired, however, that the
dead woman was not his wife, and had simply lived with him for
a short while. Her real name was Minnie Bonati (née Budd), and
her legal husband was an Italian waiter. He, too, was soon
cleared of suspicion. Further inquiries revealed that Minnie
Bonati had last been seen alive in Sydney Street, Chelsea
between 3.45 p.m. and 4 p.m. on Wednesday, 4 May. It seemed
that although she sometimes worked as a cook or cleaner, her
main income was from prostitution. This vastly increased the
field of possible killers.

Meanwhile, the police had interviewed the staff at Charing Cross
left-luggage and issued a description of the man who had left the
trunk:

Height 5ft 7 in or 5ft 8 in; military build; dark, sunburnt
complexion; a closely cropped black moustache. Speaks with a

slight Midland accent. Believed to be wearing a navy dark suit.
Handsome face; features sharply defined; piercing black eyes.

Photographs of the trunk were issued to the press, and printed
under sensational headlines. The publicity had two immediate
results. A Brixton Road dealer named Ward came forward to report
that he sold the trunk for 12s 6d on 6 May to a dark man with a
slight moustache. His daughter was able to confirm this as she
could point to two strips of leather that she had dyed and added to
the casing. Then a taxi driver reported that on or about 6 May he
had driven a man with such a trunk from an office building, No.
86, in Rochester Row to Charing Cross Station. The taxi-driver had
helped the man to carry the trunk downstairs from the third floor
landing. He had remarked on the trunk's weight, and the fare had
informed him that it was full of books.

Most of 86 Rochester Row was occupied by a firm of solicitors,
but two furnished rooms on the second floor had been sublet to
'Edwards & Co., Estate and Business Transfer Agents'. The owner
of the business was John Robinson, whom nobody had seen since 9
May, the day he had vacated the building, leaving behind a note for
his landlord which informed him: 'I am sorry to inform you that I
have gone broke, so cannot use your offices further. Let the people
who supplied the typewriter take it away.'

It was discovered that Mr Robinson had a typist, Miss Moore,
who was traced. She said that on 4 May Robinson had returned to
the office drunk, with a man in military uniform. Frightened by his
behaviour, she left and never returned.

Inquiries at Robinson's lodgings in Kensington showed that he
had gone away, without leaving a forwarding address. However, in
his room was a notice from the Post Office to say that a telegram to
'Robinson, Greyhound Hotel, Hammersmith' could not be delivered as no person of that name was known there. This, as it turned
out, was an error: *Mrs* Robinson did work there, and the telegram
had been returned by a new maid who did not recognize the name.
For her part, Mrs Robinson was ignorant of the fact that she had
been deceived by her 'husband'; it was a bigamous marriage, and
there was another, earlier, wife. 'Mrs Robinson' agreed to cooper-
ate with the police and escorted Chief Inspector Cornish of Scotland
Yard to the Elephant & Castle Public house, where she was to meet
her 'husband'.

If the police expected John Robinson to be a nervous and
guilty-seeming man they were wrong. The 36-year-old Robinson
was agreeable to being interviewed at the Yard, where he made a
statement. Mostly this recounted his past and roving life, from
his birth in Leigh in Lancashire, to his time as a bus conductor,
and butcher's apprenticeship, his army service in Egypt and later
in Ireland fighting the IRA and his failed business ventures. The

statement made no reference to the murder of Mrs Bonati, other than to say he knew nothing about it. Robinson was amenable to taking part in an identity parade. Neither the taxi-driver, the dealer nor the Charing Cross porter who helped the murderer with the trunk recognized him. Robinson was allowed to go.

Nevertheless he was still under suspicion. His story was false in vital details. On 21 May, senior detectives held a conference on the Bonati case. It was at this point that Chief Inspector Cornish had one of those inexplicable but necessary policeman's 'hunches'. The dead woman's head had been wrapped in a yellow duster, which had not yet been touched. It was washed to see if it might give some useful mark. It did: the word 'Greyhound', the name of the public house at which Mrs Robinson worked, was visible. A fresh search of Robinson's office produced a blood-stained match. All clues again pointed to John Robinson, who was invited back to the Yard.

He went but was nothing of his former self. Seemingly fearful of what the police might know, he elected to make a confession. 'I realize this is serious,' he said. 'I met her at Victoria and took her to my office. I want to tell you all about it. I done it and cut her up.'

He then made the following statement:

I left my office at 86 Rochester Row about 4 p.m. on Wednesday May 4th, and went to the post office at Victoria for some stamps. As I left a strange woman spoke to me. She asked me where I was going. I said: 'I am going back to my office to do some more work.' She suggested coming with me and we went to Rochester Row and into my office on the second floor. As far as I know no-one saw us go in. She sat in my office while I wrote some letters. She told me she was not well. She said she was hard-up and asked for a pound. I told her she would not get it and that I had got nothing for her.

She said: 'You must have some money in a place like this and I am going to have some before I leave here.' She became very abusive and said she would create a scene. She flew into a temper and came towards the chair where I was sitting.

I pushed her away. She bent down as though to pick up something from the fireplace and came towards me. I hit her on the face with my right hand. I think I hit the left side of her face, but at this time I was also in a temper and I am not certain.

She fell backwards. She struck a chair in falling and it fell over. As she fell she sort of sat down and rolled over with her hand in the fireplace. I left her there and came out closing the office door behind me. That would be between 5 and 5.30 p.m.

I went straight home to Queen's Row, Camberwell, where I was living. I returned to my office about 10 o'clock the following morning. I was surprised to find that she was still there. She was dead. I was in a hopeless position then. I did not know what to do.

I sat down and thought it all out as to how best to dispose of the body. I decided to cut up the pieces and cart it away in parcels.

I went to a big stationer's shop in Victoria Street and bought six sheets of brown paper and a ball of string, for which I think I paid 1s 9d. I went to a shop in the street, nearer Victoria Station, and bought a chef's knife. It is a big shop where they sell tools and cutlery.

I then went to my office, and of course, I did the job – that is, I cut off her legs and arms. I made it up into four parcels and tied them up in the brown paper and string which I had just bought. I finished the job as quickly as possible before dinner.

I put the three small parcels in the cupboard and the trunk in the corner of the room. I then went to the Artillery public house and had a drink. I was only gone about ten minutes. I stayed at the office till 5 p.m. and then went home. I afterwards met my wife at 6 p.m., and left her about 9 p.m. I then went to my club.

Friday morning, May 6th, I went to my office as usual, about 10 o'clock. I then began to think how I could best get rid of the parcels; and my difficulty was the trunk and head. I decided the only way out of it was to buy a trunk or bags to pack it in. I went to a shop in Brixton Road, where I knew they sold second-hand bags and trunks, and bought a big black trunk with an oval lid. I paid 12s 6d for it.

That would be about 11 o'clock in the morning. I now know it was Mr Ward's shop, near the big garage in Brixton Road.

I carried the trunk to the end of Brixton Road, by Kennington Church, where I got a bus to Rochester Row. I took the trunk up to my office. There I put the parcels into it, strapped it up, and went to the Artillery Arms and had a drink in the saloon bar.

I got into conversation with a man [Mr Judd] I had seen there twice before. I asked him to come up and have a look at my office with me, and whilst he was there I said to him, 'Now you are here, will you give me a hand downstairs with this trunk?' And he did. We got to the bottom of the stairs and he went away. We left the trunk in the passage and between the stairs and the street.

I went into the street and saw, I think, two men getting out of a taxi at the police court on the opposite side of the road. I called the taxi over and asked the driver to give me a hand with the trunk and to put it in the cab, which he did. I told him to drive to Charing Cross Station. I don't know the exact time, but I think it was between 1 p.m. and 2 p.m.

When we got to the station a porter took the trunk off the cab. I told him to put it in the cloakroom and he did so. I got a ticket at the cloakroom, and returned to my office by bus. When on the bus I felt for the ticket which I had put in my pocket, but I could

not find it. I had intended to tear it up. Upon arrival at my office
I stayed there.

On Saturday I went to Clapham Common and buried the knife
under a tree. I cannot describe where I left it, but I can show you.
The towels and dusters which I used for wrapping belonged to
me and were in my office.

The police were able to verify much of Robinson's statement. His
typist confirmed that the 'Greyhound' duster had been used in the
office. Judd agreed that he had helped with the removal of the
trunk. Escorted to Clapham Common, Robinson retrieved the
knife, which he had buried under a hawthorn bush. It is perhaps
more than coincidence that Robinson bought the knife from the
very shop, Staine's Kitchen Equipment Company, where dismemberer Patrick Mahon bought his, and remembered the earlier case
when faced with the problem of the inert Mrs Bonati.

The trial of John Robinson began at the Old Bailey on Monday,
11 July, and was presided over by Mr Justice Swift. Robinson
himself gave evidence, in which he admitted more or less everything, except an intention to kill. Accordingly, much of the trial
centred on Sir Bernard Spilsbury's forensic evidence.

The defence, in arguing that Robinson had killed Bonati accidentally, without intent, put forward several theories. Firstly, there
was the suggestion that the victim had died because of a gas-leak
from the fire in Robinson's office. Defence and prosecution agreed
that some gas was escaping from the fire. But Spilsbury could find
no evidence of poisoning by CARBON MONOXIDE, the lethal
element in coal gas. Secondly, there was the possibility that she had
died of shock, but Spilsbury considered this unlikely, as Bonati's
heart was in good condition. Next, the defence theorized that
Bonati had died from epileptic seizure, brought on by a blow from
Robinson. In support of this, the defence called Mr Rolls, the
ex-lover of Bonati, who confirmed that Minnie Bonati was violent
when under the influence of alcohol. There was little evidence to
support this; certainly, the condition had never been serious
enough for her to have had medical treatment. More persuasive was
the defence's claim that Minnie Bonati had suffocated in the fold of
her own clothing or arm, or even the carpet, when she was lying
face down on the floor. Against this, Spilsbury pointed out that the
blood in the victim's lungs had settled towards the back, which
ruled out any possibility that she had been lying on her front when
she died. The cushion in Robinson's office was the much more
likely cause of death, and the bruises on the deceased's chest were
consistent with the pressure of a knee pinning her to the ground as
she was suffocated with it.

In the witness box, Robinson did little for his own cause.
Questioned by Mr Justice Swift as to why he did not simply report

the 'accidental' death of Mrs Bonati, Robinson replied: 'The situation I was in was terrible.' He added: 'I was in a blue funk and did not know what to do.'

MR JUSTICE SWIFT: Why was it so terrible? It was unpleasant to find somebody dead in your room, but where was the difficulty, if you had done nothing wrong, in going to the police station across the road and saying, 'I had a few words with a woman in my office, and this morning I found her dead'?
ROBINSON: I did not look at it in that light.

Unfortunately for Robinson, the jury did look at it in that light. Anybody who could dismember a body would seem to be more than capable of murder. The jury, to nobody's surprise, brought in a verdict of guilty and Robinson was sentenced to death. Insisting that he had not killed Bonati intentionally, Robinson was hanged on 12 August 1927. In his last days he was much comforted by Annie Robinson, the woman who had led the police to him.

CASE FILE: The Phoenix Trunk Murders

If anything sent John Robinson to the gallows, it was probably his coolness, the deliberate buying of the artefacts he needed to commit a 'trunk murder'. Like Robinson, Winnie Ruth Judd had to tackle the problem of removing bodies from a building in a busy urban area. However, whereas Robinson was calculating, Judd panicked and set in train one of the more ludicrous of trunk murders.

'The Phoenix Trunk Murders', as Winnie Ruth Judd's crimes were dubbed, took place in an apartment at North 2nd Street in the Arizona capital just after breakfast on the morning of 17 October 1931. A violent argument between Judd, a 26-year-old medical secretary, and her two friends who rented the flat, Hedvig Samuelson and Agnes LeRoi, over a nurse at the clinic where they all worked, erupted into a gunfight. Hedvig Samuelson had threatened Judd with a gun. Judd had grabbed the gun, which had gone off injuring Judd in the hand. Once Judd had the gun, she began firing until Samuelson and LeRoi were quite dead.

In a blind panic, Judd stuffed both Samuelson and LeRoi into a large trunk, and called a removal firm to take it away. The two men from the Phoenix Transfer Company who arrived that evening were surprised to find the North 2nd street apartment in darkness, but Judd explained that the power was off because she was leaving. When Judd asked the removal men to take the trunk to the railway station they told her it was too heavy to go as baggage. Instead the trunk was taken to an apartment on East Brill Street, which Mrs Judd – she was married, if somewhat remotely, to a Los Angeles doctor – also rented. That night Judd dismembered Samuelson's body, and repacked both corpses, this time into one large trunk, one small trunk and a suitcase, for easier transportation.

The next day, Sunday, 18 October, Judd persuaded her landlord at East Brill Street, Mr Koller, and his son to drive her down to the station with her trunks, suitcase and hatbox. The porters who put Judd's baggage on the overnight train to Los Angeles would later remember the weight of the larger trunk and the fact that it smelt unpleasant.

Not only did Judd put her cadaveral baggage on the train, she decided to chaperone it herself. Nevertheless, the journey to Los Angeles passed easily enough and the train arrived at 7.45 a.m. the following morning. Judd left the hatbox, trunks and suitcase in left-luggage while she went to arrange for their removal. But in her absence the porter noticed that a dark fluid was leaking from the largest trunk. And the smell from it was getting worse by the minute.

When Judd returned with her brother, Burton J. McKinnell, a student at the University of Southern California, the luggage official insisted that her baggage be opened. He thought that deer meat was being transported illegally.

Flustered, Judd claimed that she would have to get the keys from her husband and left the station with her brother. By 4 p.m. Judd had failed to return, so officials decided to force open the baggage themselves.

Inside the larger trunk they found the jammed body of Agnes LeRoi, the smaller trunk contained the legs, upper torso and head of Hedvig Samuelson. Hedvig's abdomen was in the suitcase.

The identification of the bodies or murder weapon, or indeed the instruments of dismemberment, posed little problem, since Judd had thoughtfully placed alongside the human flesh photographs, a breadknife complete with blood stains, a set of scalpels and a .25 Colt revolver.

McKinnell was quickly rounded up, but said that his sister had said nothing about the contents of the trunks, only that she wanted the trunks 'thrown into the ocean'. He added that his sister was prone to 'insane fits of anger'. Judd's husband was also hauled in, and made a public appeal for her to give herself up.

She did so several days later. Bizarrely enough, she chose to surrender at a funeral parlour. A bullet from the murder weapon was still lodged in her bandaged hand.

In a long and rambling letter to her husband, Judd gave her account of the murders, expressing disgust at having to reduce Samuelson's body to kit-size in order to fit it into a smaller trunk and suitcase: 'It was horrible to pack things as I did. I kept saying I've got to or I'll be hung, I've got to or I'll be hung, I've got to or I'll be hung . . .'

At the trial in January 1932 Judd, 'The Tiger Woman', as she was dubbed by the press, was found guilty of first degree murder and condemned to death. The public was fascinated by the case, not only because of the bloody nature of Judd's crime, but also by suggestions of bisexual activity at the North 2nd Street apartment. There was a vigorous campaign against the severity of her sentence, and in 1933 Judd was committed to an insane asylum. She escaped numerous times before her parole in 1971.

W

WATER

A little water clears us of this deed
Macbeth II.ii

DROWNING is not the only death which can be accomplished with water. Annie Robson, a nurse, threw boiling water over one of her patients, Mrs Kate Pochin of Barkby Hall, Leicestershire, in 1931. Mrs Pochin was so severely scalded that she died. Indicted for murder, Robson, one in a long line of killer nurses, was diagnosed by various mental specialists as suffering from 'psychic epilepsy', and during periods of amnesia was likely to make murderous, and random, attacks on people. She was found 'guilty but insane', and was ordered to be detained at HM's pleasure.

The fate of being dropped alive into a vat of boiling liquid is usually reserved for the unwary in Hammer Horror films; it does not occur with any prominence in the crime annals, except as a method of execution. The Poisoning Act of 1531 was passed for the specific purpose of ensuring that a cook named Rose, employed in the household of the Bishop of Rochester and suspected of poisoning the porridge, should be boiled alive instead of enjoying the luxury of being hanged. The boiling took place in Smithfield. On 28 March 1537, at Tuesday Market Place in King's Lynn, Margaret Davy, a maidservant, was put to death for multiple poisonings. A fire was lit beneath a huge cauldron of water and 'the terrified victim plunged in it when boiling point was reached; from a gantry a chain pulled her body up and down until life was extinct'. The Act was repealed shortly after the succession of Edward VI in 1537.

In an effort to dispose of the corpse, murderers occasionally evidence a tendency to boil dismembered limbs. When the police arrived to search the 'love bungalow' of 1924 killer Patrick Mahon (see TRUNKS), they found simmered bits of Emily Kaye in saucepans. London serial-killer Dennis Nilsen, who suffered from an embarrassment of corpses at 23 Cranley Gardens, regularly put victims' viscera on Regulo 7.

Another boiler was KIDNAPPER Gary Heidnik, the American 'Baby Farmer' and murderer. The fact that all these killers were caught with bits of humans on their stoves suggests that it lacks efficiency as a disposal method; flesh has to be boiled for a very long period before it disintegrates into an easily flushable stew. It is certainly instructive that American AXE murderer Roxanna Druse resorted to putting boiled pieces of her husband John on the fire for

BURNING in an effort to get rid of the evidence more quickly. Fellow 19th-century axe-murderess Kate Webster was obliged to consign boiled lumps of her mistress to the Thames.

Immersion of the corpse in water, be it a stream, pond, lake, river or sea is, of course, one of the staple methods killers resort to when disposing of the result of their handiwork. It is the hope of those who consign the victim to a watery grave that he or she will disappear for ever, or at least rot sufficiently to be unidentifiable. By the general principle established by John Glaister in *Medical Jurisprudence* (1953), the corpse immersed in water will decompose half as quickly as one left in open air, but around four times as quickly as one buried in earth. The singular drawback with immersion as a disposal method is that you can lead a corpse to water but you cannot necessarily make it sink. After approximately six to ten days in the water, the gases (sulphuretted hydrogen, phosphoretted hydrogen and ammonia) produced by decomposition cause the body to float. After a month, the body is greatly bloated with gases, and floats like a polystyrene children's swimming aid. For it to remain out of sight, beneath the water's surface, it must be adequately weighted, hence the Mafia's liking for dressing its victims with 'concrete overcoats'.

As well as the human body's awkward habit of floating, immersion poses two other problems, of which murderers often take too little account. The actual consigning of the body to the water has all sorts of hazards of discovery. Wayne B. Williams, convicted of a series of murders of young black children in Atlanta, Georgia, between 1979 and 1981, was arrested in May of that year after being seen in the early hours near the Chattahoochee river. Witnesses also heard a large splash. Two days later, the body of Nathaniel Carter was retrieved from the river, and his name was added to the 28-long list, which included five other victims found in the same river.

And then there is the unhappy tendency of tides in the sea to give back the dead dumped there. Gangster Brian Hume, who used an AIRCRAFT to drop pieces of his victim in the sea off Essex in 1949, is just one of many murderers to find that the tide brought the crime back to shore. To be counted amongst the most unlikely examples of the sea giving up unwanted human remains was 'The Shark-Arm Case' of 1935. Holiday crowds watching a tiger shark at the Coogee aquarium on Australia's Anzac Day, 25 April, that year were startled to see the exhibit vomit up the hand and brawny tattooed arm of a human being. The shark had been captured in the sea eight days before, and it seemed initially that it must have devoured a hapless swimmer.

Forensic work by Britain's Sir Sydney Smith, who happened to be in Australia at a pathologists' conference, and others established in fact that the arms had been dismembered by human agency, and the shark had only snatched a discarded snack. Fingerprints from stabilized fragile skin flakes revealed the victim to be James Smith, a petty thief. Mrs James Smith made a positive identification from the arm's tattoo.

In a reconstruction of the crime, Sir Sydney suggested that James Smith had been crammed inside a trunk, but since the arm could not be made to fit, it was lopped off and lashed to the outside. When the trunk was dumped at sea, the arm provided a meal for the passing tiger shark. The likely perpetrator of the deed seemed to be a Sydney racketeer called Patrick Brady. Unfortunately, the Sydney police failed to provide a key witness in the case with protective custody, with the result that the witness was shot dead and the case against Brady collapsed.

Still, immersion does have possibilities, and a steady trickle of killers head waterwards every year in the hope of adding to the secrets of the deep.

CASE FILE: The Port Hole Murder

A steward aboard the ocean liner *Durban Castle*, James Camb, considered himself something of a maritime lothario. Unattached and attractive women passengers were there to be seduced, and on the voyage which set sail from Cape Town on 10 October 1947, there was no female more attractive than the 21-year-old girl in Cabin 126, a wide-eyed English actress by the name of Gay Gibson. A seduction by the 31-year-old, Lancashire-born Camb, known as 'Don Jimmy' to his shipmates, was in order.

On the morning of 18 October, when the ship was 150 miles off the coast of West Africa, Gay Gibson was reported missing. Captain Arthur Patey ordered the vessel turned about and a desperate search of the shark-infested waters ensued. There was no trace of the actress, and the ship resumed its passage to England.

Captain Patey conducted an investigation aboard ship as it continued towards Southampton. A watchman, Frederick Steer, reported that the service bell of Cabin 126 had rung frantically at 2.58 a.m. on the morning of 18 October. When he arrived at the cabin he had been surprised to see that two lights were showing outside the door, indicating that the occupant had called for both the steward and stewardess. The watchman knocked, opened the cabin door and had it shut in his face. But not before he had seen a glimpse of a man in uniform – James Camb, the slick-haired Valentino of the after deck. Through the grille of the door, Camb told the watchman 'All right'.

Steer went back to his duties, thinking that Camb had answered the call. Communicating with officials of the Union Castle Line in London, Captain Patey received the radio message: 'Padlock and seal the cabin – disturb nothing – CID officers will come aboard Cowes Roads (Southampton)'. Meanwhile, Camb denied that he had ever been in Gay Gibson's cabin. He drew suspicion to himself, however, by wearing a long-sleeved jacket during the rest of the voyage, when short-sleeved uniforms were usually worn in tropical climes. When asked to bare his arms, these revealed scratches. 'Heat rash,' said Camb.

When the *Durban Castle* reached Southampton, Camb was interviewed by Police Sergeant Quinlan and now admitted going to the girl's cabin. Quinlan suggested that if he had any reasonable explanation of the girl's fate, this was the time to divulge it. Camb replied: 'You mean that Miss Gibson might have died from a cause other than being murdered, she might have had a heart attack or something?' Camb then said Gibson had invited him to her cabin that night and he brought her a drink. She was wearing a nightgown with nothing on underneath it. She had removed this, and Camb had climbed into bed with her. During sexual intercourse, Camb said that she had suddenly thrown a fit, had foamed at the mouth, and died:

> . . . I tried artificial respiration on her. While doing this, the night-watchman knocked at the door and attempted to open it. I shut the door . . . I panicked . . . I did not want to be found in such a compromising position . . . I could not find any sign of life . . . After a struggle with the limp body I managed to lift her to the port hole and push her through . . . I cannot offer any explanation as to how the bells came to be rung as I most definitely did not touch them myself.

In a later interrogation, Camb said that the body, upon hitting the water 'made a helluva splash'.

Charged with the murder of Miss Gibson, Camb's trial began at Winchester Assizes on 20 March 1948, before Mr Justice Hilbery. Expert witnesses for the prosecution, notably Dr Donald Teare, testified that stains on the pillow in the cabin were bloodstains. The blood was type O. Since Camb's blood was Type A, it could be assumed that this was blood from Gay Gibson's body, not Camb's. Dr Teare stated that these stains, along with emissions of urine found on the bedsheet could be expected from one who had been strangled to death. Dr Griffiths, the ship's surgeon, testified that the marks on Camb's arms were scratches made, in his opinion, by a woman defending herself.

Camb stuck to his story that the evidence given in his defence did not rule out the possibility that the woman had died of natural causes, probably from sexual excitement. Evidence that Gay Gibson – whose real name was Eileen Isabella Ronnie Gibson – was sexually active, and not the virgin proclaimed by her mother, was suppressed. At the time of her demise she was three months' pregnant.

What went against Camb were his lies and his lack of a satisfactory reason for not seeking help. He insisted that the actress had only been wearing a yellow nightgown. Yet Gibson's black pyjama bottoms were never found, suggesting that she went overboard in them, and had not invited the steward to have sex with her. The steward's own admission that he had callously shoved the victim's body through a port hole merely suggested that he thought a murder charge could not be brought without a body as evidence. (Camb was far from alone in thinking this; Thomas Joseph Davidson was convicted of drowning his eight-year-old son in 1934, although no body was ever found; John Haigh thought that he would obliterate his victims in an ACID bath, and thus escape the law; likewise, the 'Veronica Mutineers', who murdered the captain, the first and second mates and four members of the crew aboard the barque *Veronica* and pushed their bodies into the mid-Atlantic in 1902 believed the fallacy of 'no body, no case'. It was a mistaken assumption for which Gustav Rau and Willem Smith were hanged at Liverpool.)

After four days of trial, and 45 minutes' deliberation, the jury found Camb guilty of murdering Gay Gibson. The steward was stunned by the decision. Before sentence was passed, he was asked if he had anything to say. He replied in a trembling voice: 'My Lord, at the beginning of this case . . . I pleaded not guilty. I repeat that statement now.' He escaped capital punishment because the 'no-hanging' clause was then under discussion in Parliament as part of the Criminal Justice Bill.

It was after this commutation that several women came forward to say that Camb had sexually attacked them on previous voyages of the *Durban Castle*. In one case he had begun strangling the woman, before giving up.

Camb was eventually released from prison in September 1959, and changed his name to Clarke. While working as a head waiter in May 1967 he was convicted of sexually attacking a thirteen-year-old girl. Placed on a two-year probation, he went to work in Scotland, where he was charged with sexual misconduct with three school-girls. This time he was returned to prison to serve a life sentence.

The body of Gay Gibson was never found.

CASE FILE: The Lady in the Lake

In what would turn out to be a cruel irony, 21-year-old Veronique Marre sent a postcard to her family in July 1983, telling them how beautiful Britain's Lake District was. 'I wish I could stay here for ever,' she wrote. And so she did, for after leaving the village pub in

Wasdale and setting off for Wast Water, the holidaying French student was never seen again.

It was doubly cruel that Wast Water, a black four-mile stretch of water on the western edge of Cumbria, is not one of Lakeland's prettiest sights, and hardly figures in tourist board literature. But what it lacks in beauty it makes up for in depth. It was too deep for police frogmen to trawl for the missing girl, although they did periodically search the surface of the lake for the rest of the year in case her corpse should arise from the inky darkness.

In February 1984, an amateur diver Nigel Prith, decided to get in some unseasonal sub-aqua practice, and entered the cold of Wast Water. Swimming around in the silent waters he spotted a 'bundle' lying on a ledge, about 100 ft beneath the surface. Prith reported his sighting to the police, who dived down on 29 February and retrieved it.

Dragged to the lake's shore, the bundle proved to be weighted-down with CONCRETE, and covered with slimy fronds. Inside the plastic sheeting was a body – but to the surprise of most it was not that of Veronique Marre. This body was that of a plump middle-aged woman, not a petite French girl.

One of the laws of police work is that most bodies are identified sooner or later, and in the case of the plump stranger it was very soon indeed. The person who had dumped her – who was surely also the person who put the nasty evidence of STRANGULATION on her decayed neck – had omitted to remove a gold wedding ring on her finger, which bore the legend 'Margaret 11.11.63 Peter' on its inside surface.

The case was reported in the newspapers, and one of those who read it was Mrs Gillian Seddon of Guildford. Mrs Seddon had once acted as housekeeper to a couple called Margaret and Peter Hogg who had married on that date. Additional evidence that the 'Lady in the Lake' was Mrs Margaret Hogg came from dental records.

Mr Hogg, it turned out, was alive and well. An airline pilot, he had reported his wife missing from their Cranleigh home in October 1976, expressing the opinion that she had run off with businessman Graham Ryan, with whom she had been having a quite open affair. Hogg had even successfully cited Ryan as a co-respondent in a divorce case, despite bitter protestations from Ryan that Margaret had not eloped with him. Ryan, furthermore, was obliged to pay the legal costs of Mr Hogg's action.

Picked up by the Surrey police on 4 March 1984, Peter Hogg was arrested and charged with the murder of his wife, the concealment of her body, and of making false statements when filing for divorce. According to police he was 'most co-operative' and admitted his guilt on all counts. At his trial in March 1985, the defence tried to show that his wife's constant infidelity provoked him into murder. It was related how in the week leading up to her killing on Sunday,

17 October 1976, Mrs Hogg had spent the week with her lover at a cottage in Dorset. On her return to the marital home, a brawl developed. 'I lost control completely,' said Hogg in his statement to police, 'grabbed her throat and squeezed until she stopped squirming around. Then I looked into one of her eyes . . . and knew immediately that she was dead.'

The next day, Hogg telephoned his son's school at Taunton and arranged to collect the boy by car at the start of the half-term holiday, giving a strong hint that he would be staying overnight in Taunton. An alibi thus made, Hogg actually drove 350 miles through the night to the Lake District, and rowed a dingy out into Wast Water and dumped his wife, weighted with concrete, over the side.

It was murderous bad luck on Hogg that he did not row just 25 ft further, for then his wife would have missed the ledge on which she settled and disappeared into a dramatic ten-fathom deep oblivion. In which case she would never have been found. Told by the police that Mrs Hogg's remains had been discovered by an amateur diver doing a spot of practice, Hogg replied: 'That was unlucky, wasn't it?'

There was some sympathy for Hogg at his trial, and he was finally convicted on the lesser charge of manslaughter. He received a comparatively light sentence of four years' detention.

Veronique Marre's body was never found.

However, the Lakes have since divulged another Lady. An underwater diving enthusiast (a definite bane to the murderer intent on the immersion method of disposal) discovered the remains of 41-year-old Sheena Owlett in Crummock Water in September 1988. She had been strangled by spouse Kevin after a drunken argument over sexual infidelity. With Mr Hogg's much publicized endeavour apparently in mind, Mr Owlett had, finding a dead wife on his hands, decided that much the best thing to do was put her in the boot of the car and drive the 100 miles from Wetherby in East Yorkshire to Crummock Water. He then weighted his wife with a metal tow-chain and a car's cylinder block. Ingeniously, he then tied this ensemble to a plastic beer barrel so that it was buoyant enough to tow behind him as he swam to the centre of the lake. When he reached the centre of the lake he removed the barrel's screw top, which enabled the barrel to fill with water, and the whole gruesome bundle to sink. And there it might have lain undisturbed, save for the passing amateur diver. Unfortunately for Mr Owlett, the jury took a dim view of such premeditation, and he was found guilty of the greater charge of murder.

WEEDKILLER *See* **NICOTINE, PARAQUAT, POISON**

Select Bibliography

ABBOTT, Jack Henry *In the Belly of the Beast*, London (1982)
ASKILL, John & SHARPE, Martyn *Angel of Death*, London (1993)
BANKS, Harold K. *The Strangler!*, New York (1967)
BARTON, George *The True Stories of Celebrated Crimes* (n.d.)
BERRY, James *My Experiences as an Executioner*, Newton Abbot (1972)
BLOCK, Eugene B. *The Chemist of Crime*, London (1959)
BOUCHER, Anthony *The Quality of Murder*, New York (1962)
BROCK, Alan *A Casebook of Crime*, London (1948)
BROWNE, Douglas C. & TULLETT, E.V. *Sir Bernard Spilsbury: His Life and Cases*, London (1951)
CAMP, John *One Hundred years of Medical Murder*, London (1982)
CAMPS, Francis E. *Camps on Crime*, Newton Abbot (1973)
CHERRILL, Fred *Cherrill of the Yard*, London (1954)
COHEN, Sam D. *One Hundred True Crime Stories*, Cleveland, USA (1946)
COTTRELL, Richard *Blood on their Hands*, London (1987)
DOWER, Alan *Crime Chemist*, London (1965)
DUNNING, John *Mindless Murders*, London (1987)
EATON, Harold *Famous Poison Trials*, London (1923)
FIDO, Martin *Murder Guide to London*, London (1986)
FRANKE, David *Torture Doctor*, New York (1975)
FURNEAUX, Rupert *They Died by the Gun*, London (1962)
GAUTE, J.H.H. & ODELL, Robin *Murder: Whatdunit?*, London (1982)
The New Murderers' Who's Who, London (1989)
GLAISTER, John *The Power of Poison*, London (1954)
GOODMAN, Jonathan (ed.) *Medical Murders*, London (1991)
The Railway Murders, London (1984)
GRIBBLE, Leonard *Clues That Spelled Guilty*, London (1961)
Murders Most Strange, London (1959)
HEIMER, Mel *The Cannibal*, New York (1971)
HILL, Paul *Portrait of a Sadist*, London (1960)
HOLMES, Paul *The Trials of Dr Coppolino*, New York (1968)
HONEYCOMBE, Gordon *The Murders of the Black Museum*, London (1982)
HYDE, H. Montgomery & KISCH, John *An International Casebook of Crime*, London (1962)
JACOBS, T.C.H. *Cavalcade of Murder*, London (1955)
JONES, Frank *White-collar Killers*, London (1992)
JONES, Richard Glynn (ed.) *Poison!*, London (1987)
KENNEDY, Ludovic *Ten Rillington Place*, London (1961)
KLAUSNER, L.D. *Son of Sam*, New York (1981)
LANE, Brian *The Encyclopedia of Forensic Science*, London (1992)
The Murder Guide to Great Britain, London (1993)
LAURENCE, J. *Extraordinary Crimes*, London (1931)
LEFEBURE, Molly *Evidence for the Crown*, London (1975)
LUCAS, Norman *The Laboratory Detectives*, London (1971)
McCONNELL, Brian & BENCE, Douglas *The Nilsen File*, London (1983)
McLAUGHLIN, Terence *The Coward's Weapon*, London (1980)

MARRINER, Brian *Murder with Venom*, London (1993)
MORLAND, Nigel *Background to Murder*, London (1955)
MORTIMER, John *Famous Trials*, London (1984)
NOTABLE BRITISH TRIALS (83 titles)
O'DONNELL, Bernard *The World's Strangest Murders*, London (1957)
PARRISH, J.M. & CROSSLAND, J.R. *The Fifty Most Amazing Crimes of the Last Hundred Years*, London (1936)
PICTON, Bernard *Murder, Accident or Suicide*, London (1971)
PIERREPOINT, Albert *Executioner Pierrepoint*, London (1974)
RAE, George W. *Confessions of the Boston Strangler*, London (1967)
ROBINS, Joyce *Lady Killers*, London (1993)
ROWLAND, John *Poisoner in the Dock*, London (1960)
SHEW, E. Spencer *Companion to Murder*, London (1962)
Second Companion to Murder, London (1961)
SIFAKIS, Carl *The Encyclopedia of American Crime*, New York (1982)
SIMPSON, Keith *Forty Years of Murder*, London (1978)
Forensic Medicine, London (1981)
SINGER, Kurt *Crime Omnibus*, London (1961)
SMYTH, Frank *Cause of Death*, London (1980)
SPARROW, Gerald *Vintage Victorian and Edwardian Murder*, London (1971)
STEIGER, Brad *Mass Murderer*, New York (1967)
TAYLOR, Bernard & KNIGHT, Stephen *Perfect Murder*, London (1987)
THOMPSON, C.J.S. *Poison Mysteries in History, Romance and Crime*, London (1925)
WILSON, Colin & PITMAN, Pat *Encyclopedia of Murder*, London (1961)
YOUNG, Winifred *Obsessive Poisoner*, London (1973)

Index

acetylcholine 191
acid 5-8, 52, 190
aconitine 9-12, 20, 21
Adams, Dr John Bodkin 167
Adams, William 205-6
aircraft 12-13, 85
air embolism 13-14, 34, 77, 157
airguns *see* firearms
alcohol 15-16, 34, 36, 51, 64, 190
Allitt, Beverley 139-42
animals 16-18, 191
anti-freeze 16
antimony 10, 18-23, 32, 44, 113, 143, 185, 190, 246
antipyrine 24
Armstrong, Major Herbert Rowse 25, 26, 29-31, 191
Armstrong, John 45-6
arsenic 18, 24-33, 43, 44, 143, 185, 186, 188, 190
asphyxia 33-5, 162
atropine 24, 35, 167, 186
'Axeman of New Orleans' 37-9
axes 35-9

bacterial poisoning 40-4, 65, 191
Bamber, Jeremy 112
Barber, Susan 178-80, 192
barbiturates 34, 43, 44-6, 62, 172, 189, 190, 254
Bartlett, Adelaide 68-71
Beard, Arthur 237-8
belladonna *see* atropine
Berkowitz, David 111
Besnard, Marie, the 'Black Widow of Loudon' 31-2
Birkett KC, Norman 32, 92, 170, 253
Birzer, Heinrich 210-11

biting 46-7
bludgeoning *see* blunt instruments
blunt instruments 47-51, 220, 251
boiling 264
boiling alive 264
Bompard, Gabrielle 123
Bonaparte, Napoleon 26
Borden, Lizzie 35, 36
botulism 40, 201, 208
Bougrat, Dr Pierre 60, 165
Bravo, Florence 19
Brownrigg, Elizabeth 214
brucine 190
Brudos, Jerry 199
Buchanan, Robert 166-8
bullets *see* firearms
burial *see* interring
Burke, William and Hare, William 15, 34
burning 18, 37, 51-7, 195, 252

Camb, James 266
cancer 189
cannibalism 47, 58, 152, 198, 199
cantharidin 17, 60-1
carbon monoxide poisoning 34, 44, 52, 54, 61-5, 190, 260
Castaing, Edme 165
caustic potash 65-7, 190
caustic soda 52, 190
chainsaws 73
Chantrelle, Eugene Marie 165
Chapman, George 21-3
chisels 73, 153, 202, 206
chloral hydrate 67
chlorinated lime *see* quicklime
chloroform 43, 67-71, 190, 217
choking 34, 71, 77
Christie, Agatha 243, 250

Christie, John Reginald
  Halliday 63-4, 172
Christison, Professor Robert 9,
  185
concrete 71-2, 269
coniine 129
Constanzo, Adolfo de Jesus
  151-2
copper 188, 190
Coppolino, Carl 232-4
Corll, Dean 218
Crafts, Richard 199-200
Cream, Dr Neill 226, 227-32
Crippen, Dr Hawley Harvey
  132-6, 191, 194
curare 74-7, 110, 191
cut-throat 37, 47, 77-8, 240
cyanide 5, 34, 40, 78-83, 190,
  191

Dahmer, Jeffrey 198, 204
da Vinci, Leonardo 78
de Bocarme, Hippolyte 175-7
de Brinvilliers, Marquise Marie
  33, 186-7
decomposition 80
defenestration 2, 13, 36, 61,
  84-5, 249
de Kaplany, Dr Geza 5, 8-9
de la Pommerais, Couty 86-7
De Quincey, Thomas 15
de Sade, Marquis 60
DeSalvo, Albert, the 'Boston
  Strangler' 2, 216, 219-23
digitalis 85-7, 161
dismemberment 12, 36, 37, 59,
  73, 87-93, 127, 134, 136,
  154, 158, 195, 252, 255, 262
drowning 34, 93-7, 118, 122,
  202, 209
Duffy, John 217

electrocution 34, 97-101, 154
embolism see air embolism
Emmett-Dunne, Frederick 125,
  147-8
explosives 13, 101-4, 130

Eyraud, Michael 123

Finlay, James, the 'Rochdale
  Mummy' 171-4
fire see burning
firearms 1, 7, 74, 105-20, 149,
  261, 262
Fish, Albert 58
Ford, Arthur 60
fungi 42, 71, 120-1, 185, 191

Gacy, John Wayne 68
gas see carbon monoxide
  poisoning
Gein, Ed 199
gelsemium 24
Girard, Henri 40, 41-2
Glaister, Professor John 90, 93,
  118, 225, 265
glass 122, 161
gold 185
Graham, John Gilbert 13, 101,
  103-4
Grills, Caroline 244
Guay, Albert 13, 101
guns see firearms

Haarmann, Fritz 46-7, 58
hacksaws 88
Haigh, John George 6-8, 52, 240
Hall, Edward Marshall 29
hanging 34, 123-7, 147, 150
Heath, Neville 238-41
Heidnik, Gary 151, 153-5, 264
hemlock 127-9, 181, 190
Hill, John 41, 129
Hirasawa, Sadamichi 81-3
hit-and-run 15, 41, 49, 65,
  129-32
Hogg, Peter 269
Holmes, H.H. (a.k.a. H.W.
  Mudgett) 5, 63
Hume, Brian Donald 12-13,
  265
Hyde, Dr Bennett Clarke 40,
  227
hydrochloric acid 5, 8

hyoscine 132-6, 161
hypothermia 65

immersion *see* drowning and
    water
insulin 137-42, 189
interring 63, 135, 143-5, 170

Jack the Ripper 22, 23, 58, 77,
    158, 232
James, Robert 208-10, 213
Johnson, Russell 238
Jones, Genene 234-5
Judd, Winnie Ruth 249, 252,
    261-3

karate 146-8
kicking 49, 148-9
kidnapping 149-55
knives 1, 2, 37, 88, 89, 93, 145,
    152, 153, 155-63, 221-2, 260
Kurten, Peter 58, 77, 158

Labbé, Denise 94-9
Lamson, Dr George Henry
    10-12
laurel water *see* cyanide
Laurens, Carolyn 3, 15, 130,
    212-13
lead 190
lead acetate 188
Lee, Minnie Freeman 241-2
Leonski, Edward 217-8
Leopold, Nathan and Loeb,
    Richard 203
Lipski, Israel 5
Loughans, Harold 223-4
Lowenstein, Martha 243-4
Luetgart, Adolph Louis 65-7

Mahon, Patrick 252, 264
Mancini, Tony 253-4
Manning, Frederick and Maria
    193
Markov, Georgi 200-201
Marsh, James *see* Marsh test for
    arsenic

Marsh test for arsenic 19, 26,
    188
Matushka, Sylvestre 250
Maybrick, Florence 28
mercuric cyanide 79, 80, 164,
    165
mercury 164-5, 185, 187, 190
'Mercy Killing Trial' 13-14
Merrett, John Donald 116-17
Merrifield, Louisa 180-2
Metesky, George 101-2
morphine 10, 12, 34, 165-70,
    188, 190, 192
Mortimer, Charles 129, 131-2
Mudgett, Hermann Webster *see*
    H.H. Holmes
Muller, Franz 251
mummification 170-4, 193
Munchausen Syndrome 76,
    140, 235
mushrooms *see* fungi

Neilson, Donald 149-50
nicotine 175-7, 190
Nilsen, Dennis 89, 94, 172, 264
nitric acid 5, 8

Oakes, Sir Harry 49
Onufrejczyk, Michael 16
Orwell, George 24
opium 165, 187

Palmer, Dr William 19, 226,
    249
paraquat 178-80, 192
Parker, Pauline and Hulme,
    Janet 48, 49-51
Pasolini, Pier Paolo 130
Petiot, Dr Marcel 194-7
phosphorus 180-5, 190
Pierrepoint, Albert 8, 64, 124
pigs *see* animals
poisoning 17, 185-92 *see also*
    aconitine, animals, antimony,
    arsenic, atropine, bacterial
    poisoning, barbiturates,
    cantharidin, carbon

monoxide poisoning,
chloroform, cyanide, fungi,
hemlock, hyoscine,
mercury, morphine,
nicotine, phosphorus, ricin,
snakes, spiders, strychnine,
thallium
potassium chloride 140
potassium cyanide *see* cyanide
potassium hydroxide 190
powdered glass *see* glass
Powers, Gary 17
Pritchard, Dr Edward William
10, 19-21
prussic acid *see* cyanide

quicklime 135, 143, 193

Reed, Les 148-9
refrigeration 59, 60, 73,
198-200
'Rhyl Mummy' case 171
ricin 200-202
Robinson, John 238, 252,
256-61
Rouse, Alfred Arthur 53-4,
129
Ruxton, Dr Buck 88, 89-93
Ryan, Michael 2, 108, 112

Sams, Michael 152-3
Sandhu, Suchnam Singh 254-5
Sangret, August 49, 158
Sarret, Georges 5, 6
scalding *see* water
scopolamine *see* hyoscine
Seddon, Frederick 25, 26, 27-9,
191
Seymour, Henry 206-8
'Shark Arm' case 261
sharp instruments 1, 203-7 *see
also* knives
Sheppard, Marilyn 48
silver 185
Simpson, Professor Keith 49,
144, 157, 171, 194, 216,
223-4, 237, 239

slaked lime *see* quicklime
Smith, George, the 'Brides
in the Bath' murderer 93,
95-7
snakes 59, 191, 207-11
Snyder, Ruth 217
Socrates 127-8, 185
sodium cyanide *see* cyanide
Spanish Fly *see* cantharidin
spiders 3, 59, 191, 212-14
Spilsbury, Sir Bernard 28, 30,
53, 54, 96, 118, 127, 135,
158, 162, 171, 206, 224, 256,
260
stabbing *see* knives, *also* sharp
instruments
starvation 214-16
Stas, Professor Jean Servais 10,
86, 176-7, 188, 226
Staunton, Harriet 214,
215-16
Stevenson, Dr Thomas 12, 23,
70
strangulation 34, 63, 64, 78,
92, 125, 194, 216-24, 238,
269
strychnine 40, 44, 188, 190,
191, 208, 224-32, 249
succinylcholine chloride 189,
232-5
suffocation 34, 79, 125, 141,
235-42, 260
sulphuric acid 5, 8
Sutcliffe, Peter 58, 203

Tardieu, Professor Ambrose
86, 87
Thackeray, William Makepeace
248
thallium 188, 190, 192, 243
Thompson, Edith and
Bywaters, Frederick 122,
159-62
Thorn, Fred 87
Thorne, Norman 125-7
throat-cutting *see* cut-throat
trains 248-51

Trotsky, Leon 202-3
trunks 59, 123, 242, 249, 251, 266

Unruh, Howard 2, 108, 114-16

Vaquier, Jean-Pierre 227

Waddingham, Dorothea 168-70, 192
Wainewright, Thomas 225-6

Waite, Arthur Warren 41, 42-4, 45, 68
water 94, 264-7 *see also* drowning
Weber, Jeanne 218
Webster, Kate 36, 265
Whittle, Lesley 149-50
Wilde, Oscar 193
Wilson, Mary, the 'Widow of Windy Nook' 183-5

Young, Graham 243, 245-8